BUT THERE'S PLENTY OF TIME TO *WORRY LATER!* WHAT COUNTS *HERE AND NOW* IS, WE *WON* OUR FIRST *BATTLE!*

EARTH IS *SURELY* GOING TO KNOW THAT THE *GREEN LANTERN CORPS* HAS *ARRIVED!*

TALES OF THE
GREEN LANTERN CORPS

VOLUME 3

Steve Englehart WRITER

Joe Staton PENCILLER

Mark Farmer INKER

L. Lois Buhalis / Bob Lappan / Pete Costanza LETTERERS

Carl Gafford / Anthony Tollin ORIGINAL SERIES COLORS

Joe Staton and **Bruce Patterson** with **Allen Passalaqua** COLLECTION COVER

TALES OF THE
GREEN LANTERN CORPS

VOLUME 3

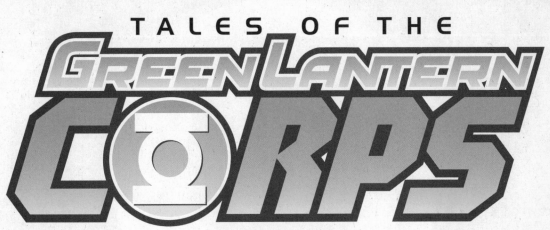

Andy Helfer Editor-Original Series
Bob Harras Group Editor-Collected Editions
Bob Joy Editor
Robbin Brosterman Design Director-Books

DC COMICS
Diane Nelson President
Dan DiDio and **Jim Lee** Co-Publishers
Geoff Johns Chief Creative Officer
Patrick Caldon EVP-Finance and Administration
John Rood EVP-Sales, Marketing and Business Development
Amy Genkins SVP-Business and Legal Affairs
Steve Rotterdam SVP-Sales and Marketing
John Cunningham VP-Marketing
Terri Cunningham VP-Managing Editor
Alison Gill VP-Manufacturing
David Hyde VP-Publicity
Sue Pohja VP-Book Trade Sales
Alysse Soll VP-Advertising and Custom Publishing
Bob Wayne VP-Sales
Mark Chiarello Art Director

Color reproduction by Joe Ketterer.

TALES OF THE GREEN LANTERN CORPS Vol. 3
Published by DC Comics. Cover and compilation Copyright © 2010 DC Comics.
All Rights Reserved.

Originally published in single magazine form in GREEN LANTERN CORPS 201-206 Copyright © 1986 DC Comics.
All Rights Reserved. All characters, their distinctive likenesses and related elements featured in this publication are trademarks of DC Comics.
The stories, characters and incidents featured in this publication are entirely fictional.
DC Comics does not read or accept unsolicited submissions of ideas, stories or artwork.

DC Comics, 1700 Broadway, New York, NY 10019
A Warner Bros. Entertainment Company
Printed by Quad/Graphics, Dubuque, IA, USA (11/17/10)

ISBN: 978-1-4012-2934-4

TABLE OF CONTENTS

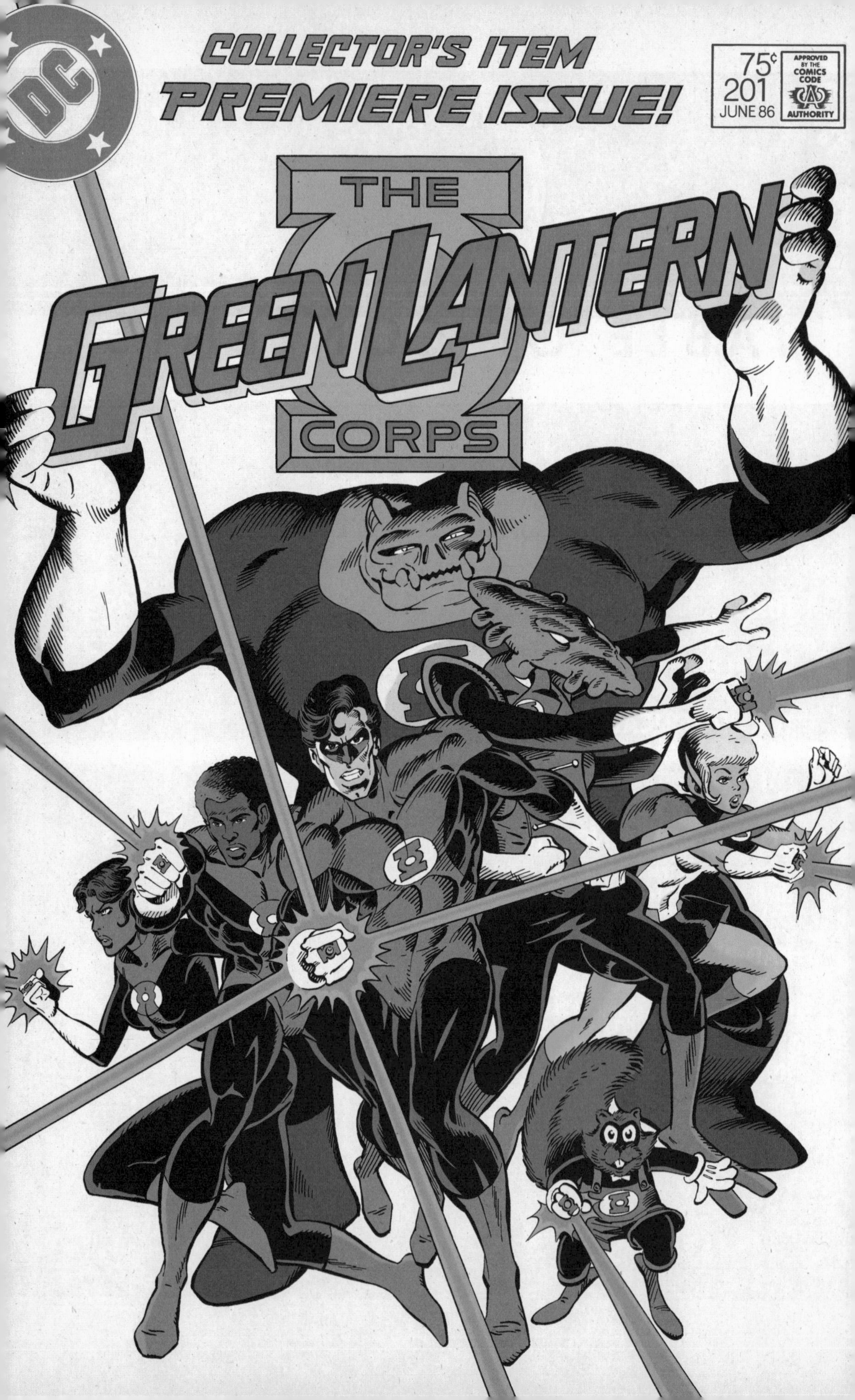

DC
COLLECTOR'S ITEM
PREMIERE ISSUE!
75¢
201
JUNE 86
APPROVED BY THE COMICS CODE AUTHORITY
THE GREEN LANTERN CORPS

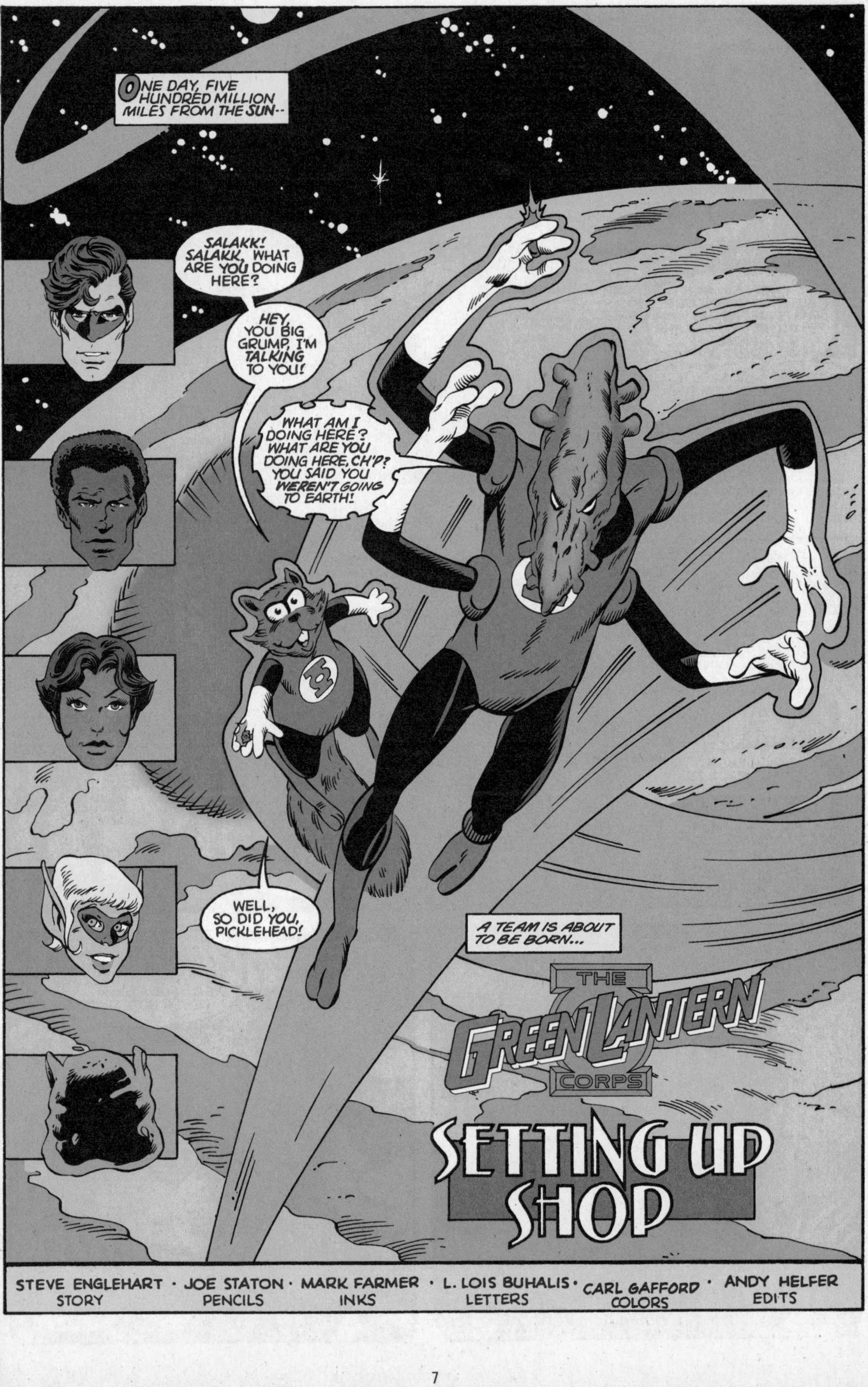

ONE DAY, FIVE HUNDRED MILLION MILES FROM THE SUN--
SALAKK! SALAKK, WHAT ARE YOU DOING HERE?
HEY, YOU BIG GRUMP, I'M TALKING TO YOU!
WHAT AM I DOING HERE? WHAT ARE YOU DOING HERE, CH'P? YOU SAID YOU WEREN'T GOING TO EARTH!
WELL, SO DID YOU, PICKLEHEAD!
A TEAM IS ABOUT TO BE BORN...
THE GREEN LANTERN CORPS
SETTING UP SHOP
STEVE ENGLEHART · JOE STATON · MARK FARMER · L. LOIS BUHALIS · CARL GAFFORD · ANDY HELFER
STORY PENCILS INKS LETTERS COLORS EDITS

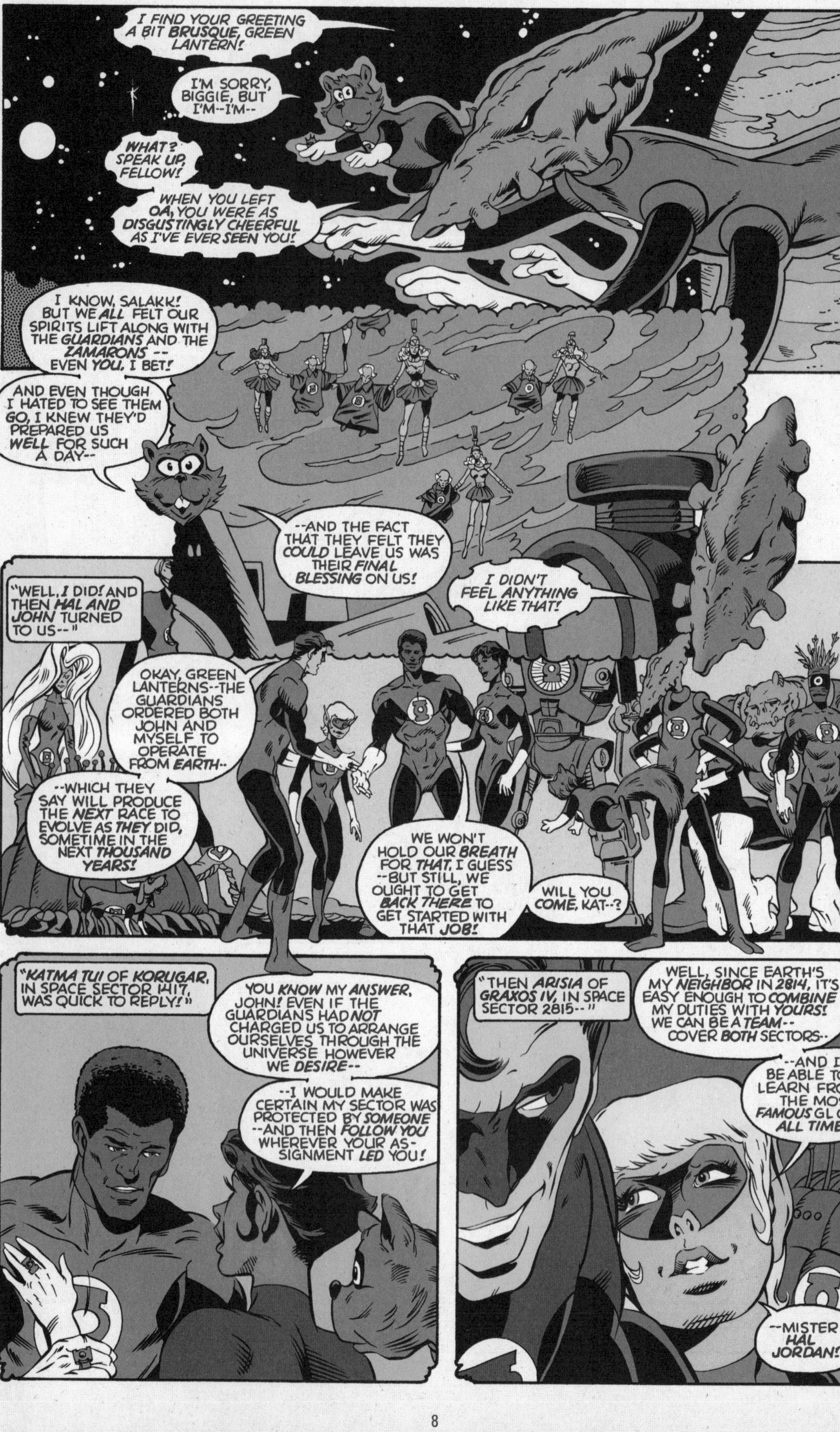

I FIND YOUR GREETING A BIT BRUSQUE, GREEN LANTERN!
I'M SORRY, BIGGIE, BUT I'M--I'M--
WHAT? SPEAK UP, FELLOW!
WHEN YOU LEFT OA, YOU WERE AS DISGUSTINGLY CHEERFUL AS I'VE EVER SEEN YOU!
I KNOW, SALAKK! BUT WE ALL FELT OUR SPIRITS LIFT ALONG WITH THE GUARDIANS AND THE ZAMARONS -- EVEN YOU, I BET!
AND EVEN THOUGH I HATED TO SEE THEM GO, I KNEW THEY'D PREPARED US WELL FOR SUCH A DAY--
--AND THE FACT THAT THEY FELT THEY COULD LEAVE US WAS THEIR FINAL BLESSING ON US!
I DIDN'T FEEL ANYTHING LIKE THAT!
"WELL, I DID! AND THEN HAL AND JOHN TURNED TO US--"
OKAY, GREEN LANTERNS--THE GUARDIANS ORDERED BOTH JOHN AND MYSELF TO OPERATE FROM EARTH--
--WHICH THEY SAY WILL PRODUCE THE NEXT RACE TO EVOLVE AS THEY DID, SOMETIME IN THE NEXT THOUSAND YEARS!
WE WON'T HOLD OUR BREATH FOR THAT, I GUESS --BUT STILL, WE OUGHT TO GET BACK THERE TO GET STARTED WITH THAT JOB!
WILL YOU COME, KAT--?
"KATMA TUI OF KORUGAR, IN SPACE SECTOR 1417, WAS QUICK TO REPLY!"
YOU KNOW MY ANSWER, JOHN! EVEN IF THE GUARDIANS HAD NOT CHARGED US TO ARRANGE OURSELVES THROUGH THE UNIVERSE HOWEVER WE DESIRE--
--I WOULD MAKE CERTAIN MY SECTOR WAS PROTECTED BY SOMEONE --AND THEN FOLLOW YOU WHEREVER YOUR AS-SIGNMENT LED YOU!
"THEN ARISIA OF GRAXOS IV, IN SPACE SECTOR 2815--"
WELL, SINCE EARTH'S MY NEIGHBOR IN 2814, IT'S EASY ENOUGH TO COMBINE MY DUTIES WITH YOURS! WE CAN BE A TEAM-- COVER BOTH SECTORS--
--AND I'LL BE ABLE TO LEARN FROM THE MOST FAMOUS GL OF ALL TIME--
--MISTER HAL JORDAN!

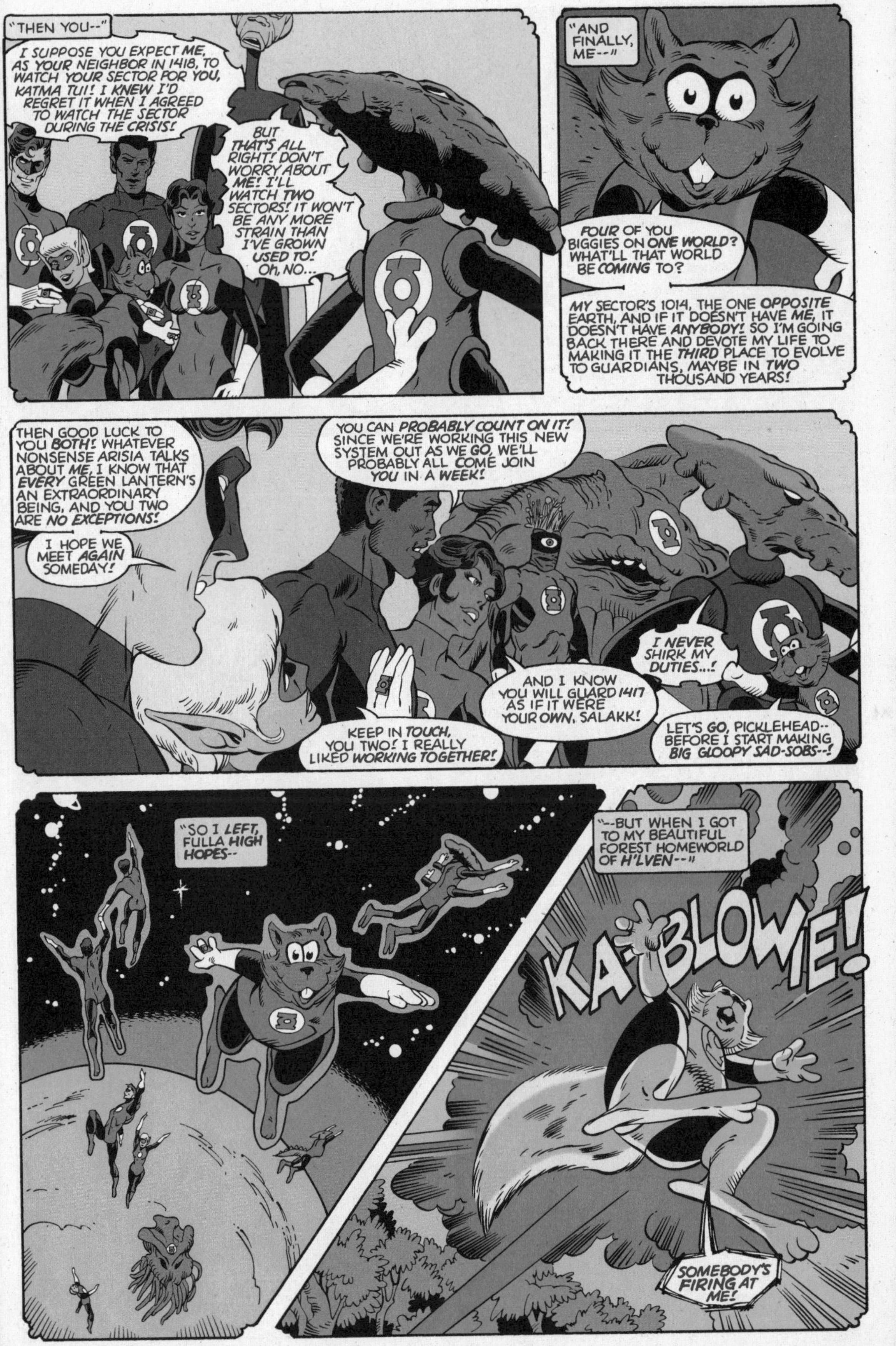
"THEN YOU--"
I SUPPOSE YOU EXPECT ME, AS YOUR NEIGHBOR IN 1418, TO WATCH YOUR SECTOR FOR YOU, KATMA TUI! I KNEW I'D REGRET IT WHEN I AGREED TO WATCH THE SECTOR DURING THE CRISIS!
BUT THAT'S ALL RIGHT! DON'T WORRY ABOUT ME! I'LL WATCH TWO SECTORS! IT WON'T BE ANY MORE STRAIN THAN I'VE GROWN USED TO! Oh, NO...
"AND FINALLY, ME--"
FOUR OF YOU BIGGIES ON ONE WORLD? WHAT'LL THAT WORLD BE COMING TO?
MY SECTOR'S 1014, THE ONE OPPOSITE EARTH, AND IF IT DOESN'T HAVE ME, IT DOESN'T HAVE ANYBODY! SO I'M GOING BACK THERE AND DEVOTE MY LIFE TO MAKING IT THE THIRD PLACE TO EVOLVE TO GUARDIANS, MAYBE IN TWO THOUSAND YEARS!
THEN GOOD LUCK TO YOU BOTH! WHATEVER NONSENSE ARISIA TALKS ABOUT ME, I KNOW THAT EVERY GREEN LANTERN'S AN EXTRAORDINARY BEING, AND YOU TWO ARE NO EXCEPTIONS!
I HOPE WE MEET AGAIN SOMEDAY!
YOU CAN PROBABLY COUNT ON IT! SINCE WE'RE WORKING THIS NEW SYSTEM OUT AS WE GO, WE'LL PROBABLY ALL COME JOIN YOU IN A WEEK!
KEEP IN TOUCH, YOU TWO! I REALLY LIKED WORKING TOGETHER!
AND I KNOW YOU WILL GUARD 1417 AS IF IT WERE YOUR OWN, SALAKK!
I NEVER SHIRK MY DUTIES...!
LET'S GO, PICKLEHEAD-- BEFORE I START MAKING BIG GLOOPY SAD-SOBS--!
"SO I LEFT, FULLA HIGH HOPES--
"--BUT WHEN I GOT TO MY BEAUTIFUL FOREST HOMEWORLD OF H'LVEN--"
KA-BLOWIE!
SOMEBODY'S FIRING AT ME!

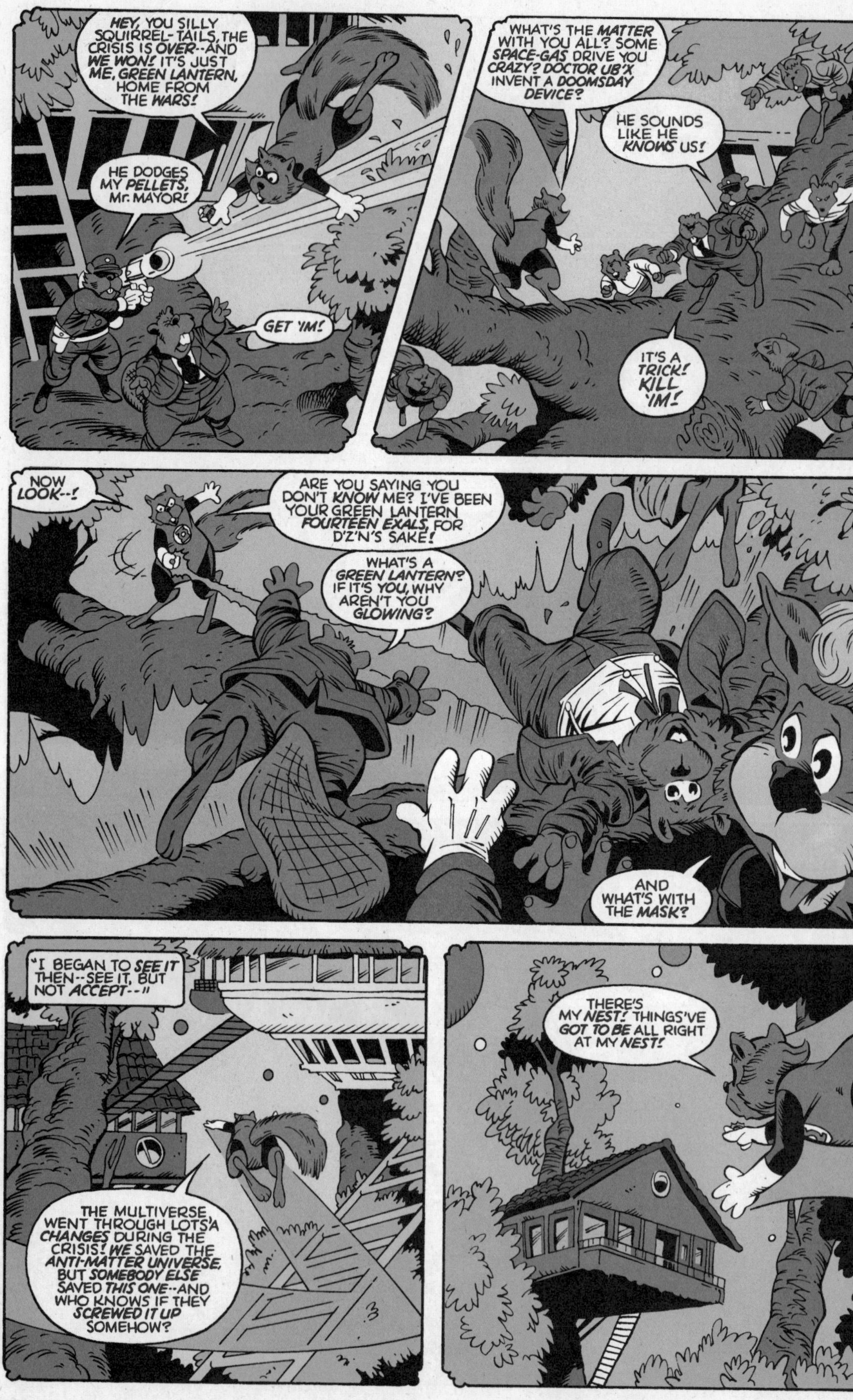
HEY, YOU SILLY SQUIRREL-TAILS, THE CRISIS IS OVER--AND WE WON! IT'S JUST ME, GREEN LANTERN, HOME FROM THE WARS!
HE DODGES MY PELLETS, Mr. MAYOR!
GET 'IM!
WHAT'S THE MATTER WITH YOU ALL? SOME SPACE-GAS DRIVE YOU CRAZY? DOCTOR UB'X INVENT A DOOMSDAY DEVICE?
HE SOUNDS LIKE HE KNOWS US!
IT'S A TRICK! KILL 'IM!
NOW LOOK--!
ARE YOU SAYING YOU DON'T KNOW ME? I'VE BEEN YOUR GREEN LANTERN FOURTEEN EXALS, FOR D'Z'N'S SAKE!
WHAT'S A GREEN LANTERN? IF IT'S YOU, WHY AREN'T YOU GLOWING?
AND WHAT'S WITH THE MASK?
"I BEGAN TO SEE IT THEN--SEE IT, BUT NOT ACCEPT--"
THE MULTIVERSE WENT THROUGH LOTS'A CHANGES DURING THE CRISIS! WE SAVED THE ANTI-MATTER UNIVERSE, BUT SOMEBODY ELSE SAVED THIS ONE--AND WHO KNOWS IF THEY SCREWED IT UP SOMEHOW?
THERE'S MY NEST! THINGS'VE GOT TO BE ALL RIGHT AT MY NEST!

Panel 1:
G'BYE, HONEY! I'LL BRING YOU SOME NUTS-- =OOOFF!=

D'LL! WHAT ARE YOU DOING HERE?

Panel 2:
DO I *KNOW* YOU, SILKY BOY?

WHAT'S GOING ON, D'LL? WHO *IS* THIS MONK?

M'NN'E?

Panel 3:

M'NN'E, IT'S ME-- CH'P!

EEEEEEKK!!

BY THE TREE SPIRIT!

LISTEN, YOU-- YOU *SCAMP!* THIS IS *NOT* FUNNY! MY WIFE WAS IN *LOVE* WITH C'HP BEFORE HE *DIED!*

DIED--?

HE WAS ALSO *MY* BEST FRIEND, AND EVEN IF M'NN'E AND I FOUND *ANOTHER* KIND OF HAPPINESS *WITHOUT* HIM, I MISS HIM A LOT, *TOO*--SO JUST *GET OUT* OF HERE!

Panel 4:
"IT WAS *CLEAR*, SALAKK--ALL *TOO* CLEAR! THE POSITIVE-MATTER UNIVERSE *WAS* PUT BACK TOGETHER WRONG--AND ALL THE *ALTERNATIVES* CEASED TO *EXIST!*

"I SCOURED THE *PLANET*, YOU BETTER *BELIEVE*--AND THEN THE *SECTOR!* BUT THE STORY WAS THE SAME EVERY-WHERE--

"--I FELL FROM A TREE *NINETEEN EXALS* AGO, BEFORE I MARRIED M'NN'E --AND THEY NEVER *HAD* A GREEN LANTERN THERE!"

Panel 5:
THERE'S AN *ALTERNATE* SECTOR THERE NOW--A 1014-2 OR SOMETHING!

THAT MEANS THAT IT'S *ONLY* WITH THE *CORPS* THAT I AM --*WHAT I AM* AND CONTINUE TO BE!

I CAN SEE HOW THAT MIGHT BOTHER A TINY MIND LIKE YOURS!

IT WOULDN'T BOTHER MY MIND-- BECAUSE I *ALWAYS EXPECT THE WORST!*

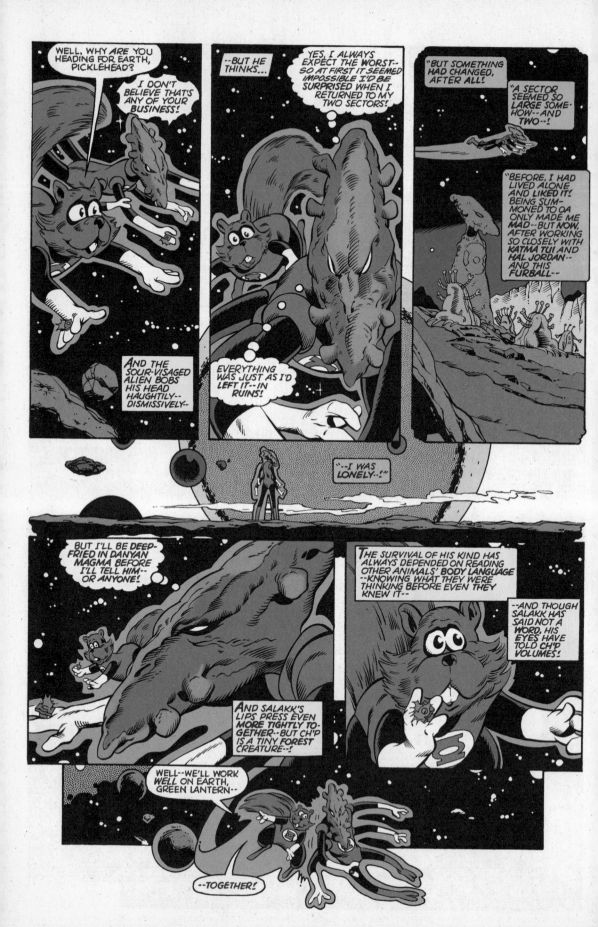

WELL, WHY *ARE* YOU HEADING FOR EARTH, PICKLEHEAD?

I DON'T BELIEVE THAT'S ANY OF YOUR BUSINESS!

AND THE SOUR-VISAGED ALIEN BOBS HIS HEAD HAUGHTILY-- DISMISSIVELY--

--BUT HE THINKS...

YES, I ALWAYS EXPECT THE WORST-- SO AT FIRST IT SEEMED IMPOSSIBLE I'D BE SURPRISED WHEN I RETURNED TO MY TWO SECTORS!

EVERYTHING WAS JUST AS I'D LEFT IT--IN RUINS!

"BUT SOMETHING HAD CHANGED, AFTER ALL!

"A SECTOR SEEMED SO LARGE SOME-HOW--AND TWO--!

"BEFORE, I HAD LIVED ALONE AND LIKED IT! BEING SUM-MONED TO OA ONLY MADE ME MAD--BUT NOW, AFTER WORKING SO CLOSELY WITH KATMA TUI AND HAL JORDAN-- AND THIS FURBALL--

--I WAS LONELY--!

BUT I'LL BE DEEP-FRIED IN DANYAN MAGMA BEFORE I'LL TELL HIM-- OR ANYONE!

THE SURVIVAL OF HIS KIND HAS ALWAYS DEPENDED ON READING OTHER ANIMALS' BODY LANGUAGE --KNOWING WHAT THEY WERE THINKING BEFORE EVEN THEY KNEW IT--

--AND THOUGH SALAKK HAS SAID NOT A WORD, HIS EYES HAVE TOLD CH'P VOLUMES!

AND SALAKK'S LIPS PRESS EVEN MORE TIGHTLY TO-GETHER--BUT CH'P IS A TINY FOREST CREATURE--!

WELL--WE'LL WORK WELL ON EARTH, GREEN LANTERN--

--TOGETHER!

LIGHTLY THEY SKIM INTO OUR PLANET'S ATMOSPHERE, THE GREEN LIGHT THEY COMMAND PROTECTING THEM FROM FRICTION AND THE GASES THAT OTHERWISE WOULD POISON THEM!

AT A WORD FROM THEM, THEIR POWER RINGS HOME IN ON THE OTHER RINGS HERE, AND THEY QUICKEN THEIR PACE--

--TOWARD THE LAND-MASS THEY WILL LEARN TO CALL AMERICA--

--AND THE HOME CLUSTER THEY WILL CALL LOS ANGELES--

LOS ANGELE
DOWNTO
NEXT 10 EX

--AND THE GREEN LANTERN CORPS!

WELL, LOOK WHO'S HERE!

CH'P! SALAKK!

OH, BOY! YOU CHANGED YOUR MINDS!

13

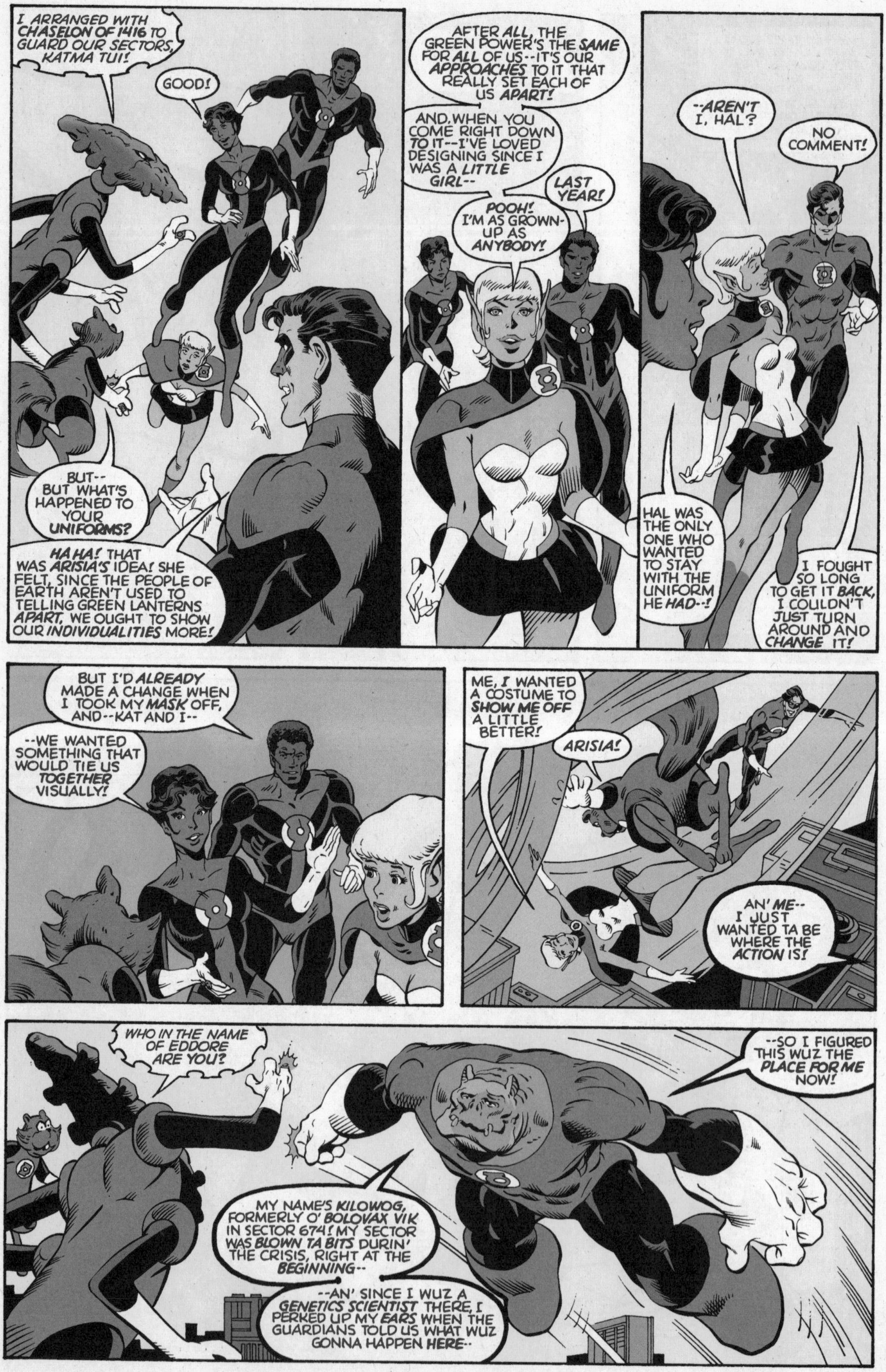
I ARRANGED WITH CHASELON OF 1416 TO GUARD OUR SECTORS, KATMA TUI!
GOOD!
BUT-- BUT WHAT'S HAPPENED TO YOUR UNIFORMS?
HA HA! THAT WAS ARISIA'S IDEA! SHE FELT, SINCE THE PEOPLE OF EARTH AREN'T USED TO TELLING GREEN LANTERNS APART, WE OUGHT TO SHOW OUR INDIVIDUALITIES MORE!
AFTER ALL, THE GREEN POWER'S THE SAME FOR ALL OF US--IT'S OUR APPROACHES TO IT THAT REALLY SET EACH OF US APART!
AND.WHEN YOU COME RIGHT DOWN TO IT--I'VE LOVED DESIGNING SINCE I WAS A LITTLE GIRL--
LAST YEAR!
POOH! I'M AS GROWN-UP AS ANYBODY!
--AREN'T I, HAL?
NO COMMENT!
HAL WAS THE ONLY ONE WHO WANTED TO STAY WITH THE UNIFORM HE HAD--!
I FOUGHT SO LONG TO GET IT BACK, I COULDN'T JUST TURN AROUND AND CHANGE IT!
BUT I'D ALREADY MADE A CHANGE WHEN I TOOK MY MASK OFF, AND--KAT AND I--
--WE WANTED SOMETHING THAT WOULD TIE US TOGETHER VISUALLY!
ME, I WANTED A COSTUME TO SHOW ME OFF A LITTLE BETTER!
ARISIA!
AN' ME-- I JUST WANTED TA BE WHERE THE ACTION IS!
WHO IN THE NAME OF EDDORE ARE YOU?
MY NAME'S KILOWOG, FORMERLY O' BOLOVAX VIK IN SECTOR 674! MY SECTOR WAS BLOWN TA BITS DURIN' THE CRISIS, RIGHT AT THE BEGINNING--
--AN' SINCE I WUZ A GENETICS SCIENTIST THERE, I PERKED UP MY EARS WHEN THE GUARDIANS TOLD US WHAT WUZ GONNA HAPPEN HERE--
--SO I FIGURED THIS WUZ THE PLACE FOR ME NOW!

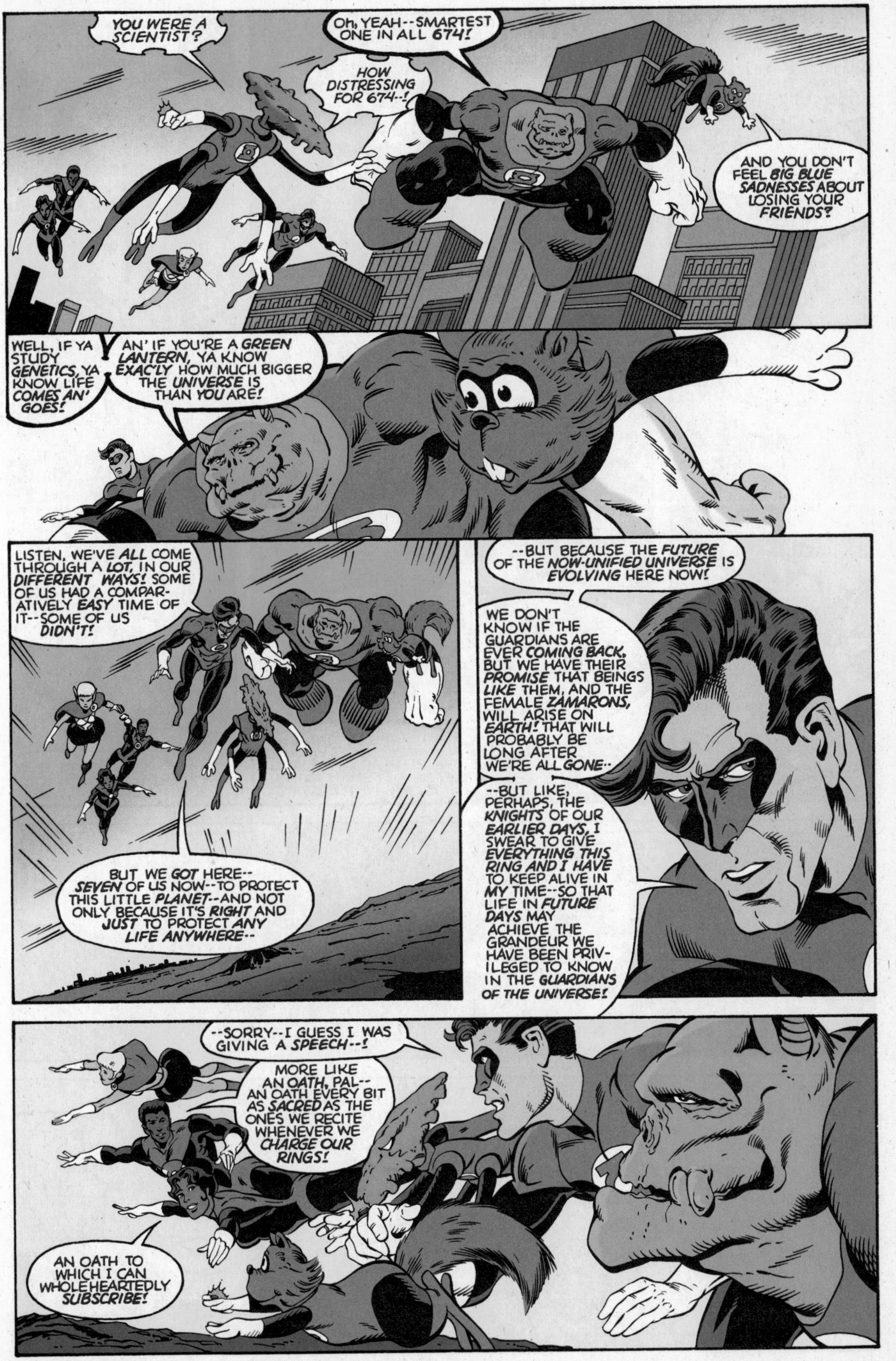
YOU WERE A SCIENTIST?
Oh, YEAH--SMARTEST ONE IN ALL 674!
HOW DISTRESSING FOR 674--!
AND YOU DON'T FEEL BIG BLUE SADNESSES ABOUT LOSING YOUR FRIENDS?
WELL, IF YA STUDY GENETICS, YA KNOW LIFE COMES AN' GOES!
AN' IF YOU'RE A GREEN LANTERN, YA KNOW EXAC'LY HOW MUCH BIGGER THE UNIVERSE IS THAN YOU ARE!
LISTEN, WE'VE ALL COME THROUGH A LOT, IN OUR DIFFERENT WAYS! SOME OF US HAD A COMPARATIVELY EASY TIME OF IT--SOME OF US DIDN'T!
BUT WE GOT HERE--SEVEN OF US NOW--TO PROTECT THIS LITTLE PLANET--AND NOT ONLY BECAUSE IT'S RIGHT AND JUST TO PROTECT ANY LIFE ANYWHERE--
--BUT BECAUSE THE FUTURE OF THE NOW-UNIFIED UNIVERSE IS EVOLVING HERE NOW!
WE DON'T KNOW IF THE GUARDIANS ARE EVER COMING BACK, BUT WE HAVE THEIR PROMISE THAT BEINGS LIKE THEM, AND THE FEMALE ZAMARONS, WILL ARISE ON EARTH! THAT WILL PROBABLY BE LONG AFTER WE'RE ALL GONE--
--BUT LIKE, PERHAPS, THE KNIGHTS OF OUR EARLIER DAYS, I SWEAR TO GIVE EVERYTHING THIS RING AND I HAVE TO KEEP ALIVE IN MY TIME--SO THAT LIFE IN FUTURE DAYS MAY ACHIEVE THE GRANDEUR WE HAVE BEEN PRIVILEGED TO KNOW IN THE GUARDIANS OF THE UNIVERSE!
--SORRY--I GUESS I WAS GIVING A SPEECH--!
MORE LIKE AN OATH, PAL--AN OATH EVERY BIT AS SACRED AS THE ONES WE RECITE WHENEVER WE CHARGE OUR RINGS!
AN OATH TO WHICH I CAN WHOLEHEARTEDLY SUBSCRIBE!

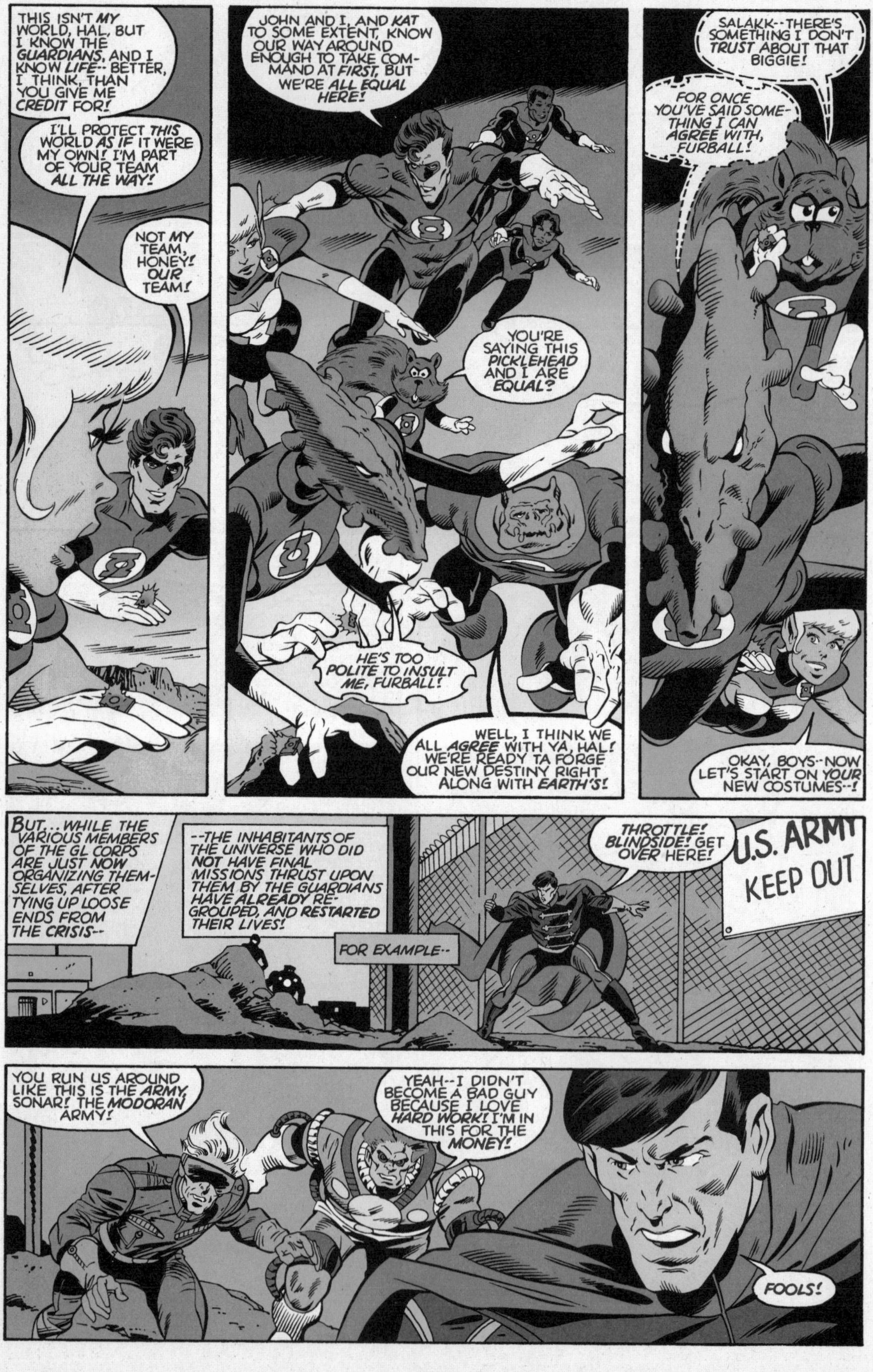
THIS ISN'T MY WORLD, HAL, BUT I KNOW THE GUARDIANS. AND I KNOW LIFE-- BETTER, I THINK, THAN YOU GIVE ME CREDIT FOR!
I'LL PROTECT THIS WORLD AS IF IT WERE MY OWN! I'M PART OF YOUR TEAM ALL THE WAY!
NOT MY TEAM, HONEY! OUR TEAM!
JOHN AND I, AND KAT TO SOME EXTENT, KNOW OUR WAY AROUND ENOUGH TO TAKE COMMAND AT FIRST, BUT WE'RE ALL EQUAL HERE!
YOU'RE SAYING THIS PICKLEHEAD AND I ARE EQUAL?
HE'S TOO POLITE TO INSULT ME, FURBALL!
WELL, I THINK WE ALL AGREE WITH YA, HAL! WE'RE READY TA FORGE OUR NEW DESTINY RIGHT ALONG WITH EARTH'S!
SALAKK--THERE'S SOMETHING I DON'T TRUST ABOUT THAT BIGGIE!
FOR ONCE YOU'VE SAID SOMETHING I CAN AGREE WITH, FURBALL!
OKAY, BOYS--NOW LET'S START ON YOUR NEW COSTUMES--!
BUT... WHILE THE VARIOUS MEMBERS OF THE GL CORPS ARE JUST NOW ORGANIZING THEMSELVES, AFTER TYING UP LOOSE ENDS FROM THE CRISIS--
--THE INHABITANTS OF THE UNIVERSE WHO DID NOT HAVE FINAL MISSIONS THRUST UPON THEM BY THE GUARDIANS HAVE ALREADY REGROUPED, AND RESTARTED THEIR LIVES!
FOR EXAMPLE--
THROTTLE! BLINDSIDE! GET OVER HERE!
U.S. ARMY
KEEP OUT
YOU RUN US AROUND LIKE THIS IS THE ARMY, SONAR! THE MODORAN ARMY!
YEAH--I DIDN'T BECOME A BAD GUY BECAUSE I LOVE HARD WORK! I'M IN THIS FOR THE MONEY!
FOOLS!

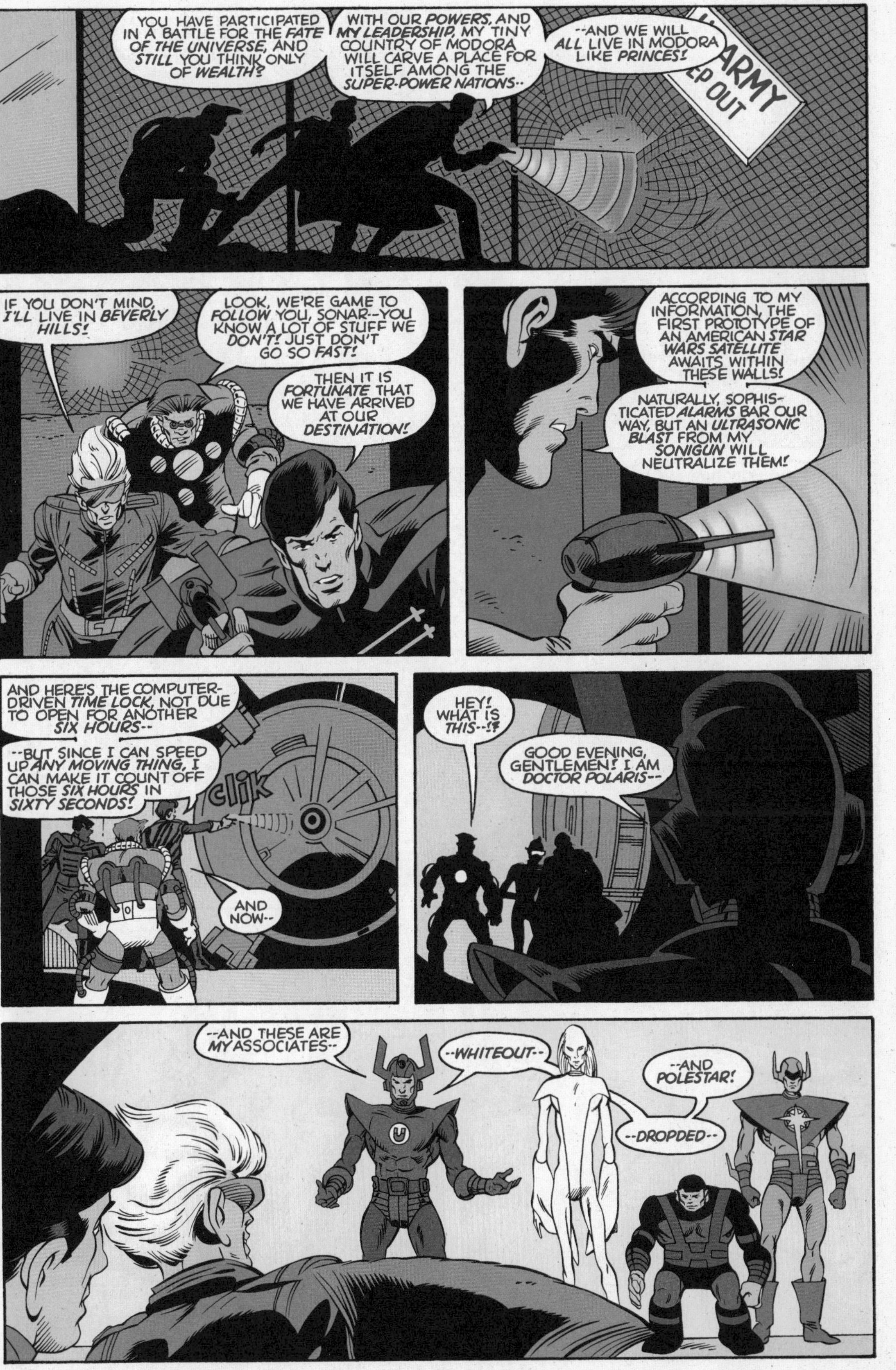
YOU HAVE PARTICIPATED IN A BATTLE FOR THE FATE OF THE UNIVERSE, AND STILL YOU THINK ONLY OF WEALTH?
WITH OUR POWERS, AND MY LEADERSHIP, MY TINY COUNTRY OF MODORA WILL CARVE A PLACE FOR ITSELF AMONG THE SUPER-POWER NATIONS--
--AND WE WILL ALL LIVE IN MODORA LIKE PRINCES!
ARMY
P OUT
IF YOU DON'T MIND, I'LL LIVE IN BEVERLY HILLS!
LOOK, WE'RE GAME TO FOLLOW YOU, SONAR--YOU KNOW A LOT OF STUFF WE DON'T! JUST DON'T GO SO FAST!
THEN IT IS FORTUNATE THAT WE HAVE ARRIVED AT OUR DESTINATION!
ACCORDING TO MY INFORMATION, THE FIRST PROTOTYPE OF AN AMERICAN STAR WARS SATELLITE AWAITS WITHIN THESE WALLS!
NATURALLY, SOPHISTICATED ALARMS BAR OUR WAY, BUT AN ULTRASONIC BLAST FROM MY SONIGUN WILL NEUTRALIZE THEM!
AND HERE'S THE COMPUTER-DRIVEN TIME LOCK, NOT DUE TO OPEN FOR ANOTHER SIX HOURS--
--BUT SINCE I CAN SPEED UP ANY MOVING THING, I CAN MAKE IT COUNT OFF THOSE SIX HOURS IN SIXTY SECONDS!
CLIK
AND NOW--
HEY! WHAT IS THIS--!?
GOOD EVENING, GENTLEMEN! I AM DOCTOR POLARIS--
--AND THESE ARE MY ASSOCIATES--
--WHITEOUT--
--DROPDED--
--AND POLESTAR!

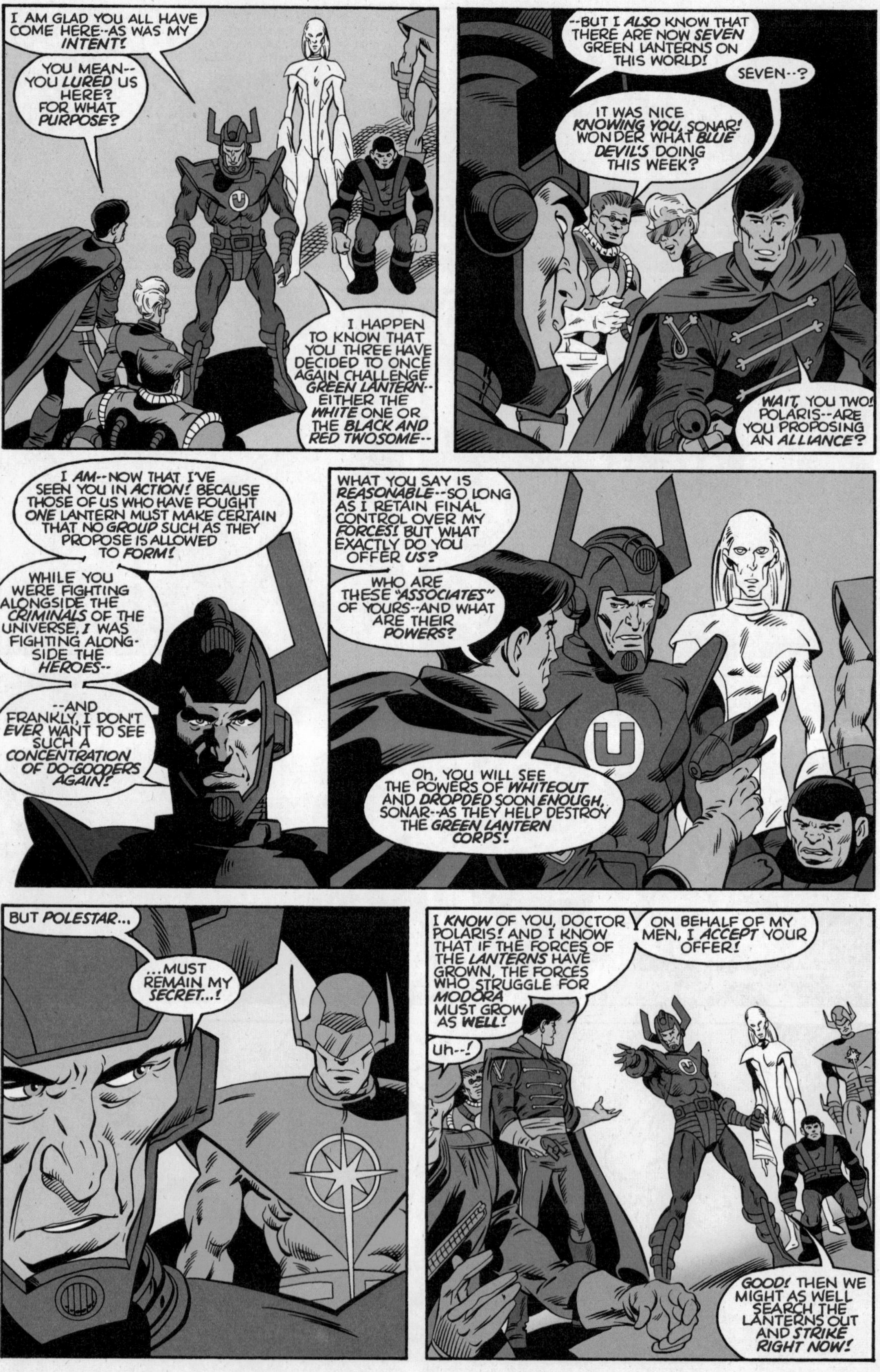
I AM GLAD YOU ALL HAVE COME HERE--AS WAS MY INTENT!
YOU MEAN--YOU LURED US HERE? FOR WHAT PURPOSE?
I HAPPEN TO KNOW THAT YOU THREE HAVE DECIDED TO ONCE AGAIN CHALLENGE GREEN LANTERN--EITHER THE WHITE ONE OR THE BLACK AND RED TWOSOME--
--BUT I ALSO KNOW THAT THERE ARE NOW SEVEN GREEN LANTERNS ON THIS WORLD!
SEVEN--?
IT WAS NICE KNOWING YOU, SONAR! WONDER WHAT BLUE DEVIL'S DOING THIS WEEK?
WAIT, YOU TWO! POLARIS--ARE YOU PROPOSING AN ALLIANCE?
I AM--NOW THAT I'VE SEEN YOU IN ACTION! BECAUSE THOSE OF US WHO HAVE FOUGHT ONE LANTERN MUST MAKE CERTAIN THAT NO GROUP SUCH AS THEY PROPOSE IS ALLOWED TO FORM!
WHILE YOU WERE FIGHTING ALONGSIDE THE CRIMINALS OF THE UNIVERSE, I WAS FIGHTING ALONG-SIDE THE HEROES--
--AND FRANKLY, I DON'T EVER WANT TO SEE SUCH A CONCENTRATION OF DO-GOODERS AGAIN!
WHAT YOU SAY IS REASONABLE--SO LONG AS I RETAIN FINAL CONTROL OVER MY FORCES! BUT WHAT EXACTLY DO YOU OFFER US?
WHO ARE THESE "ASSOCIATES" OF YOURS--AND WHAT ARE THEIR POWERS?
Oh, YOU WILL SEE THE POWERS OF WHITEOUT AND DROPDED SOON ENOUGH, SONAR--AS THEY HELP DESTROY THE GREEN LANTERN CORPS!
BUT POLESTAR...
...MUST REMAIN MY SECRET...!
I KNOW OF YOU, DOCTOR POLARIS! AND I KNOW THAT IF THE FORCES OF THE LANTERNS HAVE GROWN, THE FORCES WHO STRUGGLE FOR MODORA MUST GROW AS WELL!
ON BEHALF OF MY MEN, I ACCEPT YOUR OFFER!
Uh--!
GOOD! THEN WE MIGHT AS WELL SEARCH THE LANTERNS OUT AND STRIKE RIGHT NOW!

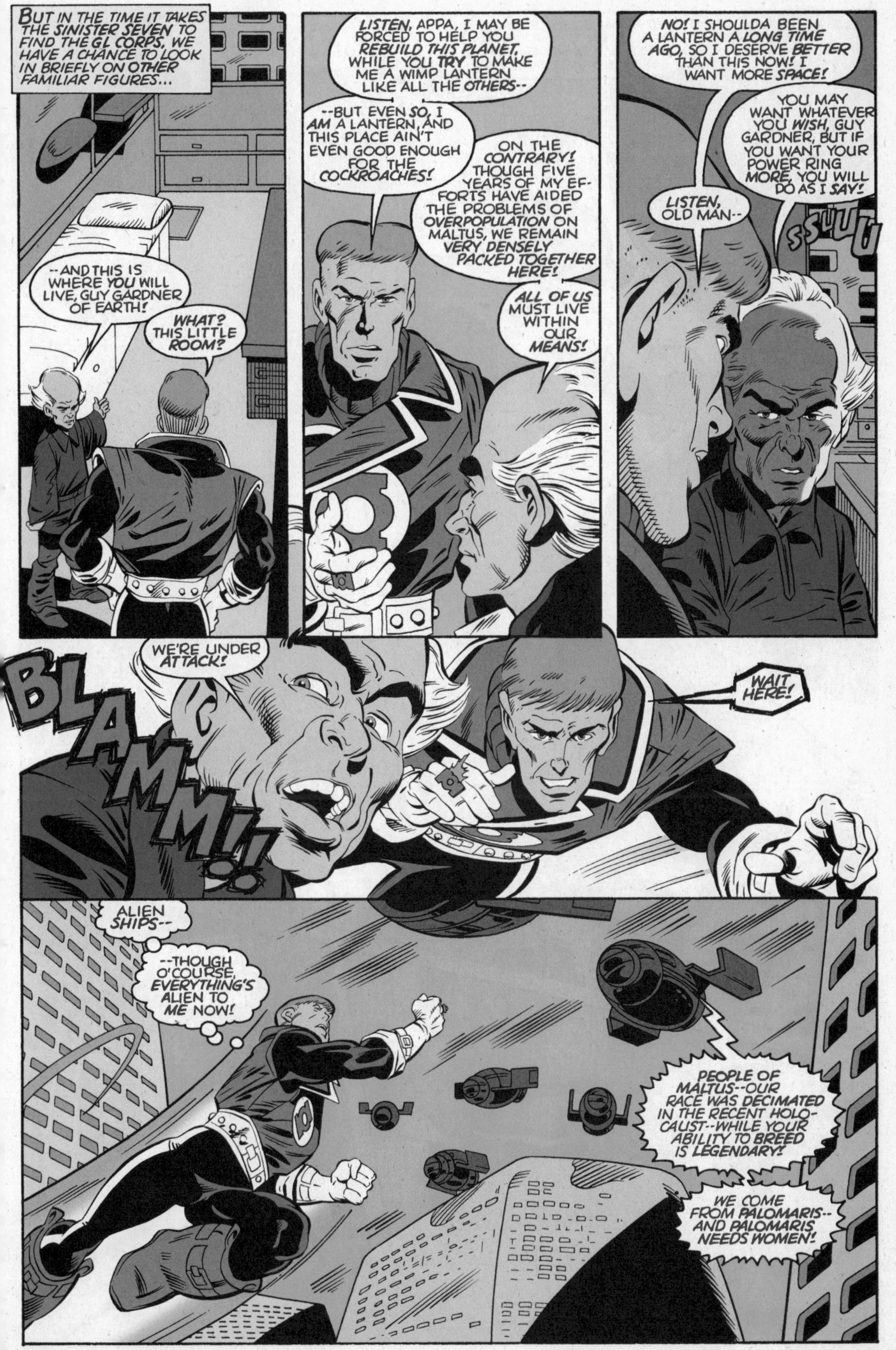
BUT IN THE TIME IT TAKES THE SINISTER SEVEN TO FIND THE GL CORPS, WE HAVE A CHANCE TO LOOK IN BRIEFLY ON OTHER FAMILIAR FIGURES...
--AND THIS IS WHERE YOU WILL LIVE, GUY GARDNER OF EARTH!
WHAT? THIS LITTLE ROOM?
LISTEN, APPA, I MAY BE FORCED TO HELP YOU REBUILD THIS PLANET, WHILE YOU TRY TO MAKE ME A WIMP LANTERN LIKE ALL THE OTHERS--
--BUT EVEN SO, I AM A LANTERN, AND THIS PLACE AIN'T EVEN GOOD ENOUGH FOR THE COCKROACHES!
ON THE CONTRARY! THOUGH FIVE YEARS OF MY EFFORTS HAVE AIDED THE PROBLEMS OF OVERPOPULATION ON MALTUS, WE REMAIN VERY DENSELY PACKED TOGETHER HERE!
ALL OF US MUST LIVE WITHIN OUR MEANS!
NO! I SHOULDA BEEN A LANTERN A LONG TIME AGO, SO I DESERVE BETTER THAN THIS NOW! I WANT MORE SPACE!
YOU MAY WANT WHATEVER YOU WISH, GUY GARDNER, BUT IF YOU WANT YOUR POWER RING MORE, YOU WILL DO AS I SAY!
LISTEN, OLD MAN--
SSUUU
BLAMM!!
WE'RE UNDER ATTACK!
WAIT HERE!
ALIEN SHIPS--
--THOUGH O'COURSE, EVERYTHING'S ALIEN TO ME NOW!
PEOPLE OF MALTUS--OUR RACE WAS DECIMATED IN THE RECENT HOLOCAUST--WHILE YOUR ABILITY TO BREED IS LEGENDARY!
WE COME FROM PALOMARIS--AND PALOMARIS NEEDS WOMEN!

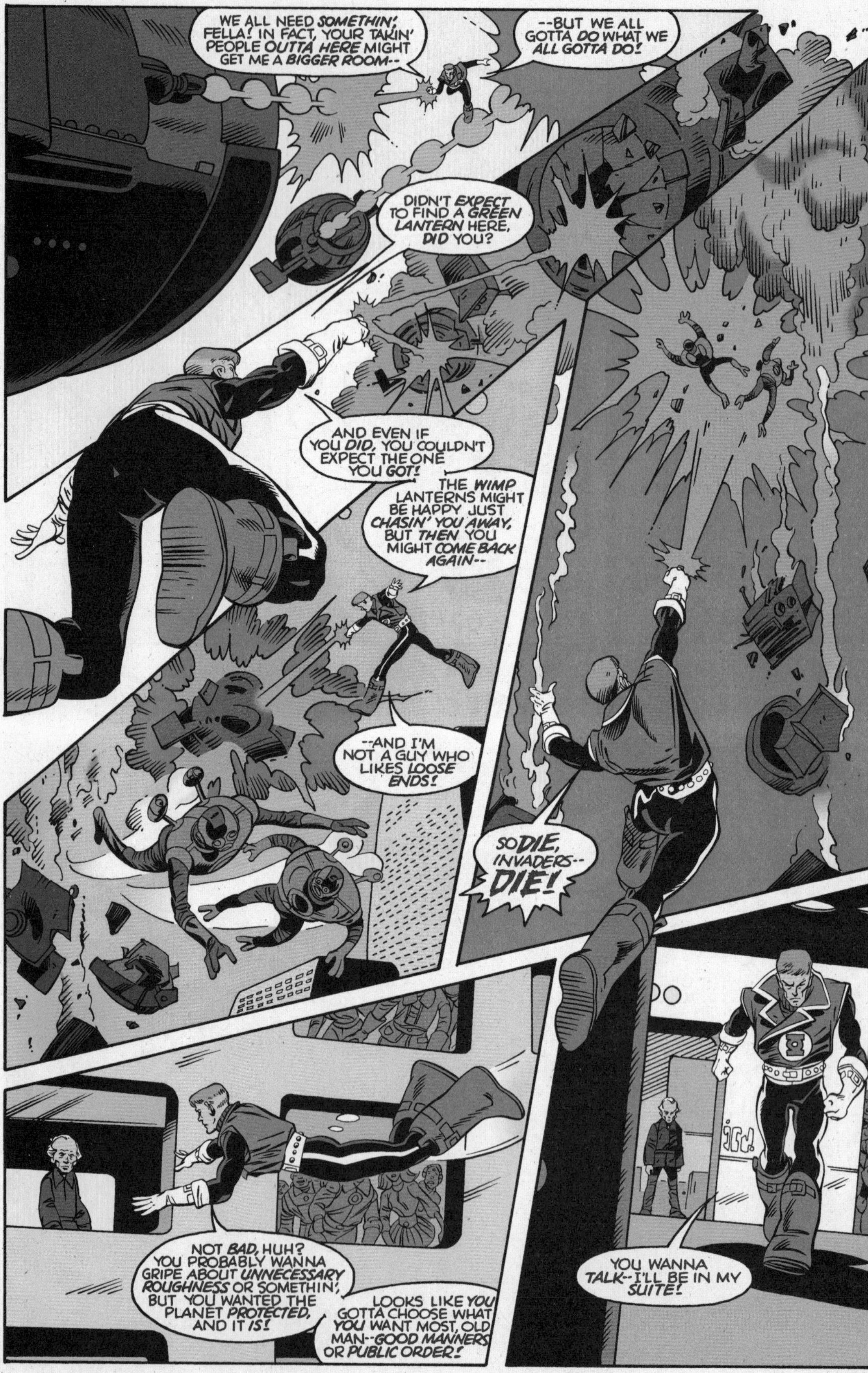
WE ALL NEED SOMETHIN', FELLA! IN FACT, YOUR TAKIN' PEOPLE OUTTA HERE MIGHT GET ME A BIGGER ROOM--
--BUT WE ALL GOTTA DO WHAT WE ALL GOTTA DO!
DIDN'T EXPECT TO FIND A GREEN LANTERN HERE, DID YOU?
AND EVEN IF YOU DID, YOU COULDN'T EXPECT THE ONE YOU GOT!
THE WIMP LANTERNS MIGHT BE HAPPY JUST CHASIN' YOU AWAY, BUT THEN YOU MIGHT COME BACK AGAIN--
--AND I'M NOT A GUY WHO LIKES LOOSE ENDS!
SO DIE, INVADERS-- DIE!
NOT BAD, HUH? YOU PROBABLY WANNA GRIPE ABOUT UNNECESSARY ROUGHNESS OR SOMETHIN', BUT YOU WANTED THE PLANET PROTECTED, AND IT IS!
LOOKS LIKE YOU GOTTA CHOOSE WHAT YOU WANT MOST, OLD MAN--GOOD MANNERS OR PUBLIC ORDER!
YOU WANNA TALK--I'LL BE IN MY SUITE!

AND ELSEWHERE IN THE UNIVERSE-- SPECIFICALLY, THE PLANET ZAMARON--

I'M *BACK!*

BUT THEN, WHERE *ELSE* WAS STAR SAPPHIRE TO GO--?

MY ENTIRE *WORLD* IS *DESERTED*, SINCE MY WARRIORS LEFT THE UNIVERSE WITH THE GUARDIANS! I AM A *QUEEN* WITHOUT *SUBJECTS*--

--BUT A QUEEN *NONETHELESS!* IT WAS *UNTHINKABLE* THAT I SHOULD RETURN TO THE WORLD OF MY *HUMBLE ORIGINS*-- *EARTH!*

I *BECAME* QUEEN FOR THE *REST* OF MY *NATURAL* LIFE, AND THE POWERS AVAILABLE TO ME REMAIN LARGELY *UNEXPLORED!*

GIVEN TIME, THOUGH, I WILL *MASTER* THEM! GIVEN TIME, I WILL DISCOVER *ALL* THE SECRETS OF THE *ZAMARONS*--

--AND THEN THE *UNIVERSE* WILL LEARN THAT I DON'T NEED *WARRIORS* TO MAKE MY *PRESENCE* FELT!

MOST *PARTICULARLY*, THE *GREEN LANTERN CORPS* WILL LEARN WHAT IT MEANS TO TREAT ME AS THEY HAVE!

BEFORE I'M *FINISHED*, HAL AND JOHN AND KATMA WILL EACH *KISS MY FOOT!*

AND I KNOW JUST HOW TO *BEGIN*--!

BUDALUMM

DADALAAAAAAAAAAAAAAAAAA

IF THERE IS SUCH A THING AS THE *MUSIC OF THE SPHERES*--IT NOW HAS *COMPETITION*...

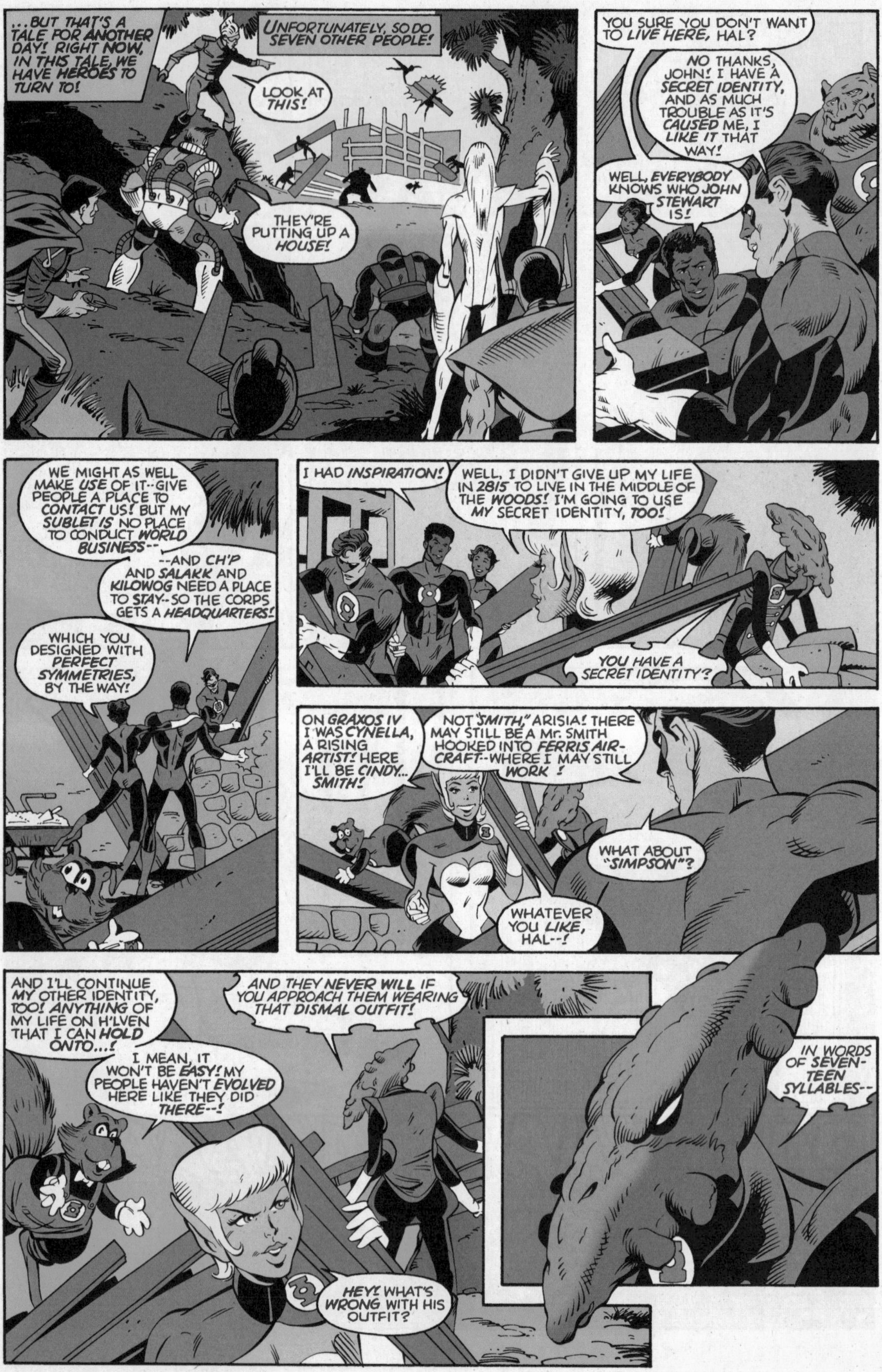
...BUT THAT'S A TALE FOR ANOTHER DAY! RIGHT NOW, IN THIS TALE, WE HAVE HEROES TO TURN TO!
UNFORTUNATELY, SO DO SEVEN OTHER PEOPLE!
LOOK AT THIS!
THEY'RE PUTTING UP A HOUSE!
YOU SURE YOU DON'T WANT TO LIVE HERE, HAL?
NO THANKS, JOHN! I HAVE A SECRET IDENTITY, AND AS MUCH TROUBLE AS IT'S CAUSED ME, I LIKE IT THAT WAY!
WELL, EVERYBODY KNOWS WHO JOHN STEWART IS!
WE MIGHT AS WELL MAKE USE OF IT--GIVE PEOPLE A PLACE TO CONTACT US! BUT MY SUBLET IS NO PLACE TO CONDUCT WORLD BUSINESS--
--AND CH'P AND SALAKK AND KILOWOG NEED A PLACE TO STAY--SO THE CORPS GETS A HEADQUARTERS!
WHICH YOU DESIGNED WITH PERFECT SYMMETRIES, BY THE WAY!
I HAD INSPIRATION!
WELL, I DIDN'T GIVE UP MY LIFE IN 2815 TO LIVE IN THE MIDDLE OF THE WOODS! I'M GOING TO USE MY SECRET IDENTITY, TOO!
YOU HAVE A SECRET IDENTITY?
ON GRAXOS IV I WAS CYNELLA, A RISING ARTIST! HERE I'LL BE CINDY... SMITH!
NOT "SMITH," ARISIA! THERE MAY STILL BE A Mr. SMITH HOOKED INTO FERRIS AIR-CRAFT--WHERE I MAY STILL WORK!
WHAT ABOUT "SIMPSON"?
WHATEVER YOU LIKE, HAL--!
AND I'LL CONTINUE MY OTHER IDENTITY, TOO! ANYTHING OF MY LIFE ON H'LVEN THAT I CAN HOLD ONTO...!
I MEAN, IT WON'T BE EASY! MY PEOPLE HAVEN'T EVOLVED HERE LIKE THEY DID THERE--!
AND THEY NEVER WILL IF YOU APPROACH THEM WEARING THAT DISMAL OUTFIT!
IN WORDS OF SEVEN-TEEN SYLLABLES--
HEY! WHAT'S WRONG WITH HIS OUTFIT?

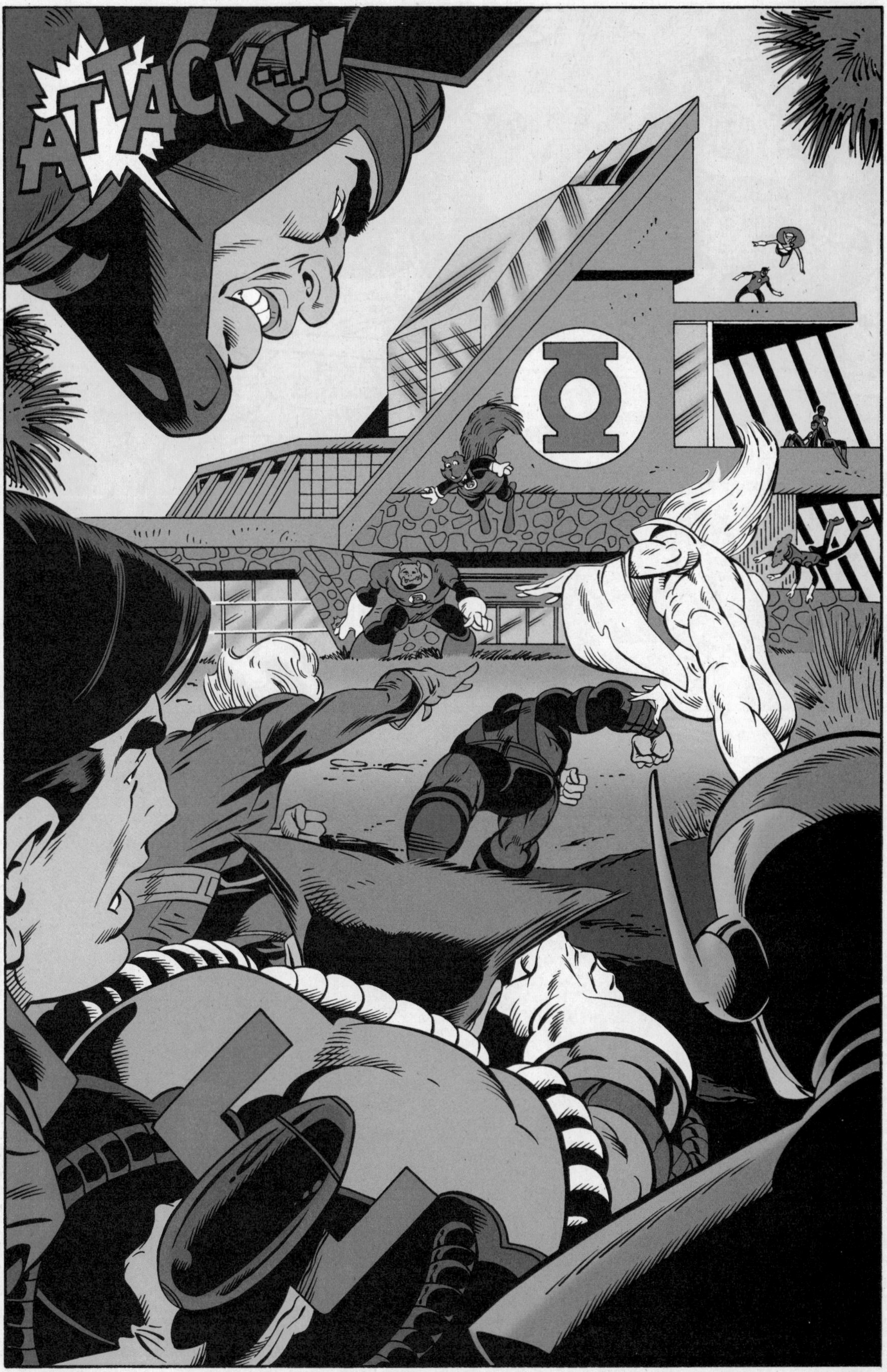
ATTACK..!!!

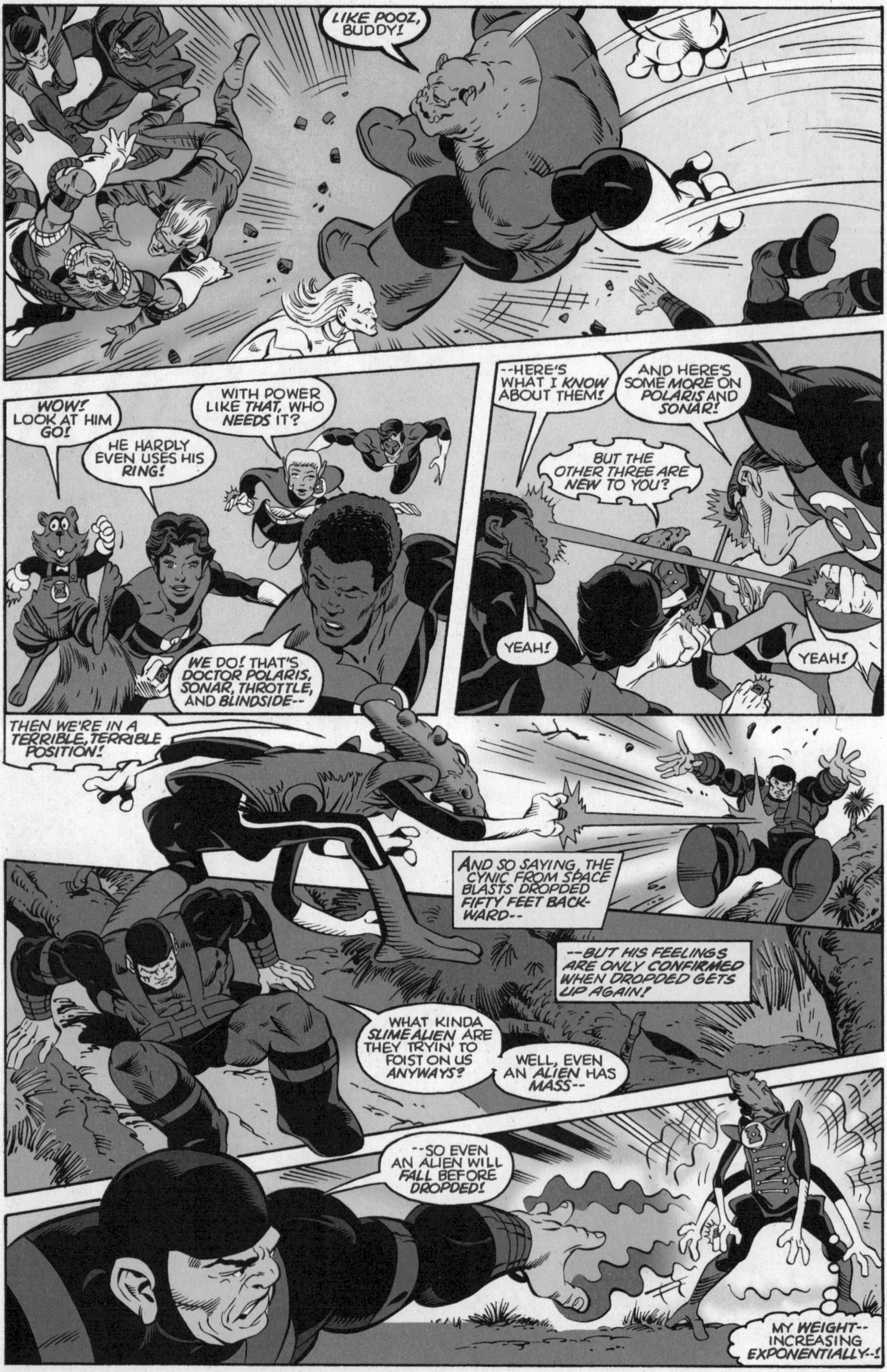
LIKE POOZ, BUDDY!
WOW! LOOK AT HIM GO!
HE HARDLY EVEN USES HIS RING!
WITH POWER LIKE THAT, WHO NEEDS IT?
WE DO! THAT'S DOCTOR POLARIS, SONAR, THROTTLE, AND BLINDSIDE--
--HERE'S WHAT I KNOW ABOUT THEM!
AND HERE'S SOME MORE ON POLARIS AND SONAR!
BUT THE OTHER THREE ARE NEW TO YOU?
YEAH!
YEAH!
THEN WE'RE IN A TERRIBLE, TERRIBLE POSITION!
AND SO SAYING, THE CYNIC FROM SPACE BLASTS DROPDED FIFTY FEET BACKWARD--
--BUT HIS FEELINGS ARE ONLY CONFIRMED WHEN DROPDED GETS UP AGAIN!
WHAT KINDA SLIME ALIEN ARE THEY TRYIN' TO FOIST ON US ANYWAYS?
WELL, EVEN AN ALIEN HAS MASS--
--SO EVEN AN ALIEN WILL FALL BEFORE DROPDED!
MY WEIGHT-- INCREASING EXPONENTIALLY--!

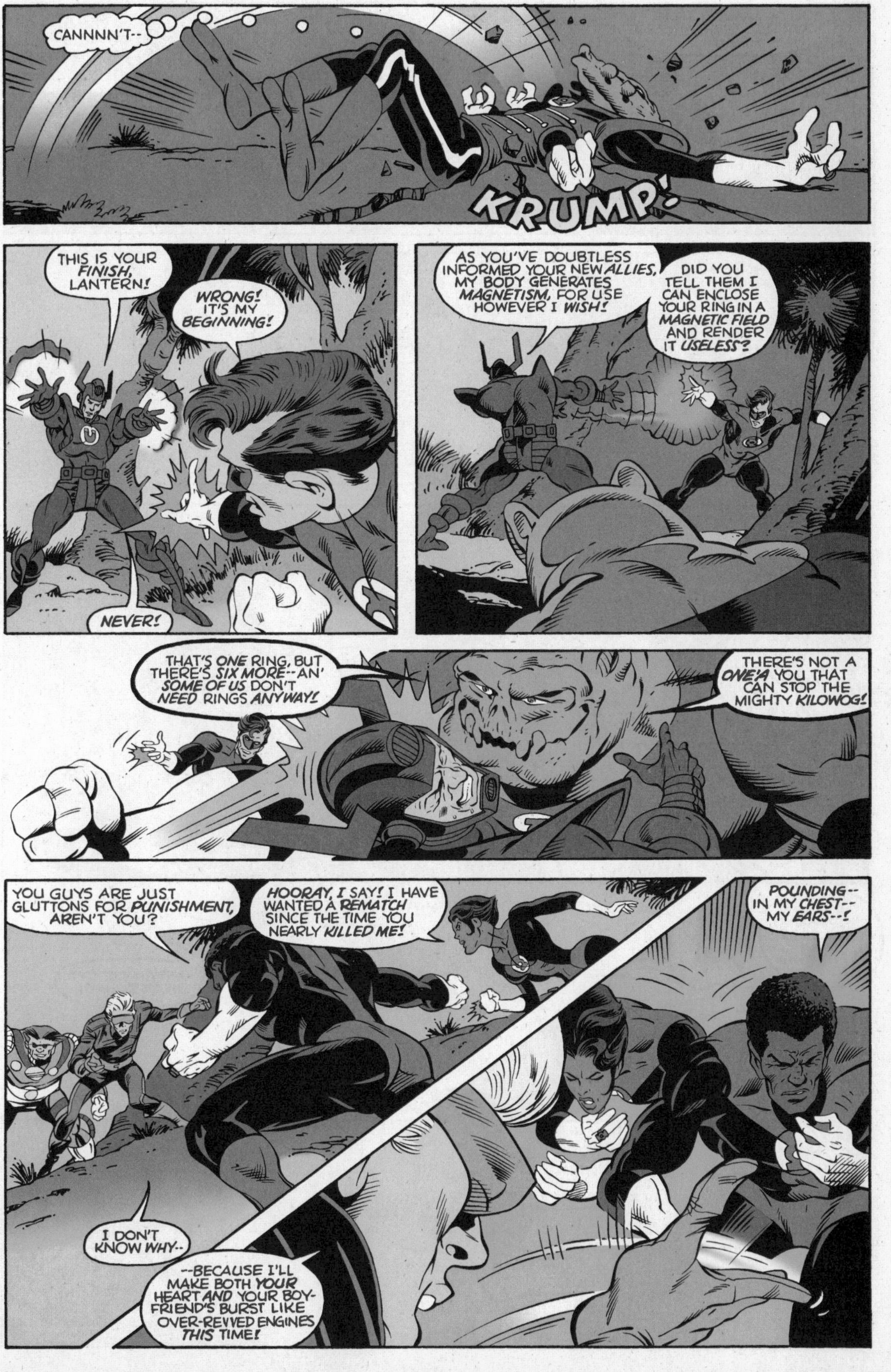
CANNNN'T--
KRUMP!
THIS IS YOUR FINISH, LANTERN!
WRONG! IT'S MY BEGINNING!
NEVER!
AS YOU'VE DOUBTLESS INFORMED YOUR NEW ALLIES, MY BODY GENERATES MAGNETISM, FOR USE HOWEVER I WISH!
DID YOU TELL THEM I CAN ENCLOSE YOUR RING IN A MAGNETIC FIELD AND RENDER IT USELESS?
THAT'S ONE RING, BUT THERE'S SIX MORE--AN' SOME OF US DON'T NEED RINGS ANYWAY!
THERE'S NOT A ONE'A YOU THAT CAN STOP THE MIGHTY KILOWOG!
YOU GUYS ARE JUST GLUTTONS FOR PUNISHMENT, AREN'T YOU?
HOORAY, I SAY! I HAVE WANTED A REMATCH SINCE THE TIME YOU NEARLY KILLED ME!
POUNDING-- IN MY CHEST-- MY EARS--!
I DON'T KNOW WHY--
--BECAUSE I'LL MAKE BOTH YOUR HEART AND YOUR BOY-FRIEND'S BURST LIKE OVER-REVVED ENGINES THIS TIME!

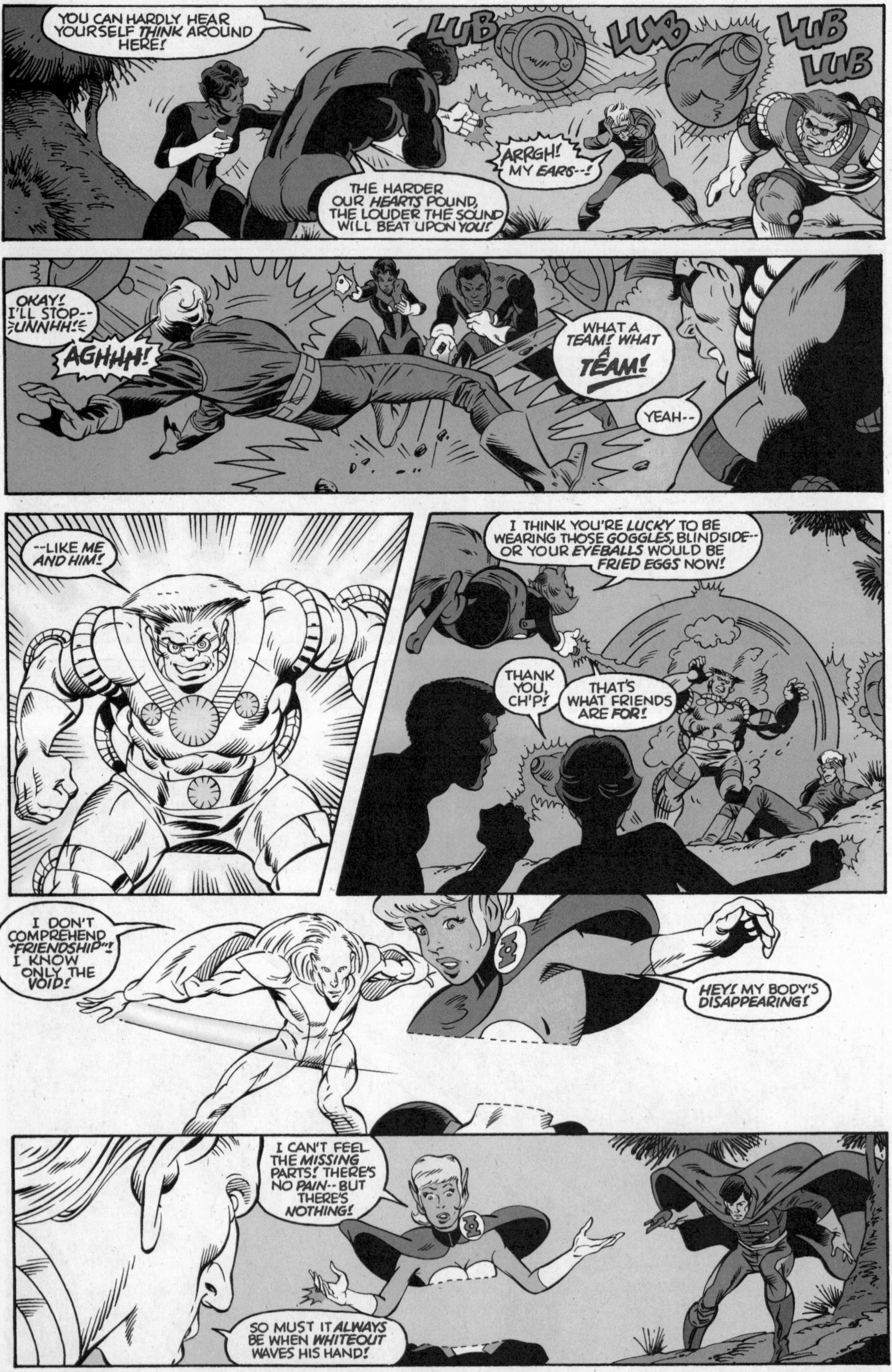

YOU CAN HARDLY HEAR YOURSELF THINK AROUND HERE!
LUB
LUB
LUB LUB
ARRGH! MY EARS--!
THE HARDER OUR HEARTS POUND, THE LOUDER THE SOUND WILL BEAT UPON YOU!
OKAY! I'LL STOP-- UNNHH!
AGHHH!
WHAT A TEAM! WHAT A TEAM!
YEAH--
--LIKE ME AND HIM!
I THINK YOU'RE LUCKY TO BE WEARING THOSE GOGGLES, BLINDSIDE-- OR YOUR EYEBALLS WOULD BE FRIED EGGS NOW!
THANK YOU, CH'P!
THAT'S WHAT FRIENDS ARE FOR!
I DON'T COMPREHEND "FRIENDSHIP"! I KNOW ONLY THE VOID!
HEY! MY BODY'S DISAPPEARING!
I CAN'T FEEL THE MISSING PARTS! THERE'S NO PAIN-- BUT THERE'S NOTHING!
SO MUST IT ALWAYS BE WHEN WHITEOUT WAVES HIS HAND!

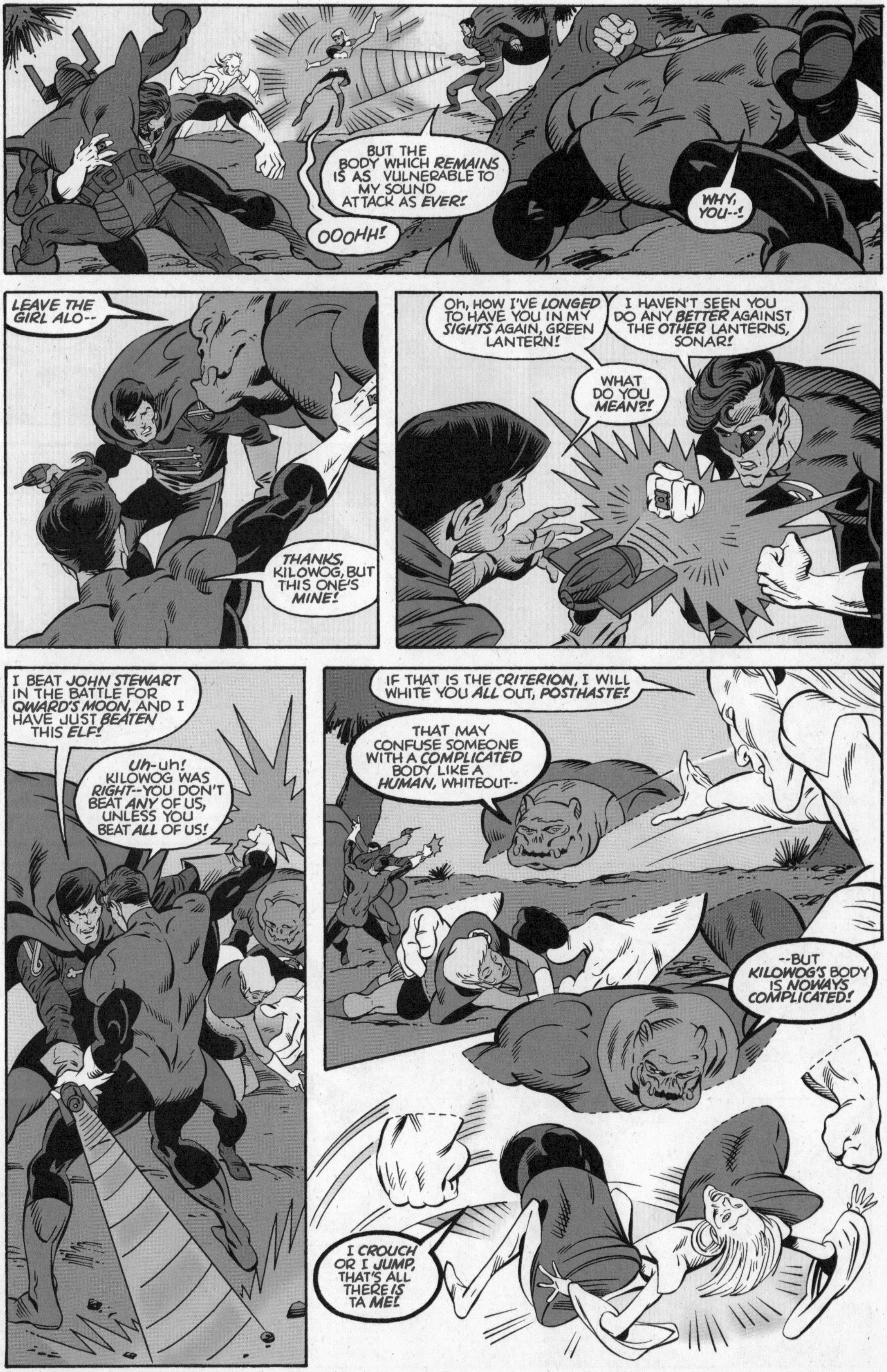
BUT THE BODY WHICH REMAINS IS AS VULNERABLE TO MY SOUND ATTACK AS EVER!
OOOHH!
WHY, YOU--!
LEAVE THE GIRL ALO--
THANKS, KILOWOG, BUT THIS ONE'S MINE!
Oh, HOW I'VE LONGED TO HAVE YOU IN MY SIGHTS AGAIN, GREEN LANTERN!
I HAVEN'T SEEN YOU DO ANY BETTER AGAINST THE OTHER LANTERNS, SONAR!
WHAT DO YOU MEAN?!
I BEAT JOHN STEWART IN THE BATTLE FOR QWARD'S MOON, AND I HAVE JUST BEATEN THIS ELF!
Uh-uh! KILOWOG WAS RIGHT--YOU DON'T BEAT ANY OF US, UNLESS YOU BEAT ALL OF US!
IF THAT IS THE CRITERION, I WILL WHITE YOU ALL OUT, POSTHASTE!
THAT MAY CONFUSE SOMEONE WITH A COMPLICATED BODY LIKE A HUMAN, WHITEOUT--
--BUT KILOWOG'S BODY IS NOWAYS COMPLICATED!
I CROUCH OR I JUMP, THAT'S ALL THERE IS TA ME!

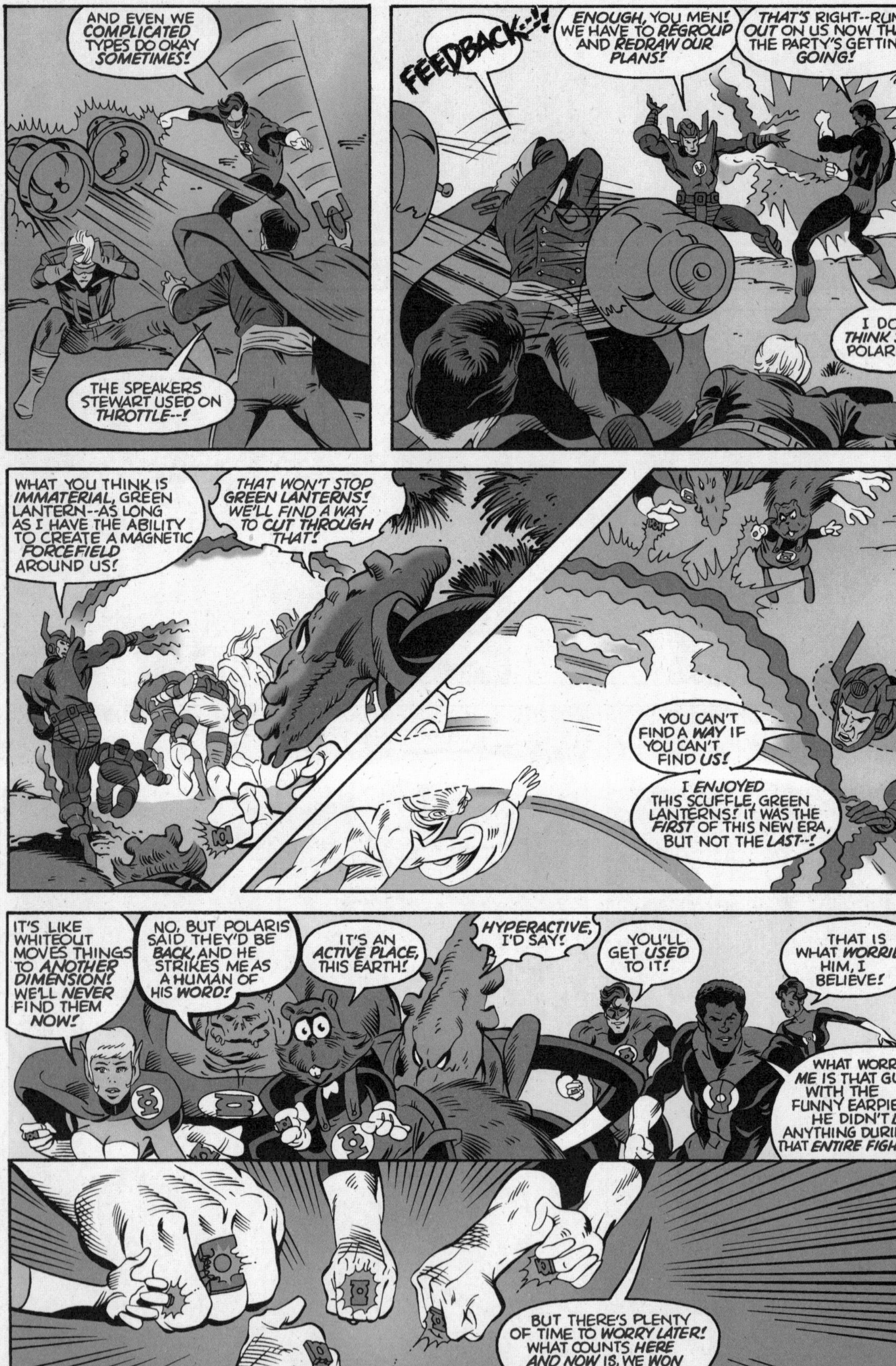
AND EVEN WE COMPLICATED TYPES DO OKAY SOMETIMES!
THE SPEAKERS STEWART USED ON THROTTLE--!
FEEDBACK--!
ENOUGH, YOU MEN! WE HAVE TO REGROUP AND REDRAW OUR PLANS!
THAT'S RIGHT--RUN OUT ON US NOW THAT THE PARTY'S GETTING GOING!
I DON'T THINK SO, POLARIS!
WHAT YOU THINK IS IMMATERIAL, GREEN LANTERN--AS LONG AS I HAVE THE ABILITY TO CREATE A MAGNETIC FORCEFIELD AROUND US!
THAT WON'T STOP GREEN LANTERNS! WE'LL FIND A WAY TO CUT THROUGH THAT!
YOU CAN'T FIND A WAY IF YOU CAN'T FIND US!
I ENJOYED THIS SCUFFLE, GREEN LANTERNS! IT WAS THE FIRST OF THIS NEW ERA, BUT NOT THE LAST--!
IT'S LIKE WHITEOUT MOVES THINGS TO ANOTHER DIMENSION! WE'LL NEVER FIND THEM NOW!
NO, BUT POLARIS SAID THEY'D BE BACK, AND HE STRIKES ME AS A HUMAN OF HIS WORD!
IT'S AN ACTIVE PLACE, THIS EARTH!
HYPERACTIVE, I'D SAY!
YOU'LL GET USED TO IT!
THAT IS WHAT WORRIES HIM, I BELIEVE!
WHAT WORRIES ME IS THAT GUY WITH THE FUNNY EARPIECES! HE DIDN'T DO ANYTHING DURING THAT ENTIRE FIGHT!
BUT THERE'S PLENTY OF TIME TO WORRY LATER! WHAT COUNTS HERE AND NOW IS, WE WON OUR FIRST BATTLE!
EARTH IS SURELY GOING TO KNOW THAT THE GREEN LANTERN CORPS HAS ARRIVED!

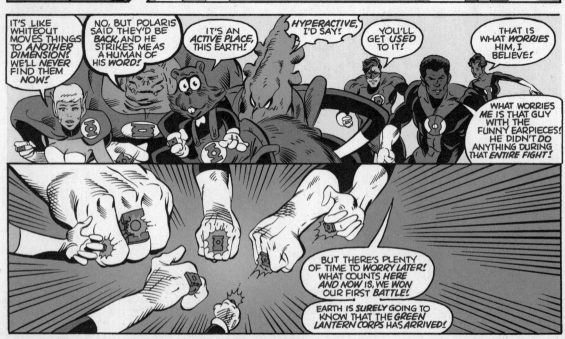

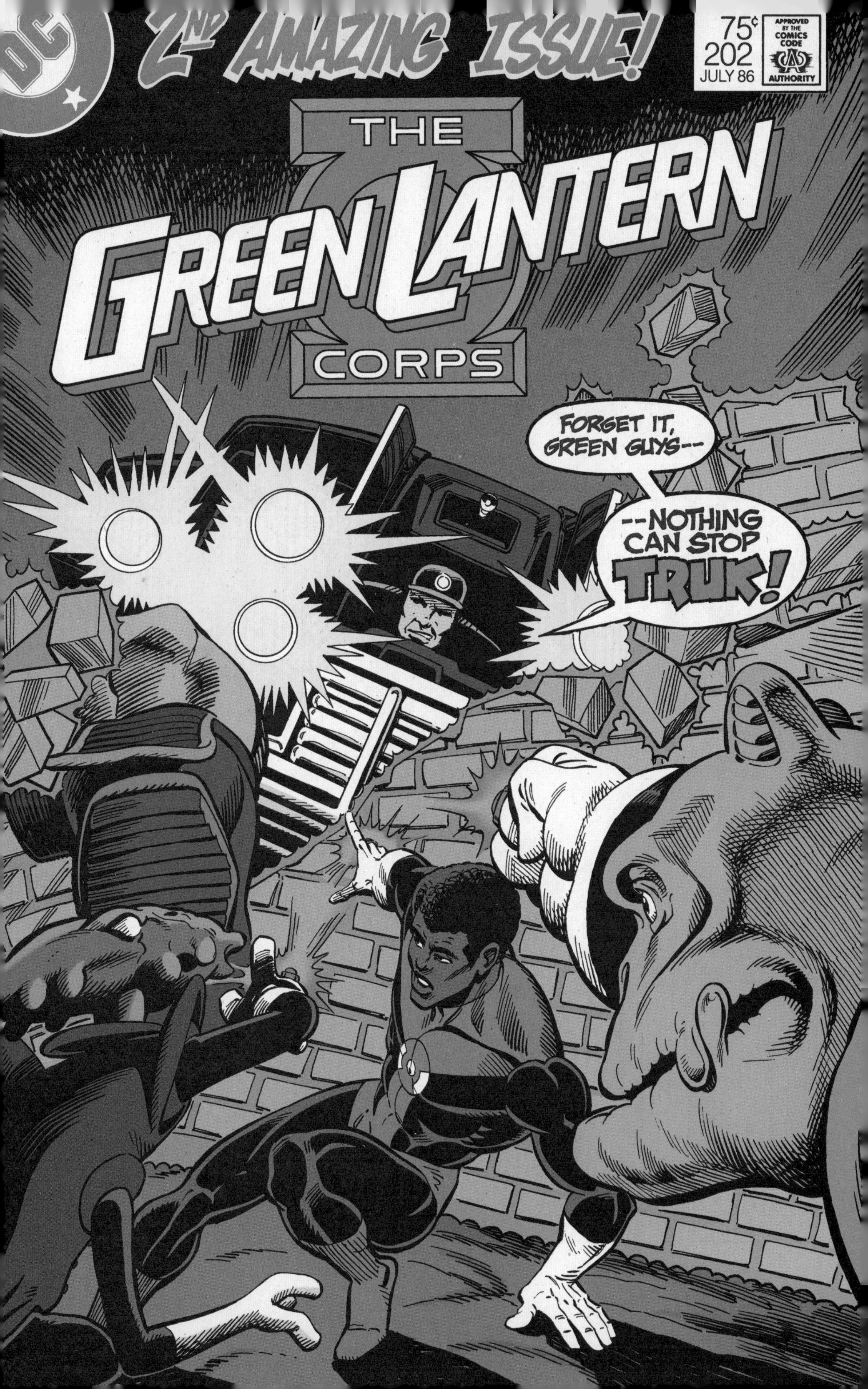
2ND AMAZING ISSUE!
75¢
202
JULY 86
APPROVED BY THE COMICS CODE AUTHORITY
THE GREEN LANTERN CORPS
FORGET IT, GREEN GUYS--
--NOTHING CAN STOP TRUK!

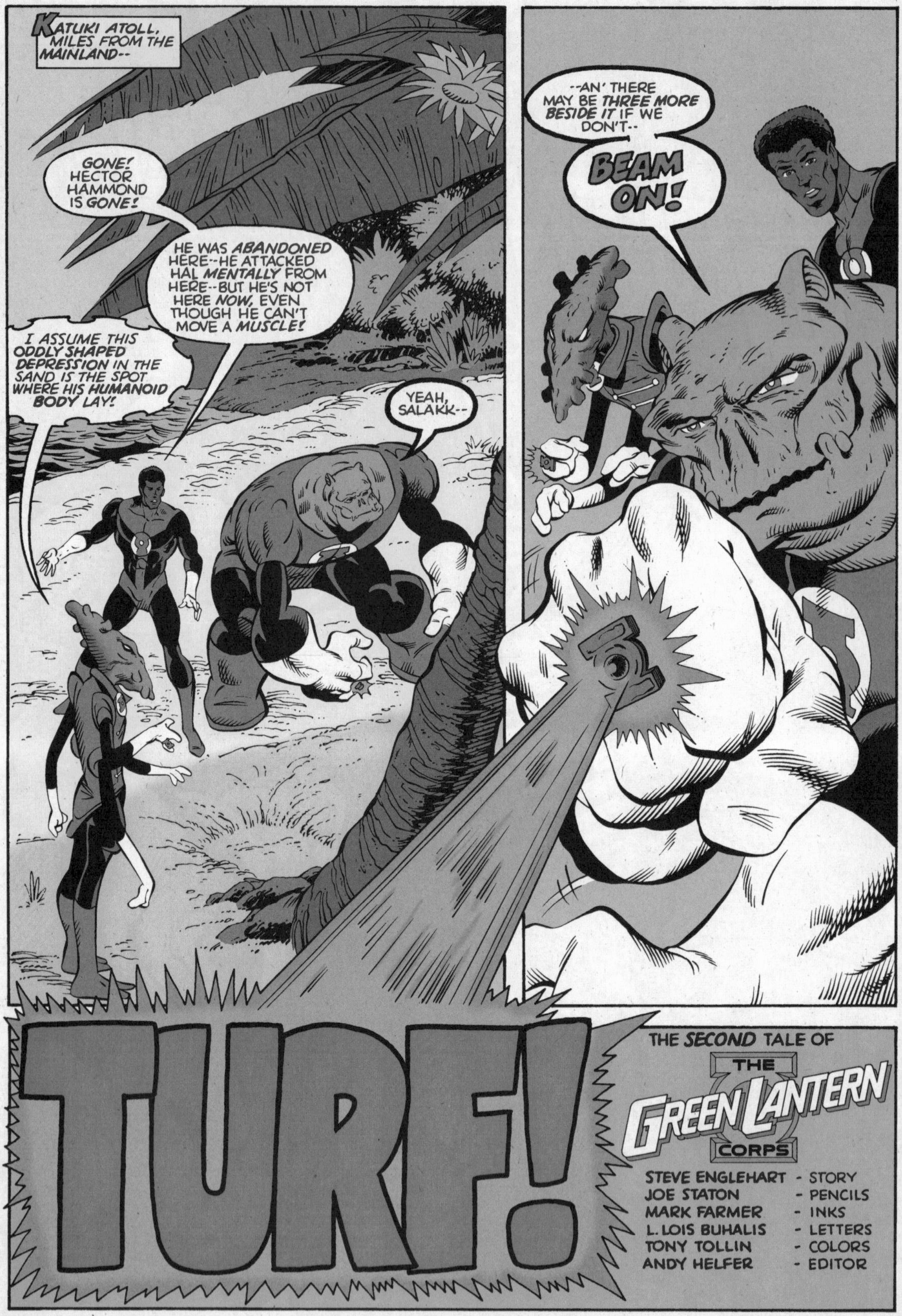
KATUKI ATOLL, MILES FROM THE MAINLAND--
GONE! HECTOR HAMMOND IS GONE!
HE WAS ABANDONED HERE--HE ATTACKED HAL MENTALLY FROM HERE--BUT HE'S NOT HERE NOW, EVEN THOUGH HE CAN'T MOVE A MUSCLE!
I ASSUME THIS ODDLY SHAPED DEPRESSION IN THE SAND IS THE SPOT WHERE HIS HUMANOID BODY LAY!
YEAH, SALAKK--
--AN' THERE MAY BE THREE MORE BESIDE IT IF WE DON'T--
BEAM ON!
TURF!
THE SECOND TALE OF THE GREEN LANTERN CORPS
STEVE ENGLEHART - STORY
JOE STATON - PENCILS
MARK FARMER - INKS
L. LOIS BUHALIS - LETTERS
TONY TOLLIN - COLORS
ANDY HELFER - EDITOR

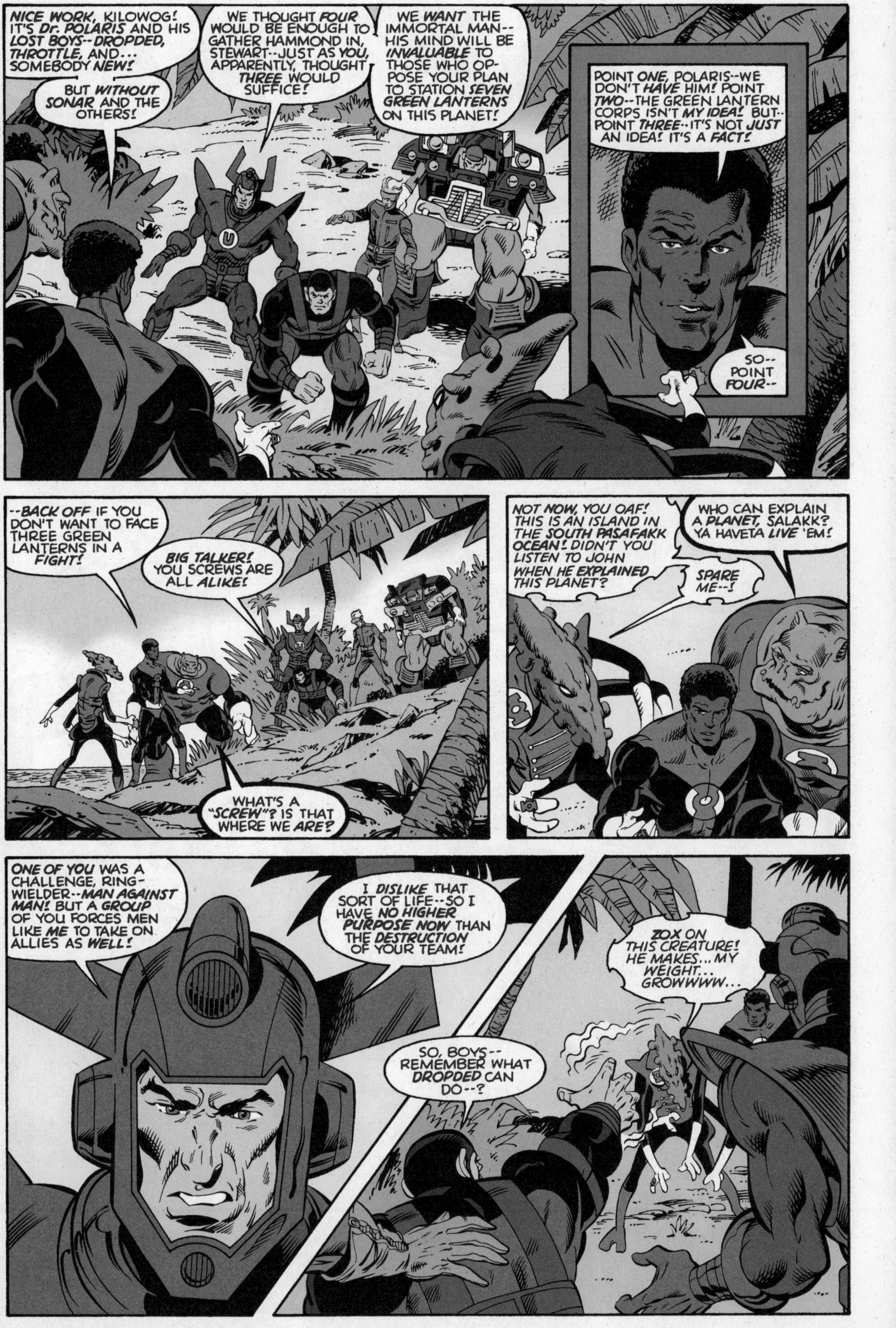

NICE WORK, KILOWOG! IT'S Dr. POLARIS AND HIS LOST BOYS--DROPDED, THROTTLE, AND... SOMEBODY NEW!
BUT WITHOUT SONAR AND THE OTHERS!
WE THOUGHT FOUR WOULD BE ENOUGH TO GATHER HAMMOND IN, STEWART--JUST AS YOU, APPARENTLY, THOUGHT THREE WOULD SUFFICE!
WE WANT THE IMMORTAL MAN--HIS MIND WILL BE INVALUABLE TO THOSE WHO OPPOSE YOUR PLAN TO STATION SEVEN GREEN LANTERNS ON THIS PLANET!
POINT ONE, POLARIS--WE DON'T HAVE HIM! POINT TWO--THE GREEN LANTERN CORPS ISN'T MY IDEA! BUT--POINT THREE--IT'S NOT JUST AN IDEA! IT'S A FACT!
SO--POINT FOUR--
--BACK OFF IF YOU DON'T WANT TO FACE THREE GREEN LANTERNS IN A FIGHT!
BIG TALKER! YOU SCREWS ARE ALL ALIKE!
WHAT'S A "SCREW"? IS THAT WHERE WE ARE?
NOT NOW, YOU OAF! THIS IS AN ISLAND IN THE SOUTH PASAFAKK OCEAN! DIDN'T YOU LISTEN TO JOHN WHEN HE EXPLAINED THIS PLANET?
WHO CAN EXPLAIN A PLANET, SALAKK? YA HAVETA LIVE 'EM!
SPARE ME--!
ONE OF YOU WAS A CHALLENGE, RING-WIELDER--MAN AGAINST MAN! BUT A GROUP OF YOU FORCES MEN LIKE ME TO TAKE ON ALLIES AS WELL!
I DISLIKE THAT SORT OF LIFE--SO I HAVE NO HIGHER PURPOSE NOW THAN THE DESTRUCTION OF YOUR TEAM!
ZOX ON THIS CREATURE! HE MAKES... MY WEIGHT... GROWWWW...
SO, BOYS--REMEMBER WHAT DROPDED CAN DO--?

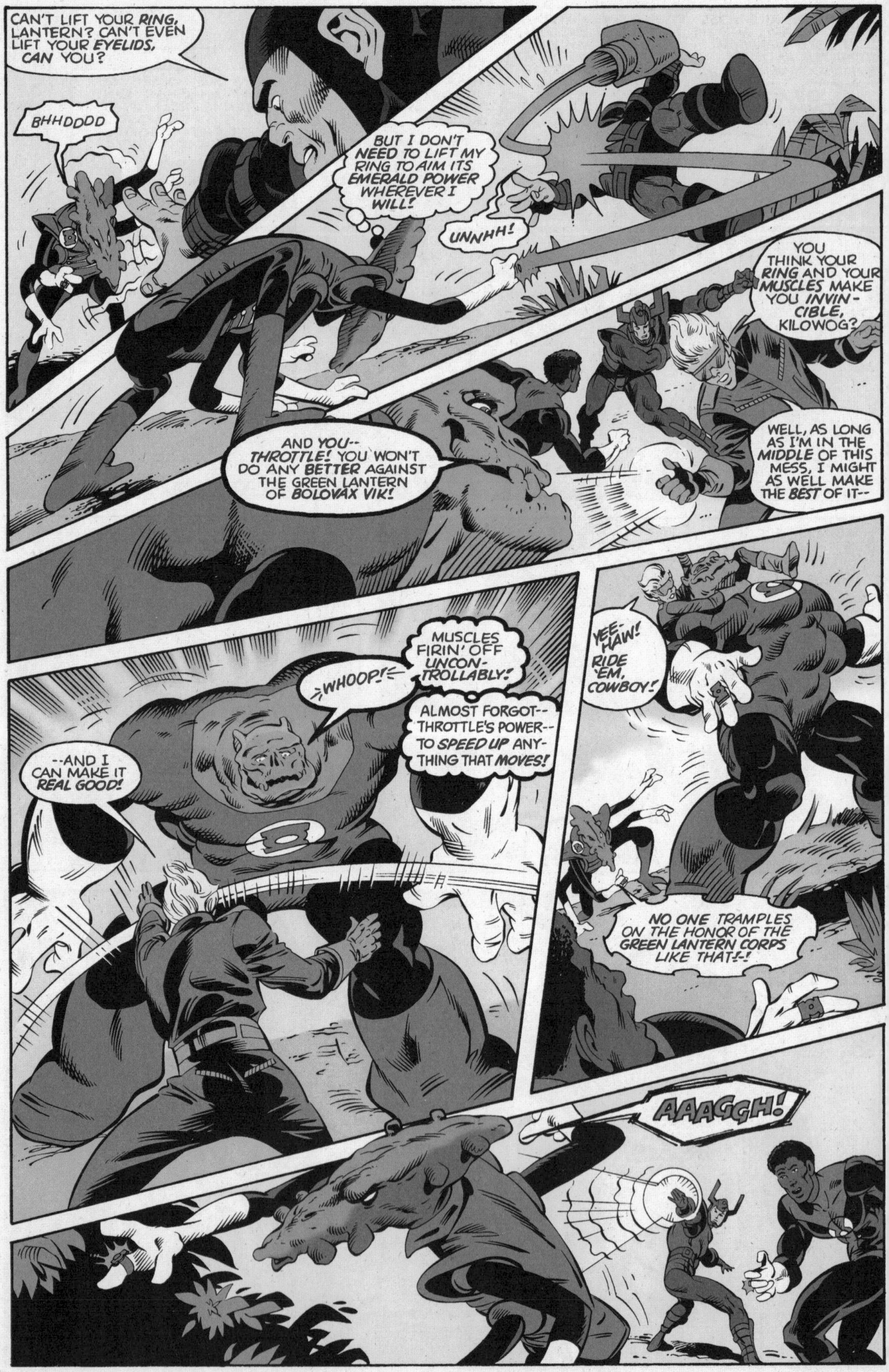
CAN'T LIFT YOUR RING, LANTERN? CAN'T EVEN LIFT YOUR EYELIDS, CAN YOU?
BHHDDDD
BUT I DON'T NEED TO LIFT MY RING TO AIM ITS EMERALD POWER WHEREVER I WILL!
UNNHH!
YOU THINK YOUR RING AND YOUR MUSCLES MAKE YOU INVIN-CIBLE, KILOWOG?
AND YOU--THROTTLE! YOU WON'T DO ANY BETTER AGAINST THE GREEN LANTERN OF BOLOVAX VIK!
WELL, AS LONG AS I'M IN THE MIDDLE OF THIS MESS, I MIGHT AS WELL MAKE THE BEST OF IT--
--AND I CAN MAKE IT REAL GOOD!
WHOOP!
MUSCLES FIRIN' OFF UNCON-TROLLABLY!
ALMOST FORGOT--THROTTLE'S POWER--TO SPEED UP ANY-THING THAT MOVES!
YEE-HAW! RIDE 'EM, COWBOY!
NO ONE TRAMPLES ON THE HONOR OF THE GREEN LANTERN CORPS LIKE THAT!-!
AAAGGH!

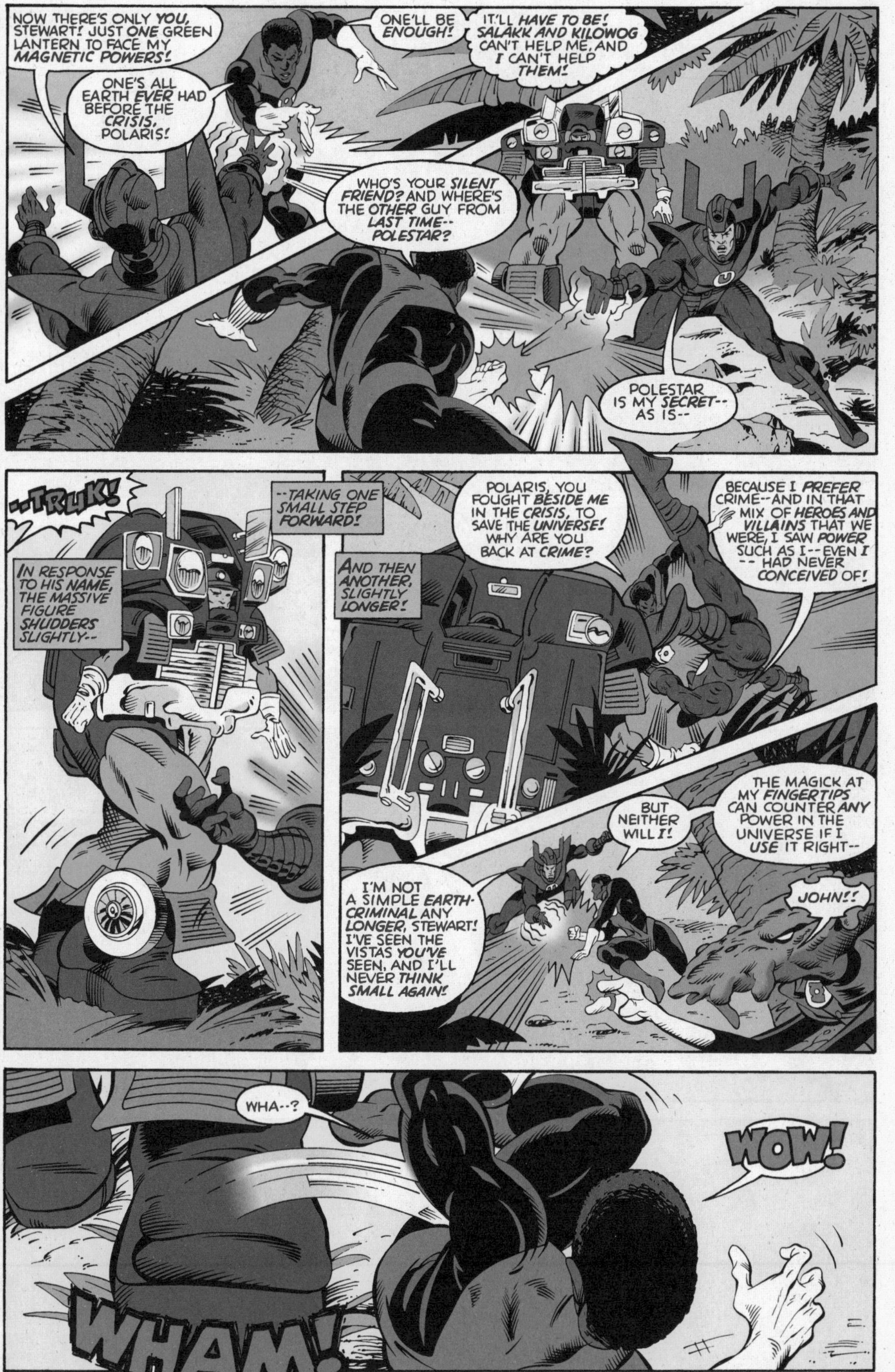
NOW THERE'S ONLY YOU, STEWART! JUST ONE GREEN LANTERN TO FACE MY MAGNETIC POWERS!
ONE'LL BE ENOUGH!
IT'LL HAVE TO BE! SALAKK AND KILOWOG CAN'T HELP ME, AND I CAN'T HELP THEM!
ONE'S ALL EARTH EVER HAD BEFORE THE CRISIS, POLARIS!
WHO'S YOUR SILENT FRIEND? AND WHERE'S THE OTHER GUY FROM LAST TIME-- POLESTAR?
POLESTAR IS MY SECRET-- AS IS--
--TRUK!
--TAKING ONE SMALL STEP FORWARD!
IN RESPONSE TO HIS NAME, THE MASSIVE FIGURE SHUDDERS SLIGHTLY--
AND THEN ANOTHER, SLIGHTLY LONGER!
POLARIS, YOU FOUGHT BESIDE ME IN THE CRISIS, TO SAVE THE UNIVERSE! WHY ARE YOU BACK AT CRIME?
BECAUSE I PREFER CRIME--AND IN THAT MIX OF HEROES AND VILLAINS THAT WE WERE, I SAW POWER SUCH AS I--EVEN I -- HAD NEVER CONCEIVED OF!
I'M NOT A SIMPLE EARTH-CRIMINAL ANY LONGER, STEWART! I'VE SEEN THE VISTAS YOU'VE SEEN, AND I'LL NEVER THINK SMALL AGAIN!
BUT NEITHER WILL I!
THE MAGICK AT MY FINGERTIPS CAN COUNTER ANY POWER IN THE UNIVERSE IF I USE IT RIGHT--
JOHN!!
WHA--?
WOW!
WHAM!

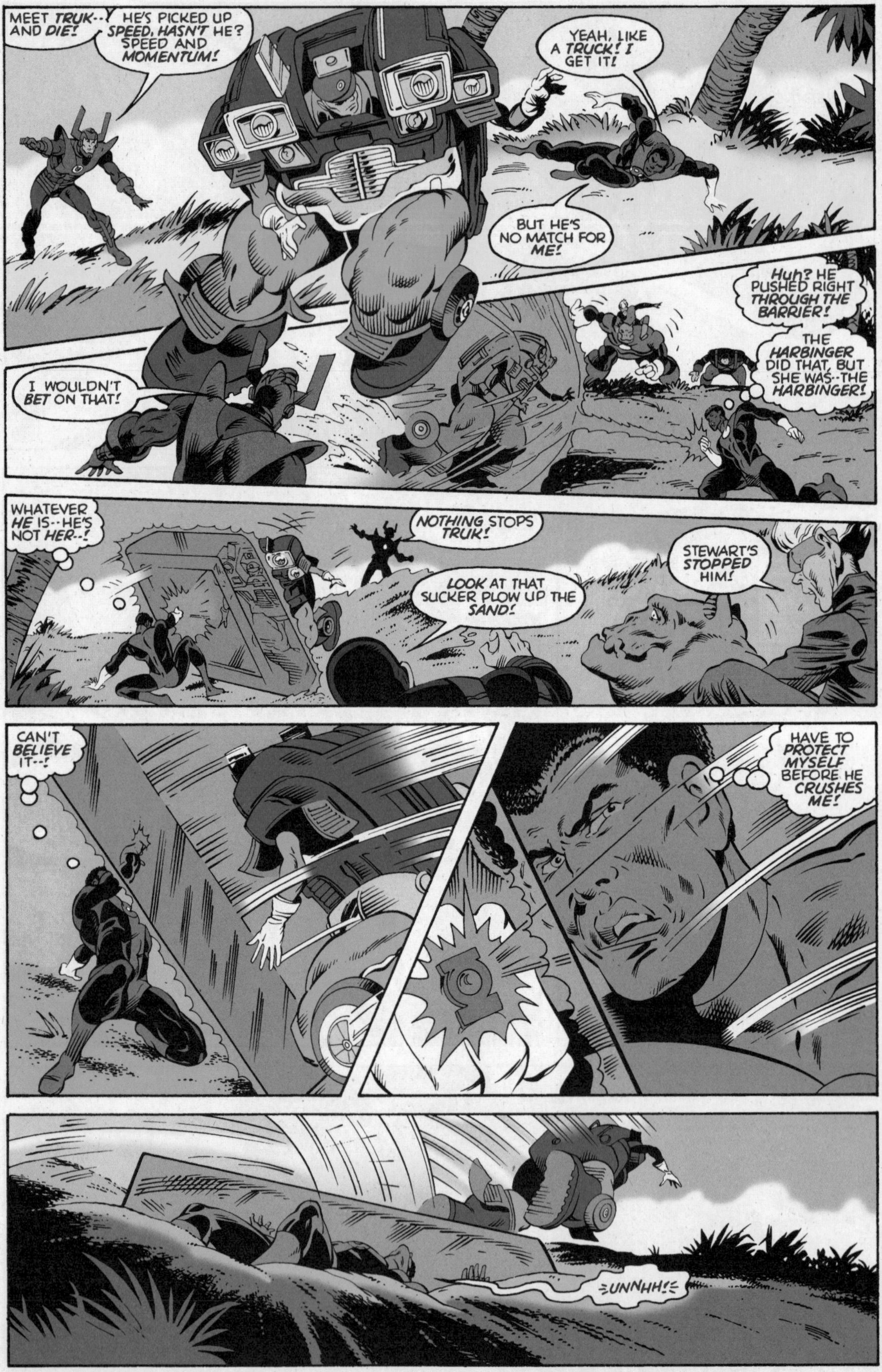

MEET TRUK--AND DIE!
HE'S PICKED UP SPEED, HASN'T HE? SPEED AND MOMENTUM!
YEAH, LIKE A TRUCK! I GET IT!
BUT HE'S NO MATCH FOR ME!
I WOULDN'T BET ON THAT!
Huh? HE PUSHED RIGHT THROUGH THE BARRIER!
THE HARBINGER DID THAT, BUT SHE WAS--THE HARBINGER!
WHATEVER HE IS--HE'S NOT HER--!
NOTHING STOPS TRUK!
LOOK AT THAT SUCKER PLOW UP THE SAND!
STEWART'S STOPPED HIM!
CAN'T BELIEVE IT--!
HAVE TO PROTECT MYSELF BEFORE HE CRUSHES ME!
UNNHH!

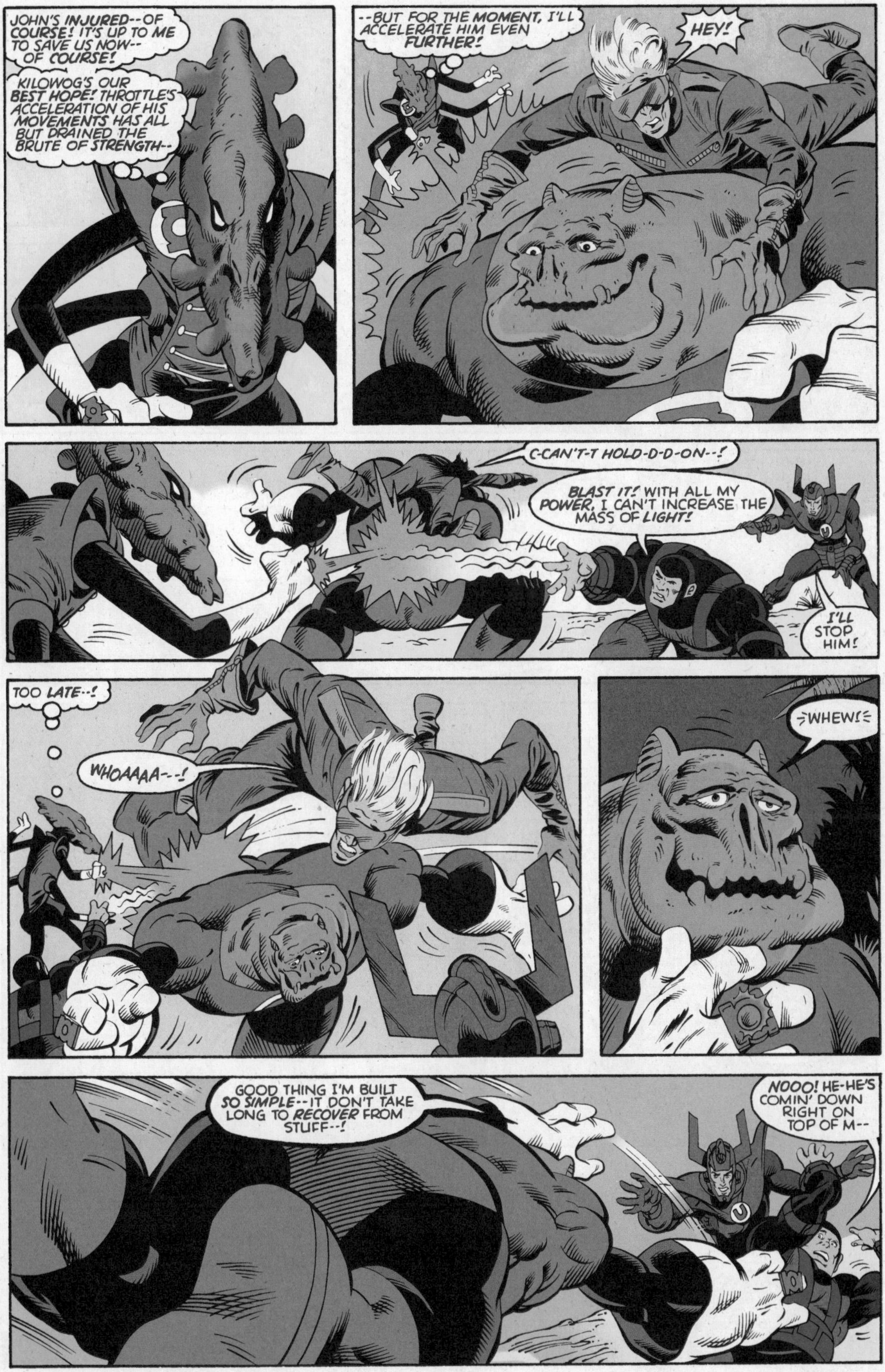

JOHN'S INJURED--OF COURSE! IT'S UP TO ME TO SAVE US NOW--OF COURSE!
KILOWOG'S OUR BEST HOPE! THROTTLE'S ACCELERATION OF HIS MOVEMENTS HAS ALL BUT DRAINED THE BRUTE OF STRENGTH--
--BUT FOR THE MOMENT, I'LL ACCELERATE HIM EVEN FURTHER!
HEY!
C-CAN'T-T HOLD-D-D-ON--!
BLAST IT! WITH ALL MY POWER, I CAN'T INCREASE THE MASS OF LIGHT!
I'LL STOP HIM!
TOO LATE--!
WHOAAAA---!
WHEW!
GOOD THING I'M BUILT SO SIMPLE--IT DON'T TAKE LONG TO RECOVER FROM STUFF--!
NOOO! HE-HE'S COMIN' DOWN RIGHT ON TOP OF M--

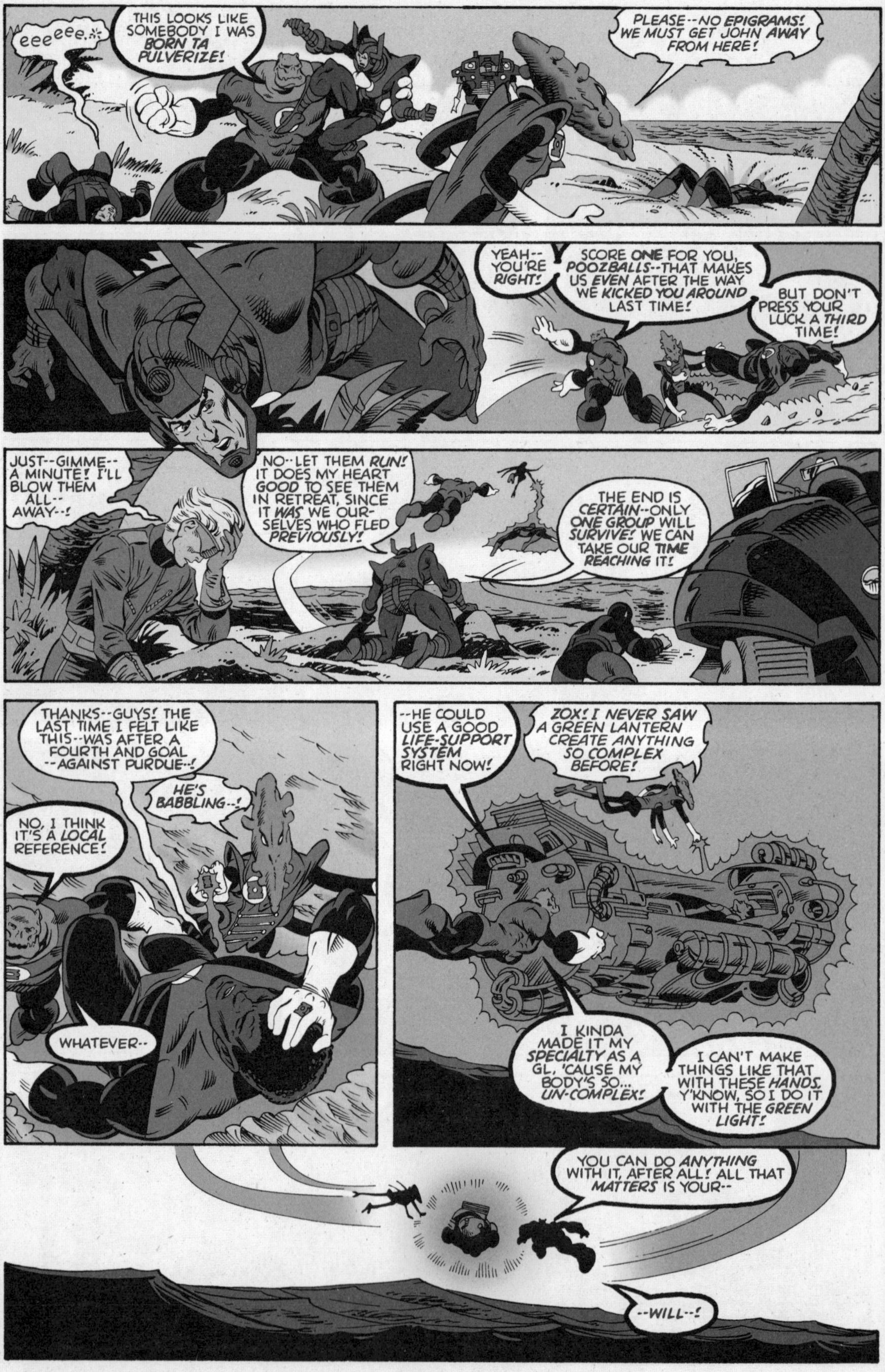
eeeeeee..
THIS LOOKS LIKE SOMEBODY I WAS BORN TA PULVERIZE!
PLEASE--NO EPIGRAMS! WE MUST GET JOHN AWAY FROM HERE!
YEAH--YOU'RE RIGHT!
SCORE ONE FOR YOU, POOZBALLS--THAT MAKES US EVEN AFTER THE WAY WE KICKED YOU AROUND LAST TIME!
BUT DON'T PRESS YOUR LUCK A THIRD TIME!
JUST--GIMME--A MINUTE! I'LL BLOW THEM ALL--AWAY--!
NO--LET THEM RUN! IT DOES MY HEART GOOD TO SEE THEM IN RETREAT, SINCE IT WAS WE OURSELVES WHO FLED PREVIOUSLY!
THE END IS CERTAIN--ONLY ONE GROUP WILL SURVIVE! WE CAN TAKE OUR TIME REACHING IT!
THANKS--GUYS! THE LAST TIME I FELT LIKE THIS--WAS AFTER A FOURTH AND GOAL--AGAINST PURDUE--!
HE'S BABBLING--!
NO, I THINK IT'S A LOCAL REFERENCE!
WHATEVER--
--HE COULD USE A GOOD LIFE-SUPPORT SYSTEM RIGHT NOW!
ZOX! I NEVER SAW A GREEN LANTERN CREATE ANYTHING SO COMPLEX BEFORE!
I KINDA MADE IT MY SPECIALTY AS A GL, 'CAUSE MY BODY'S SO... UN-COMPLEX!
I CAN'T MAKE THINGS LIKE THAT WITH THESE HANDS, Y'KNOW, SO I DO IT WITH THE GREEN LIGHT!
YOU CAN DO ANYTHING WITH IT, AFTER ALL! ALL THAT MATTERS IS YOUR--
--WILL--!

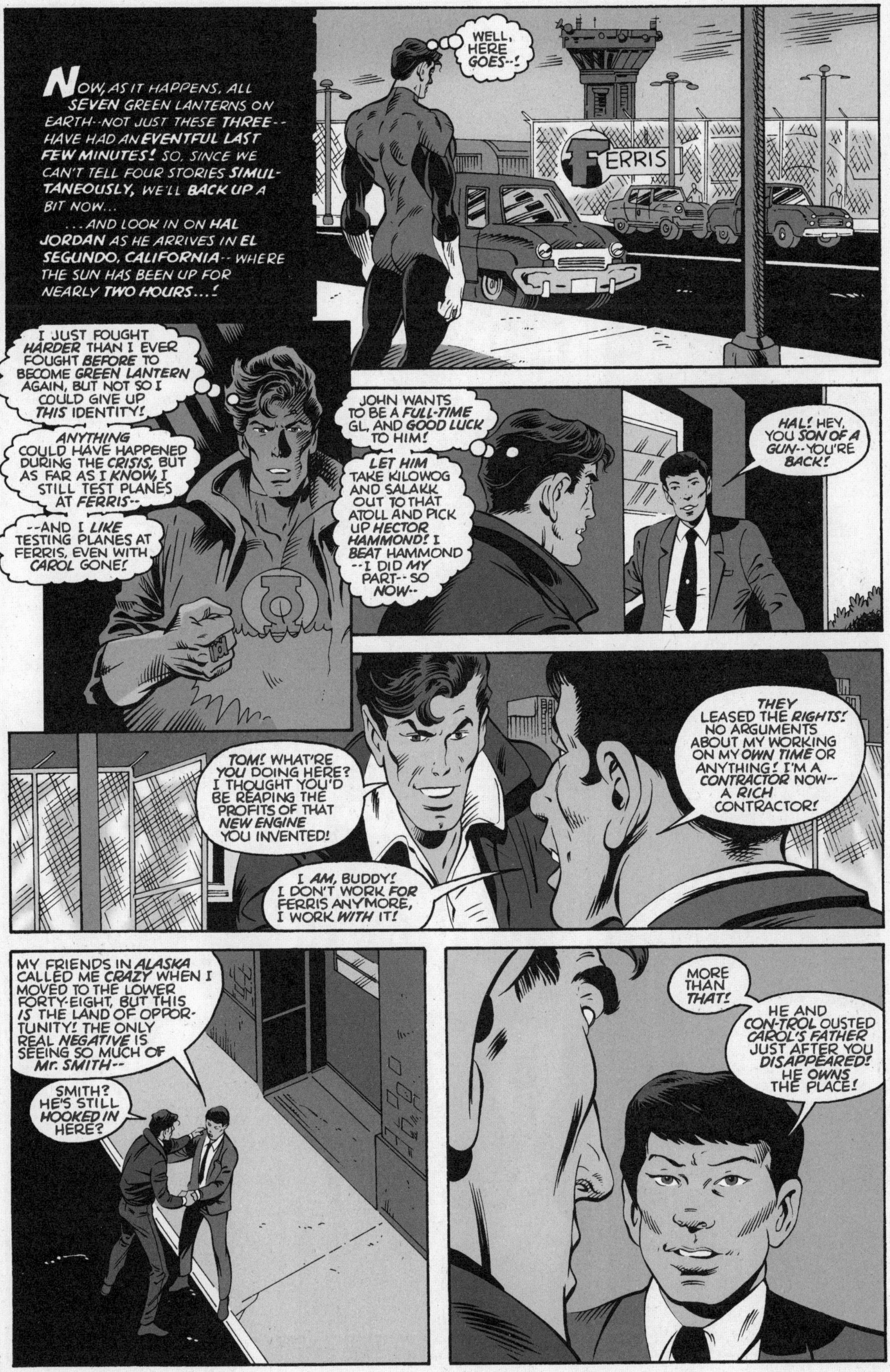
NOW, AS IT HAPPENS, ALL SEVEN GREEN LANTERNS ON EARTH--NOT JUST THESE THREE--HAVE HAD AN EVENTFUL LAST FEW MINUTES! SO, SINCE WE CAN'T TELL FOUR STORIES SIMULTANEOUSLY, WE'LL BACK UP A BIT NOW...
...AND LOOK IN ON HAL JORDAN AS HE ARRIVES IN EL SEGUNDO, CALIFORNIA-- WHERE THE SUN HAS BEEN UP FOR NEARLY TWO HOURS...!
WELL, HERE GOES--!
FERRIS
I JUST FOUGHT HARDER THAN I EVER FOUGHT BEFORE TO BECOME GREEN LANTERN AGAIN, BUT NOT SO I COULD GIVE UP THIS IDENTITY!
ANYTHING COULD HAVE HAPPENED DURING THE CRISIS, BUT AS FAR AS I KNOW, I STILL TEST PLANES AT FERRIS--
--AND I LIKE TESTING PLANES AT FERRIS, EVEN WITH CAROL GONE!
JOHN WANTS TO BE A FULL-TIME GL, AND GOOD LUCK TO HIM!
LET HIM TAKE KILOWOG AND SALAKK OUT TO THAT ATOLL AND PICK UP HECTOR HAMMOND! I BEAT HAMMOND--I DID MY PART--SO NOW--
HAL! HEY, YOU SON OF A GUN--YOU'RE BACK!
TOM! WHAT'RE YOU DOING HERE? I THOUGHT YOU'D BE REAPING THE PROFITS OF THAT NEW ENGINE YOU INVENTED!
I AM, BUDDY! I DON'T WORK FOR FERRIS ANYMORE, I WORK WITH IT!
THEY LEASED THE RIGHTS! NO ARGUMENTS ABOUT MY WORKING ON MY OWN TIME OR ANYTHING! I'M A CONTRACTOR NOW--A RICH CONTRACTOR!
MY FRIENDS IN ALASKA CALLED ME CRAZY WHEN I MOVED TO THE LOWER FORTY-EIGHT, BUT THIS IS THE LAND OF OPPORTUNITY! THE ONLY REAL NEGATIVE IS SEEING SO MUCH OF Mr. SMITH--
SMITH? HE'S STILL HOOKED IN HERE?
MORE THAN THAT!
HE AND CON-TROL OUSTED CAROL'S FATHER JUST AFTER YOU DISAPPEARED! HE OWNS THE PLACE!

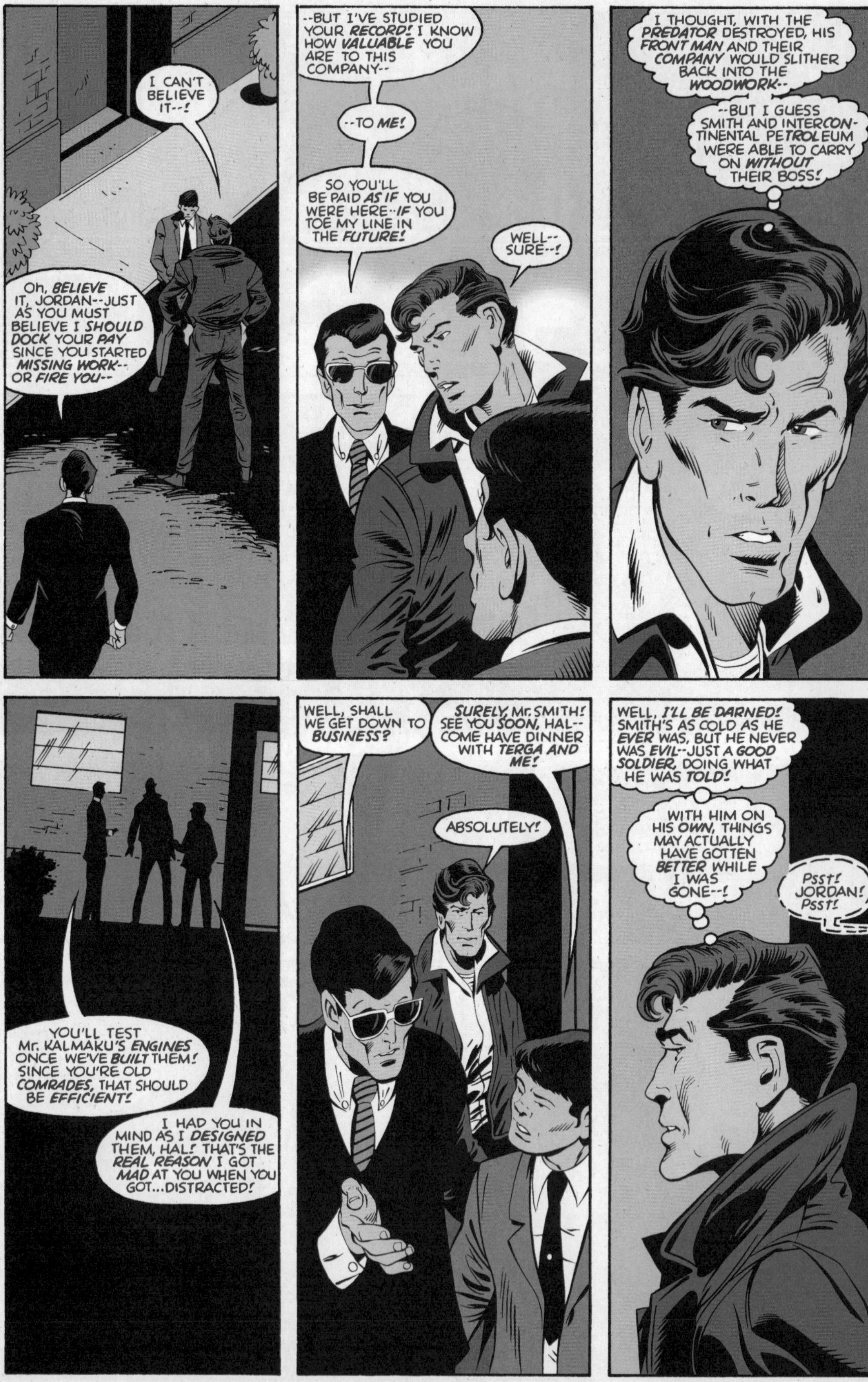
I CAN'T BELIEVE IT--!
Oh, BELIEVE IT, JORDAN--JUST AS YOU MUST BELIEVE I SHOULD DOCK YOUR PAY SINCE YOU STARTED MISSING WORK--OR FIRE YOU--
--BUT I'VE STUDIED YOUR RECORD! I KNOW HOW VALUABLE YOU ARE TO THIS COMPANY--
--TO ME!
SO YOU'LL BE PAID AS IF YOU WERE HERE--IF YOU TOE MY LINE IN THE FUTURE!
WELL--SURE--!
I THOUGHT, WITH THE PREDATOR DESTROYED, HIS FRONT MAN AND THEIR COMPANY WOULD SLITHER BACK INTO THE WOODWORK--
--BUT I GUESS SMITH AND INTERCONTINENTAL PETROLEUM WERE ABLE TO CARRY ON WITHOUT THEIR BOSS!
YOU'LL TEST Mr. KALMAKU'S ENGINES ONCE WE'VE BUILT THEM! SINCE YOU'RE OLD COMRADES, THAT SHOULD BE EFFICIENT!
I HAD YOU IN MIND AS I DESIGNED THEM, HAL! THAT'S THE REAL REASON I GOT MAD AT YOU WHEN YOU GOT...DISTRACTED!
WELL, SHALL WE GET DOWN TO BUSINESS?
SURELY, Mr. SMITH! SEE YOU SOON, HAL--COME HAVE DINNER WITH TERGA AND ME!
ABSOLUTELY!
WELL, I'LL BE DARNED! SMITH'S AS COLD AS HE EVER WAS, BUT HE NEVER WAS EVIL--JUST A GOOD SOLDIER, DOING WHAT HE WAS TOLD!
WITH HIM ON HIS OWN, THINGS MAY ACTUALLY HAVE GOTTEN BETTER WHILE I WAS GONE--!
Psst! JORDAN! Psst!

WHY-- CARL FERRIS!

OVER *HERE*! I DON'T WANT TO BE *SEEN*!

I HEARD YOU--

THEY *STOLE IT* FROM ME, JORDAN! THEY STOLE MY *COMPANY*--MY *LIFE'S WORK*--

--AND THEY *KILLED* MY DAUGHTER!

WHA-- WHAT? CAROL--?

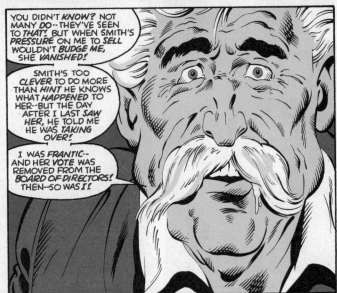

YOU DIDN'T *KNOW*? NOT MANY *DO*--THEY'VE SEEN TO *THAT*! BUT WHEN SMITH'S *PRESSURE* ON ME TO *SELL* WOULDN'T *BUDGE* ME, SHE *VANISHED*!

SMITH'S TOO *CLEVER* TO DO MORE THAN *HINT* HE KNOWS WHAT *HAPPENED* TO HER--BUT THE DAY AFTER I LAST *SAW* HER, HE TOLD ME HE WAS *TAKING OVER*!

I WAS *FRANTIC*-- AND HER *VOTE* WAS REMOVED FROM THE *BOARD OF DIRECTORS*! THEN--SO WAS *I*!

MY GOD! CAROL'S NOT DEAD--SHE'S *STAR SAPPHIRE*! BUT I CAN'T *TELL* HIM! HOW WOULD HAL JORDAN *KNOW*?

JORDAN, WE'VE HAD OUR *DIFFERENCES*, BUT I KNOW YOU *LOVED MY DAUGHTER*! YOU'VE GOT TO *HELP ME*!

USE YOUR *POSITION* HERE TO *SPY* ON SMITH! GET ME SOME *AMMUNITION* TO MAKE HIM PAY FOR HIS *CRIMES*!

I--I--

--I'LL DO WHATEVER I *CAN*!

GOOD MAN!

WE *DIDN'T* ALWAYS GET ALONG--BUT I DON'T KNOW WHAT I'D DO WITHOUT YOU *NOW*!

WELCOME *HOME*, HAL--!

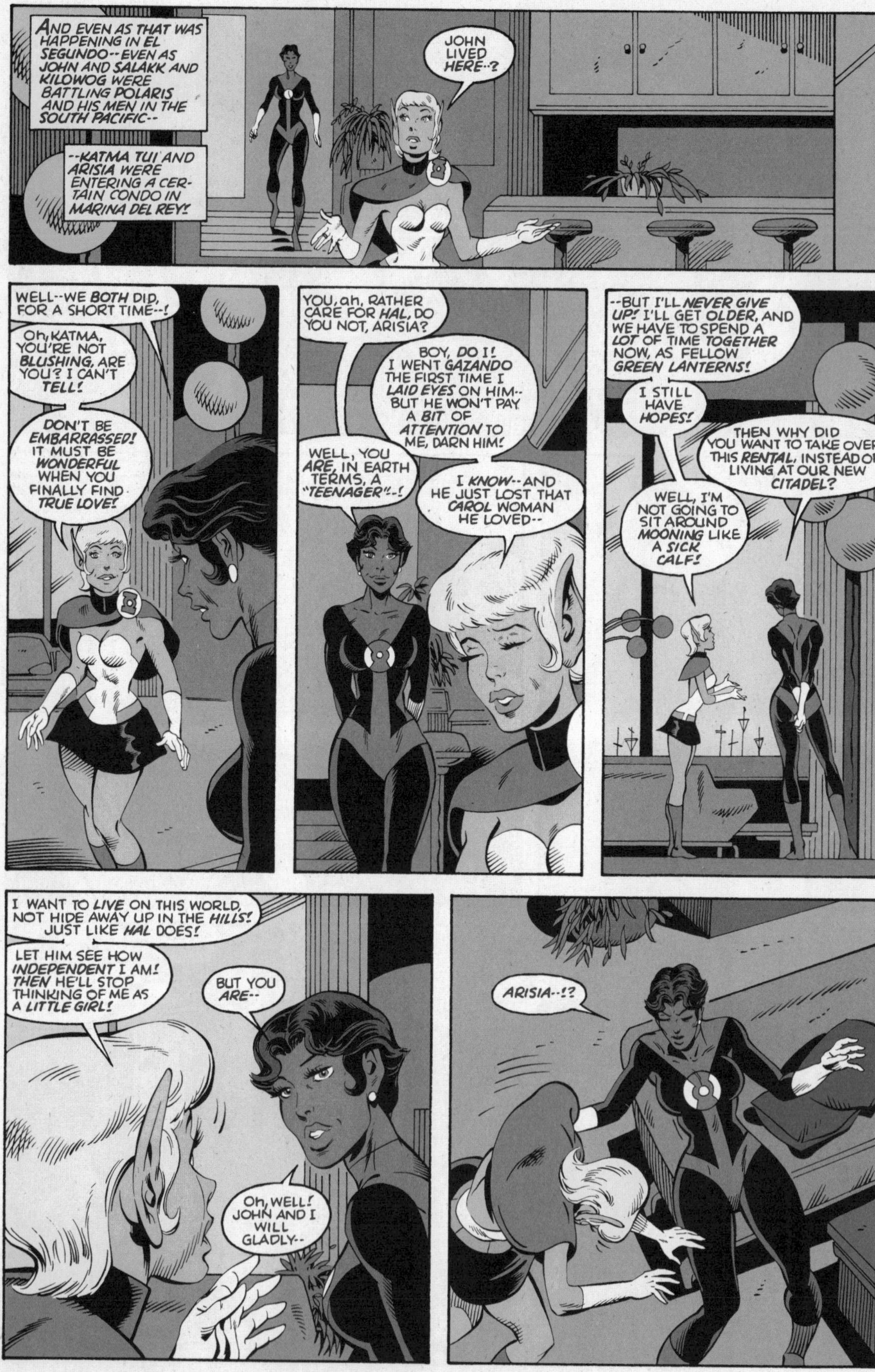
AND EVEN AS THAT WAS HAPPENING IN EL SEGUNDO--EVEN AS JOHN AND SALAKK AND KILOWOG WERE BATTLING POLARIS AND HIS MEN IN THE SOUTH PACIFIC--
--KATMA TUI AND ARISIA WERE ENTERING A CERTAIN CONDO IN MARINA DEL REY!
JOHN LIVED HERE..?
WELL--WE BOTH DID, FOR A SHORT TIME--!
Oh, KATMA, YOU'RE NOT BLUSHING, ARE YOU? I CAN'T TELL!
DON'T BE EMBARRASSED! IT MUST BE WONDERFUL WHEN YOU FINALLY FIND TRUE LOVE!
YOU, ah, RATHER CARE FOR HAL, DO YOU NOT, ARISIA?
BOY, DO I! I WENT GAZANDO THE FIRST TIME I LAID EYES ON HIM--BUT HE WON'T PAY A BIT OF ATTENTION TO ME, DARN HIM!
WELL, YOU ARE, IN EARTH TERMS, A "TEENAGER"--!
I KNOW--AND HE JUST LOST THAT CAROL WOMAN HE LOVED--
--BUT I'LL NEVER GIVE UP! I'LL GET OLDER, AND WE HAVE TO SPEND A LOT OF TIME TOGETHER NOW, AS FELLOW GREEN LANTERNS!
I STILL HAVE HOPES!
THEN WHY DID YOU WANT TO TAKE OVER THIS RENTAL, INSTEAD OF LIVING AT OUR NEW CITADEL?
WELL, I'M NOT GOING TO SIT AROUND MOONING LIKE A SICK CALF!
I WANT TO LIVE ON THIS WORLD, NOT HIDE AWAY UP IN THE HILLS! JUST LIKE HAL DOES!
LET HIM SEE HOW INDEPENDENT I AM! THEN HE'LL STOP THINKING OF ME AS A LITTLE GIRL!
BUT YOU ARE--
Oh, WELL! JOHN AND I WILL GLADLY--
ARISIA--!?

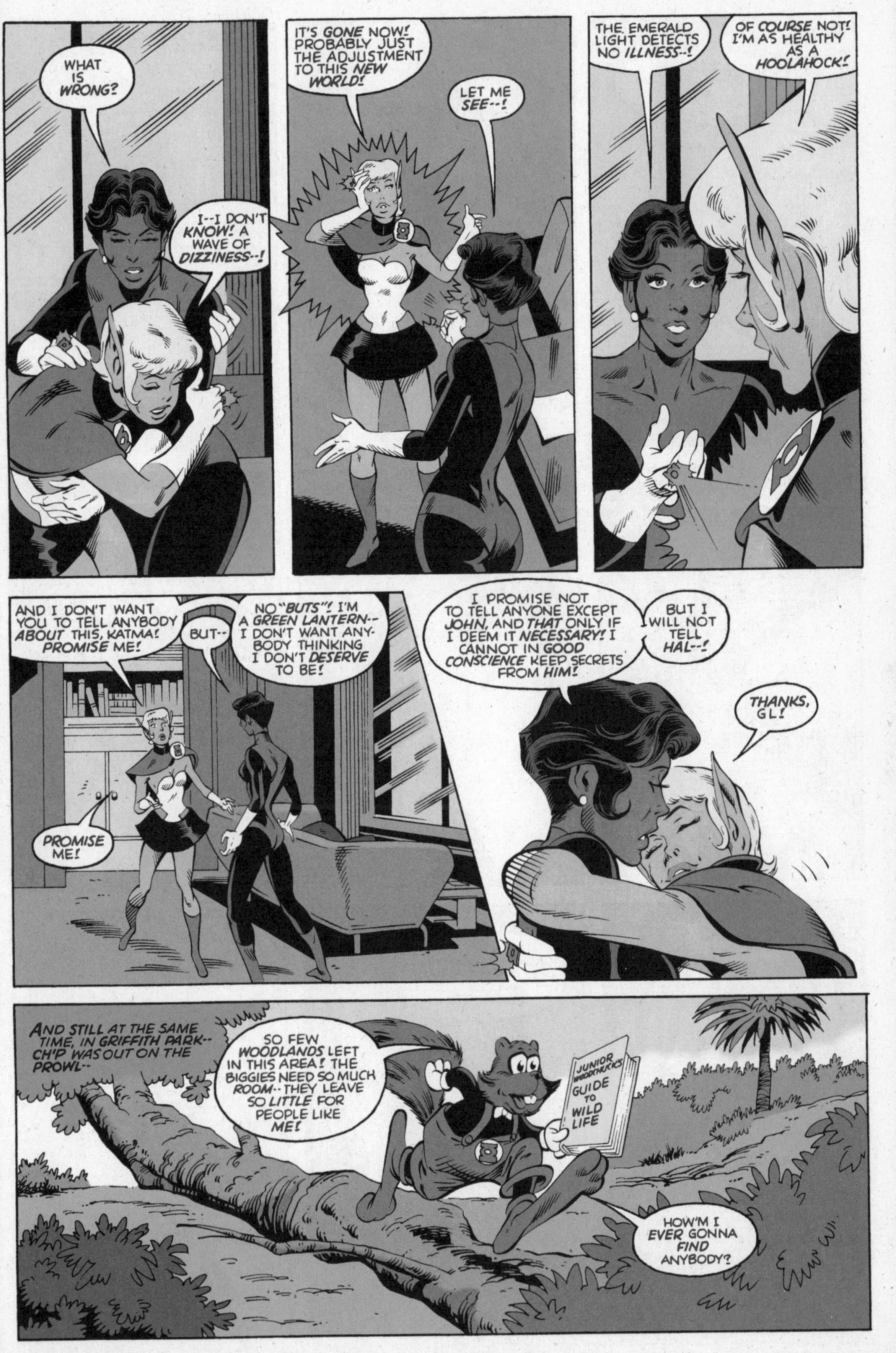
WHAT IS WRONG?
I--I DON'T KNOW! A WAVE OF DIZZINESS--!
IT'S GONE NOW! PROBABLY JUST THE ADJUSTMENT TO THIS NEW WORLD!
LET ME SEE--!
THE EMERALD LIGHT DETECTS NO ILLNESS--!
OF COURSE NOT! I'M AS HEALTHY AS A HOOLAHOCK!
AND I DON'T WANT YOU TO TELL ANYBODY ABOUT THIS, KATMA! PROMISE ME!
BUT--
NO "BUTS"! I'M A GREEN LANTERN-- I DON'T WANT ANY-BODY THINKING I DON'T DESERVE TO BE!
PROMISE ME!
I PROMISE NOT TO TELL ANYONE EXCEPT JOHN, AND THAT ONLY IF I DEEM IT NECESSARY! I CANNOT IN GOOD CONSCIENCE KEEP SECRETS FROM HIM!
BUT I WILL NOT TELL HAL--!
THANKS, GL!
AND STILL AT THE SAME TIME, IN GRIFFITH PARK-- CH'P WAS OUT ON THE PROWL--
SO FEW WOODLANDS LEFT IN THIS AREA! THE BIGGIES NEED SO MUCH ROOM-- THEY LEAVE SO LITTLE FOR PEOPLE LIKE ME!
JUNIOR WOODCHUCK'S GUIDE TO WILD LIFE
HOW'M I EVER GONNA FIND ANYBODY?

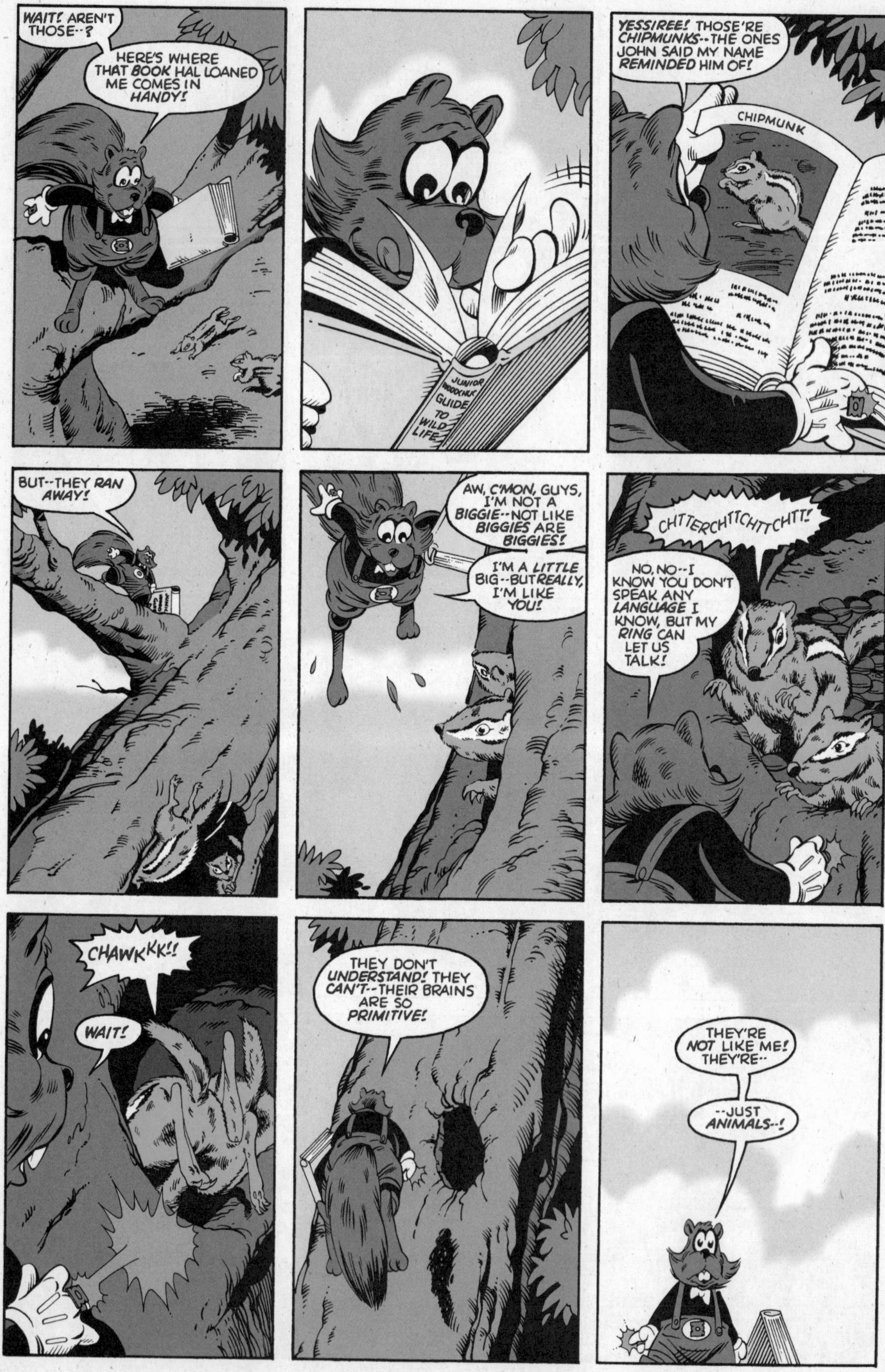
WAIT! AREN'T THOSE--?
HERE'S WHERE THAT BOOK HAL LOANED ME COMES IN HANDY!
JUNIOR WOODCHUCK GUIDE TO WILD LIFE
YESSIREE! THOSE'RE CHIPMUNKS--THE ONES JOHN SAID MY NAME REMINDED HIM OF!
CHIPMUNK
BUT--THEY RAN AWAY!
AW, C'MON, GUYS, I'M NOT A BIGGIE--NOT LIKE BIGGIES ARE BIGGIES!
I'M A LITTLE BIG--BUT REALLY, I'M LIKE YOU!
CHTTERCHTTCHTTCHTT!
NO, NO--I KNOW YOU DON'T SPEAK ANY LANGUAGE I KNOW, BUT MY RING CAN LET US TALK!
CHAWKKK!!
WAIT!
THEY DON'T UNDERSTAND! THEY CAN'T--THEIR BRAINS ARE SO PRIMITIVE!
THEY'RE NOT LIKE ME! THEY'RE--
--JUST ANIMALS--!

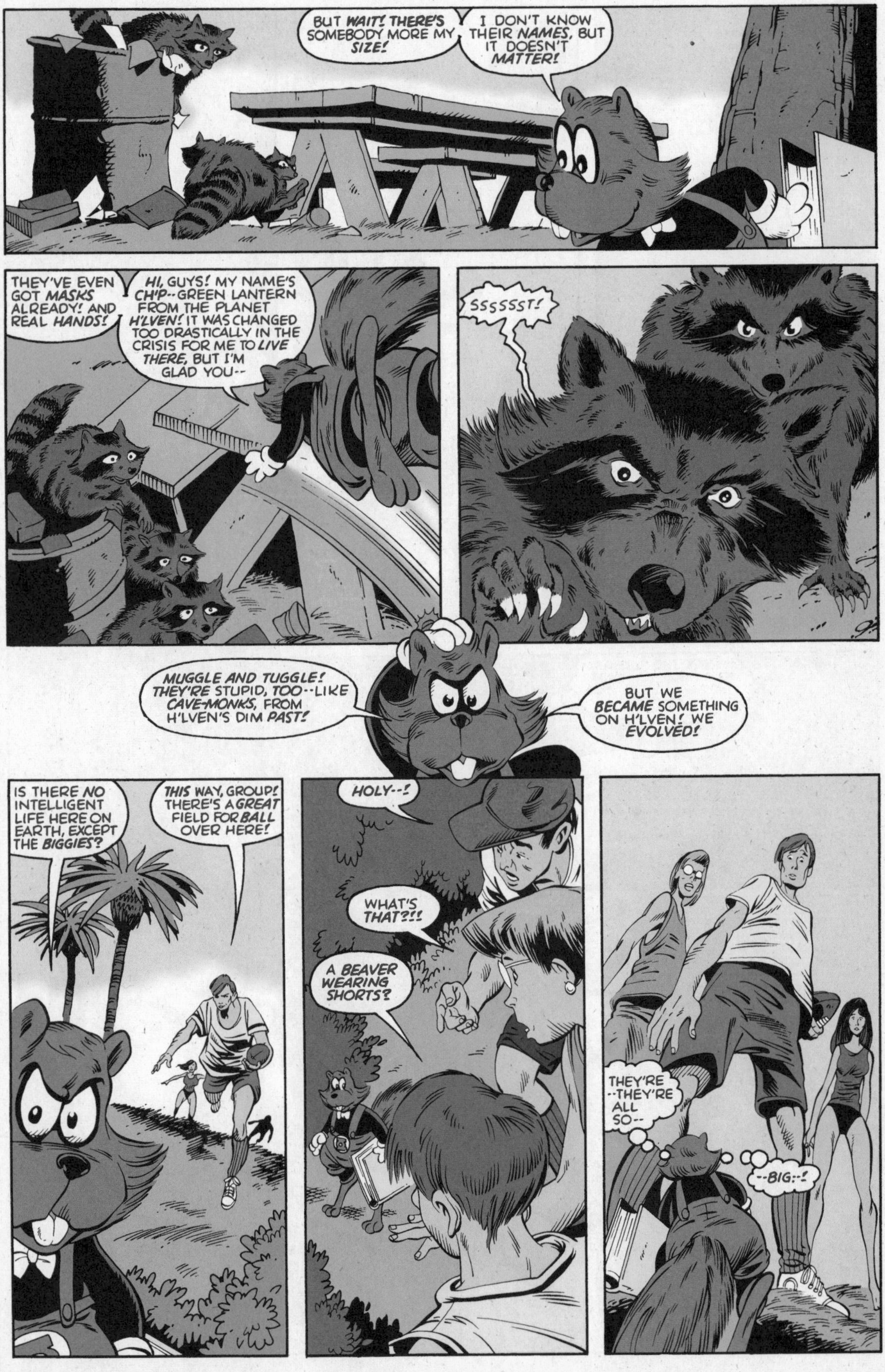
BUT WAIT! THERE'S SOMEBODY MORE MY SIZE!
I DON'T KNOW THEIR NAMES, BUT IT DOESN'T MATTER!
THEY'VE EVEN GOT MASKS ALREADY! AND REAL HANDS!
HI, GUYS! MY NAME'S CH'P--GREEN LANTERN FROM THE PLANET H'LVEN! IT WAS CHANGED TOO DRASTICALLY IN THE CRISIS FOR ME TO LIVE THERE, BUT I'M GLAD YOU--
SSSSSST!
MUGGLE AND TUGGLE! THEY'RE STUPID, TOO--LIKE CAVE-MONKS, FROM H'LVEN'S DIM PAST!
BUT WE BECAME SOMETHING ON H'LVEN! WE EVOLVED!
IS THERE NO INTELLIGENT LIFE HERE ON EARTH, EXCEPT THE BIGGIES?
THIS WAY, GROUP! THERE'S A GREAT FIELD FOR BALL OVER HERE!
HOLY--!
WHAT'S THAT?!!
A BEAVER WEARING SHORTS?
THEY'RE --THEY'RE ALL SO--
--BIG--!

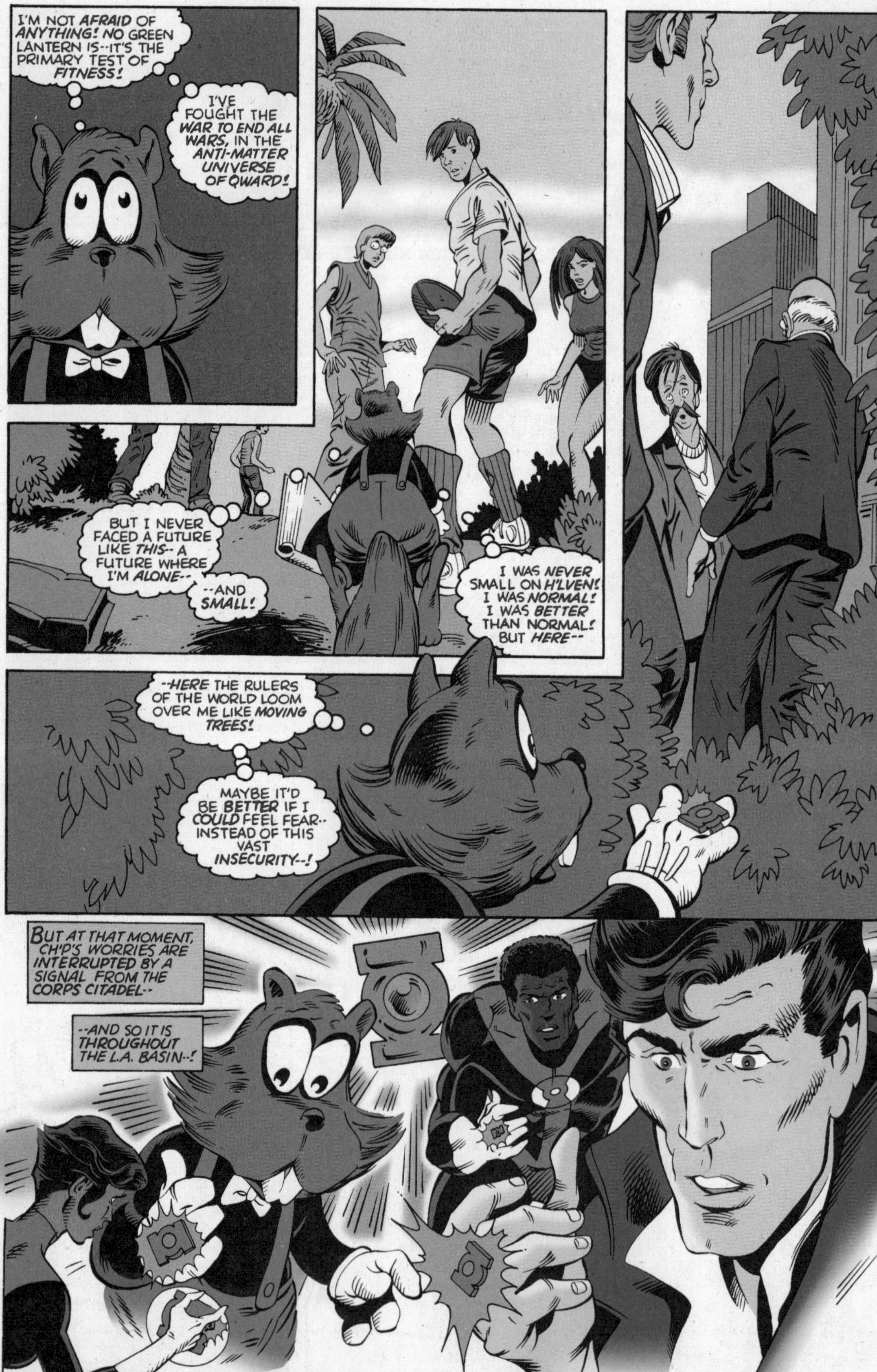
I'M NOT AFRAID OF ANYTHING! NO GREEN LANTERN IS--IT'S THE PRIMARY TEST OF FITNESS!
I'VE FOUGHT THE WAR TO END ALL WARS, IN THE ANTI-MATTER UNIVERSE OF QWARD!
BUT I NEVER FACED A FUTURE LIKE THIS-- A FUTURE WHERE I'M ALONE--
--AND SMALL!
I WAS NEVER SMALL ON H'LVEN! I WAS NORMAL! I WAS BETTER THAN NORMAL! BUT HERE--
--HERE THE RULERS OF THE WORLD LOOM OVER ME LIKE MOVING TREES!
MAYBE IT'D BE BETTER IF I COULD FEEL FEAR-- INSTEAD OF THIS VAST INSECURITY--!
BUT AT THAT MOMENT, CH'P'S WORRIES ARE INTERRUPTED BY A SIGNAL FROM THE CORPS CITADEL--
--AND SO IT IS THROUGHOUT THE L.A. BASIN--!

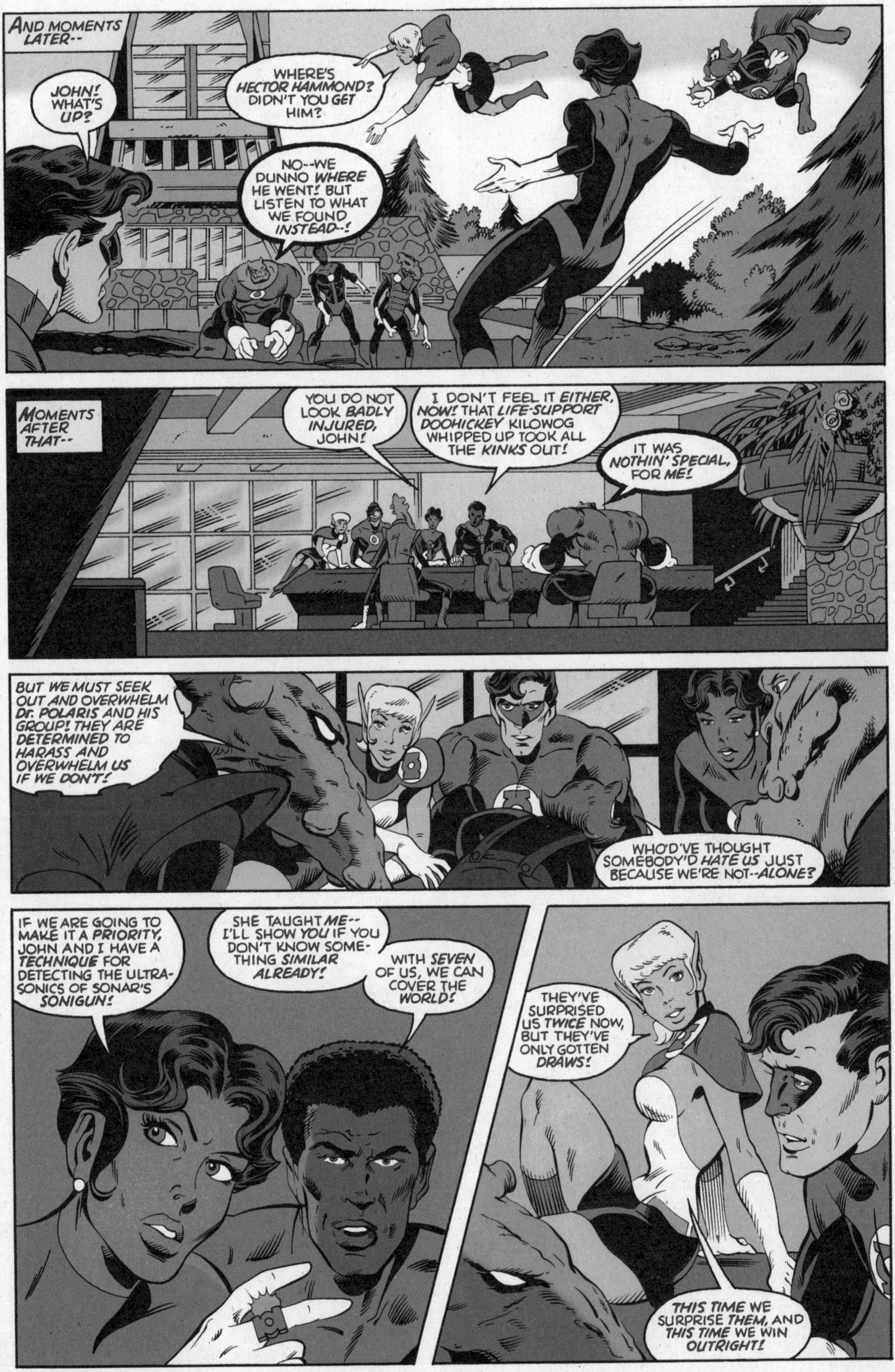
AND MOMENTS LATER--
JOHN! WHAT'S UP?
WHERE'S HECTOR HAMMOND? DIDN'T YOU GET HIM?
NO--WE DUNNO WHERE HE WENT! BUT LISTEN TO WHAT WE FOUND INSTEAD--!
MOMENTS AFTER THAT--
YOU DO NOT LOOK BADLY INJURED, JOHN!
I DON'T FEEL IT EITHER, NOW! THAT LIFE-SUPPORT DOOHICKEY KILOWOG WHIPPED UP TOOK ALL THE KINKS OUT!
IT WAS NOTHIN' SPECIAL, FOR ME!
BUT WE MUST SEEK OUT AND OVERWHELM Dr. POLARIS AND HIS GROUP! THEY ARE DETERMINED TO HARASS AND OVERWHELM US IF WE DON'T!
WHO'D'VE THOUGHT SOMEBODY'D HATE US JUST BECAUSE WE'RE NOT--ALONE?
IF WE ARE GOING TO MAKE IT A PRIORITY, JOHN AND I HAVE A TECHNIQUE FOR DETECTING THE ULTRA-SONICS OF SONAR'S SONIGUN!
SHE TAUGHT ME-- I'LL SHOW YOU IF YOU DON'T KNOW SOME-THING SIMILAR ALREADY!
WITH SEVEN OF US, WE CAN COVER THE WORLD!
THEY'VE SURPRISED US TWICE NOW, BUT THEY'VE ONLY GOTTEN DRAWS!
THIS TIME WE SURPRISE THEM, AND THIS TIME WE WIN OUTRIGHT!

THE GROUNDS OF CASTLE WLADON, DEEP IN THE CARPATHIAN MOUNTAIN REALM OF MODORA--

YOU ALLOWED THEM TO *LEAVE?!!* VICTORY OVER AN *AMERICAN GREEN LANTERN* IN YOUR *GRASP,* AND YOU DID *NOTHING?!!*

I DON'T SHARE YOUR *OBSESSION* WITH SHOWING THE WORLD AN AGENT OF MODORA CAN HUMBLE A *SUPER-POWER,* SONAR.

I WANT TO SEND OUR MESSAGE TO THE *UNIVERSE*-- "THE FORCES OF CRIME WILL *NOT ACCEPT* A *GREEN LANTERN CORPS* IN OUR MIDST!"

THAT MESSAGE IS *BEST* SENT IF THEY ALL DIE *TOGETHER!*

YOU THINK LIKE A *KING,* POLARIS--*I* THINK LIKE A *FREEDOM-FIGHTER!* TAKE *THREE* WHILE YOU *HAVE* THEM, I SAY!

THE WORLD--AND THE *UNIVERSE*--WOULD KNOW WHAT YOU'D DONE BY THE *REACTION* OF THE *FOUR REMAINING!*

THE MEDIA CAN REACH INTO THE MOST *REMOTE* CORNER OF THE GLOBE NOW!

TNNNNNNNNNNNNNNNNNNNN

WELL, *ANYWAY,* IT'S *DONE!* AND I'M READY FOR SOME OF YOUR *MODORAN* FOOD--

OH!

PARDON *ME!* MISS--?

MALIGNON!

SONAR! *LOOK!*

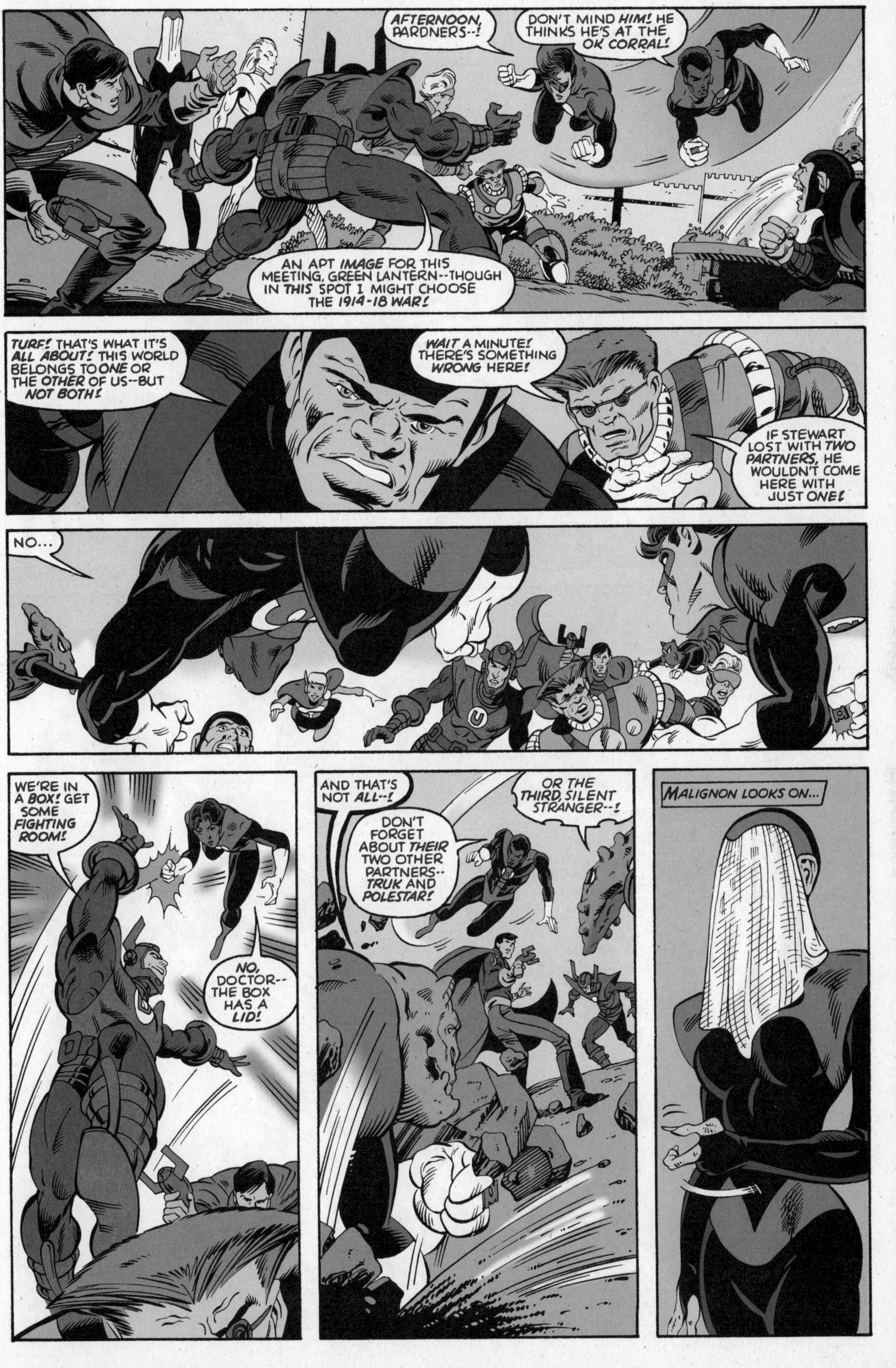

AFTERNOON, PARDNERS--!
DON'T MIND HIM! HE THINKS HE'S AT THE OK CORRAL!
AN APT IMAGE FOR THIS MEETING, GREEN LANTERN--THOUGH IN THIS SPOT I MIGHT CHOOSE THE 1914-18 WAR!
TURF! THAT'S WHAT IT'S ALL ABOUT! THIS WORLD BELONGS TO ONE OR THE OTHER OF US--BUT NOT BOTH!
WAIT A MINUTE! THERE'S SOMETHING WRONG HERE!
IF STEWART LOST WITH TWO PARTNERS, HE WOULDN'T COME HERE WITH JUST ONE!
NO...
WE'RE IN A BOX! GET SOME FIGHTING ROOM!
NO, DOCTOR--THE BOX HAS A LID!
AND THAT'S NOT ALL--!
DON'T FORGET ABOUT THEIR TWO OTHER PARTNERS--TRUK AND POLESTAR!
OR THE THIRD, SILENT STRANGER--!
MALIGNON LOOKS ON...

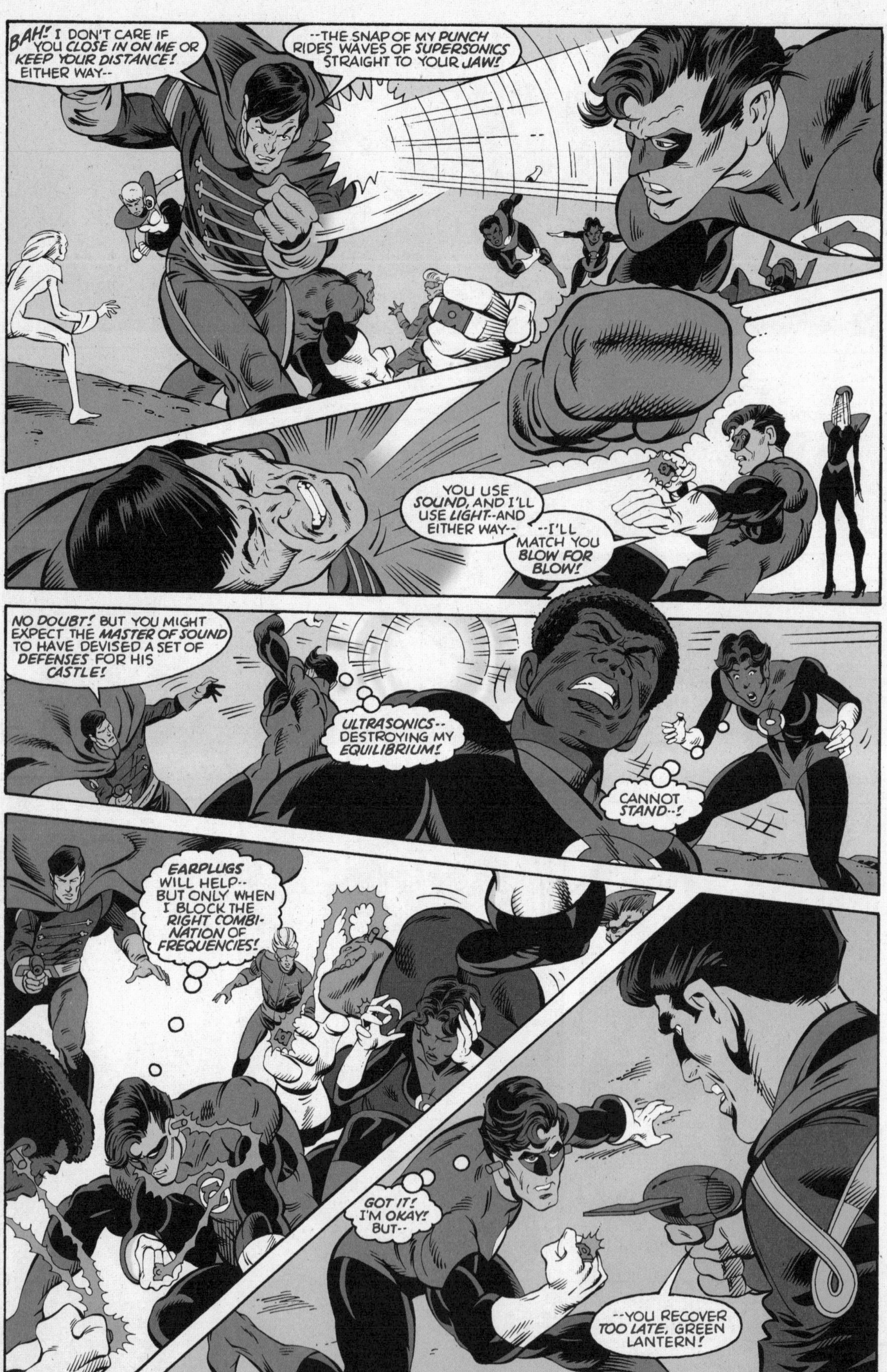
BAH! I DON'T CARE IF YOU CLOSE IN ON ME OR KEEP YOUR DISTANCE! EITHER WAY--
--THE SNAP OF MY PUNCH RIDES WAVES OF SUPERSONICS STRAIGHT TO YOUR JAW!
YOU USE SOUND, AND I'LL USE LIGHT--AND EITHER WAY--
--I'LL MATCH YOU BLOW FOR BLOW!
NO DOUBT! BUT YOU MIGHT EXPECT THE MASTER OF SOUND TO HAVE DEVISED A SET OF DEFENSES FOR HIS CASTLE!
ULTRASONICS-- DESTROYING MY EQUILIBRIUM!
CANNOT STAND--!
EARPLUGS WILL HELP-- BUT ONLY WHEN I BLOCK THE RIGHT COMBI-NATION OF FREQUENCIES!
GOT IT! I'M OKAY! BUT--
--YOU RECOVER TOO LATE, GREEN LANTERN!

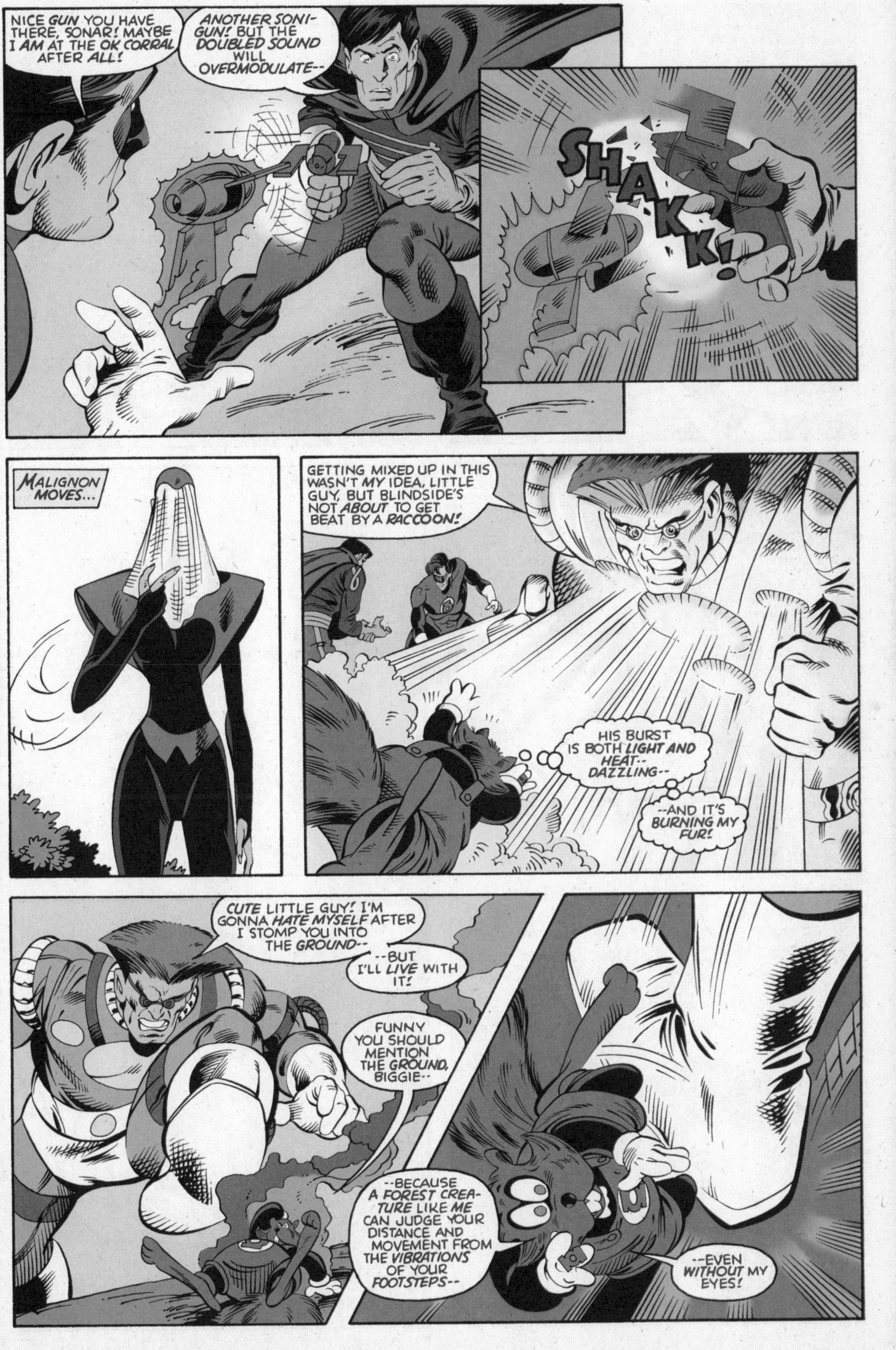

NICE GUN YOU HAVE THERE, SONAR! MAYBE I AM AT THE OK CORRAL AFTER ALL!
ANOTHER SONI-GUN! BUT THE DOUBLED SOUND WILL OVERMODULATE--
SHAKK!
MALIGNON MOVES...
GETTING MIXED UP IN THIS WASN'T MY IDEA, LITTLE GUY, BUT BLINDSIDE'S NOT ABOUT TO GET BEAT BY A RACCOON!
HIS BURST IS BOTH LIGHT AND HEAT-- DAZZLING--
--AND IT'S BURNING MY FUR!
CUTE LITTLE GUY! I'M GONNA HATE MYSELF AFTER I STOMP YOU INTO THE GROUND--
--BUT I'LL LIVE WITH IT!
FUNNY YOU SHOULD MENTION THE GROUND, BIGGIE--
--BECAUSE A FOREST CREATURE LIKE ME CAN JUDGE YOUR DISTANCE AND MOVEMENT FROM THE VIBRATIONS OF YOUR FOOTSTEPS--
--EVEN WITHOUT MY EYES!

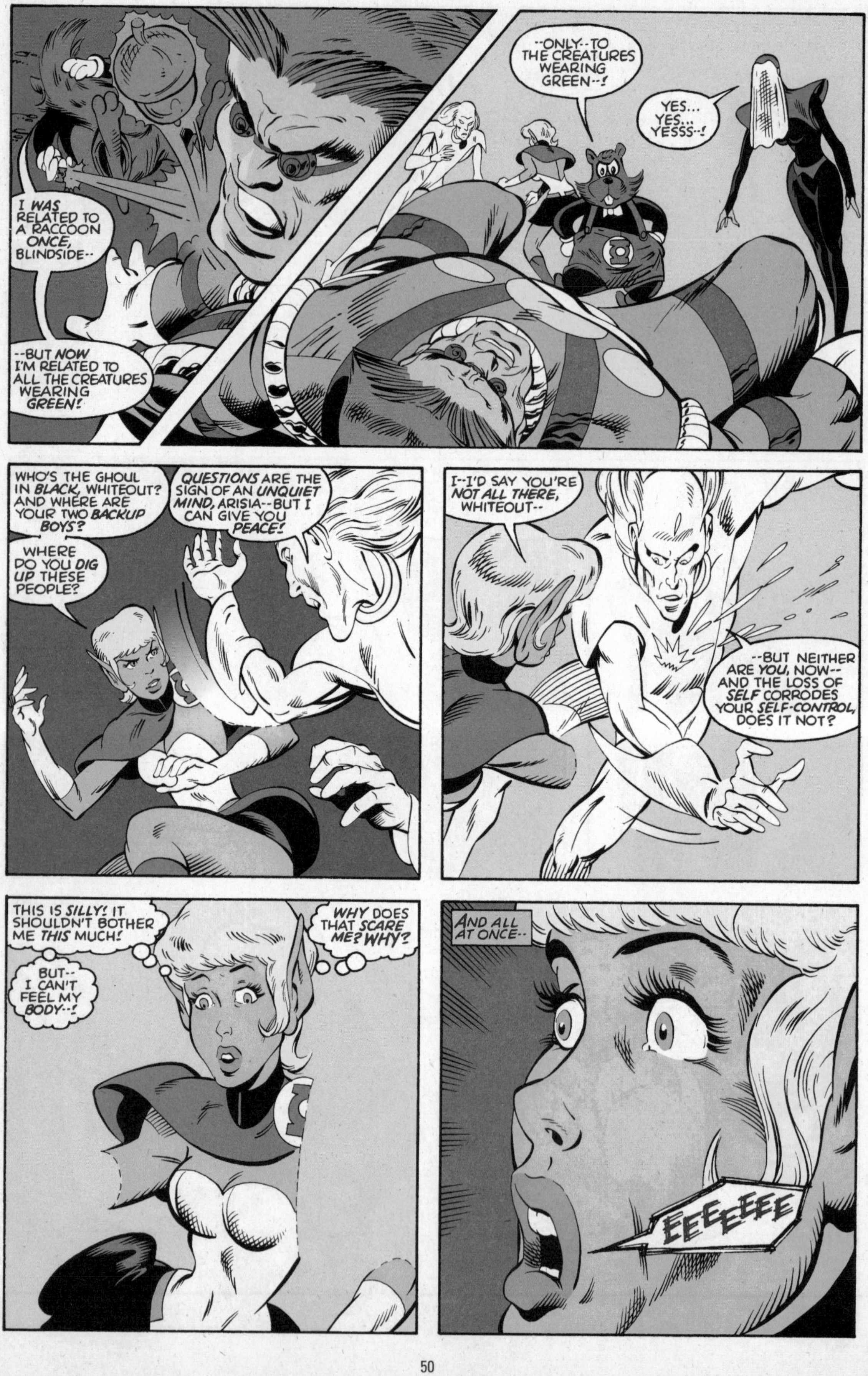
I WAS RELATED TO A RACCOON ONCE, BLINDSIDE--
--BUT NOW I'M RELATED TO ALL THE CREATURES WEARING GREEN!
--ONLY--TO THE CREATURES WEARING GREEN--!
YES... YES... YESSS--!
WHO'S THE GHOUL IN BLACK, WHITEOUT? AND WHERE ARE YOUR TWO BACKUP BOYS?
WHERE DO YOU DIG UP THESE PEOPLE?
QUESTIONS ARE THE SIGN OF AN UNQUIET MIND, ARISIA--BUT I CAN GIVE YOU PEACE!
I--I'D SAY YOU'RE NOT ALL THERE, WHITEOUT--
--BUT NEITHER ARE YOU, NOW--AND THE LOSS OF SELF CORRODES YOUR SELF-CONTROL, DOES IT NOT?
THIS IS SILLY! IT SHOULDN'T BOTHER ME THIS MUCH!
BUT--I CAN'T FEEL MY BODY--!
WHY DOES THAT SCARE ME? WHY?
AND ALL AT ONCE--
EEEEEEE

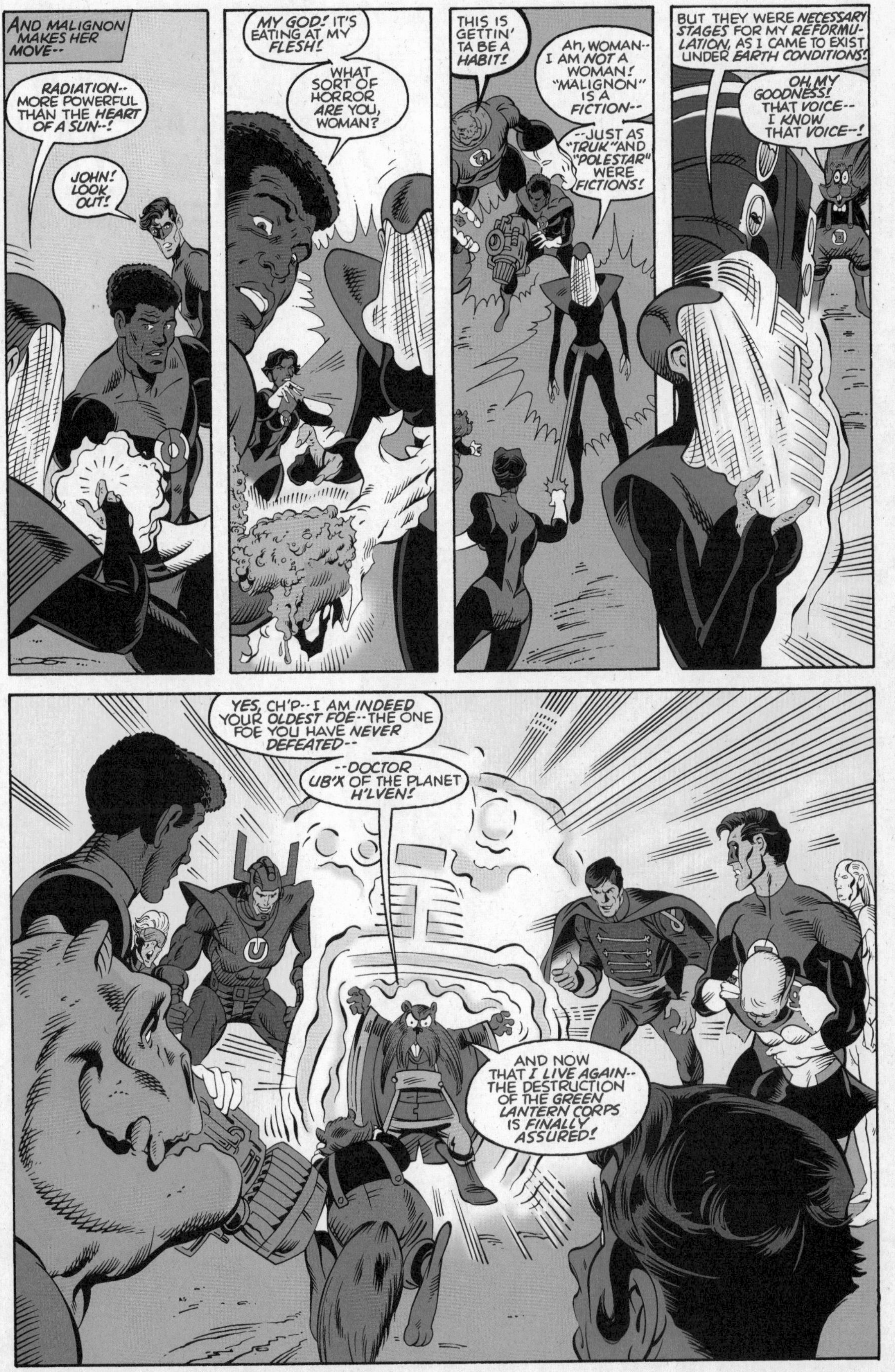
AND MALIGNON MAKES HER MOVE--
RADIATION-- MORE POWERFUL THAN THE HEART OF A SUN--!
JOHN! LOOK OUT!
MY GOD! IT'S EATING AT MY FLESH!
WHAT SORT OF HORROR ARE YOU, WOMAN?
THIS IS GETTIN' TA BE A HABIT!
Ah, WOMAN-- I AM NOT A WOMAN! "MALIGNON" IS A FICTION--
--JUST AS "TRUK" AND "POLESTAR" WERE FICTIONS!
BUT THEY WERE NECESSARY STAGES FOR MY REFORMULATION, AS I CAME TO EXIST UNDER EARTH CONDITIONS!
OH, MY GOODNESS! THAT VOICE-- I KNOW THAT VOICE--!
YES, CH'P-- I AM INDEED YOUR OLDEST FOE--THE ONE FOE YOU HAVE NEVER DEFEATED--
--DOCTOR UB'X OF THE PLANET H'LVEN!
AND NOW THAT I LIVE AGAIN-- THE DESTRUCTION OF THE GREEN LANTERN CORPS IS FINALLY ASSURED!

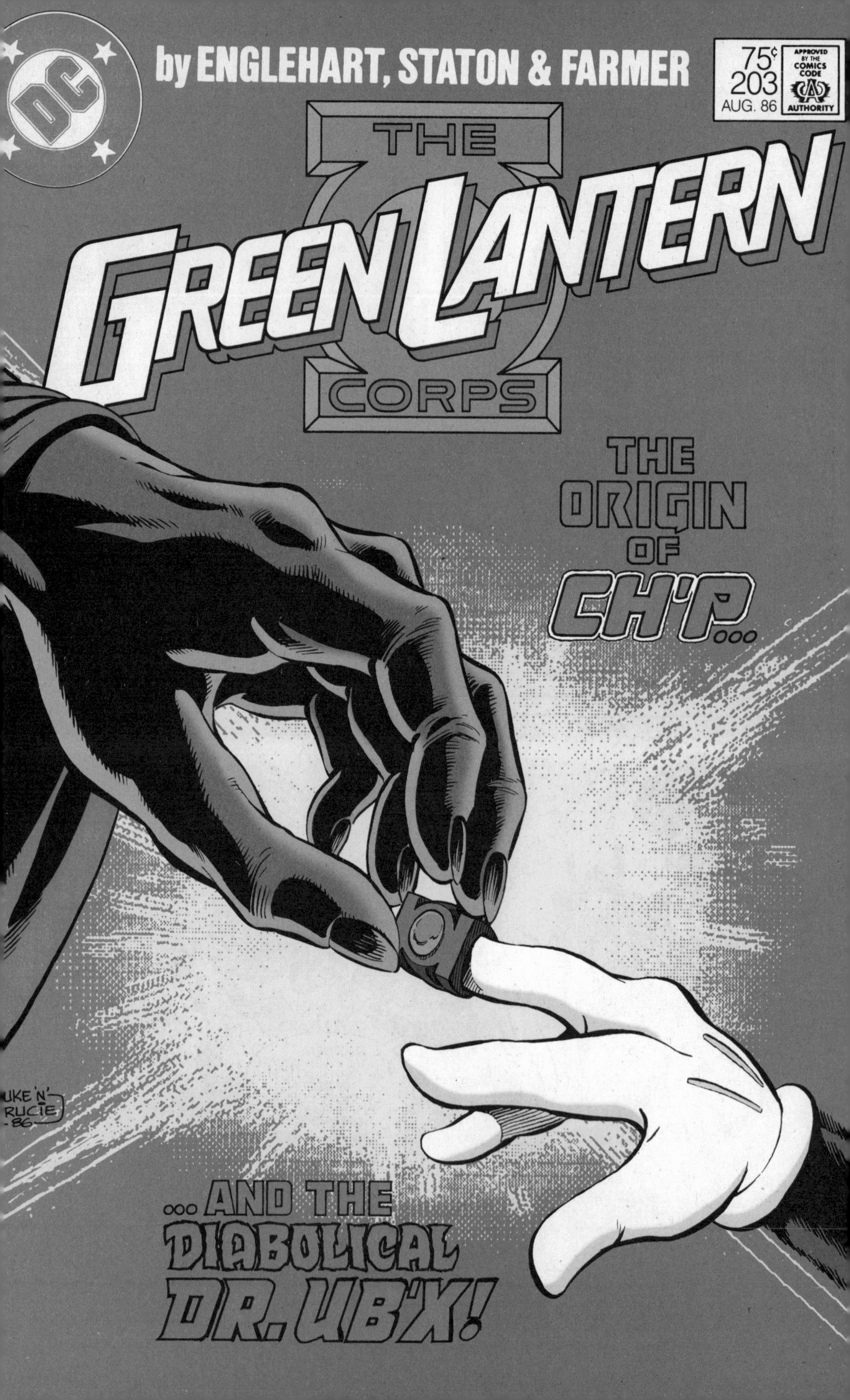
by ENGLEHART, STATON & FARMER
75¢
203
AUG. 86
APPROVED BY THE COMICS CODE AUTHORITY
THE GREEN LANTERN CORPS
THE ORIGIN OF CH'P...
...AND THE DIABOLICAL DR. UB'X!

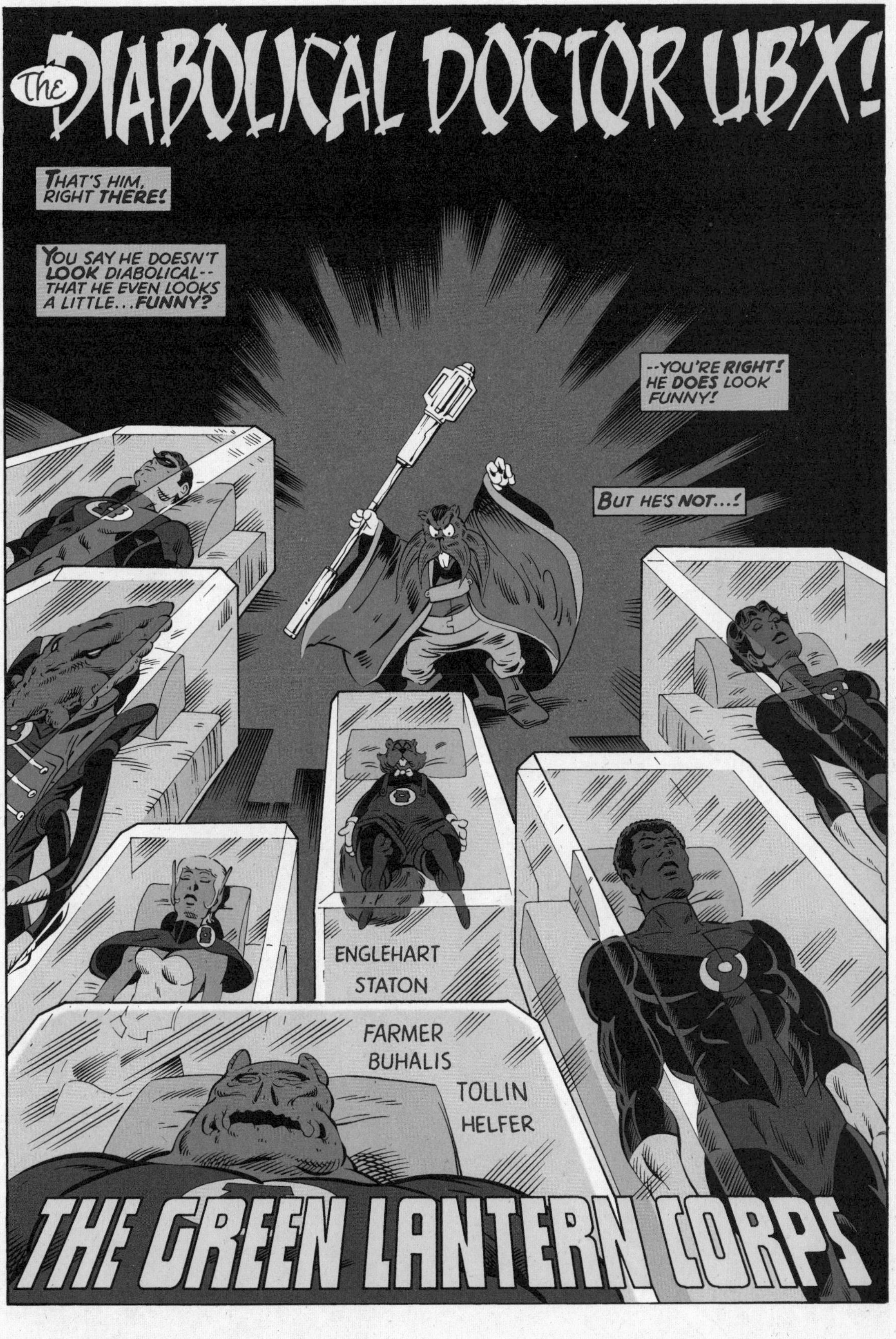
THE DIABOLICAL DOCTOR UB'X!
THAT'S HIM, RIGHT THERE!
YOU SAY HE DOESN'T LOOK DIABOLICAL-- THAT HE EVEN LOOKS A LITTLE...FUNNY?
--YOU'RE RIGHT! HE DOES LOOK FUNNY!
BUT HE'S NOT...!
ENGLEHART
STATON
FARMER
BUHALIS
TOLLIN
HELFER
THE GREEN LANTERN CORPS

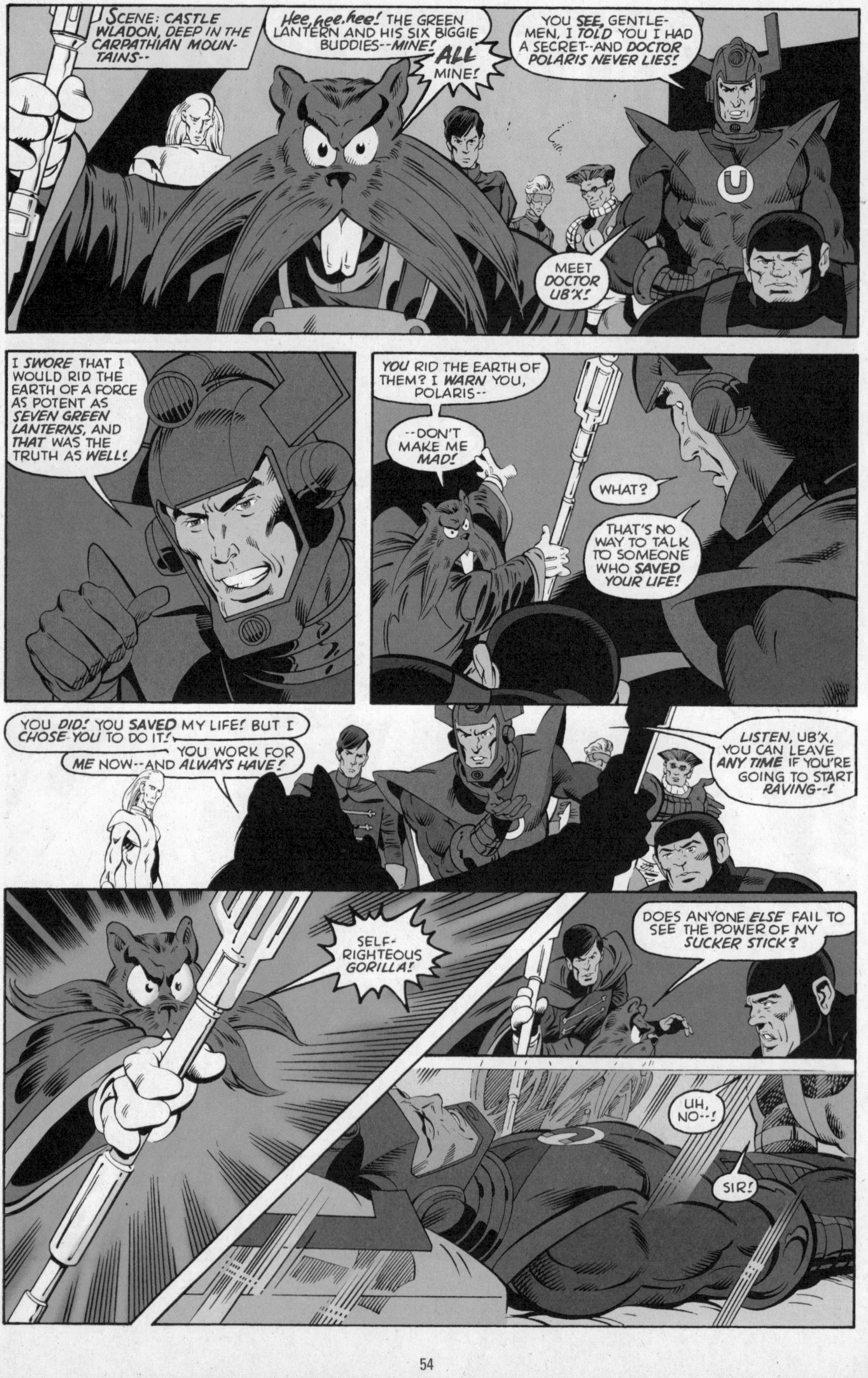
SCENE: CASTLE WLADON, DEEP IN THE CARPATHIAN MOUNTAINS--
Hee, hee, hee! THE GREEN LANTERN AND HIS SIX BIGGIE BUDDIES--MINE!
ALL MINE!
YOU SEE, GENTLEMEN, I TOLD YOU I HAD A SECRET--AND DOCTOR POLARIS NEVER LIES!
MEET DOCTOR UB'X!
I SWORE THAT I WOULD RID THE EARTH OF A FORCE AS POTENT AS SEVEN GREEN LANTERNS, AND THAT WAS THE TRUTH AS WELL!
YOU RID THE EARTH OF THEM? I WARN YOU, POLARIS--
--DON'T MAKE ME MAD!
WHAT?
THAT'S NO WAY TO TALK TO SOMEONE WHO SAVED YOUR LIFE!
YOU DID! YOU SAVED MY LIFE! BUT I CHOSE YOU TO DO IT!
YOU WORK FOR ME NOW--AND ALWAYS HAVE!
LISTEN, UB'X, YOU CAN LEAVE ANY TIME IF YOU'RE GOING TO START RAVING--!
SELF-RIGHTEOUS GORILLA!
DOES ANYONE ELSE FAIL TO SEE THE POWER OF MY SUCKER STICK?
UH, NO--!
SIR!

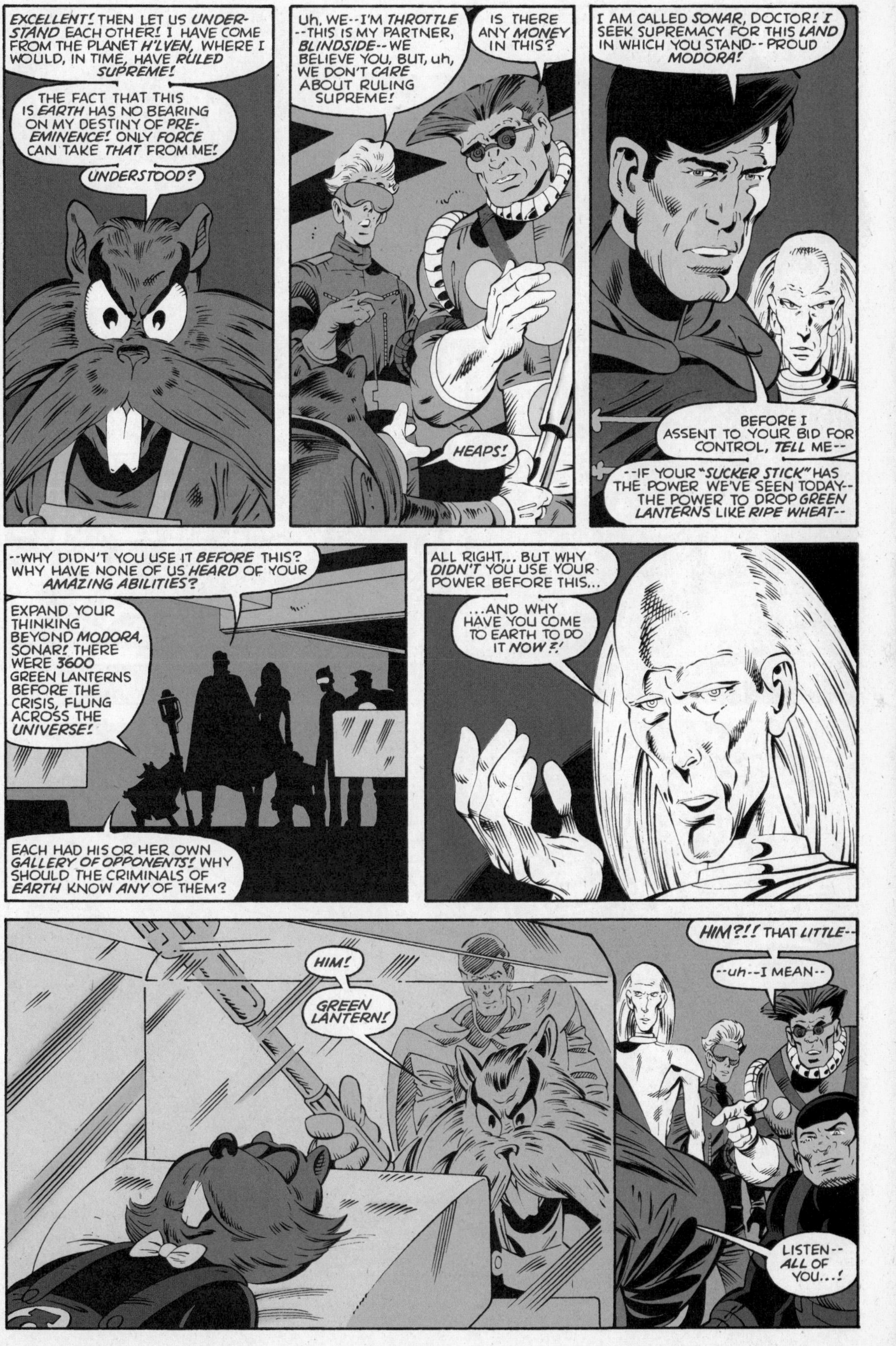
EXCELLENT! THEN LET US UNDERSTAND EACH OTHER! I HAVE COME FROM THE PLANET H'LVEN, WHERE I WOULD, IN TIME, HAVE RULED SUPREME!
THE FACT THAT THIS IS EARTH HAS NO BEARING ON MY DESTINY OF PRE-EMINENCE! ONLY FORCE CAN TAKE THAT FROM ME!
UNDERSTOOD?
Uh, WE--I'M THROTTLE --THIS IS MY PARTNER, BLINDSIDE--WE BELIEVE YOU, BUT, uh, WE DON'T CARE ABOUT RULING SUPREME!
IS THERE ANY MONEY IN THIS?
HEAPS!
I AM CALLED SONAR, DOCTOR! I SEEK SUPREMACY FOR THIS LAND IN WHICH YOU STAND--PROUD MODORA!
BEFORE I ASSENT TO YOUR BID FOR CONTROL, TELL ME--
--IF YOUR "SUCKER STICK" HAS THE POWER WE'VE SEEN TODAY--THE POWER TO DROP GREEN LANTERNS LIKE RIPE WHEAT--
--WHY DIDN'T YOU USE IT BEFORE THIS? WHY HAVE NONE OF US HEARD OF YOUR AMAZING ABILITIES?
EXPAND YOUR THINKING BEYOND MODORA, SONAR! THERE WERE 3600 GREEN LANTERNS BEFORE THE CRISIS, FLUNG ACROSS THE UNIVERSE!
EACH HAD HIS OR HER OWN GALLERY OF OPPONENTS! WHY SHOULD THE CRIMINALS OF EARTH KNOW ANY OF THEM?
ALL RIGHT,.. BUT WHY DIDN'T YOU USE YOUR POWER BEFORE THIS...
...AND WHY HAVE YOU COME TO EARTH TO DO IT NOW?!
HIM!
GREEN LANTERN!
HIM?!! THAT LITTLE--
--uh--I MEAN--
LISTEN--ALL OF YOU...!

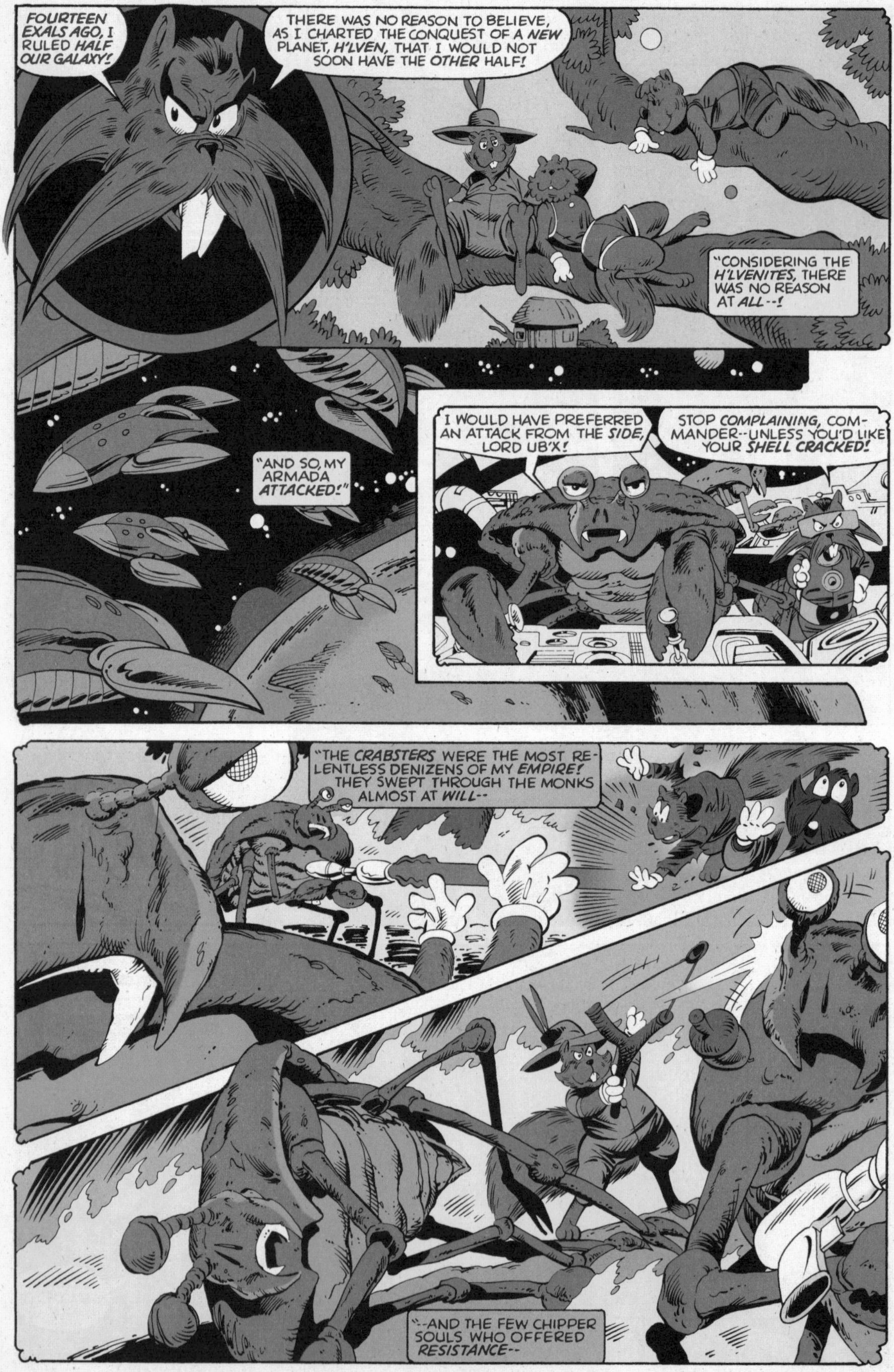
FOURTEEN EXALS AGO, I RULED HALF OUR GALAXY!
THERE WAS NO REASON TO BELIEVE, AS I CHARTED THE CONQUEST OF A NEW PLANET, H'LVEN, THAT I WOULD NOT SOON HAVE THE OTHER HALF!
"CONSIDERING THE H'LVENITES, THERE WAS NO REASON AT ALL--!
"AND SO, MY ARMADA ATTACKED!"
I WOULD HAVE PREFERRED AN ATTACK FROM THE SIDE, LORD UB'X!
STOP COMPLAINING, COMMANDER--UNLESS YOU'D LIKE YOUR SHELL CRACKED!
"THE CRABSTERS WERE THE MOST RELENTLESS DENIZENS OF MY EMPIRE! THEY SWEPT THROUGH THE MONKS ALMOST AT WILL--
"--AND THE FEW CHIPPER SOULS WHO OFFERED RESISTANCE--

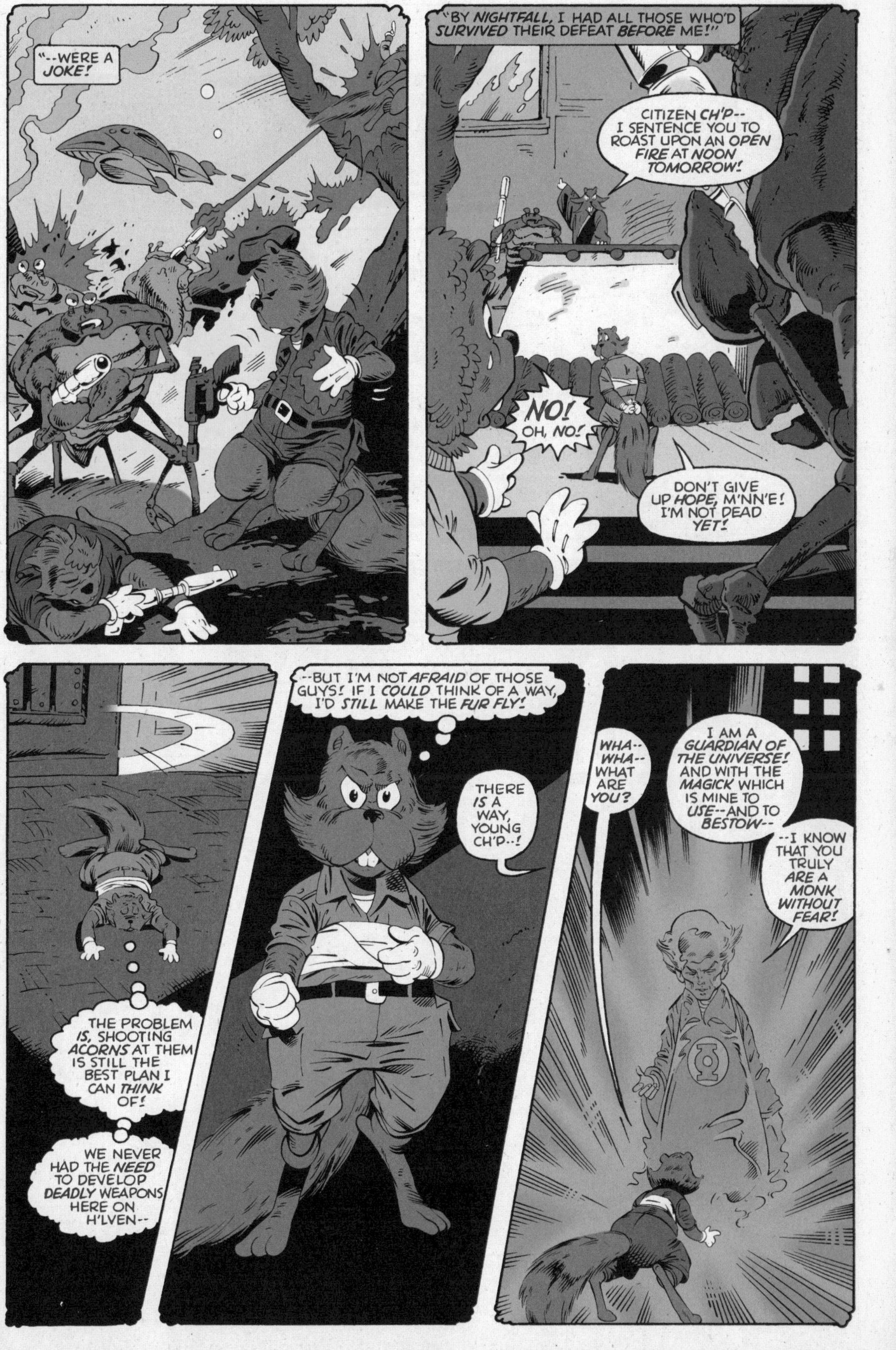
"--WERE A JOKE!
"BY NIGHTFALL, I HAD ALL THOSE WHO'D SURVIVED THEIR DEFEAT BEFORE ME!"
CITIZEN CH'P-- I SENTENCE YOU TO ROAST UPON AN OPEN FIRE AT NOON TOMORROW!
NO! OH, NO!
DON'T GIVE UP HOPE, M'NN'E! I'M NOT DEAD YET!
THE PROBLEM IS, SHOOTING ACORNS AT THEM IS STILL THE BEST PLAN I CAN THINK OF!
WE NEVER HAD THE NEED TO DEVELOP DEADLY WEAPONS HERE ON H'LVEN--
--BUT I'M NOT AFRAID OF THOSE GUYS! IF I COULD THINK OF A WAY, I'D STILL MAKE THE FUR FLY!
THERE IS A WAY, YOUNG CH'P--!
WHA-- WHA-- WHAT ARE YOU?
I AM A GUARDIAN OF THE UNIVERSE! AND WITH THE MAGICK WHICH IS MINE TO USE--AND TO BESTOW--
--I KNOW THAT YOU TRULY ARE A MONK WITHOUT FEAR!

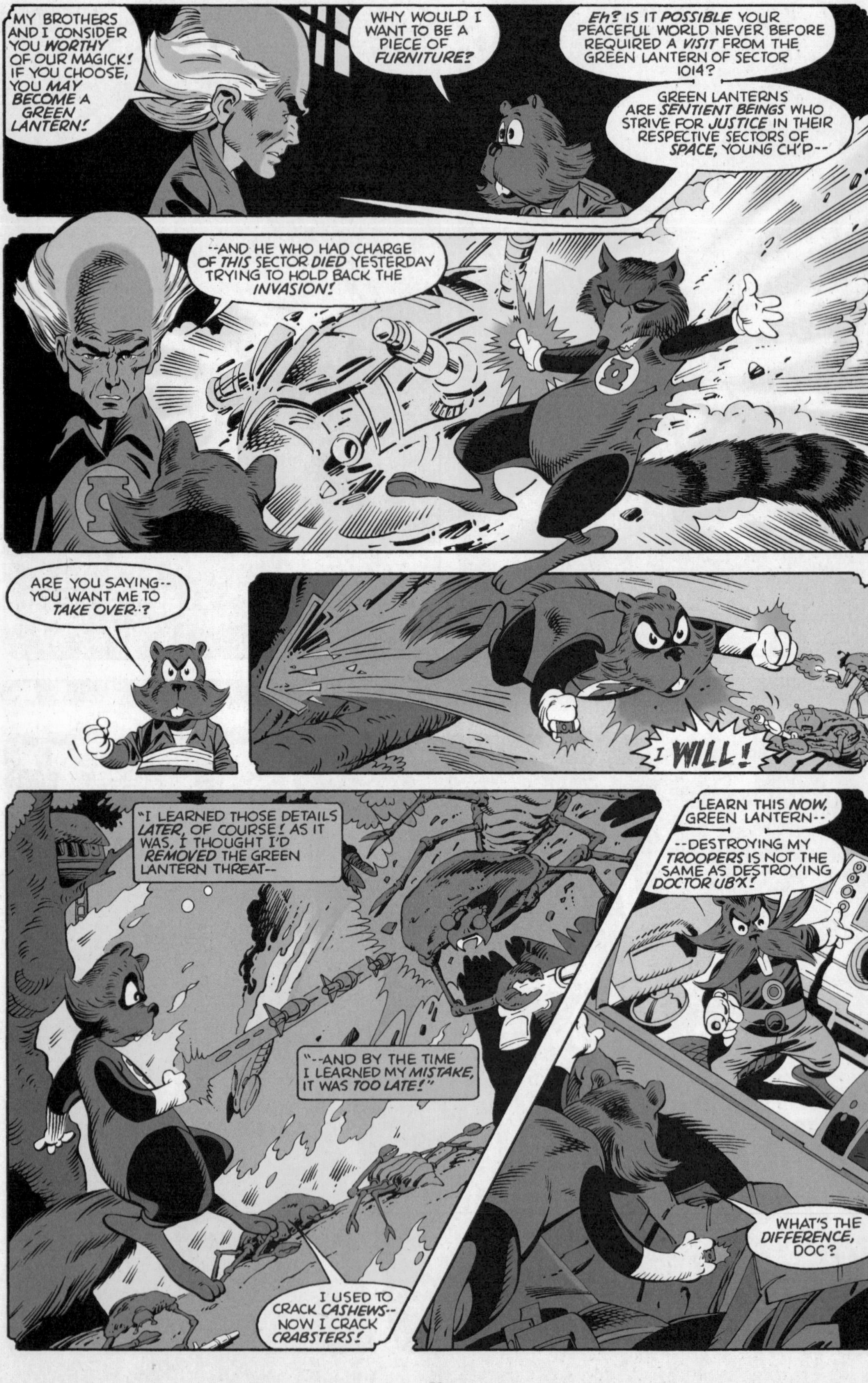

MY BROTHERS AND I CONSIDER YOU WORTHY OF OUR MAGICK! IF YOU CHOOSE, YOU MAY BECOME A GREEN LANTERN!
WHY WOULD I WANT TO BE A PIECE OF FURNITURE?
Eh? IS IT POSSIBLE YOUR PEACEFUL WORLD NEVER BEFORE REQUIRED A VISIT FROM THE GREEN LANTERN OF SECTOR 1014?
GREEN LANTERNS ARE SENTIENT BEINGS WHO STRIVE FOR JUSTICE IN THEIR RESPECTIVE SECTORS OF SPACE, YOUNG CH'P--
--AND HE WHO HAD CHARGE OF THIS SECTOR DIED YESTERDAY TRYING TO HOLD BACK THE INVASION!
ARE YOU SAYING-- YOU WANT ME TO TAKE OVER--?
I WILL!
"I LEARNED THOSE DETAILS LATER, OF COURSE! AS IT WAS, I THOUGHT I'D REMOVED THE GREEN LANTERN THREAT--
"--AND BY THE TIME I LEARNED MY MISTAKE, IT WAS TOO LATE!"
I USED TO CRACK CASHEWS-- NOW I CRACK CRABSTERS!
LEARN THIS NOW, GREEN LANTERN--
--DESTROYING MY TROOPERS IS NOT THE SAME AS DESTROYING DOCTOR UB'X!
WHAT'S THE DIFFERENCE, DOC?

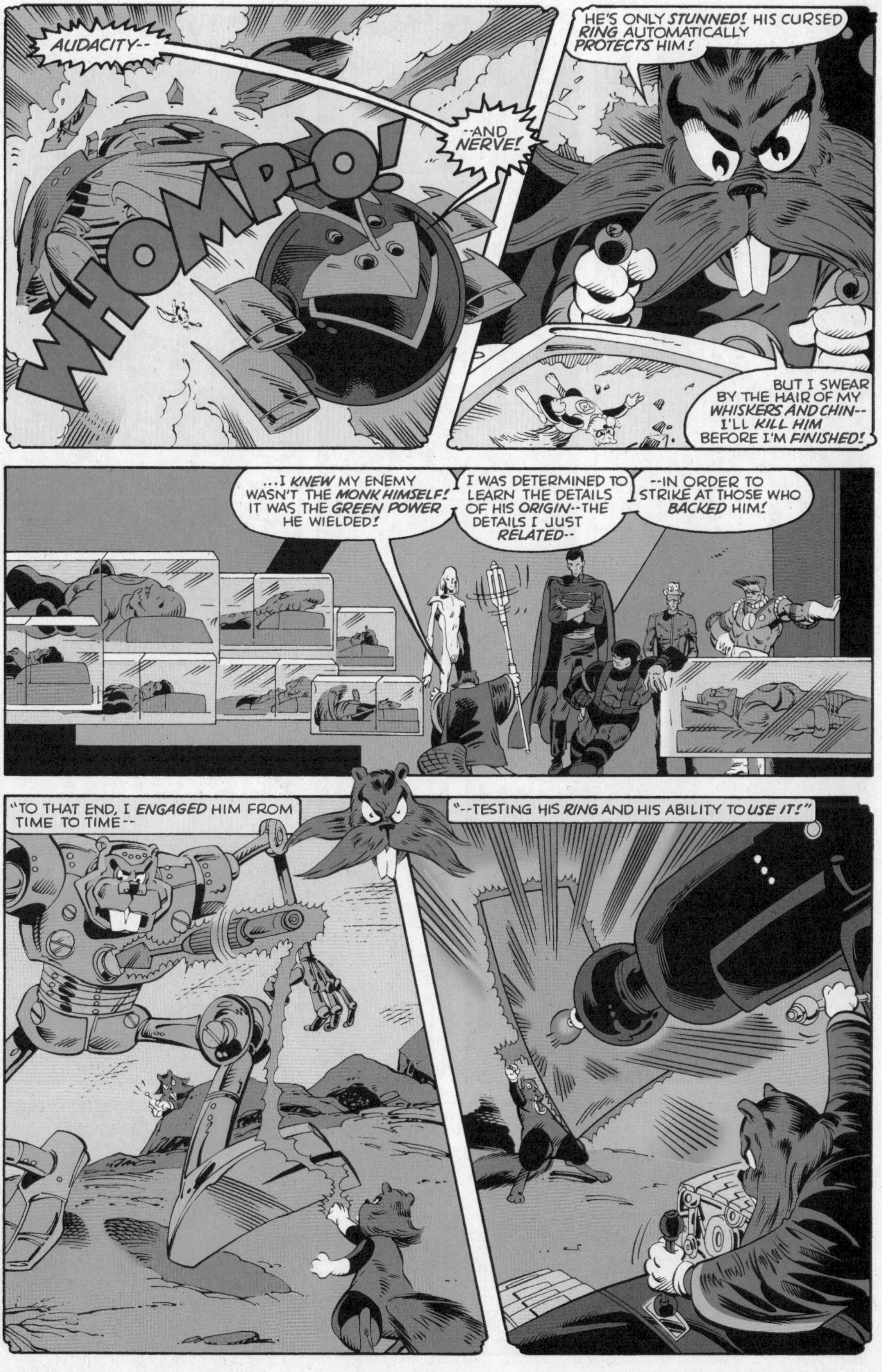
AUDACITY--
--AND NERVE!
WHOMP-O!
HE'S ONLY STUNNED! HIS CURSED RING AUTOMATICALLY PROTECTS HIM!
BUT I SWEAR BY THE HAIR OF MY WHISKERS AND CHIN-- I'LL KILL HIM BEFORE I'M FINISHED!
...I KNEW MY ENEMY WASN'T THE MONK HIMSELF! IT WAS THE GREEN POWER HE WIELDED!
I WAS DETERMINED TO LEARN THE DETAILS OF HIS ORIGIN--THE DETAILS I JUST RELATED--
--IN ORDER TO STRIKE AT THOSE WHO BACKED HIM!
"TO THAT END, I ENGAGED HIM FROM TIME TO TIME--
"--TESTING HIS RING AND HIS ABILITY TO USE IT!"

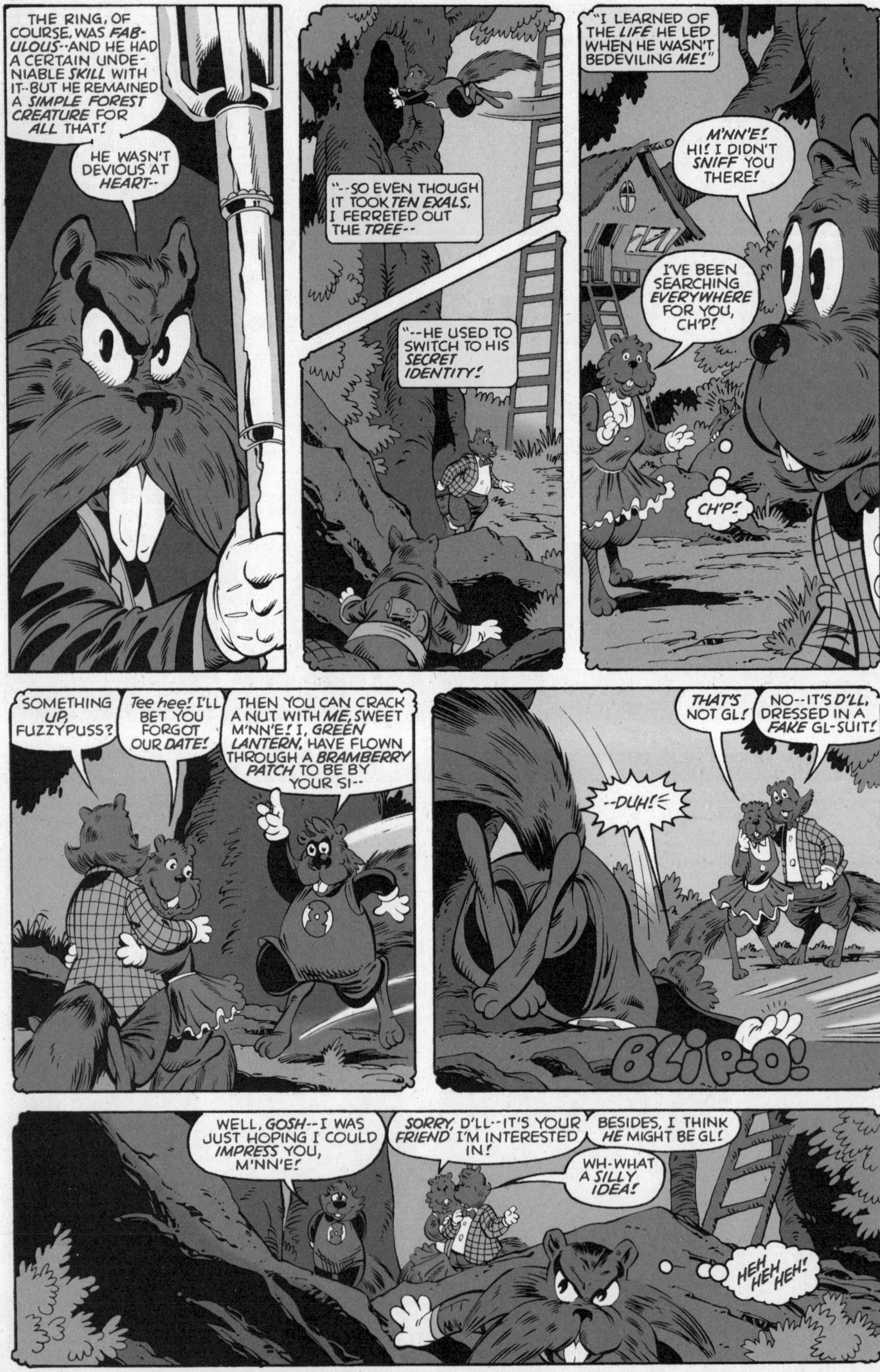
THE RING, OF COURSE, WAS FABULOUS--AND HE HAD A CERTAIN UNDENIABLE SKILL WITH IT--BUT HE REMAINED A SIMPLE FOREST CREATURE FOR ALL THAT!
HE WASN'T DEVIOUS AT HEART--
"--SO EVEN THOUGH IT TOOK TEN EXALS, I FERRETED OUT THE TREE--
"--HE USED TO SWITCH TO HIS SECRET IDENTITY!
"I LEARNED OF THE LIFE HE LED WHEN HE WASN'T BEDEVILING ME!"
M'NN'E! HI! I DIDN'T SNIFF YOU THERE!
I'VE BEEN SEARCHING EVERYWHERE FOR YOU, CH'P!
CH'P!
SOMETHING UP, FUZZYPUSS?
Tee hee! I'LL BET YOU FORGOT OUR DATE!
THEN YOU CAN CRACK A NUT WITH ME, SWEET M'NN'E! I, GREEN LANTERN, HAVE FLOWN THROUGH A BRAMBERRY PATCH TO BE BY YOUR SI--
--DUH!
THAT'S NOT GL!
NO--IT'S D'LL, DRESSED IN A FAKE GL-SUIT!
BLIP-O!
WELL, GOSH--I WAS JUST HOPING I COULD IMPRESS YOU, M'NN'E!
SORRY, D'LL--IT'S YOUR FRIEND I'M INTERESTED IN!
BESIDES, I THINK HE MIGHT BE GL!
WH-WHAT A SILLY IDEA!
HEH HEH HEH!

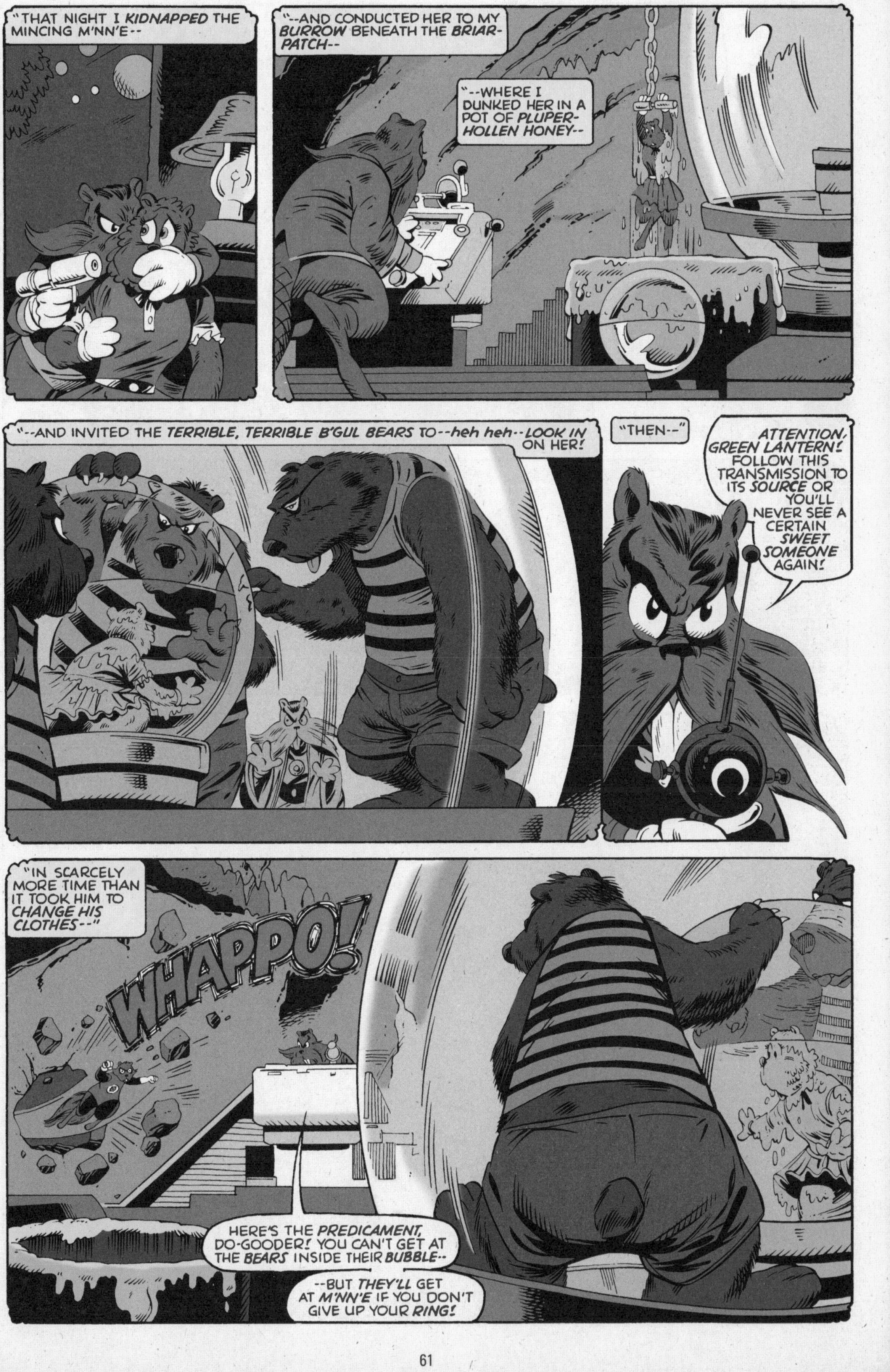
"THAT NIGHT I KIDNAPPED THE MINCING M'NN'E--
"--AND CONDUCTED HER TO MY BURROW BENEATH THE BRIAR-PATCH--
"--WHERE I DUNKED HER IN A POT OF PLUPER-HOLLEN HONEY--
"--AND INVITED THE TERRIBLE, TERRIBLE B'GUL BEARS TO--heh heh--LOOK IN ON HER!
"THEN--"
ATTENTION, GREEN LANTERN! FOLLOW THIS TRANSMISSION TO ITS SOURCE OR YOU'LL NEVER SEE A CERTAIN SWEET SOMEONE AGAIN!
"IN SCARCELY MORE TIME THAN IT TOOK HIM TO CHANGE HIS CLOTHES--"
WHAPPO!
HERE'S THE PREDICAMENT, DO-GOODER! YOU CAN'T GET AT THE BEARS INSIDE THEIR BUBBLE--
--BUT THEY'LL GET AT M'NN'E IF YOU DON'T GIVE UP YOUR RING!

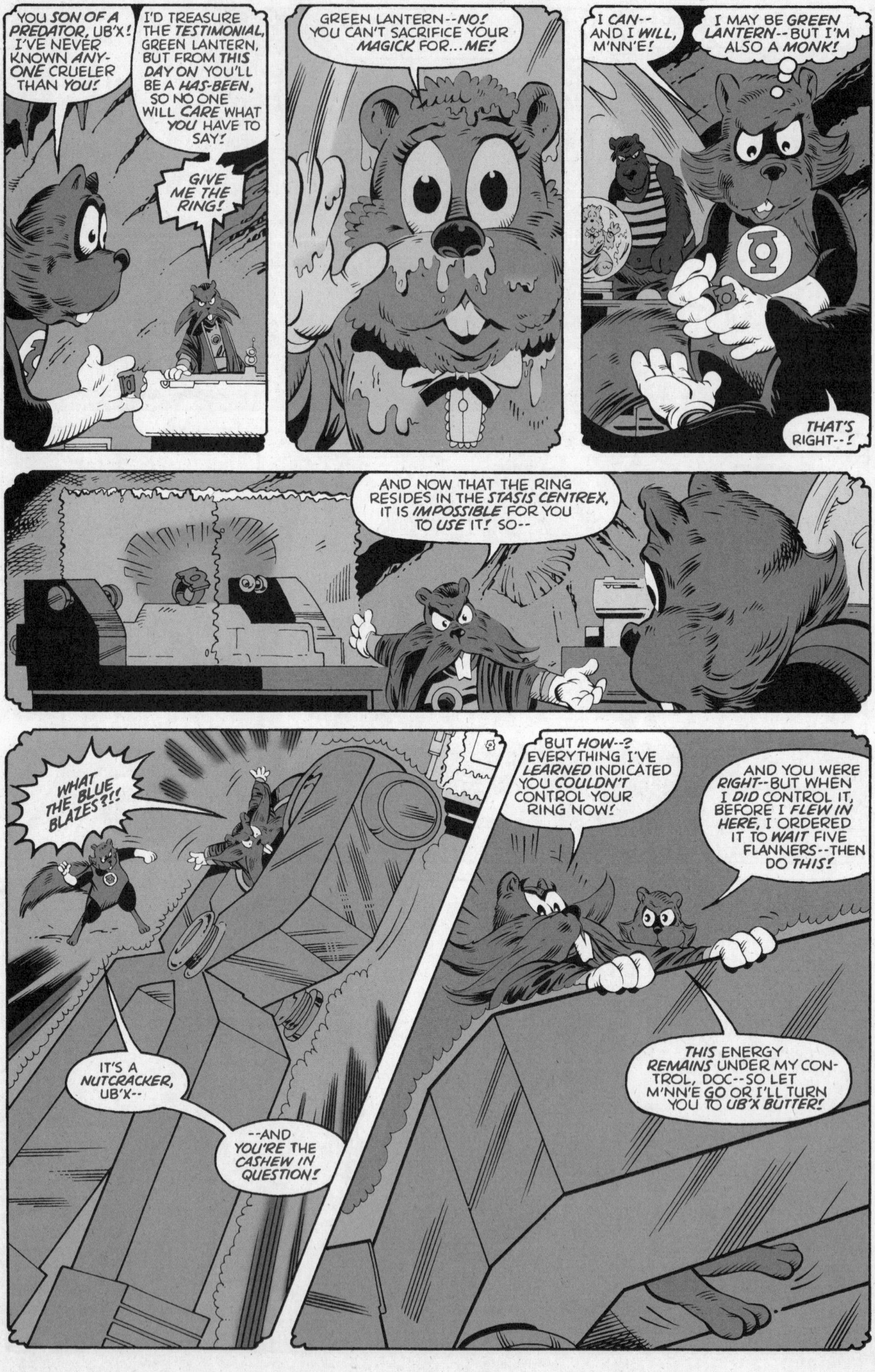
YOU SON OF A PREDATOR, UB'X! I'VE NEVER KNOWN ANY-ONE CRUELER THAN YOU!
I'D TREASURE THE TESTIMONIAL, GREEN LANTERN, BUT FROM THIS DAY ON YOU'LL BE A HAS-BEEN, SO NO ONE WILL CARE WHAT YOU HAVE TO SAY!
GIVE ME THE RING!
GREEN LANTERN--NO! YOU CAN'T SACRIFICE YOUR MAGICK FOR...ME!
I CAN-- AND I WILL, M'NN'E!
I MAY BE GREEN LANTERN--BUT I'M ALSO A MONK!
THAT'S RIGHT--!
AND NOW THAT THE RING RESIDES IN THE STASIS CENTREX, IT IS IMPOSSIBLE FOR YOU TO USE IT! SO--
WHAT THE BLUE BLAZES?!!
IT'S A NUTCRACKER, UB'X--
--AND YOU'RE THE CASHEW IN QUESTION!
BUT HOW--? EVERYTHING I'VE LEARNED INDICATED YOU COULDN'T CONTROL YOUR RING NOW!
AND YOU WERE RIGHT--BUT WHEN I DID CONTROL IT, BEFORE I FLEW IN HERE, I ORDERED IT TO WAIT FIVE FLANNERS--THEN DO THIS!
THIS ENERGY REMAINS UNDER MY CON-TROL, DOC--SO LET M'NN'E GO OR I'LL TURN YOU TO UB'X BUTTER!

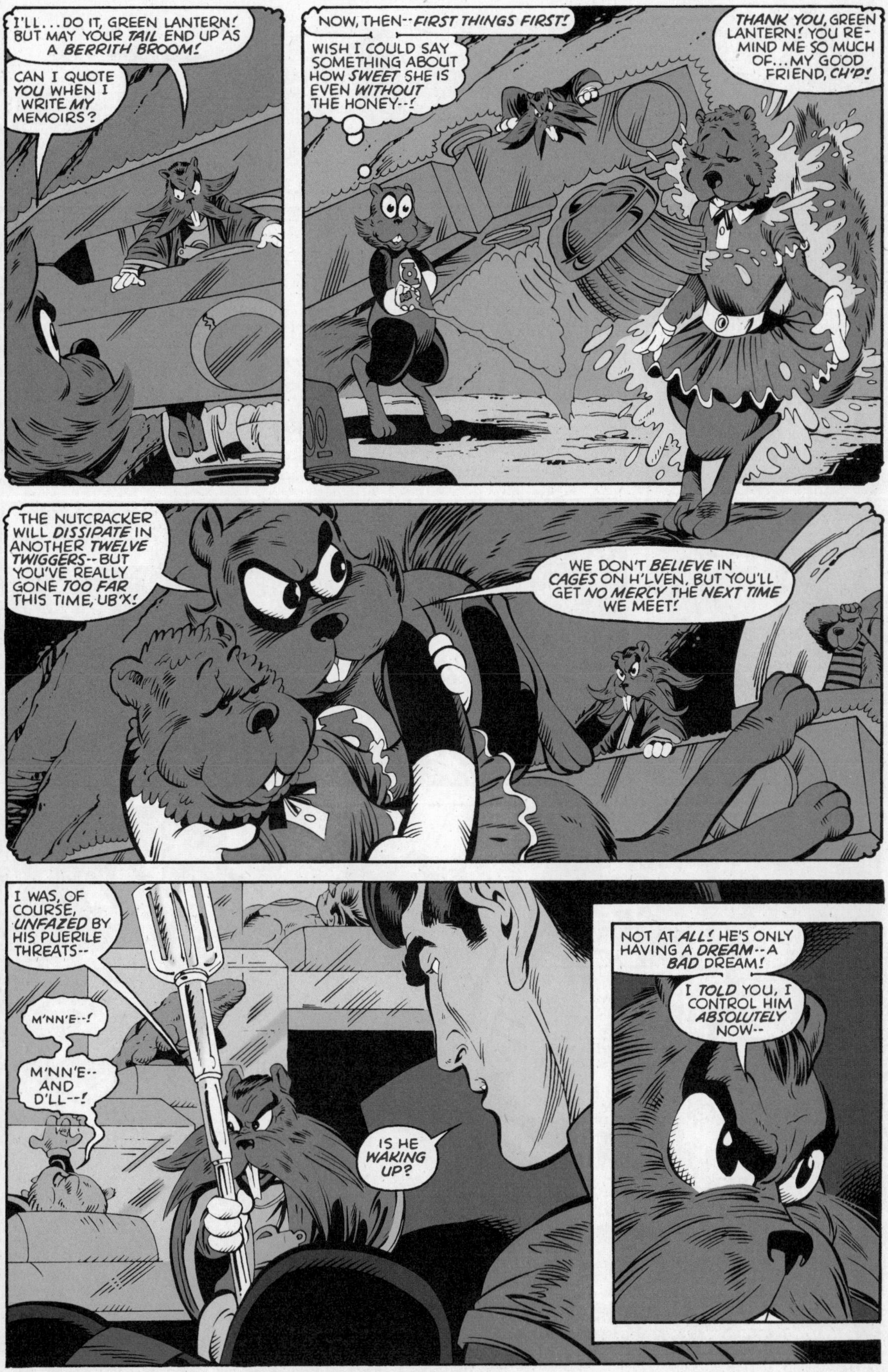
I'LL...DO IT, GREEN LANTERN! BUT MAY YOUR TAIL END UP AS A BERRITH BROOM!
CAN I QUOTE YOU WHEN I WRITE MY MEMOIRS?
NOW, THEN--FIRST THINGS FIRST!
WISH I COULD SAY SOMETHING ABOUT HOW SWEET SHE IS EVEN WITHOUT THE HONEY--!
THANK YOU, GREEN LANTERN! YOU RE-MIND ME SO MUCH OF...MY GOOD FRIEND, CH'P!
THE NUTCRACKER WILL DISSIPATE IN ANOTHER TWELVE TWIGGERS--BUT YOU'VE REALLY GONE TOO FAR THIS TIME, UB'X!
WE DON'T BELIEVE IN CAGES ON H'LVEN, BUT YOU'LL GET NO MERCY THE NEXT TIME WE MEET!
I WAS, OF COURSE, UNFAZED BY HIS PUERILE THREATS--
M'NN'E--!
M'NN'E--AND D'LL--!
IS HE WAKING UP?
NOT AT ALL! HE'S ONLY HAVING A DREAM--A BAD DREAM!
I TOLD YOU, I CONTROL HIM ABSOLUTELY NOW--

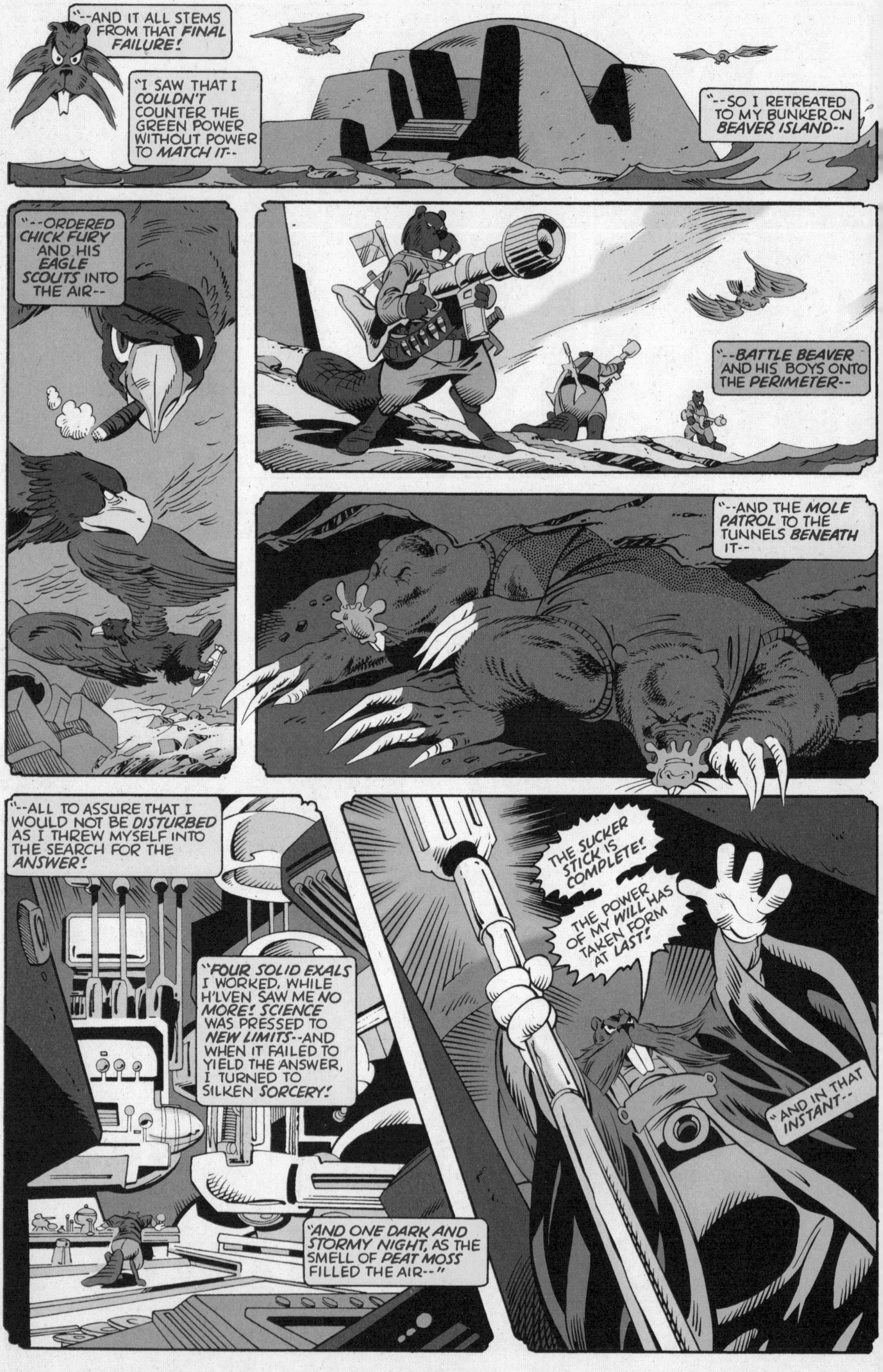
"--AND IT ALL STEMS FROM THAT FINAL FAILURE!
"I SAW THAT I COULDN'T COUNTER THE GREEN POWER WITHOUT POWER TO MATCH IT--
"--SO I RETREATED TO MY BUNKER ON BEAVER ISLAND--
"--ORDERED CHICK FURY AND HIS EAGLE SCOUTS INTO THE AIR--
"--BATTLE BEAVER AND HIS BOYS ONTO THE PERIMETER--
"--AND THE MOLE PATROL TO THE TUNNELS BENEATH IT--
"--ALL TO ASSURE THAT I WOULD NOT BE DISTURBED AS I THREW MYSELF INTO THE SEARCH FOR THE ANSWER!
"FOUR SOLID EXALS I WORKED, WHILE H'LVEN SAW ME NO MORE! SCIENCE WAS PRESSED TO NEW LIMITS--AND WHEN IT FAILED TO YIELD THE ANSWER, I TURNED TO SILKEN SORCERY!
"AND ONE DARK AND STORMY NIGHT, AS THE SMELL OF PEAT MOSS FILLED THE AIR--"
THE SUCKER STICK IS COMPLETE!
THE POWER OF MY WILL HAS TAKEN FORM AT LAST!
"AND IN THAT INSTANT--

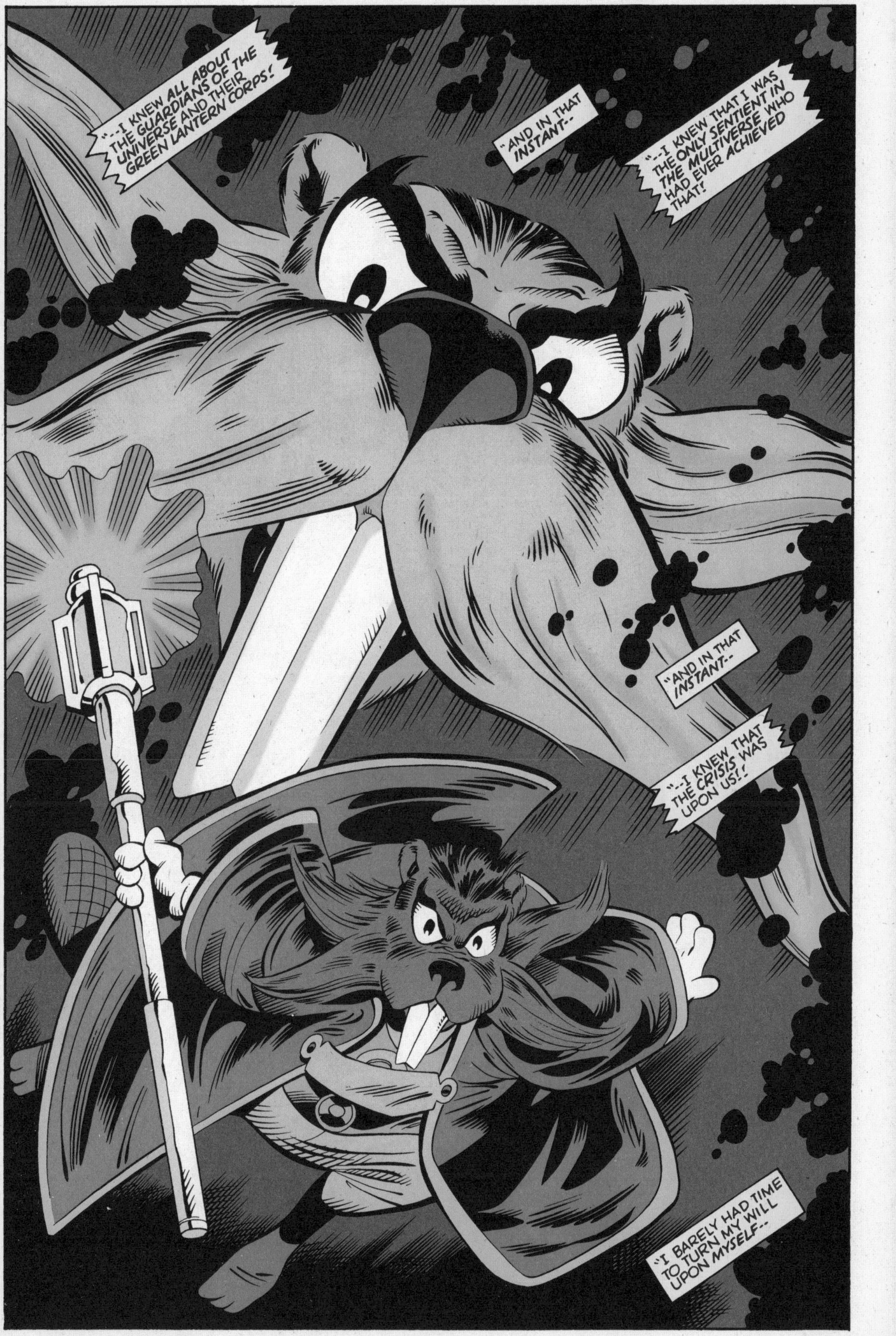
"--I KNEW ALL ABOUT THE GUARDIANS OF THE UNIVERSE AND THEIR GREEN LANTERN CORPS!
"AND IN THAT INSTANT--
"--I KNEW THAT I WAS THE ONLY SENTIENT IN THE MULTIVERSE WHO HAD EVER ACHIEVED THAT!
"AND IN THAT INSTANT--
"--I KNEW THAT THE CRISIS WAS UPON US!!
"I BARELY HAD TIME TO TURN MY WILL UPON MYSELF--

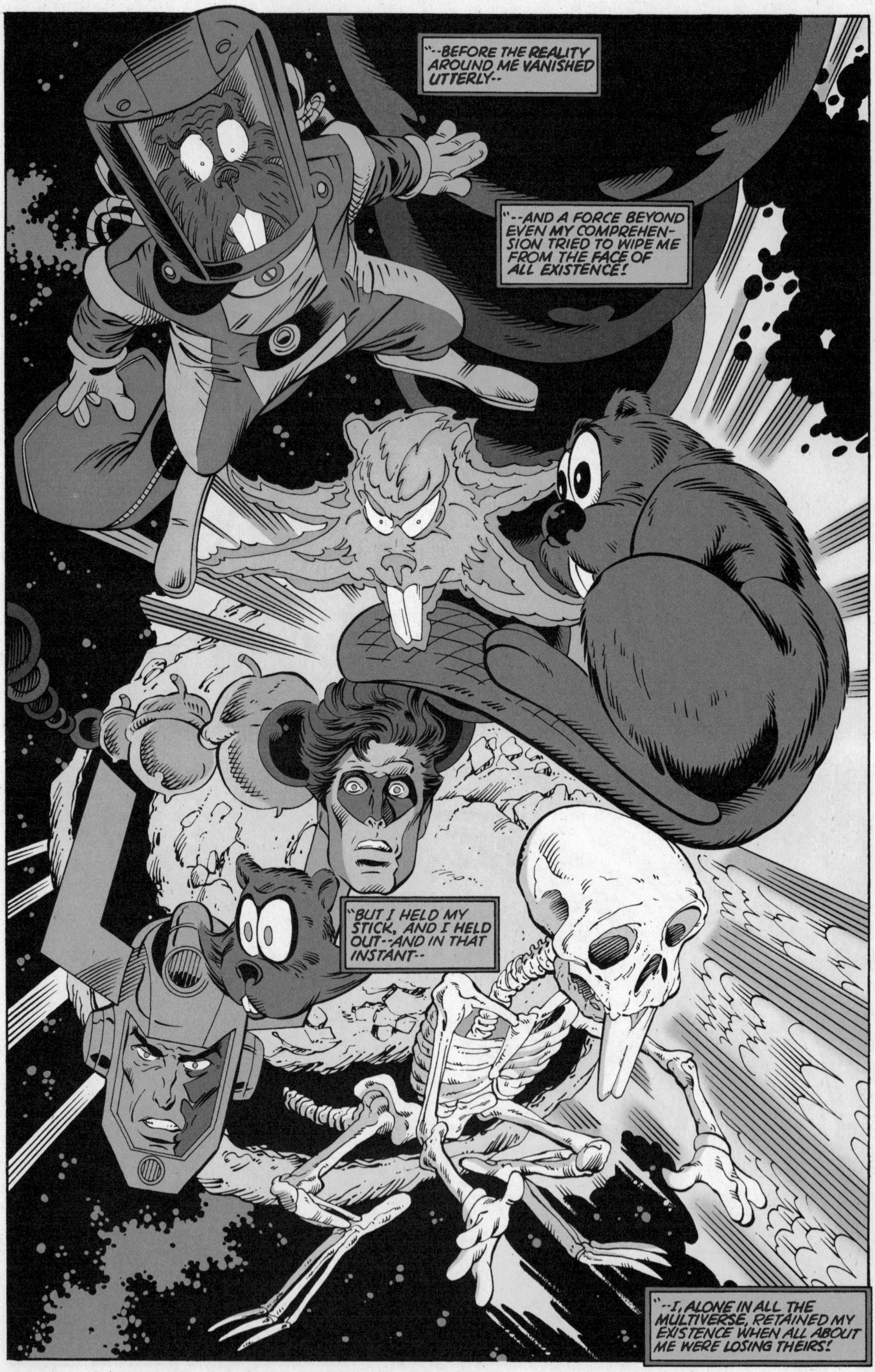
"--BEFORE THE REALITY AROUND ME VANISHED UTTERLY--
"--AND A FORCE BEYOND EVEN MY COMPREHEN-SION TRIED TO WIPE ME FROM THE FACE OF ALL EXISTENCE!
"BUT I HELD MY STICK, AND I HELD OUT--AND IN THAT INSTANT--
"--I, ALONE IN ALL THE MULTIVERSE, RETAINED MY EXISTENCE WHEN ALL ABOUT ME WERE LOSING THEIRS!

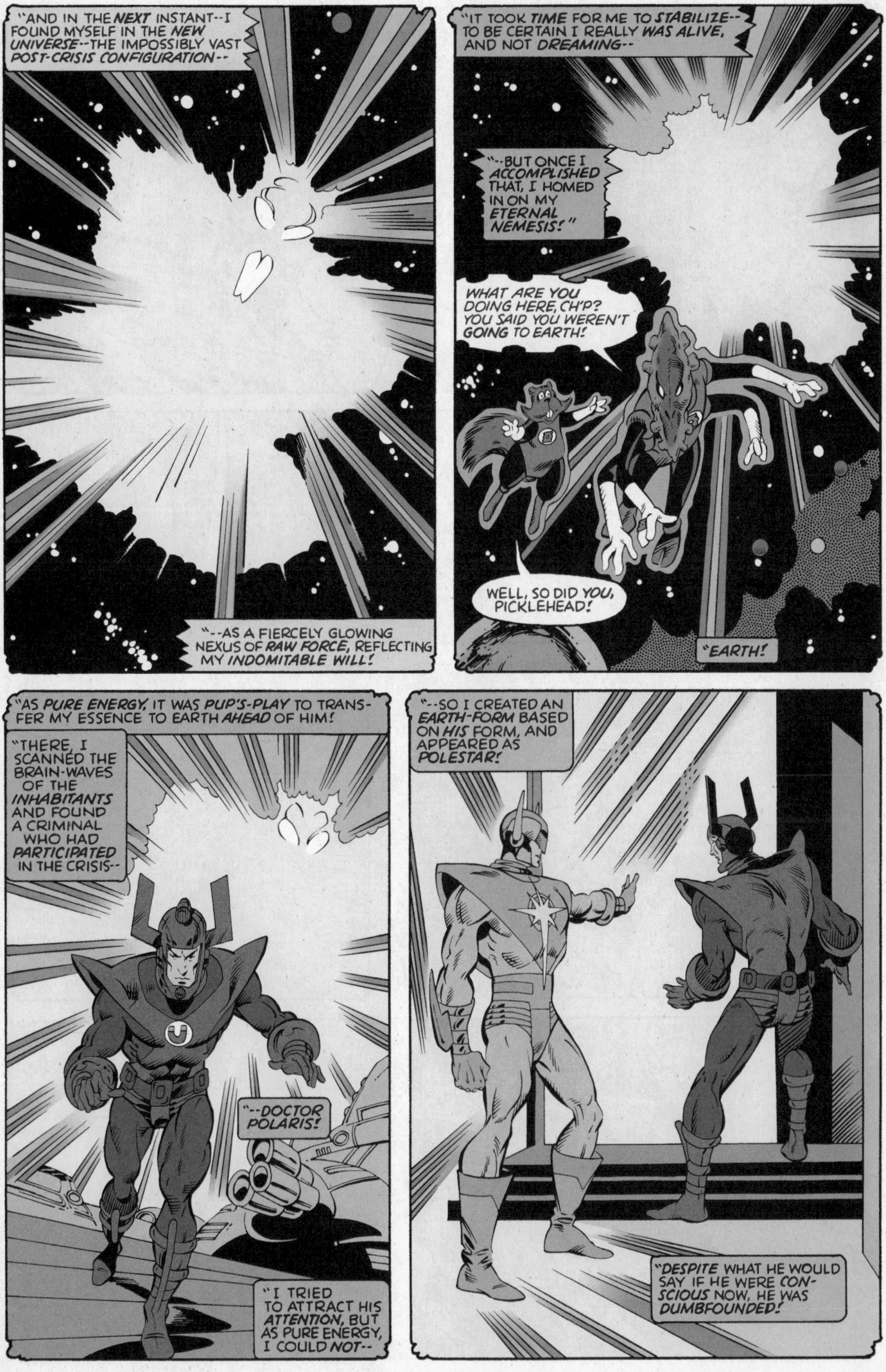
"AND IN THE NEXT INSTANT--I FOUND MYSELF IN THE NEW UNIVERSE--THE IMPOSSIBLY VAST POST-CRISIS CONFIGURATION--
"--AS A FIERCELY GLOWING NEXUS OF RAW FORCE, REFLECTING MY INDOMITABLE WILL!
"IT TOOK TIME FOR ME TO STABILIZE--TO BE CERTAIN I REALLY WAS ALIVE, AND NOT DREAMING--
"--BUT ONCE I ACCOMPLISHED THAT, I HOMED IN ON MY ETERNAL NEMESIS!"
WHAT ARE YOU DOING HERE, CH'P? YOU SAID YOU WEREN'T GOING TO EARTH!
WELL, SO DID YOU, PICKLEHEAD!
"EARTH!
"AS PURE ENERGY, IT WAS PUP'S-PLAY TO TRANSFER MY ESSENCE TO EARTH AHEAD OF HIM!
"THERE, I SCANNED THE BRAIN-WAVES OF THE INHABITANTS AND FOUND A CRIMINAL WHO HAD PARTICIPATED IN THE CRISIS--
"--DOCTOR POLARIS!
"I TRIED TO ATTRACT HIS ATTENTION, BUT AS PURE ENERGY, I COULD NOT--
"--SO I CREATED AN EARTH-FORM BASED ON HIS FORM, AND APPEARED AS POLESTAR!
"DESPITE WHAT HE WOULD SAY IF HE WERE CONSCIOUS NOW, HE WAS DUMBFOUNDED!

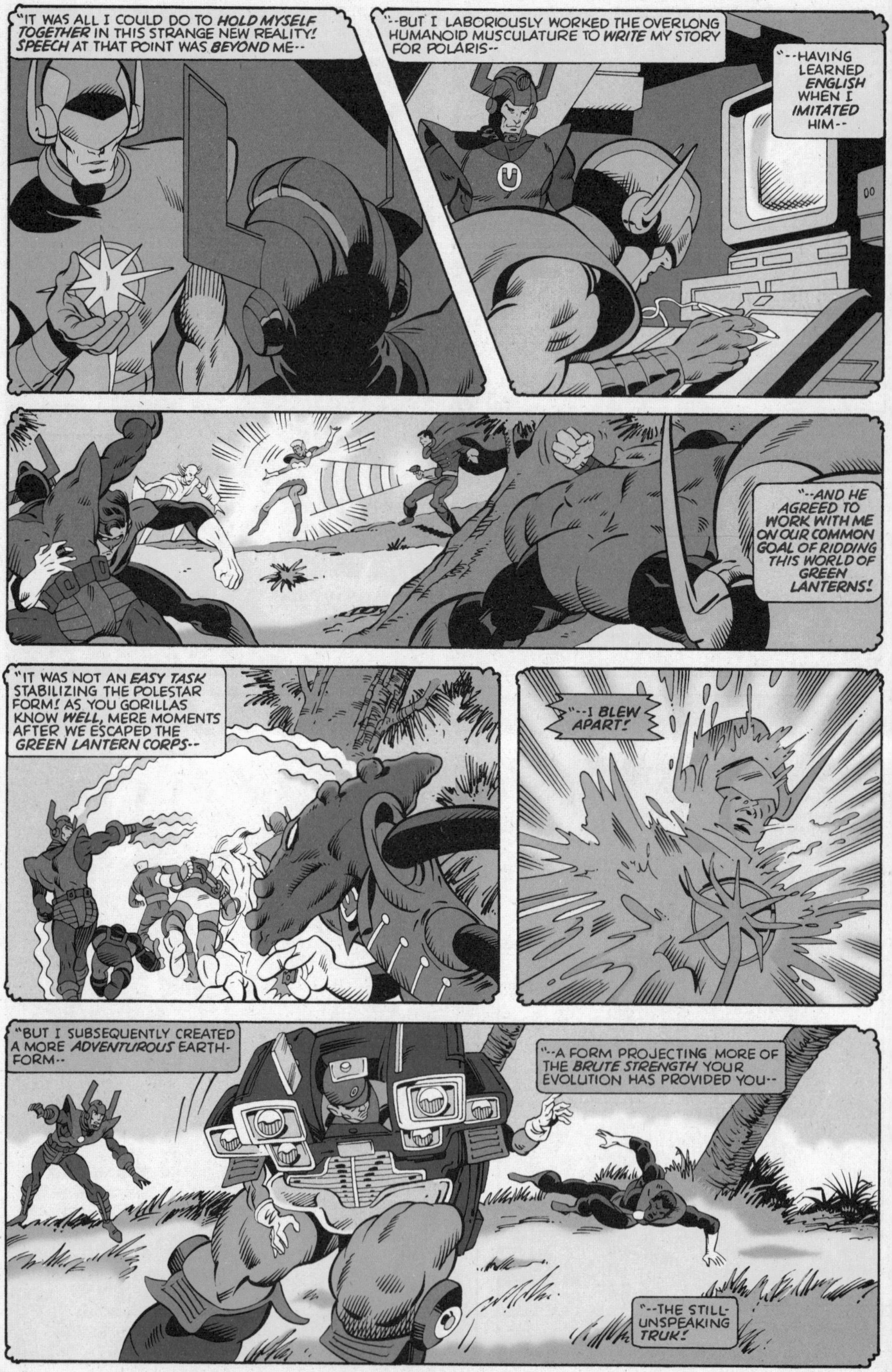
"IT WAS ALL I COULD DO TO HOLD MYSELF TOGETHER IN THIS STRANGE NEW REALITY! SPEECH AT THAT POINT WAS BEYOND ME--
"--BUT I LABORIOUSLY WORKED THE OVERLONG HUMANOID MUSCULATURE TO WRITE MY STORY FOR POLARIS--
"--HAVING LEARNED ENGLISH WHEN I IMITATED HIM--
"--AND HE AGREED TO WORK WITH ME ON OUR COMMON GOAL OF RIDDING THIS WORLD OF GREEN LANTERNS!
"IT WAS NOT AN EASY TASK STABILIZING THE POLESTAR FORM! AS YOU GORILLAS KNOW WELL, MERE MOMENTS AFTER WE ESCAPED THE GREEN LANTERN CORPS--
"--I BLEW APART!
"BUT I SUBSEQUENTLY CREATED A MORE ADVENTUROUS EARTH-FORM--
"--A FORM PROJECTING MORE OF THE BRUTE STRENGTH YOUR EVOLUTION HAS PROVIDED YOU--
"--THE STILL-UNSPEAKING TRUK!

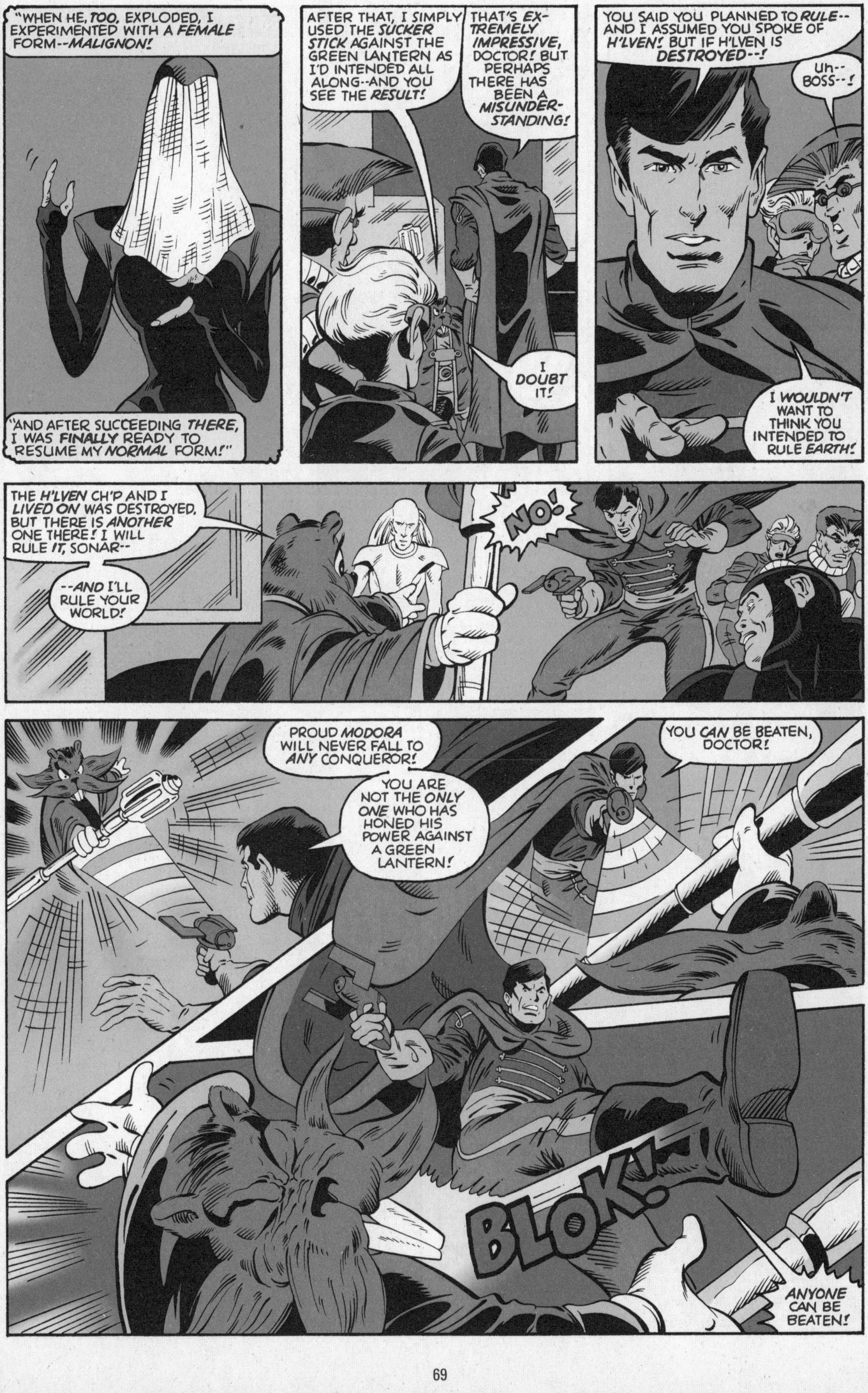
"WHEN HE, TOO, EXPLODED, I EXPERIMENTED WITH A FEMALE FORM--MALIGNON!
"AND AFTER SUCCEEDING THERE, I WAS FINALLY READY TO RESUME MY NORMAL FORM!"
AFTER THAT, I SIMPLY USED THE SUCKER STICK AGAINST THE GREEN LANTERN AS I'D INTENDED ALL ALONG--AND YOU SEE THE RESULT!
THAT'S EXTREMELY IMPRESSIVE, DOCTOR! BUT PERHAPS THERE HAS BEEN A MISUNDERSTANDING!
I DOUBT IT!
YOU SAID YOU PLANNED TO RULE--AND I ASSUMED YOU SPOKE OF H'LVEN! BUT IF H'LVEN IS DESTROYED--!
Uh--BOSS--!
I WOULDN'T WANT TO THINK YOU INTENDED TO RULE EARTH!
THE H'LVEN CH'P AND I LIVED ON WAS DESTROYED, BUT THERE IS ANOTHER ONE THERE! I WILL RULE IT, SONAR--
--AND I'LL RULE YOUR WORLD!
NO!
PROUD MODORA WILL NEVER FALL TO ANY CONQUEROR!
YOU ARE NOT THE ONLY ONE WHO HAS HONED HIS POWER AGAINST A GREEN LANTERN!
YOU CAN BE BEATEN, DOCTOR!
BLOK!
ANYONE CAN BE BEATEN!

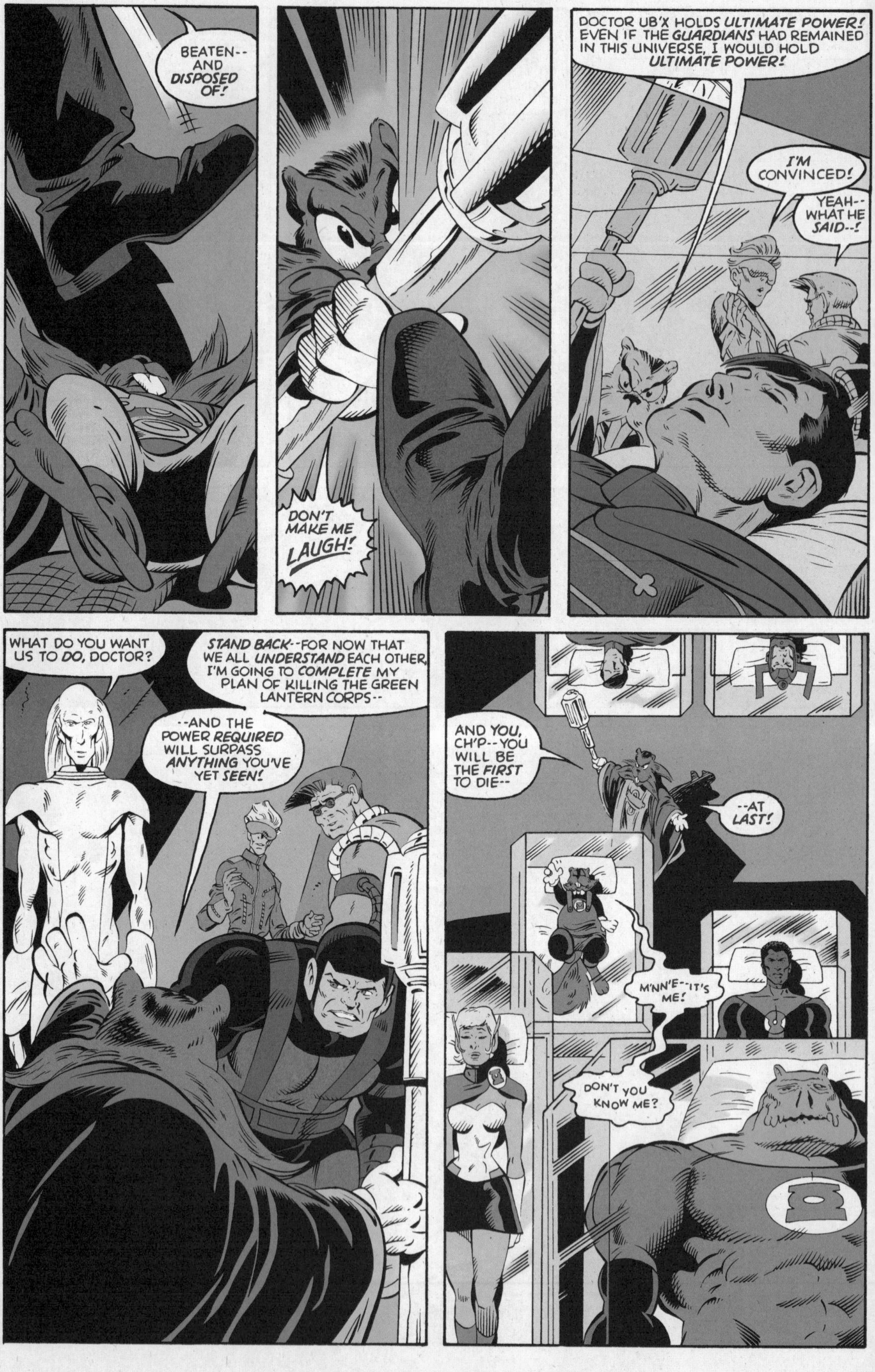
BEATEN--
AND
DISPOSED
OF!
DON'T
MAKE ME
LAUGH!
DOCTOR UB'X HOLDS ULTIMATE POWER! EVEN IF THE GUARDIANS HAD REMAINED IN THIS UNIVERSE, I WOULD HOLD ULTIMATE POWER!
I'M CONVINCED!
YEAH--
WHAT HE
SAID--!
WHAT DO YOU WANT US TO DO, DOCTOR?
STAND BACK--FOR NOW THAT WE ALL UNDERSTAND EACH OTHER, I'M GOING TO COMPLETE MY PLAN OF KILLING THE GREEN LANTERN CORPS--
--AND THE POWER REQUIRED WILL SURPASS ANYTHING YOU'VE YET SEEN!
AND YOU, CH'P--YOU WILL BE THE FIRST TO DIE--
--AT LAST!
M'NN'E--IT'S ME!
DON'T YOU KNOW ME?

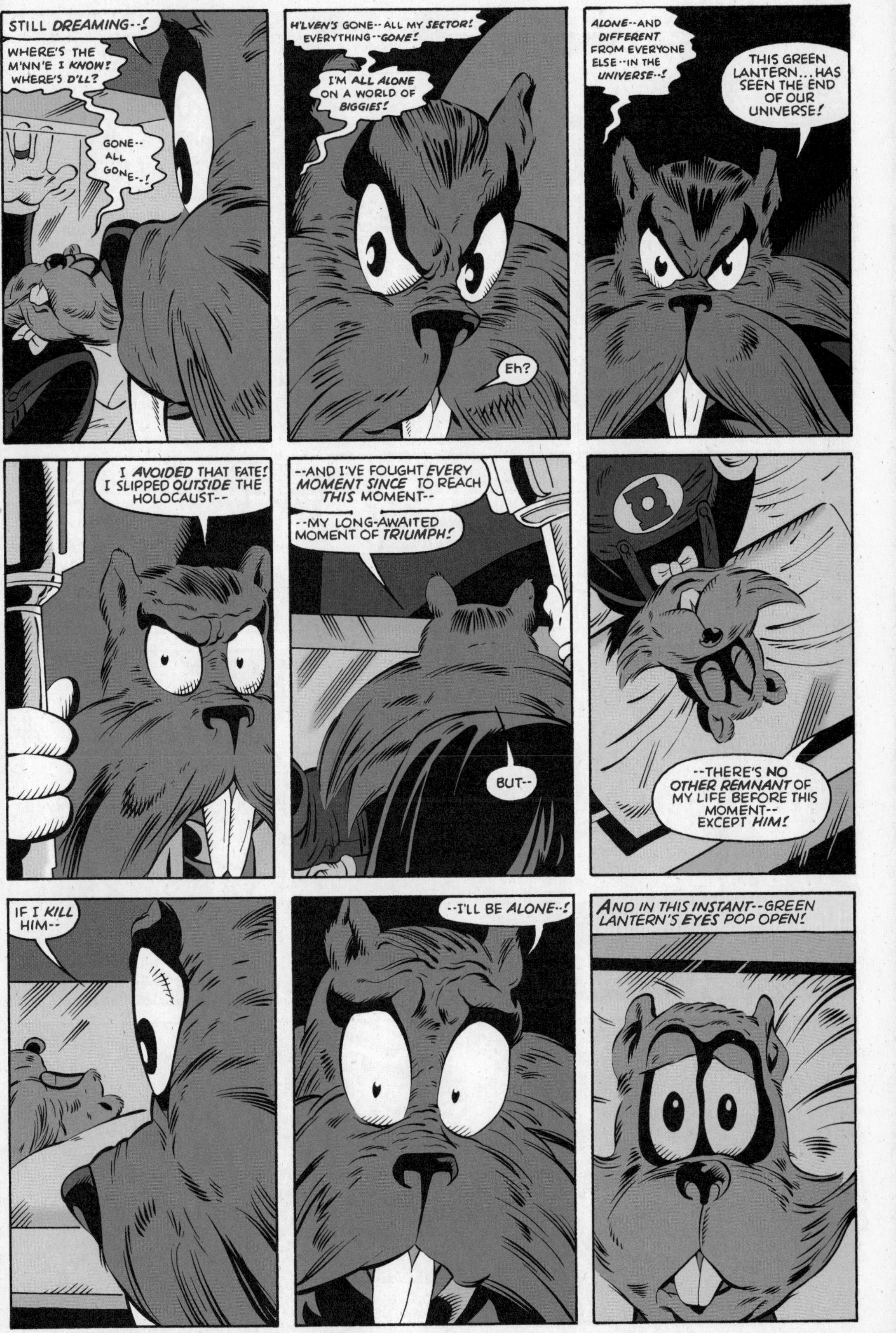
STILL DREAMING--!
WHERE'S THE M'NN'E I KNOW? WHERE'S D'LL?
GONE--ALL GONE--!
H'LVEN'S GONE--ALL MY SECTOR! EVERYTHING--GONE!
I'M ALL ALONE ON A WORLD OF BIGGIES!
Eh?
ALONE--AND DIFFERENT FROM EVERYONE ELSE--IN THE UNIVERSE--!
THIS GREEN LANTERN...HAS SEEN THE END OF OUR UNIVERSE!
I AVOIDED THAT FATE! I SLIPPED OUTSIDE THE HOLOCAUST--
--AND I'VE FOUGHT EVERY MOMENT SINCE TO REACH THIS MOMENT--
--MY LONG-AWAITED MOMENT OF TRIUMPH!
BUT--
--THERE'S NO OTHER REMNANT OF MY LIFE BEFORE THIS MOMENT--EXCEPT HIM!
IF I KILL HIM--
--I'LL BE ALONE--!
AND IN THIS INSTANT--GREEN LANTERN'S EYES POP OPEN!

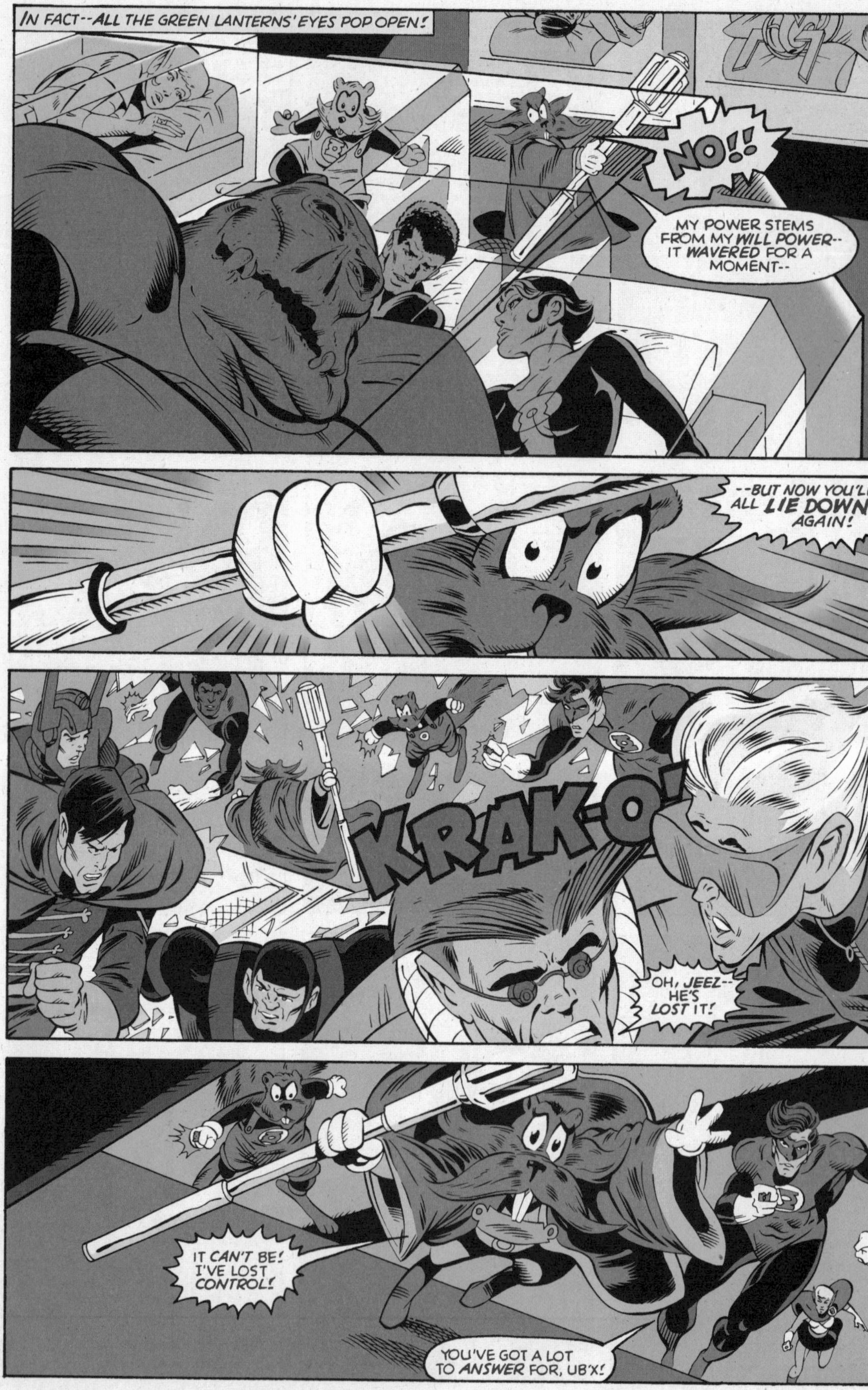
IN FACT--ALL THE GREEN LANTERNS' EYES POP OPEN!
NO!!
MY POWER STEMS FROM MY WILL POWER-- IT WAVERED FOR A MOMENT--
--BUT NOW YOU'LL ALL LIE DOWN AGAIN!
KRAK-O'
OH, JEEZ-- HE'S LOST IT!
IT CAN'T BE! I'VE LOST CONTROL!
YOU'VE GOT A LOT TO ANSWER FOR, UB'X!

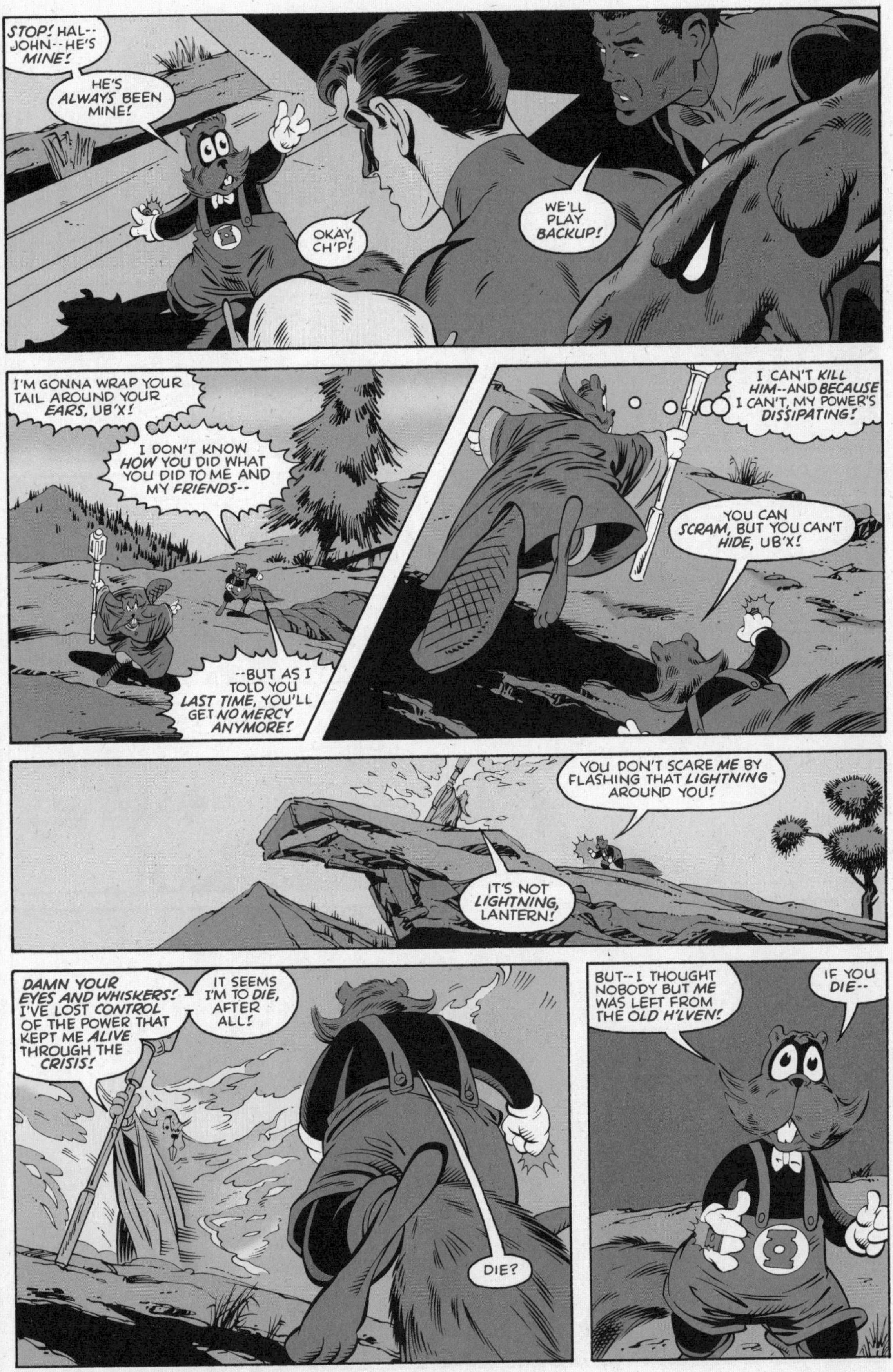
STOP! HAL--JOHN--HE'S MINE!
HE'S ALWAYS BEEN MINE!
OKAY, CH'P!
WE'LL PLAY BACKUP!
I'M GONNA WRAP YOUR TAIL AROUND YOUR EARS, UB'X!
I DON'T KNOW HOW YOU DID WHAT YOU DID TO ME AND MY FRIENDS--
--BUT AS I TOLD YOU LAST TIME, YOU'LL GET NO MERCY ANYMORE!
I CAN'T KILL HIM--AND BECAUSE I CAN'T, MY POWER'S DISSIPATING!
YOU CAN SCRAM, BUT YOU CAN'T HIDE, UB'X!
YOU DON'T SCARE ME BY FLASHING THAT LIGHTNING AROUND YOU!
IT'S NOT LIGHTNING, LANTERN!
DAMN YOUR EYES AND WHISKERS! I'VE LOST CONTROL OF THE POWER THAT KEPT ME ALIVE THROUGH THE CRISIS!
IT SEEMS I'M TO DIE, AFTER ALL!
DIE?
BUT--I THOUGHT NOBODY BUT ME WAS LEFT FROM THE OLD H'LVEN!
IF YOU DIE--

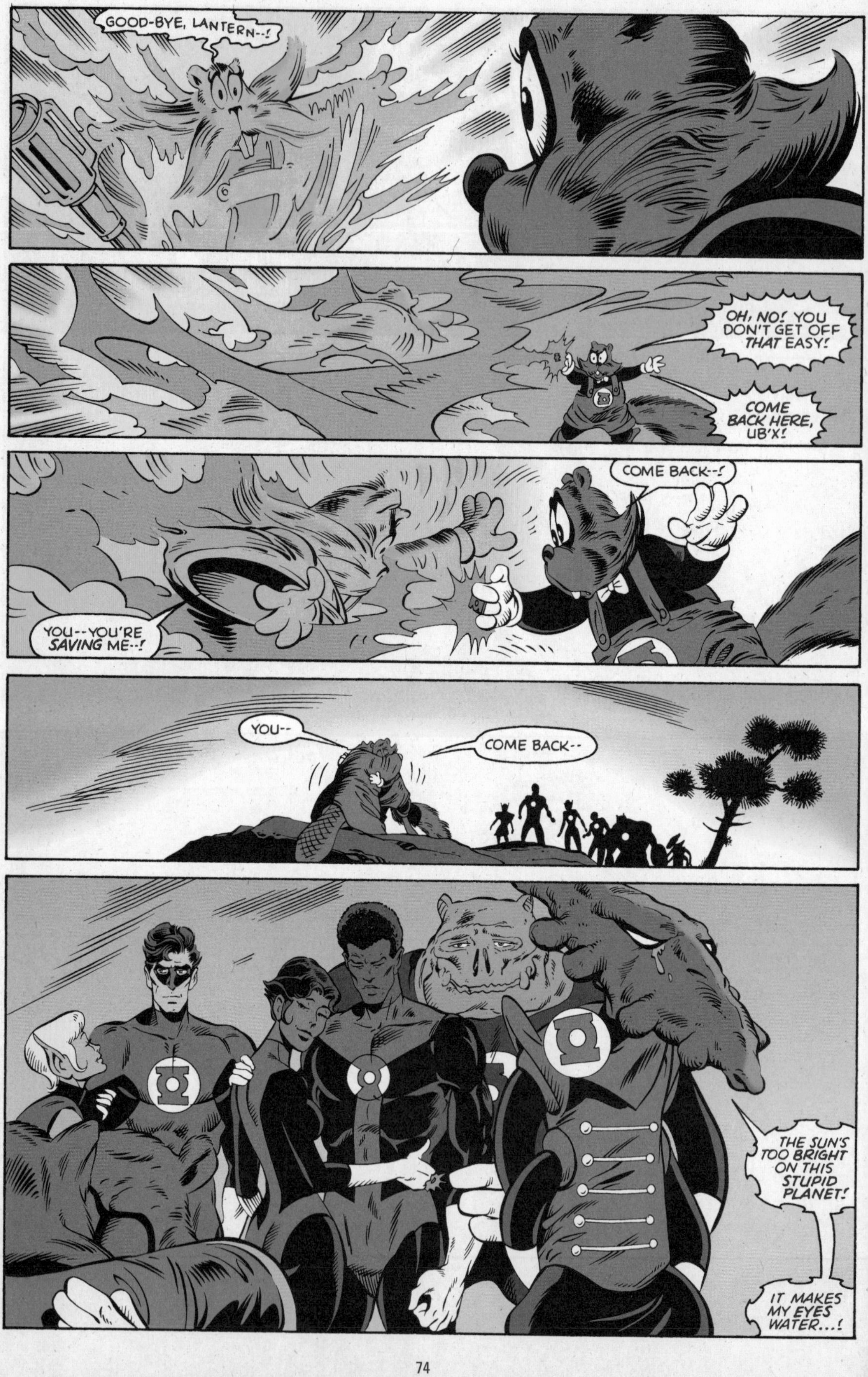
GOOD-BYE, LANTERN--!
OH, NO! YOU DON'T GET OFF THAT EASY!
COME BACK HERE, UB'X!
COME BACK--!
YOU--YOU'RE SAVING ME--!
YOU--
COME BACK--
THE SUN'S TOO BRIGHT ON THIS STUPID PLANET!
IT MAKES MY EYES WATER...!

By ENGLEHART, STATON & FARMER

75¢
204
SEPT. 86

APPROVED BY THE COMICS CODE AUTHORITY

THE Green Lantern Corps

FACES ITS DEADLIEST ENEMY...

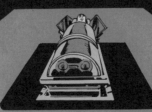

...THE MAN IN THE IRON LUNG!

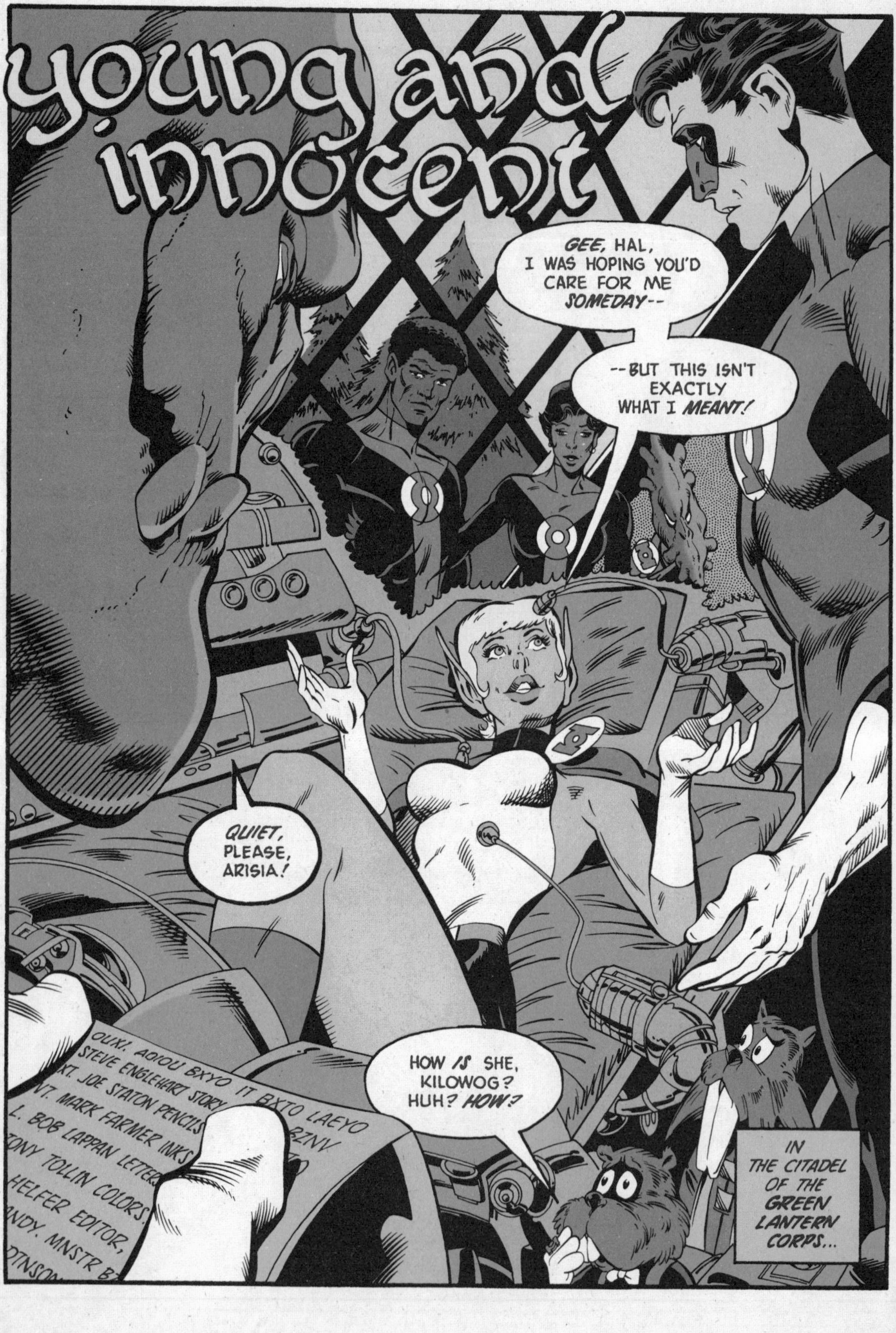
young and innocent
GEE, HAL, I WAS HOPING YOU'D CARE FOR ME SOMEDAY--
--BUT THIS ISN'T EXACTLY WHAT I MEANT!
QUIET, PLEASE, ARISIA!
IN THE CITADEL OF THE GREEN LANTERN CORPS...
HOW IS SHE, KILOWOG? HUH? HOW?
STEVE ENGLEHART STORY
JOE STATON PENCILS
MARK FARMER INKS
TOLLIN COLORS
HELFER EDITOR

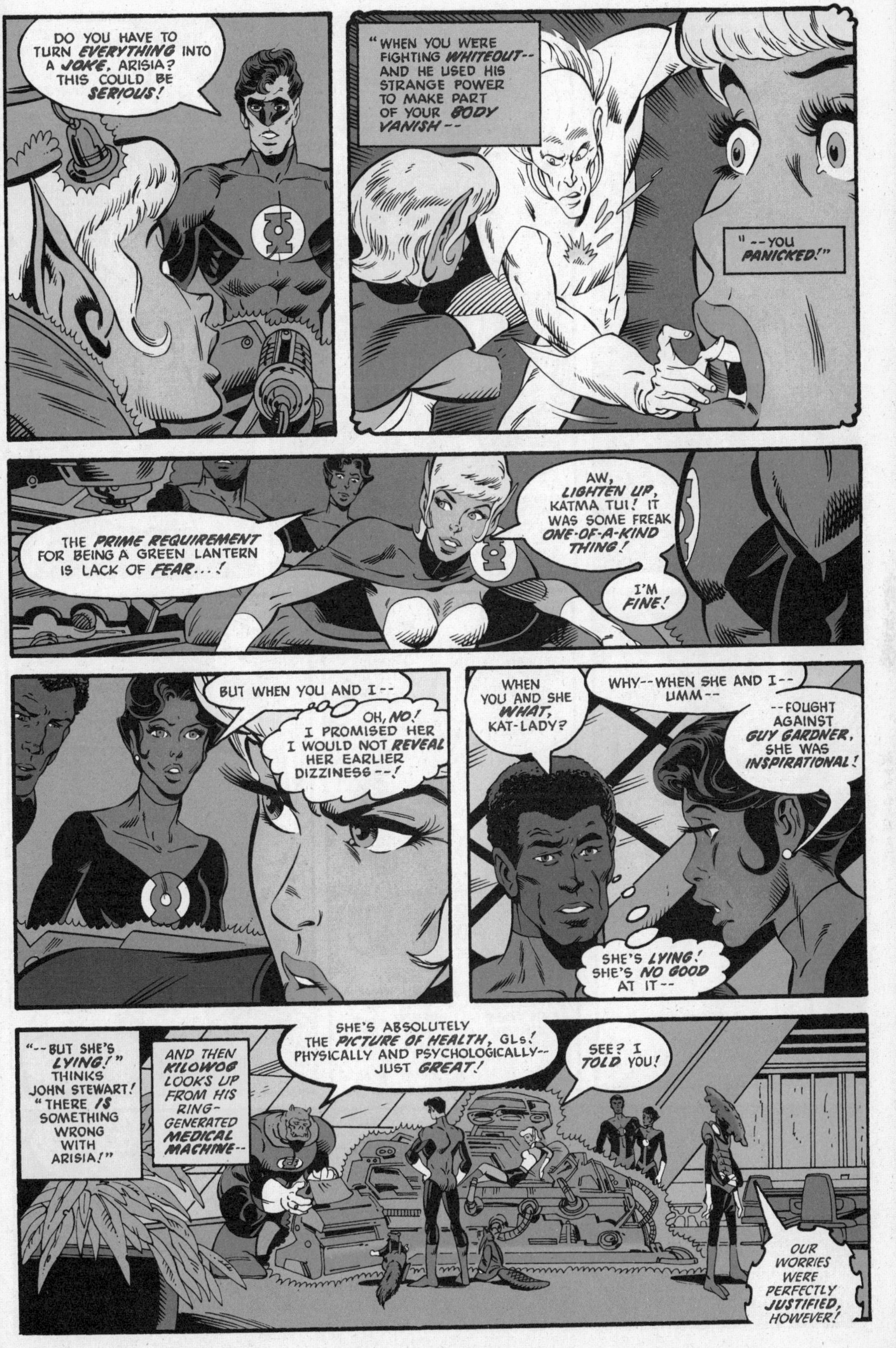
DO YOU HAVE TO TURN EVERYTHING INTO A JOKE, ARISIA? THIS COULD BE SERIOUS!
"WHEN YOU WERE FIGHTING WHITEOUT-- AND HE USED HIS STRANGE POWER TO MAKE PART OF YOUR BODY VANISH--
"--YOU PANICKED!"
THE PRIME REQUIREMENT FOR BEING A GREEN LANTERN IS LACK OF FEAR...!
AW, LIGHTEN UP, KATMA TUI! IT WAS SOME FREAK ONE-OF-A-KIND THING!
I'M FINE!
BUT WHEN YOU AND I--
OH, NO! I PROMISED HER I WOULD NOT REVEAL HER EARLIER DIZZINESS--!
WHEN YOU AND SHE WHAT, KAT-LADY?
WHY--WHEN SHE AND I-- UMM--
--FOUGHT AGAINST GUY GARDNER, SHE WAS INSPIRATIONAL!
SHE'S LYING! SHE'S NO GOOD AT IT--
"--BUT SHE'S LYING!" THINKS JOHN STEWART! "THERE IS SOMETHING WRONG WITH ARISIA!"
AND THEN KILOWOG LOOKS UP FROM HIS RING-GENERATED MEDICAL MACHINE--
SHE'S ABSOLUTELY THE PICTURE OF HEALTH, GLs! PHYSICALLY AND PSYCHOLOGICALLY-- JUST GREAT!
SEE? I TOLD YOU!
OUR WORRIES WERE PERFECTLY JUSTIFIED, HOWEVER!

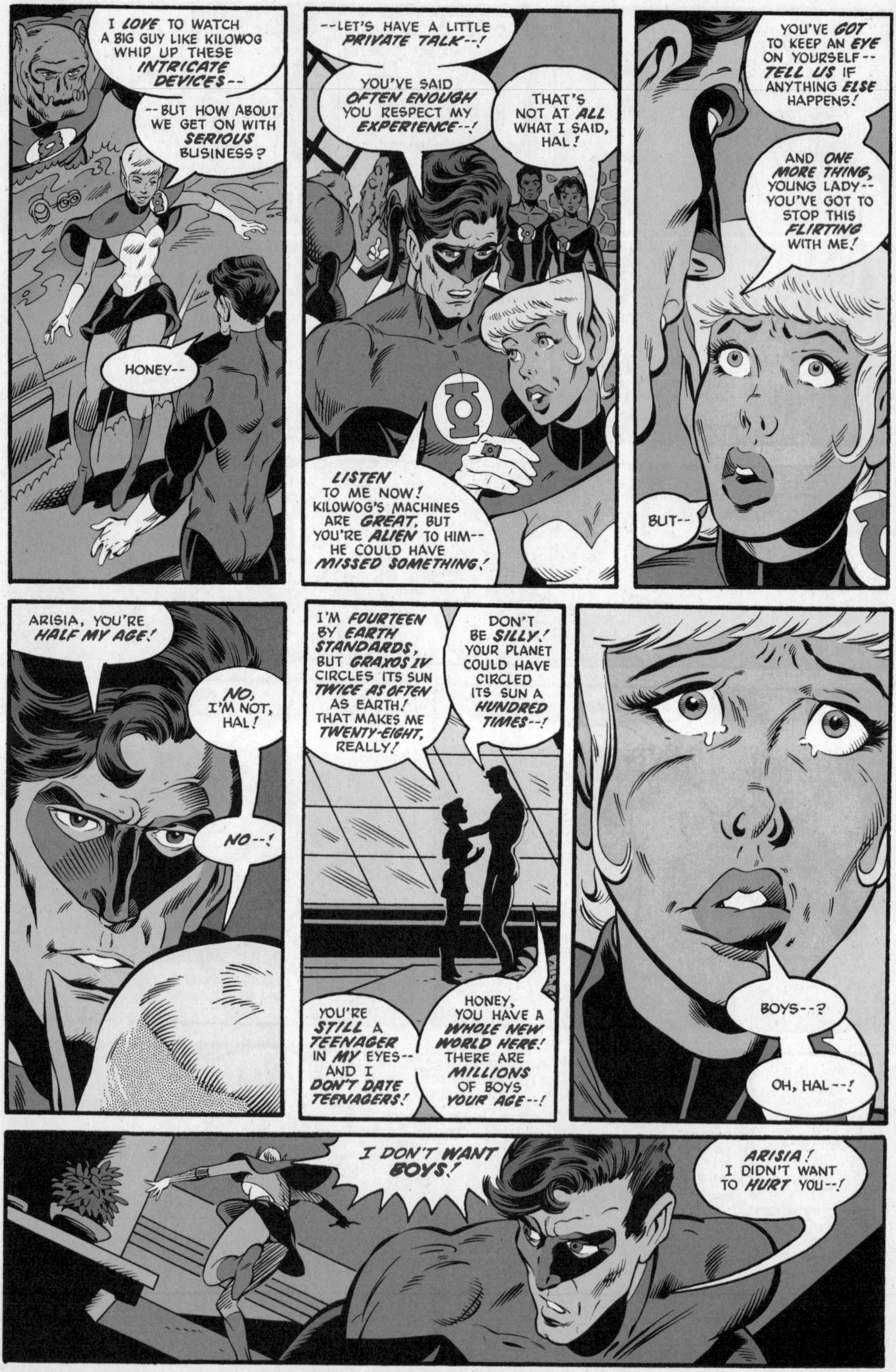

I LOVE TO WATCH A BIG GUY LIKE KILOWOG WHIP UP THESE INTRICATE DEVICES--
--BUT HOW ABOUT WE GET ON WITH SERIOUS BUSINESS?
HONEY--
--LET'S HAVE A LITTLE PRIVATE TALK--!
YOU'VE SAID OFTEN ENOUGH YOU RESPECT MY EXPERIENCE--!
THAT'S NOT AT ALL WHAT I SAID, HAL!
LISTEN TO ME NOW! KILOWOG'S MACHINES ARE GREAT, BUT YOU'RE ALIEN TO HIM-- HE COULD HAVE MISSED SOMETHING!
YOU'VE GOT TO KEEP AN EYE ON YOURSELF-- TELL US IF ANYTHING ELSE HAPPENS!
AND ONE MORE THING, YOUNG LADY-- YOU'VE GOT TO STOP THIS FLIRTING WITH ME!
BUT--
ARISIA, YOU'RE HALF MY AGE!
NO, I'M NOT, HAL!
NO--!
I'M FOURTEEN BY EARTH STANDARDS, BUT GRAXOS IV CIRCLES ITS SUN TWICE AS OFTEN AS EARTH! THAT MAKES ME TWENTY-EIGHT, REALLY!
DON'T BE SILLY! YOUR PLANET COULD HAVE CIRCLED ITS SUN A HUNDRED TIMES--!
YOU'RE STILL A TEENAGER IN MY EYES-- AND I DON'T DATE TEENAGERS!
HONEY, YOU HAVE A WHOLE NEW WORLD HERE! THERE ARE MILLIONS OF BOYS YOUR AGE--!
BOYS--?
OH, HAL--!
I DON'T WANT BOYS!
ARISIA! I DIDN'T WANT TO HURT YOU--!

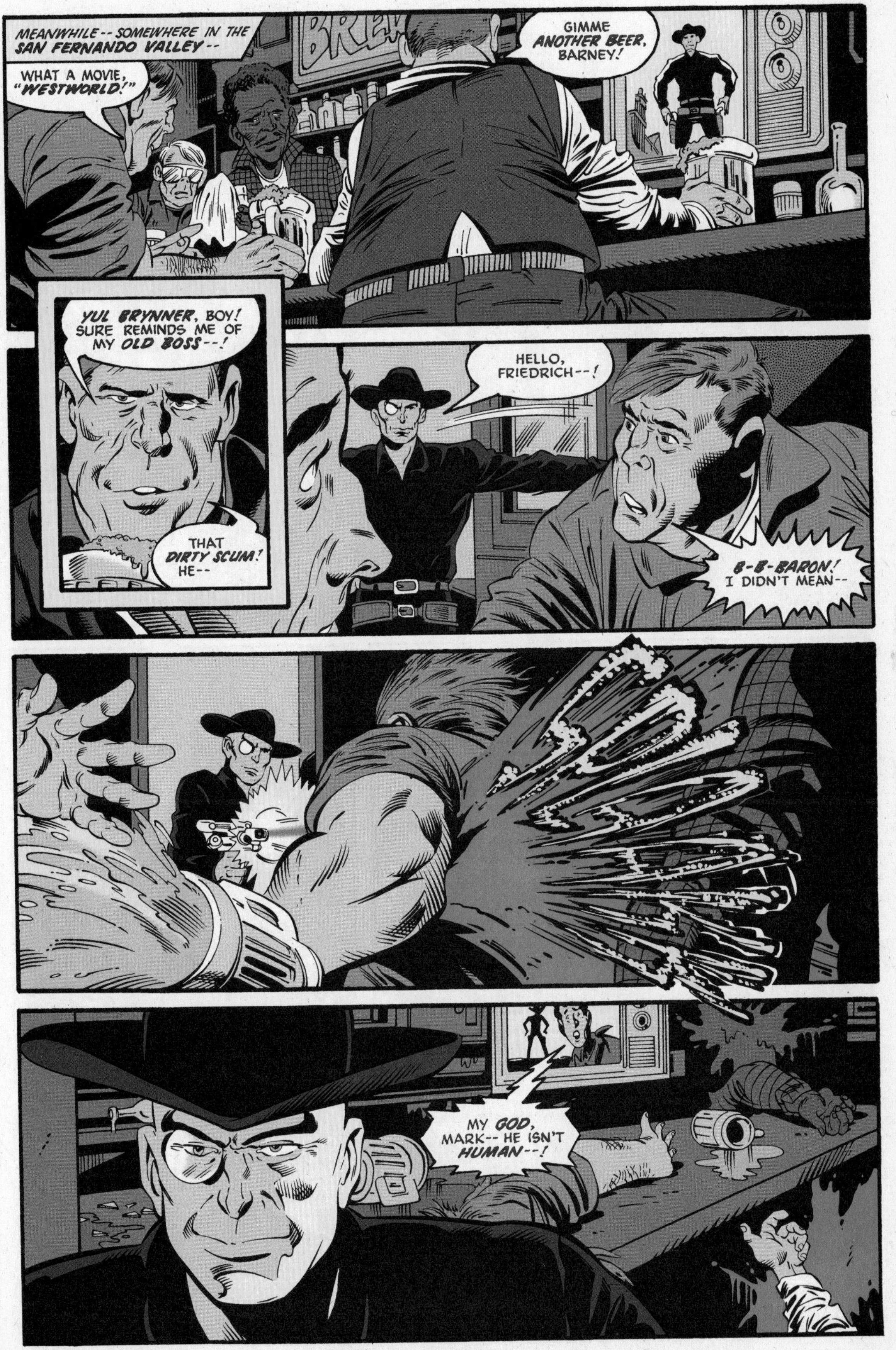
MEANWHILE-- SOMEWHERE IN THE SAN FERNANDO VALLEY--
WHAT A MOVIE, "WESTWORLD!"
GIMME ANOTHER BEER, BARNEY!
YUL BRYNNER, BOY! SURE REMINDS ME OF MY OLD BOSS--!
THAT DIRTY SCUM! HE--
HELLO, FRIEDRICH--!
B-B-BARON! I DIDN'T MEAN--
MY GOD, MARK-- HE ISN'T HUMAN--!

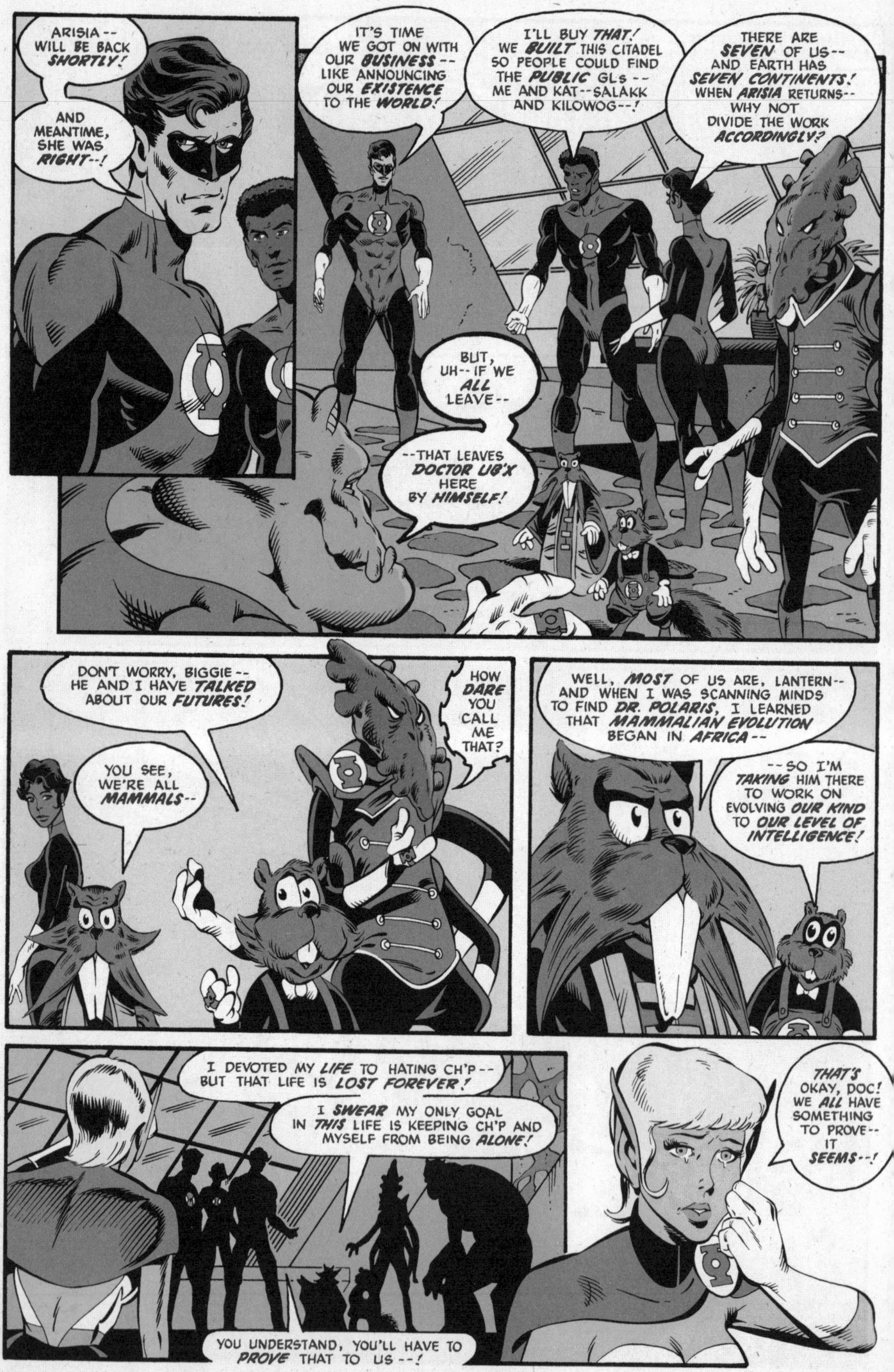
ARISIA -- WILL BE BACK SHORTLY!
AND MEANTIME, SHE WAS RIGHT--!
IT'S TIME WE GOT ON WITH OUR BUSINESS -- LIKE ANNOUNCING OUR EXISTENCE TO THE WORLD!
I'LL BUY THAT! WE BUILT THIS CITADEL SO PEOPLE COULD FIND THE PUBLIC GLs -- ME AND KAT--SALAKK AND KILOWOG--!
THERE ARE SEVEN OF US-- AND EARTH HAS SEVEN CONTINENTS! WHEN ARISIA RETURNS-- WHY NOT DIVIDE THE WORK ACCORDINGLY?
BUT, UH-- IF WE ALL LEAVE--
--THAT LEAVES DOCTOR UG'X HERE BY HIMSELF!
DON'T WORRY, BIGGIE-- HE AND I HAVE TALKED ABOUT OUR FUTURES!
HOW DARE YOU CALL ME THAT?
YOU SEE, WE'RE ALL MAMMALS--
WELL, MOST OF US ARE, LANTERN-- AND WHEN I WAS SCANNING MINDS TO FIND DR. POLARIS, I LEARNED THAT MAMMALIAN EVOLUTION BEGAN IN AFRICA--
--SO I'M TAKING HIM THERE TO WORK ON EVOLVING OUR KIND TO OUR LEVEL OF INTELLIGENCE!
I DEVOTED MY LIFE TO HATING CH'P-- BUT THAT LIFE IS LOST FOREVER!
I SWEAR MY ONLY GOAL IN THIS LIFE IS KEEPING CH'P AND MYSELF FROM BEING ALONE!
THAT'S OKAY, DOC! WE ALL HAVE SOMETHING TO PROVE-- IT SEEMS--!
YOU UNDERSTAND, YOU'LL HAVE TO PROVE THAT TO US--!

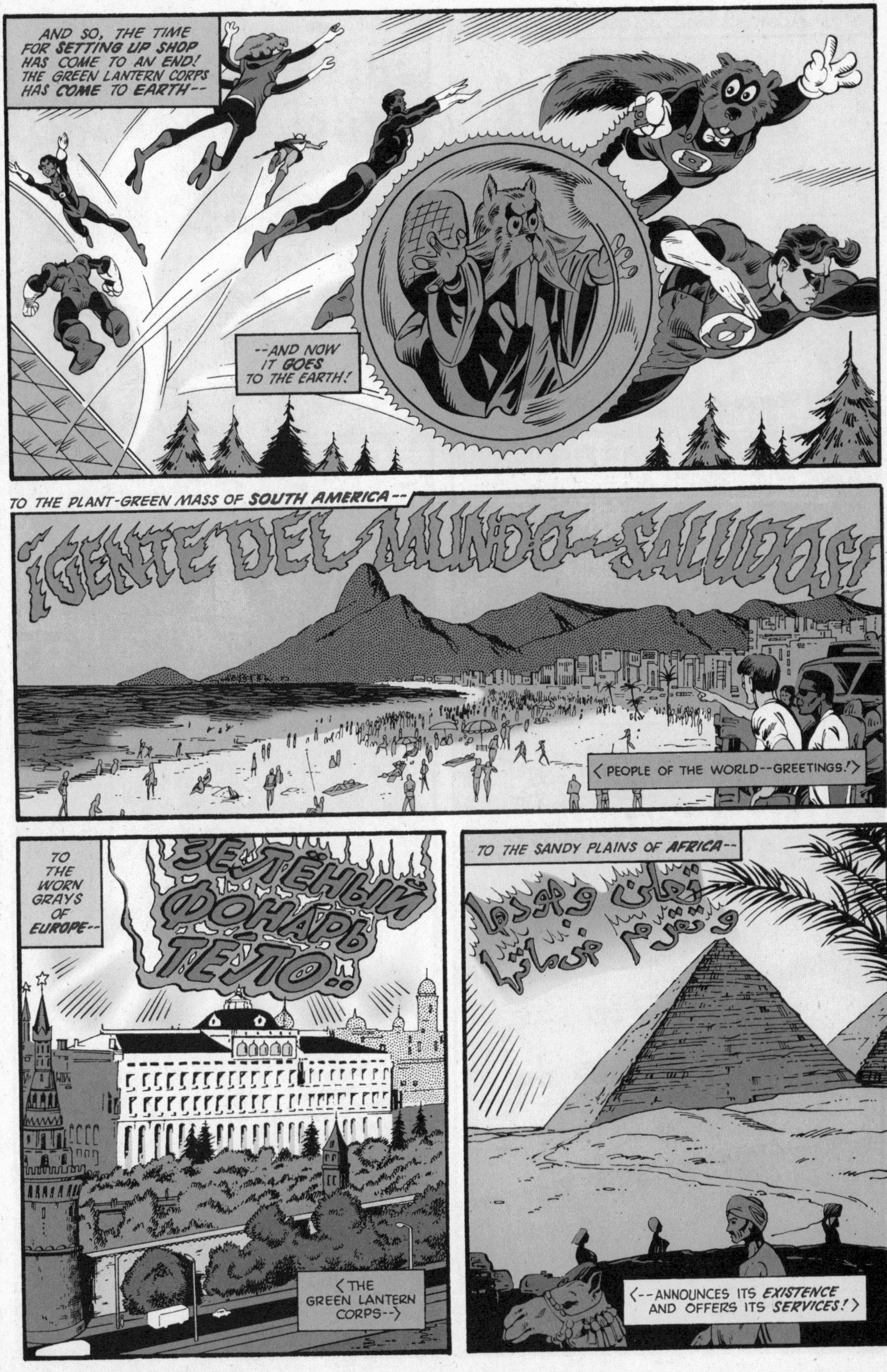
AND SO, THE TIME FOR SETTING UP SHOP HAS COME TO AN END! THE GREEN LANTERN CORPS HAS COME TO EARTH--
--AND NOW IT GOES TO THE EARTH!
TO THE PLANT-GREEN MASS OF SOUTH AMERICA--
¡GENTE DEL MUNDO--SALUDOS!
<PEOPLE OF THE WORLD--GREETINGS.!>
TO THE WORN GRAYS OF EUROPE--
ЗЕЛЁНЫЙ ФОНАРЬ ТЕЛО..
<THE GREEN LANTERN CORPS-->
TO THE SANDY PLAINS OF AFRICA--
تعلن وجودها وتقدم خدماتها
<--ANNOUNCES ITS EXISTENCE AND OFFERS ITS SERVICES!>

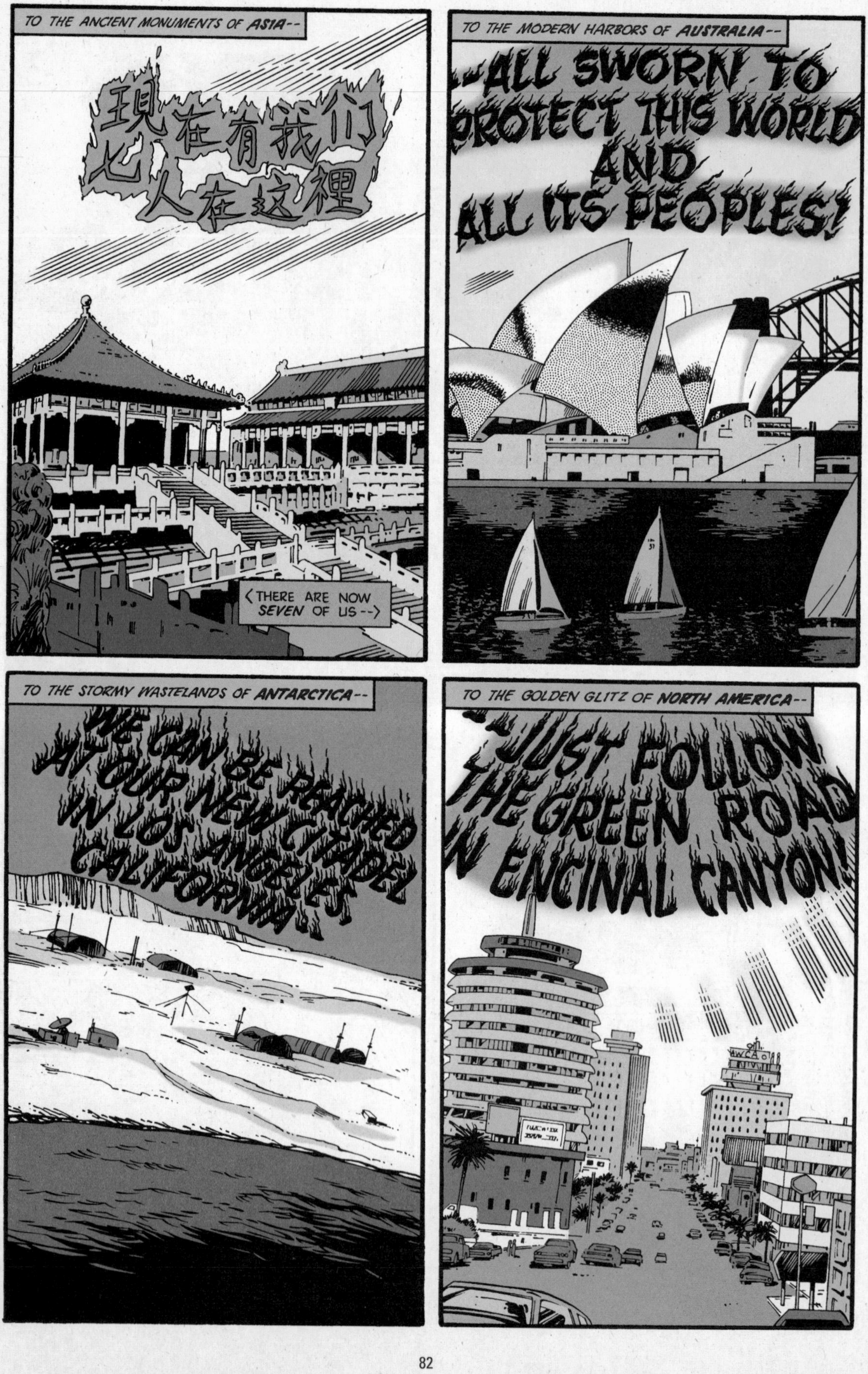
TO THE ANCIENT MONUMENTS OF ASIA--
現在有我们七人在这裡
⟨THERE ARE NOW SEVEN OF US--⟩
TO THE MODERN HARBORS OF AUSTRALIA--
--ALL SWORN TO PROTECT THIS WORLD AND ALL ITS PEOPLES!
TO THE STORMY WASTELANDS OF ANTARCTICA--
WE CAN BE REACHED AT OUR NEW CITADEL IN LOS ANGELES, CALIFORNIA...
TO THE GOLDEN GLITZ OF NORTH AMERICA--
--JUST FOLLOW THE GREEN ROAD IN ENCINAL CANYON!

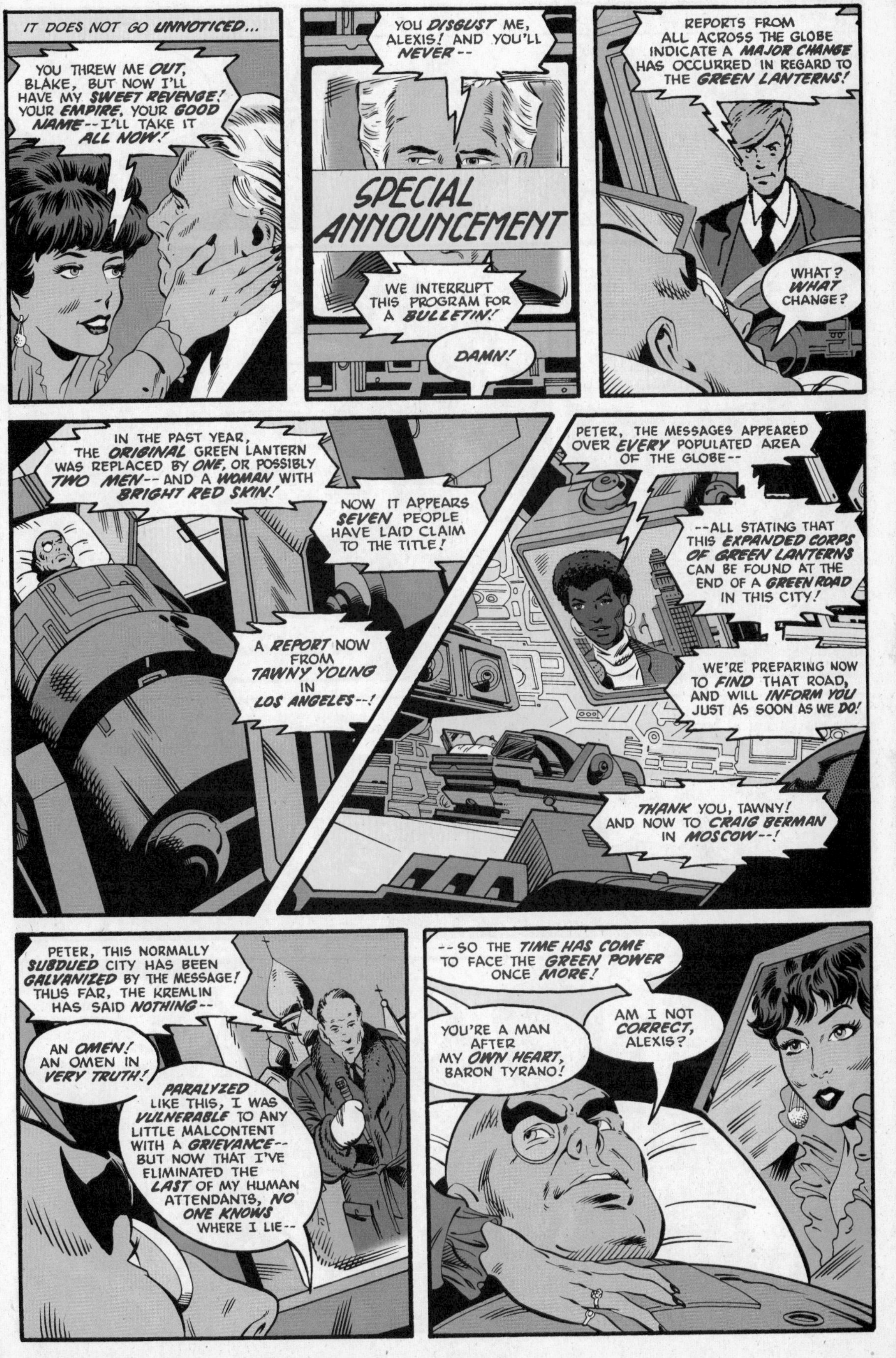

IT DOES NOT GO UNNOTICED...
YOU THREW ME OUT, BLAKE, BUT NOW I'LL HAVE MY SWEET REVENGE! YOUR EMPIRE, YOUR GOOD NAME--I'LL TAKE IT ALL NOW!
YOU DISGUST ME, ALEXIS! AND YOU'LL NEVER--
SPECIAL ANNOUNCEMENT
WE INTERRUPT THIS PROGRAM FOR A BULLETIN!
DAMN!
REPORTS FROM ALL ACROSS THE GLOBE INDICATE A MAJOR CHANGE HAS OCCURRED IN REGARD TO THE GREEN LANTERNS!
WHAT? WHAT CHANGE?
IN THE PAST YEAR, THE ORIGINAL GREEN LANTERN WAS REPLACED BY ONE, OR POSSIBLY TWO MEN-- AND A WOMAN WITH BRIGHT RED SKIN!
NOW IT APPEARS SEVEN PEOPLE HAVE LAID CLAIM TO THE TITLE!
A REPORT NOW FROM TAWNY YOUNG IN LOS ANGELES--!
PETER, THE MESSAGES APPEARED OVER EVERY POPULATED AREA OF THE GLOBE--
--ALL STATING THAT THIS EXPANDED CORPS OF GREEN LANTERNS CAN BE FOUND AT THE END OF A GREEN ROAD IN THIS CITY!
WE'RE PREPARING NOW TO FIND THAT ROAD, AND WILL INFORM YOU JUST AS SOON AS WE DO!
THANK YOU, TAWNY! AND NOW TO CRAIG BERMAN IN MOSCOW--!
PETER, THIS NORMALLY SUBDUED CITY HAS BEEN GALVANIZED BY THE MESSAGE! THUS FAR, THE KREMLIN HAS SAID NOTHING--
AN OMEN! AN OMEN IN VERY TRUTH!
PARALYZED LIKE THIS, I WAS VULNERABLE TO ANY LITTLE MALCONTENT WITH A GRIEVANCE-- BUT NOW THAT I'VE ELIMINATED THE LAST OF MY HUMAN ATTENDANTS, NO ONE KNOWS WHERE I LIE--
--SO THE TIME HAS COME TO FACE THE GREEN POWER ONCE MORE!
AM I NOT CORRECT, ALEXIS?
YOU'RE A MAN AFTER MY OWN HEART, BARON TYRANO!

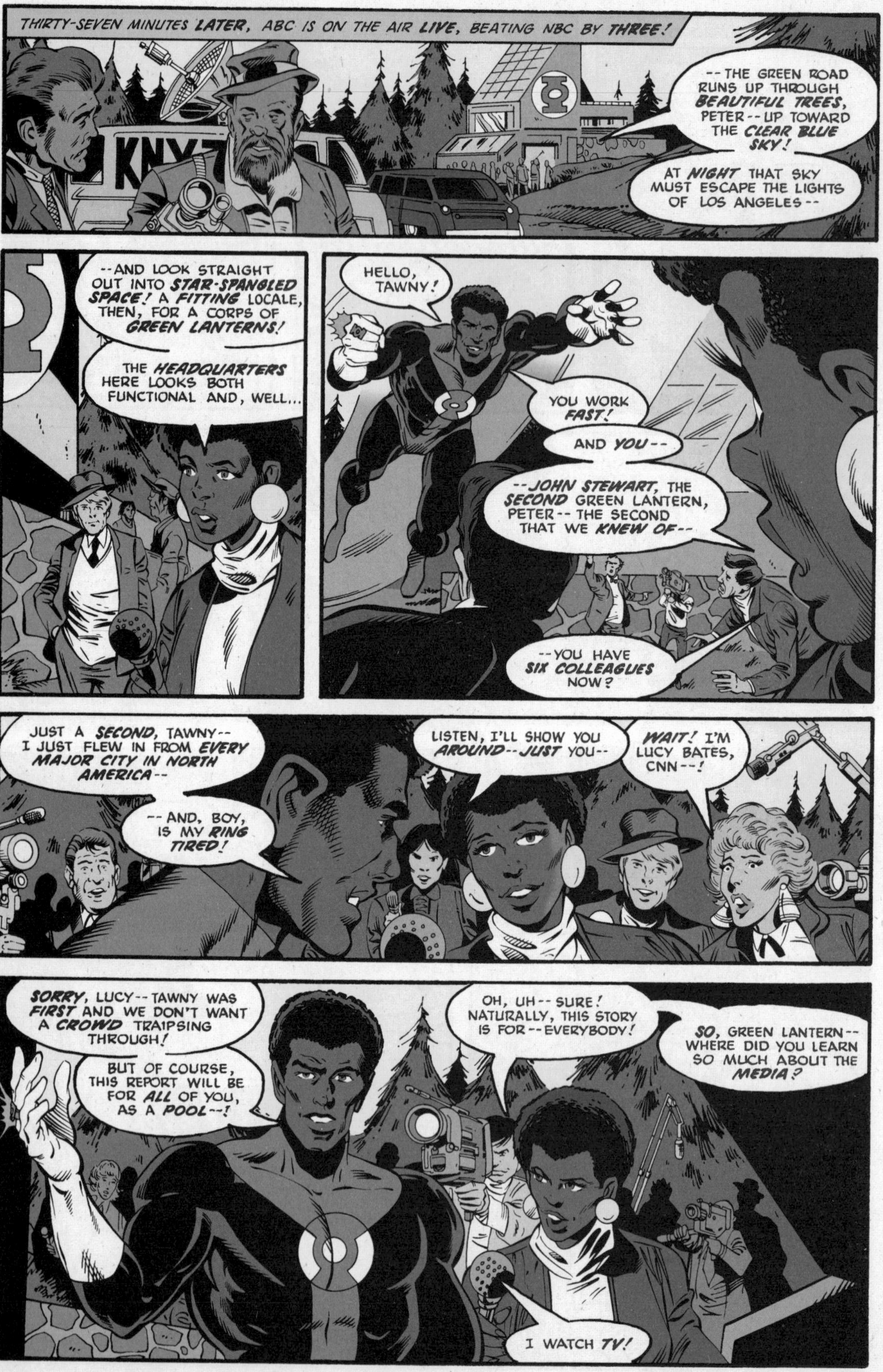

THIRTY-SEVEN MINUTES LATER, ABC IS ON THE AIR LIVE, BEATING NBC BY THREE!
--THE GREEN ROAD RUNS UP THROUGH BEAUTIFUL TREES, PETER--UP TOWARD THE CLEAR BLUE SKY!
AT NIGHT THAT SKY MUST ESCAPE THE LIGHTS OF LOS ANGELES--
--AND LOOK STRAIGHT OUT INTO STAR-SPANGLED SPACE! A FITTING LOCALE, THEN, FOR A CORPS OF GREEN LANTERNS!
THE HEADQUARTERS HERE LOOKS BOTH FUNCTIONAL AND, WELL...
HELLO, TAWNY!
YOU WORK FAST!
AND YOU--
--JOHN STEWART, THE SECOND GREEN LANTERN, PETER--THE SECOND THAT WE KNEW OF--
--YOU HAVE SIX COLLEAGUES NOW?
JUST A SECOND, TAWNY--I JUST FLEW IN FROM EVERY MAJOR CITY IN NORTH AMERICA--
--AND, BOY, IS MY RING TIRED!
LISTEN, I'LL SHOW YOU AROUND--JUST YOU--
WAIT! I'M LUCY BATES, CNN--!
SORRY, LUCY--TAWNY WAS FIRST AND WE DON'T WANT A CROWD TRAIPSING THROUGH!
BUT OF COURSE, THIS REPORT WILL BE FOR ALL OF YOU, AS A POOL--!
OH, UH--SURE! NATURALLY, THIS STORY IS FOR--EVERYBODY!
SO, GREEN LANTERN--WHERE DID YOU LEARN SO MUCH ABOUT THE MEDIA?
I WATCH TV!

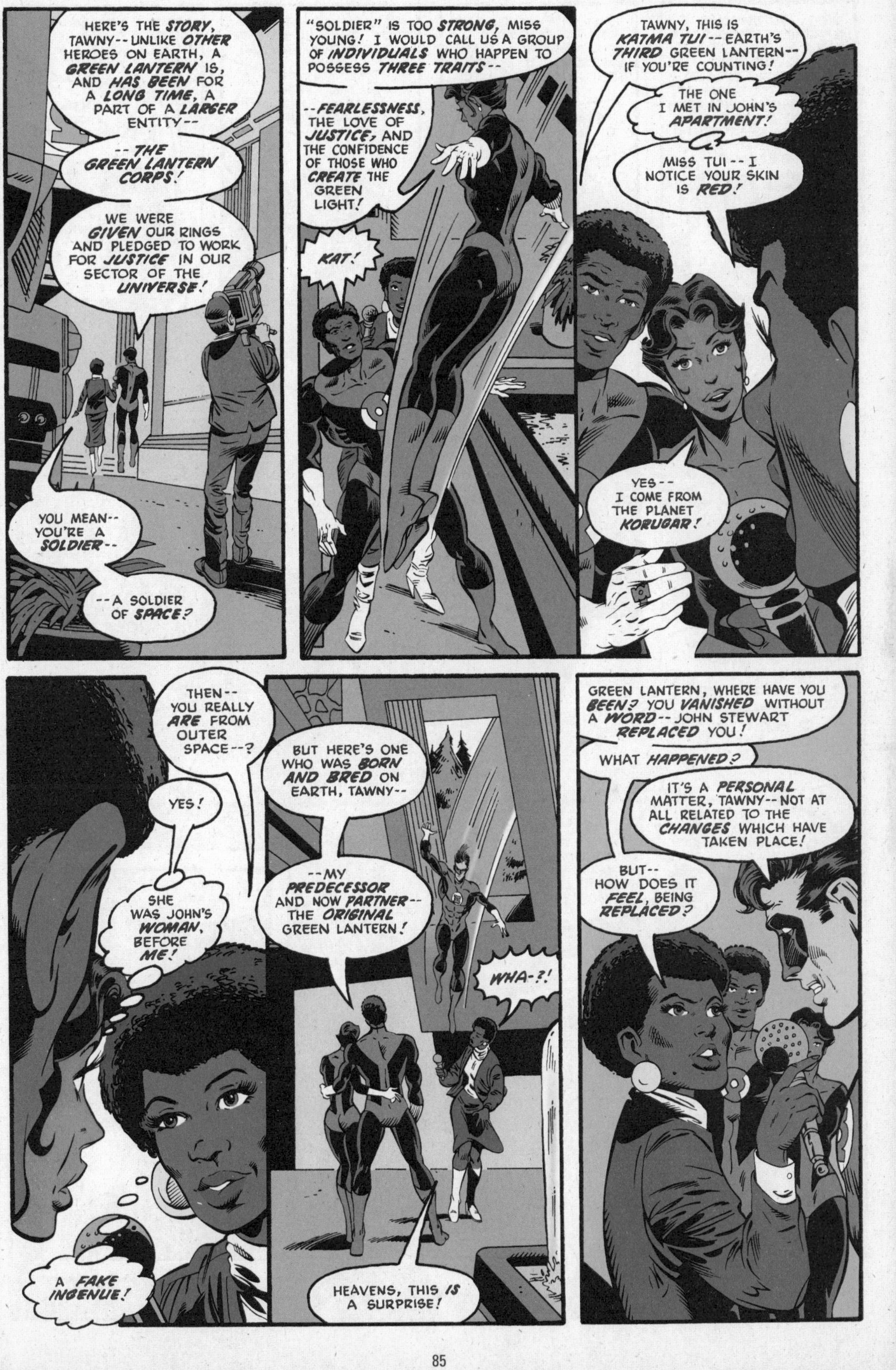
HERE'S THE STORY, TAWNY-- UNLIKE OTHER HEROES ON EARTH, A GREEN LANTERN IS, AND HAS BEEN FOR A LONG TIME, A PART OF A LARGER ENTITY--
--THE GREEN LANTERN CORPS!
WE WERE GIVEN OUR RINGS AND PLEDGED TO WORK FOR JUSTICE IN OUR SECTOR OF THE UNIVERSE!
YOU MEAN-- YOU'RE A SOLDIER--
--A SOLDIER OF SPACE?
"SOLDIER" IS TOO STRONG, MISS YOUNG! I WOULD CALL US A GROUP OF INDIVIDUALS WHO HAPPEN TO POSSESS THREE TRAITS--
--FEARLESSNESS, THE LOVE OF JUSTICE, AND THE CONFIDENCE OF THOSE WHO CREATE THE GREEN LIGHT!
KAT!
TAWNY, THIS IS KATMA TUI -- EARTH'S THIRD GREEN LANTERN-- IF YOU'RE COUNTING!
THE ONE I MET IN JOHN'S APARTMENT!
MISS TUI -- I NOTICE YOUR SKIN IS RED!
YES -- I COME FROM THE PLANET KORUGAR!
THEN-- YOU REALLY ARE FROM OUTER SPACE--?
YES!
SHE WAS JOHN'S WOMAN, BEFORE ME!
A FAKE INGENUE!
BUT HERE'S ONE WHO WAS BORN AND BRED ON EARTH, TAWNY--
--MY PREDECESSOR AND NOW PARTNER-- THE ORIGINAL GREEN LANTERN!
WHA-?!
HEAVENS, THIS IS A SURPRISE!
GREEN LANTERN, WHERE HAVE YOU BEEN? YOU VANISHED WITHOUT A WORD-- JOHN STEWART REPLACED YOU!
WHAT HAPPENED?
IT'S A PERSONAL MATTER, TAWNY-- NOT AT ALL RELATED TO THE CHANGES WHICH HAVE TAKEN PLACE!
BUT-- HOW DOES IT FEEL, BEING REPLACED?

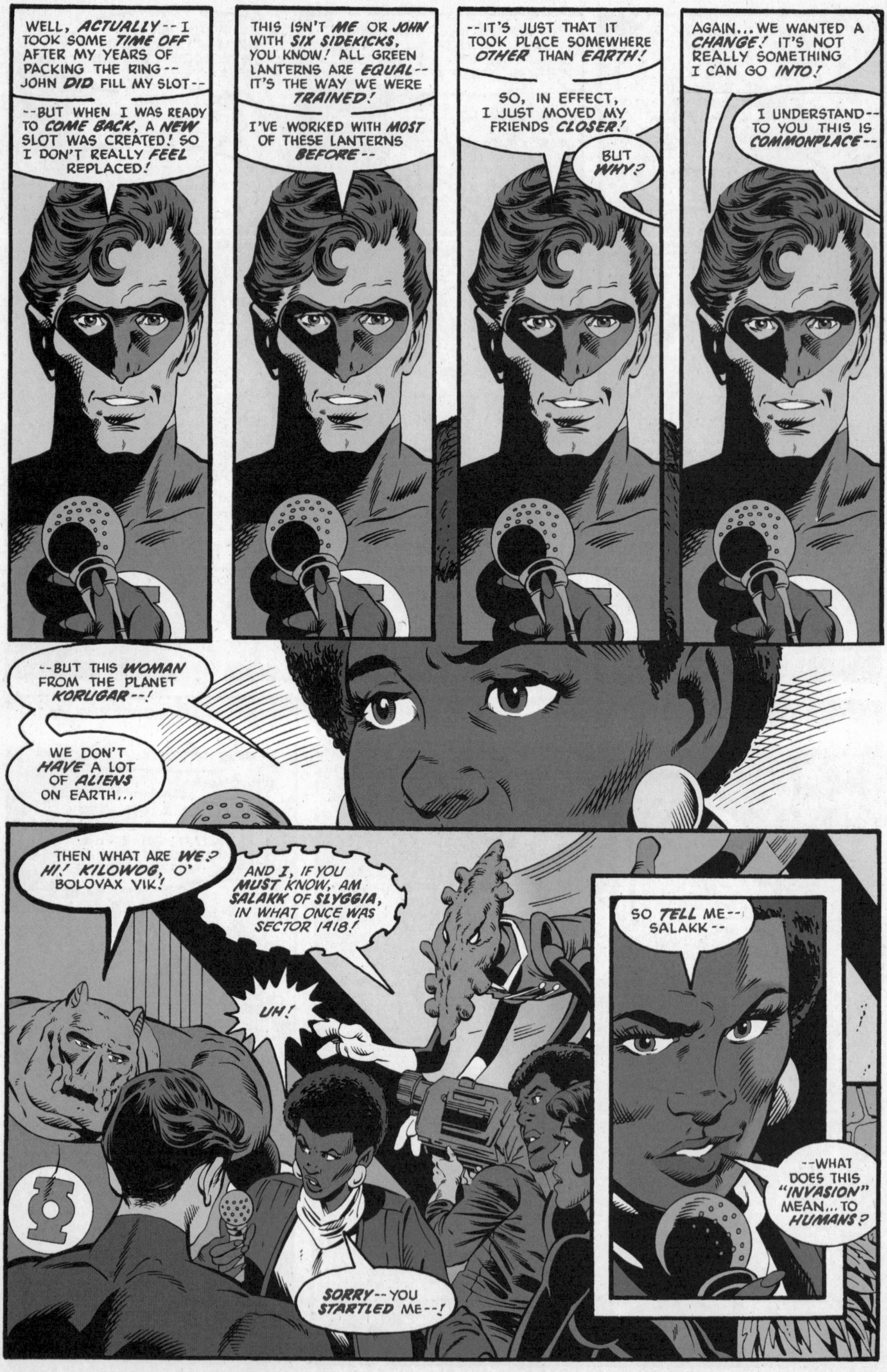
WELL, ACTUALLY-- I TOOK SOME TIME OFF AFTER MY YEARS OF PACKING THE RING-- JOHN DID FILL MY SLOT--
--BUT WHEN I WAS READY TO COME BACK, A NEW SLOT WAS CREATED! SO I DON'T REALLY FEEL REPLACED!
THIS ISN'T ME OR JOHN WITH SIX SIDEKICKS, YOU KNOW! ALL GREEN LANTERNS ARE EQUAL-- IT'S THE WAY WE WERE TRAINED!
I'VE WORKED WITH MOST OF THESE LANTERNS BEFORE--
--IT'S JUST THAT IT TOOK PLACE SOMEWHERE OTHER THAN EARTH!
SO, IN EFFECT, I JUST MOVED MY FRIENDS CLOSER!
BUT WHY?
AGAIN... WE WANTED A CHANGE! IT'S NOT REALLY SOMETHING I CAN GO INTO!
I UNDERSTAND-- TO YOU THIS IS COMMONPLACE--
--BUT THIS WOMAN FROM THE PLANET KORUGAR--!
WE DON'T HAVE A LOT OF ALIENS ON EARTH...
THEN WHAT ARE WE? HI! KILOWOG, O' BOLOVAX VIK!
AND I, IF YOU MUST KNOW, AM SALAKK OF SLYGGIA, IN WHAT ONCE WAS SECTOR 1418!
UH!
SORRY-- YOU STARTLED ME--!
SO TELL ME-- SALAKK--
--WHAT DOES THIS "INVASION" MEAN... TO HUMANS?

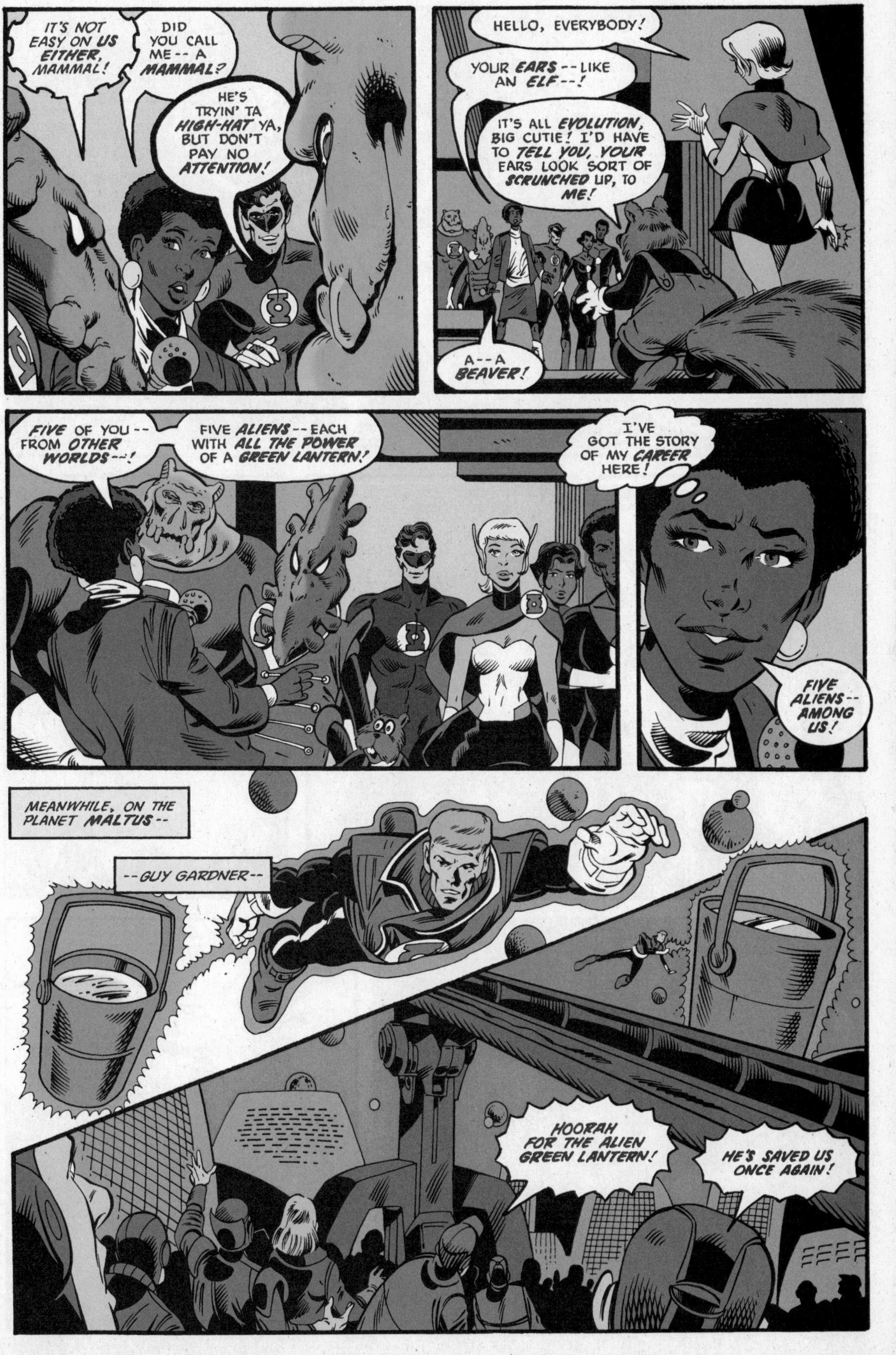
IT'S NOT EASY ON US EITHER, MAMMAL!
DID YOU CALL ME-- A MAMMAL?
HE'S TRYIN' TA HIGH-HAT YA, BUT DON'T PAY NO ATTENTION!
HELLO, EVERYBODY!
YOUR EARS--LIKE AN ELF--!
IT'S ALL EVOLUTION, BIG CUTIE! I'D HAVE TO TELL YOU, YOUR EARS LOOK SORT OF SCRUNCHED UP, TO ME!
A--A BEAVER!
FIVE OF YOU-- FROM OTHER WORLDS--!
FIVE ALIENS--EACH WITH ALL THE POWER OF A GREEN LANTERN!
I'VE GOT THE STORY OF MY CAREER HERE!
FIVE ALIENS-- AMONG US!
MEANWHILE, ON THE PLANET MALTUS--
--GUY GARDNER--
HOORAH FOR THE ALIEN GREEN LANTERN!
HE'S SAVED US ONCE AGAIN!

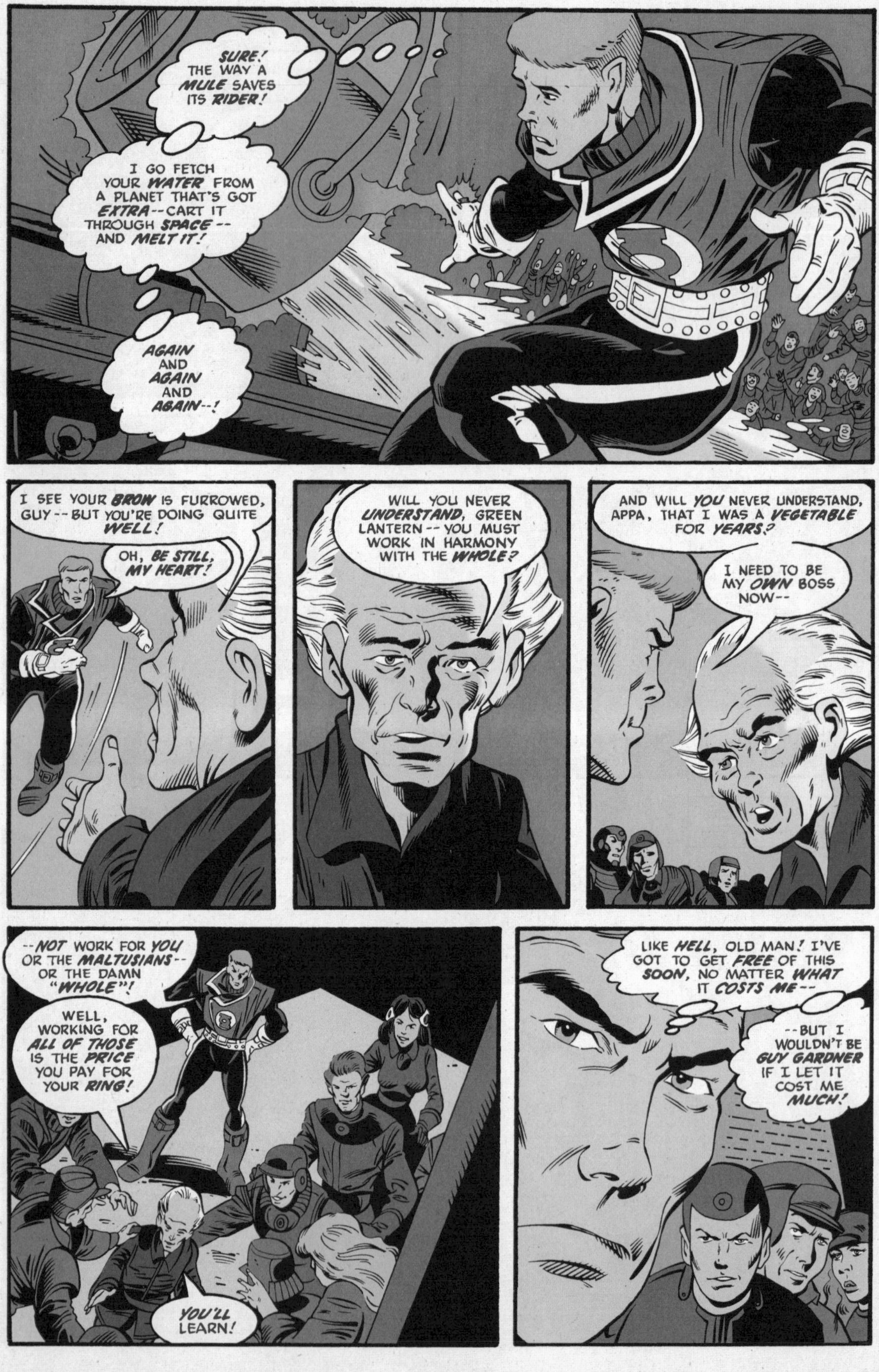
SURE! THE WAY A MULE SAVES ITS RIDER!
I GO FETCH YOUR WATER FROM A PLANET THAT'S GOT EXTRA--CART IT THROUGH SPACE--AND MELT IT!
AGAIN AND AGAIN AND AGAIN--!
I SEE YOUR BROW IS FURROWED, GUY--BUT YOU'RE DOING QUITE WELL!
OH, BE STILL, MY HEART!
WILL YOU NEVER UNDERSTAND, GREEN LANTERN--YOU MUST WORK IN HARMONY WITH THE WHOLE?
AND WILL YOU NEVER UNDERSTAND, APPA, THAT I WAS A VEGETABLE FOR YEARS?
I NEED TO BE MY OWN BOSS NOW--
--NOT WORK FOR YOU OR THE MALTUSIANS--OR THE DAMN "WHOLE"!
WELL, WORKING FOR ALL OF THOSE IS THE PRICE YOU PAY FOR YOUR RING!
YOU'LL LEARN!
LIKE HELL, OLD MAN! I'VE GOT TO GET FREE OF THIS SOON, NO MATTER WHAT IT COSTS ME--
--BUT I WOULDN'T BE GUY GARDNER IF I LET IT COST ME MUCH!

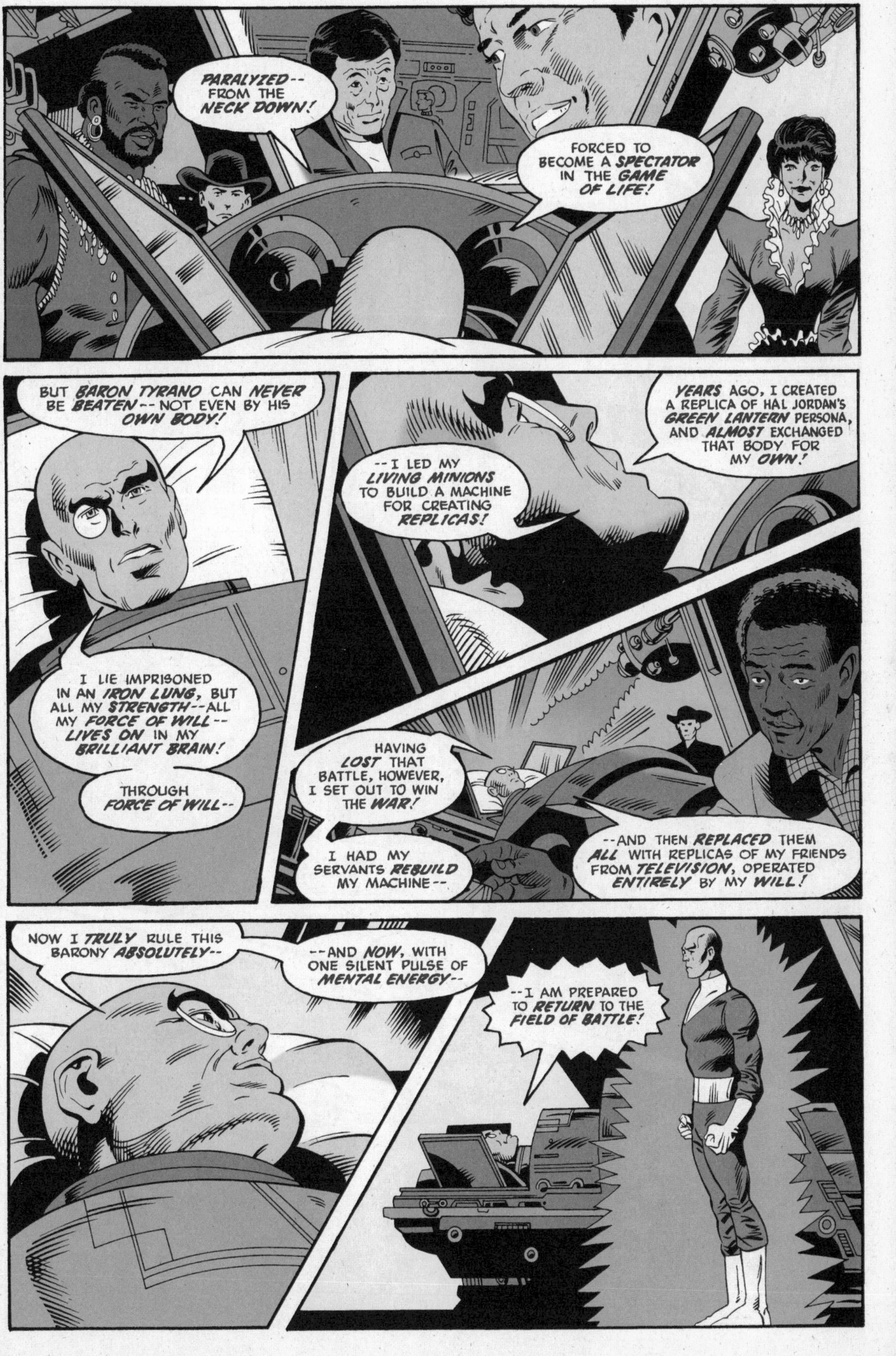
PARALYZED-- FROM THE NECK DOWN!
FORCED TO BECOME A SPECTATOR IN THE GAME OF LIFE!
BUT BARON TYRANO CAN NEVER BE BEATEN-- NOT EVEN BY HIS OWN BODY!
I LIE IMPRISONED IN AN IRON LUNG, BUT ALL MY STRENGTH--ALL MY FORCE OF WILL-- LIVES ON IN MY BRILLIANT BRAIN!
THROUGH FORCE OF WILL--
--I LED MY LIVING MINIONS TO BUILD A MACHINE FOR CREATING REPLICAS!
YEARS AGO, I CREATED A REPLICA OF HAL JORDAN'S GREEN LANTERN PERSONA, AND ALMOST EXCHANGED THAT BODY FOR MY OWN!
HAVING LOST THAT BATTLE, HOWEVER, I SET OUT TO WIN THE WAR!
I HAD MY SERVANTS REBUILD MY MACHINE--
--AND THEN REPLACED THEM ALL WITH REPLICAS OF MY FRIENDS FROM TELEVISION, OPERATED ENTIRELY BY MY WILL!
NOW I TRULY RULE THIS BARONY ABSOLUTELY--
--AND NOW, WITH ONE SILENT PULSE OF MENTAL ENERGY--
--I AM PREPARED TO RETURN TO THE FIELD OF BATTLE!

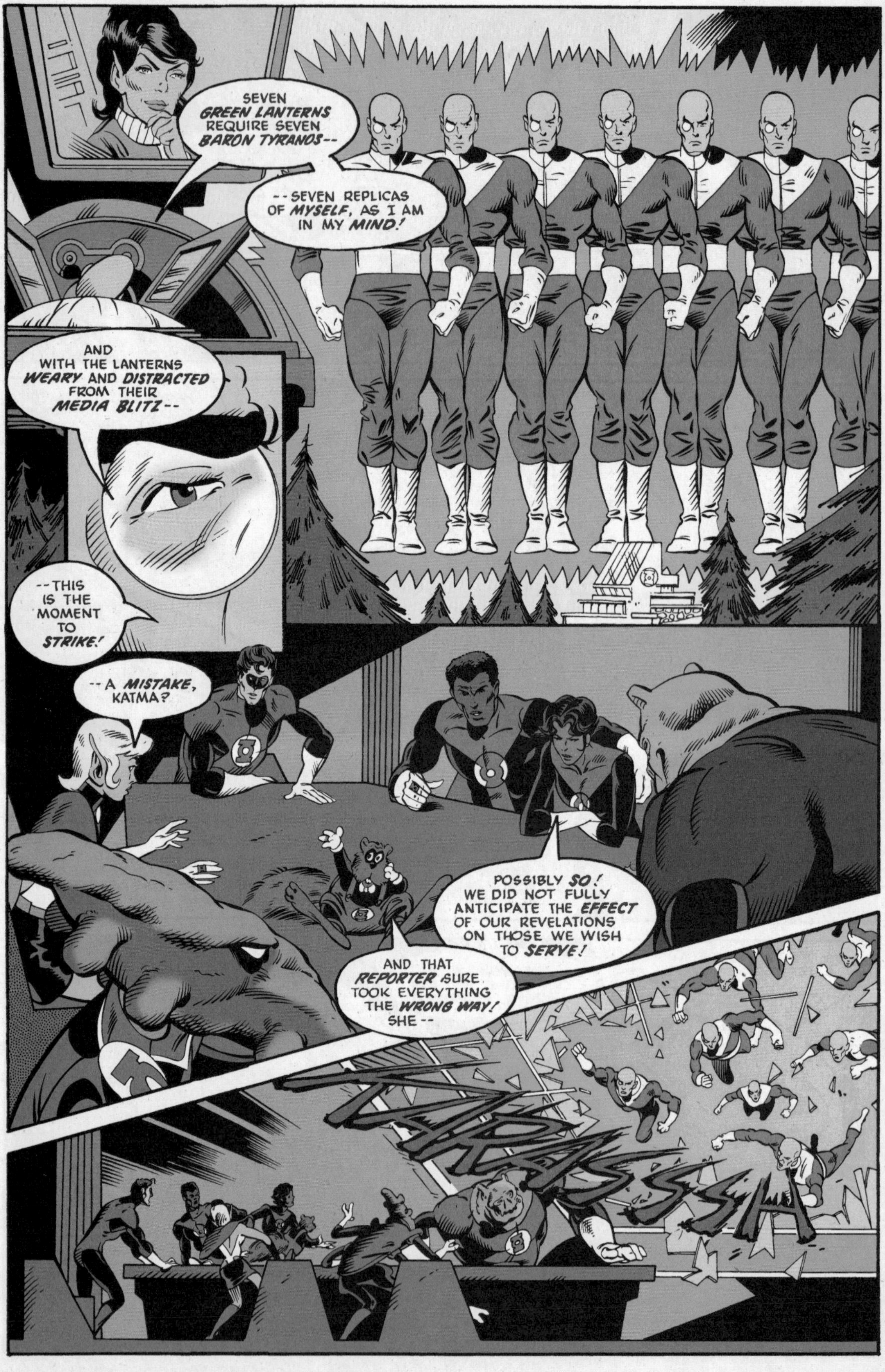
SEVEN GREEN LANTERNS REQUIRE SEVEN BARON TYRANOS--
--SEVEN REPLICAS OF MYSELF, AS I AM IN MY MIND!
AND WITH THE LANTERNS WEARY AND DISTRACTED FROM THEIR MEDIA BLITZ--
--THIS IS THE MOMENT TO STRIKE!
--A MISTAKE, KATMA?
POSSIBLY SO! WE DID NOT FULLY ANTICIPATE THE EFFECT OF OUR REVELATIONS ON THOSE WE WISH TO SERVE!
AND THAT REPORTER SURE TOOK EVERYTHING THE WRONG WAY! SHE--
KARASSSSH

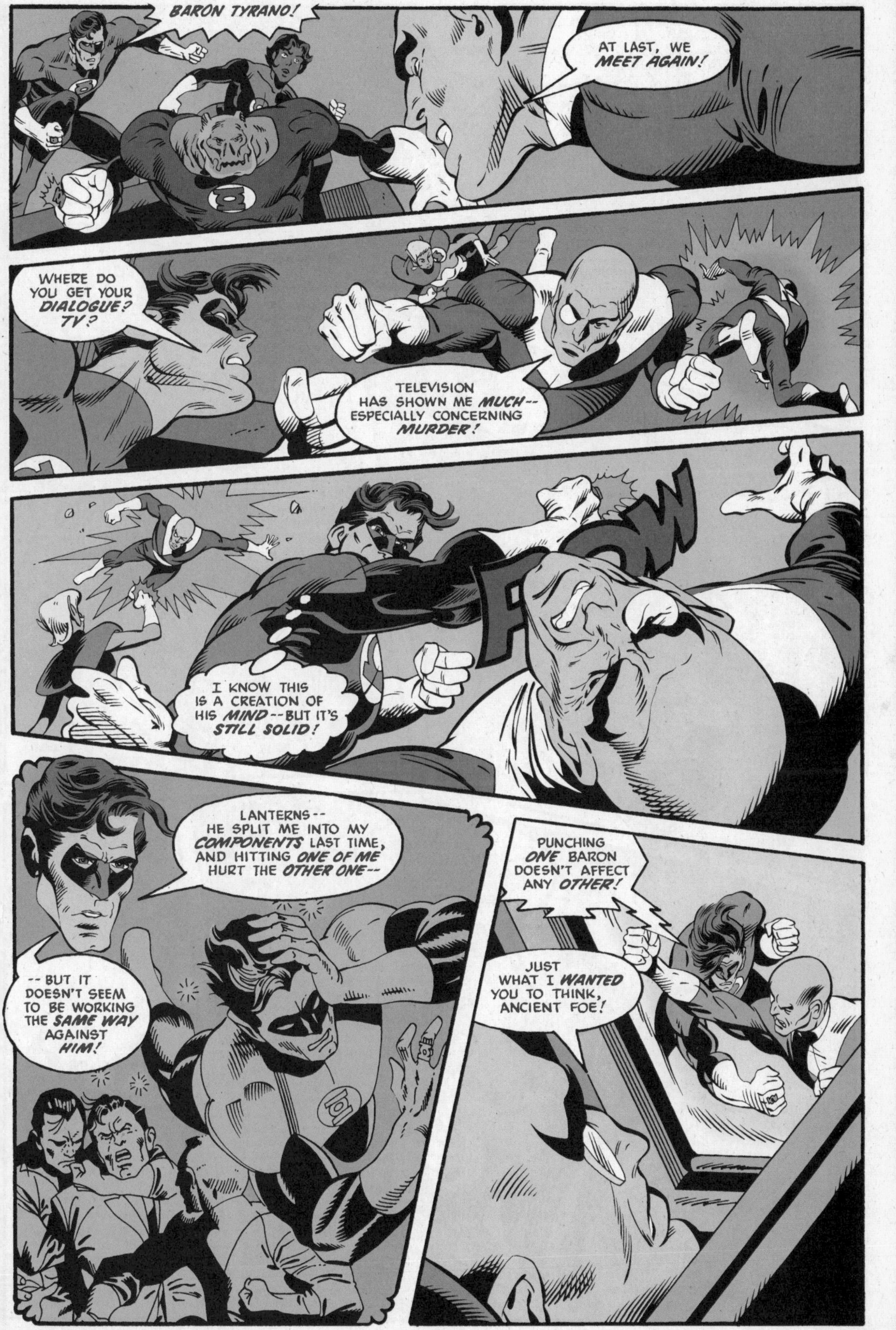
BARON TYRANO!
AT LAST, WE MEET AGAIN!
WHERE DO YOU GET YOUR DIALOGUE? TV?
TELEVISION HAS SHOWN ME MUCH-- ESPECIALLY CONCERNING MURDER!
I KNOW THIS IS A CREATION OF HIS MIND--BUT IT'S STILL SOLID!
POW
LANTERNS-- HE SPLIT ME INTO MY COMPONENTS LAST TIME, AND HITTING ONE OF ME HURT THE OTHER ONE--
--BUT IT DOESN'T SEEM TO BE WORKING THE SAME WAY AGAINST HIM!
PUNCHING ONE BARON DOESN'T AFFECT ANY OTHER!
JUST WHAT I WANTED YOU TO THINK, ANCIENT FOE!

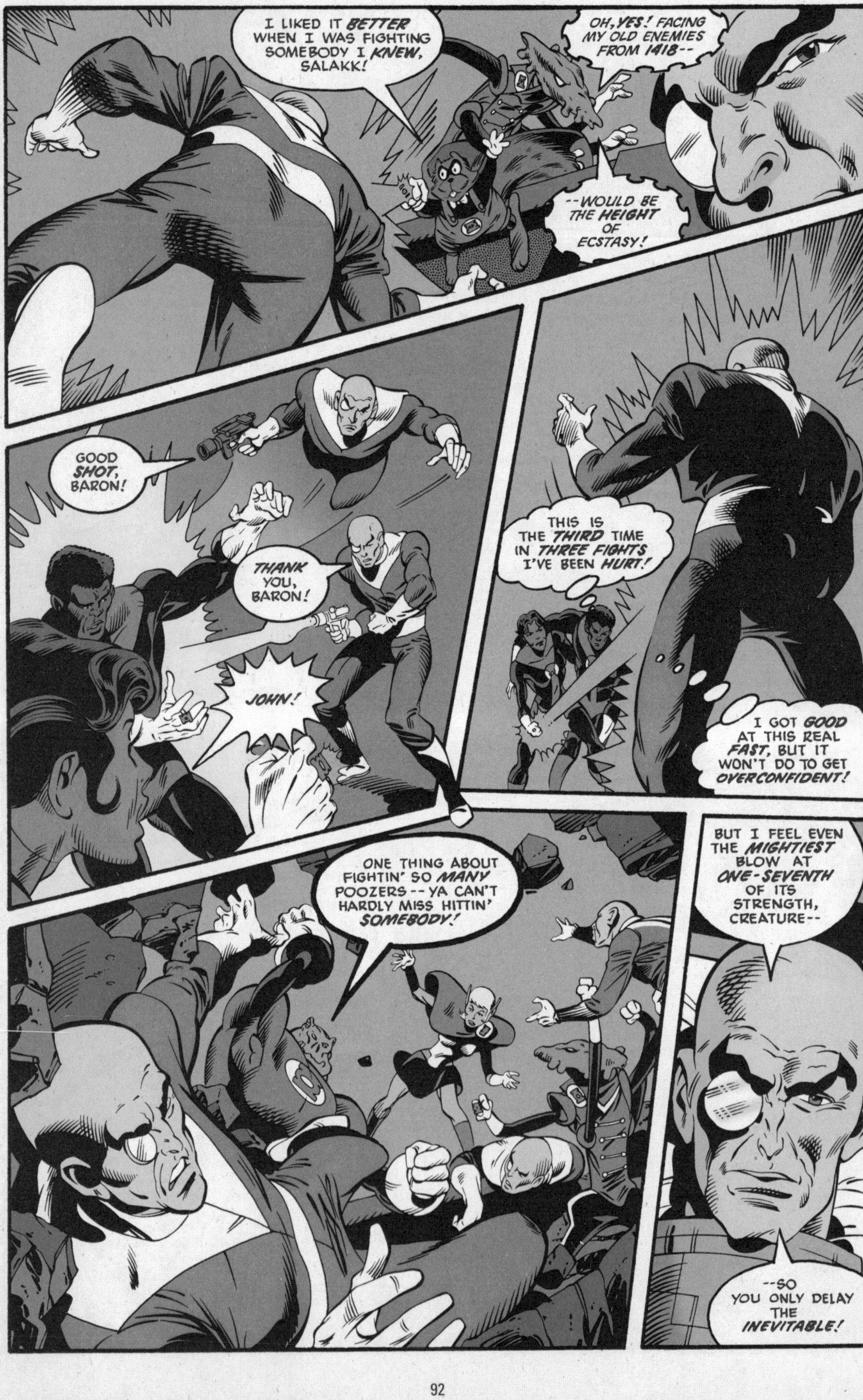
I LIKED IT BETTER WHEN I WAS FIGHTING SOMEBODY I KNEW, SALAKK!
OH, YES! FACING MY OLD ENEMIES FROM 1418--
--WOULD BE THE HEIGHT OF ECSTASY!
GOOD SHOT, BARON!
THANK YOU, BARON!
JOHN!
THIS IS THE THIRD TIME IN THREE FIGHTS I'VE BEEN HURT!
I GOT GOOD AT THIS REAL FAST, BUT IT WON'T DO TO GET OVERCONFIDENT!
ONE THING ABOUT FIGHTIN' SO MANY POOZERS -- YA CAN'T HARDLY MISS HITTIN' SOMEBODY!
BUT I FEEL EVEN THE MIGHTIEST BLOW AT ONE-SEVENTH OF ITS STRENGTH, CREATURE--
--SO YOU ONLY DELAY THE INEVITABLE!

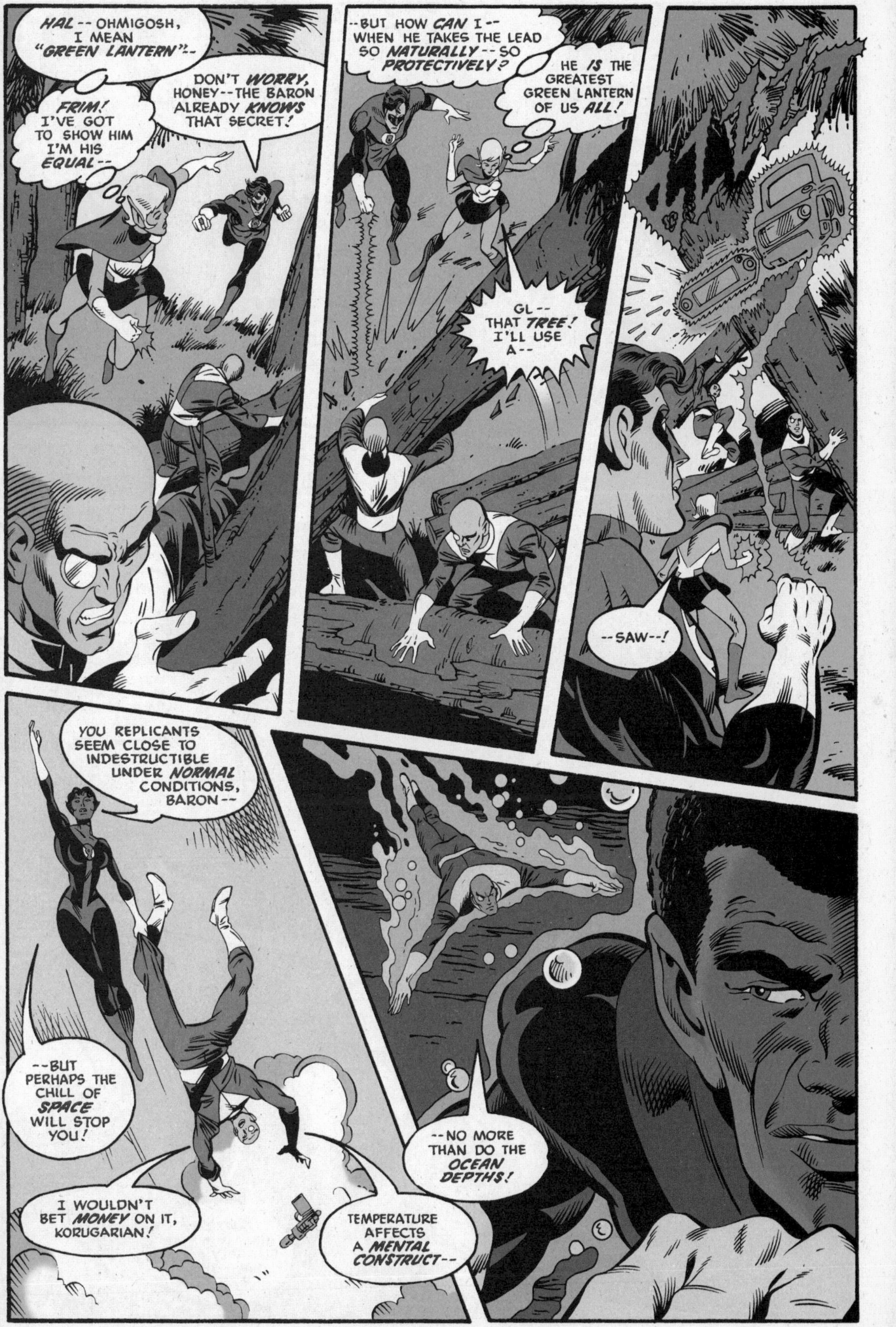

HAL -- OHMIGOSH, I MEAN "GREEN LANTERN"--
FRIM! I'VE GOT TO SHOW HIM I'M HIS EQUAL--
DON'T WORRY, HONEY--THE BARON ALREADY KNOWS THAT SECRET!
--BUT HOW CAN I -- WHEN HE TAKES THE LEAD SO NATURALLY -- SO PROTECTIVELY?
HE IS THE GREATEST GREEN LANTERN OF US ALL!
GL -- THAT TREE! I'LL USE A--
--SAW--!
YOU REPLICANTS SEEM CLOSE TO INDESTRUCTIBLE UNDER NORMAL CONDITIONS, BARON--
--BUT PERHAPS THE CHILL OF SPACE WILL STOP YOU!
I WOULDN'T BET MONEY ON IT, KORUGARIAN!
TEMPERATURE AFFECTS A MENTAL CONSTRUCT--
--NO MORE THAN DO THE OCEAN DEPTHS!

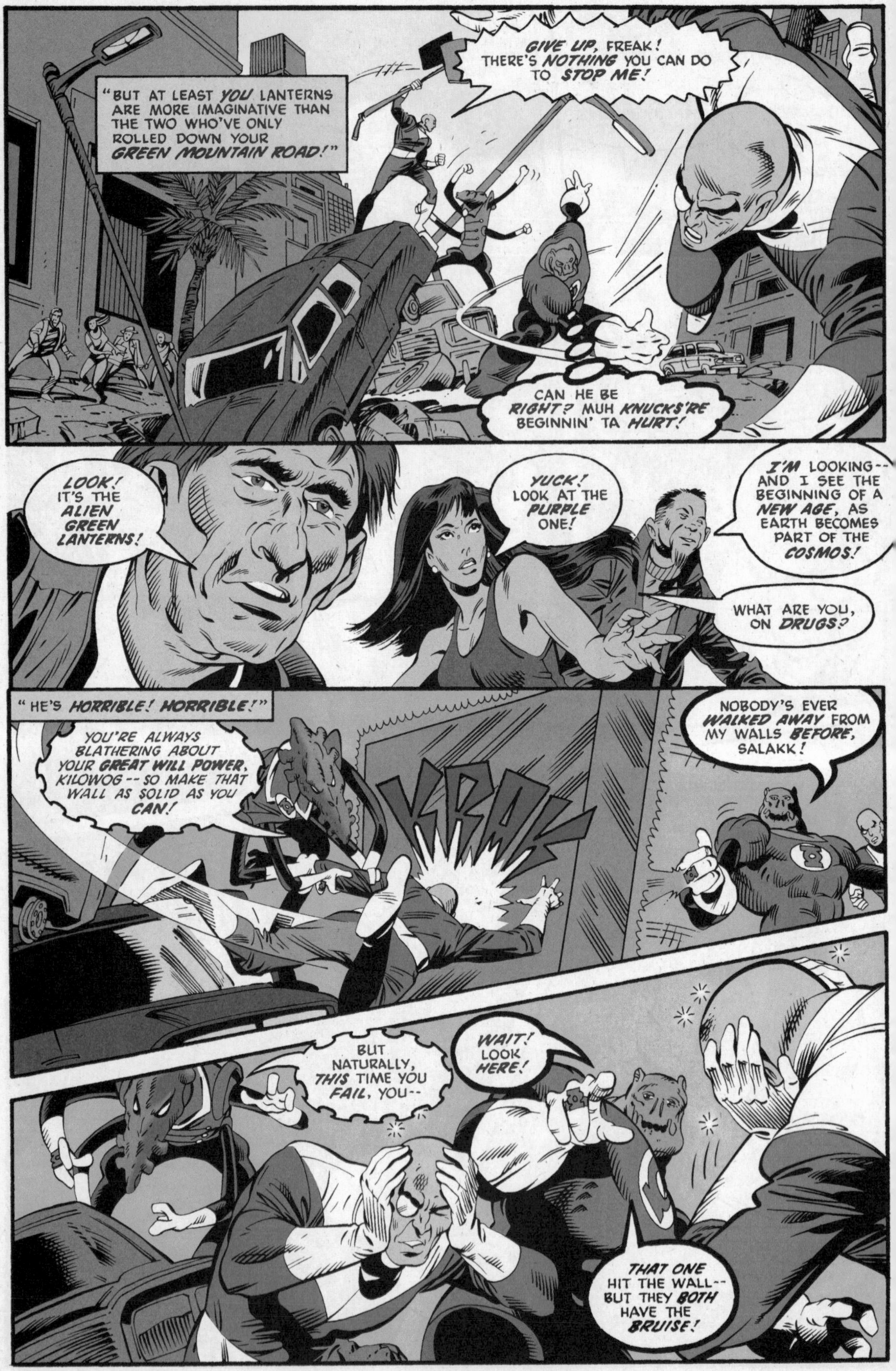
"BUT AT LEAST YOU LANTERNS ARE MORE IMAGINATIVE THAN THE TWO WHO'VE ONLY ROLLED DOWN YOUR GREEN MOUNTAIN ROAD!"
GIVE UP, FREAK! THERE'S NOTHING YOU CAN DO TO STOP ME!
CAN HE BE RIGHT? MUH KNUCKS'RE BEGINNIN' TA HURT!
LOOK! IT'S THE ALIEN GREEN LANTERNS!
YUCK! LOOK AT THE PURPLE ONE!
I'M LOOKING-- AND I SEE THE BEGINNING OF A NEW AGE, AS EARTH BECOMES PART OF THE COSMOS!
WHAT ARE YOU, ON DRUGS?
"HE'S HORRIBLE! HORRIBLE!"
YOU'RE ALWAYS BLATHERING ABOUT YOUR GREAT WILL POWER, KILOWOG-- SO MAKE THAT WALL AS SOLID AS YOU CAN!
KRAK
NOBODY'S EVER WALKED AWAY FROM MY WALLS BEFORE, SALAKK!
BUT NATURALLY, THIS TIME YOU FAIL, YOU--
WAIT! LOOK HERE!
THAT ONE HIT THE WALL-- BUT THEY BOTH HAVE THE BRUISE!

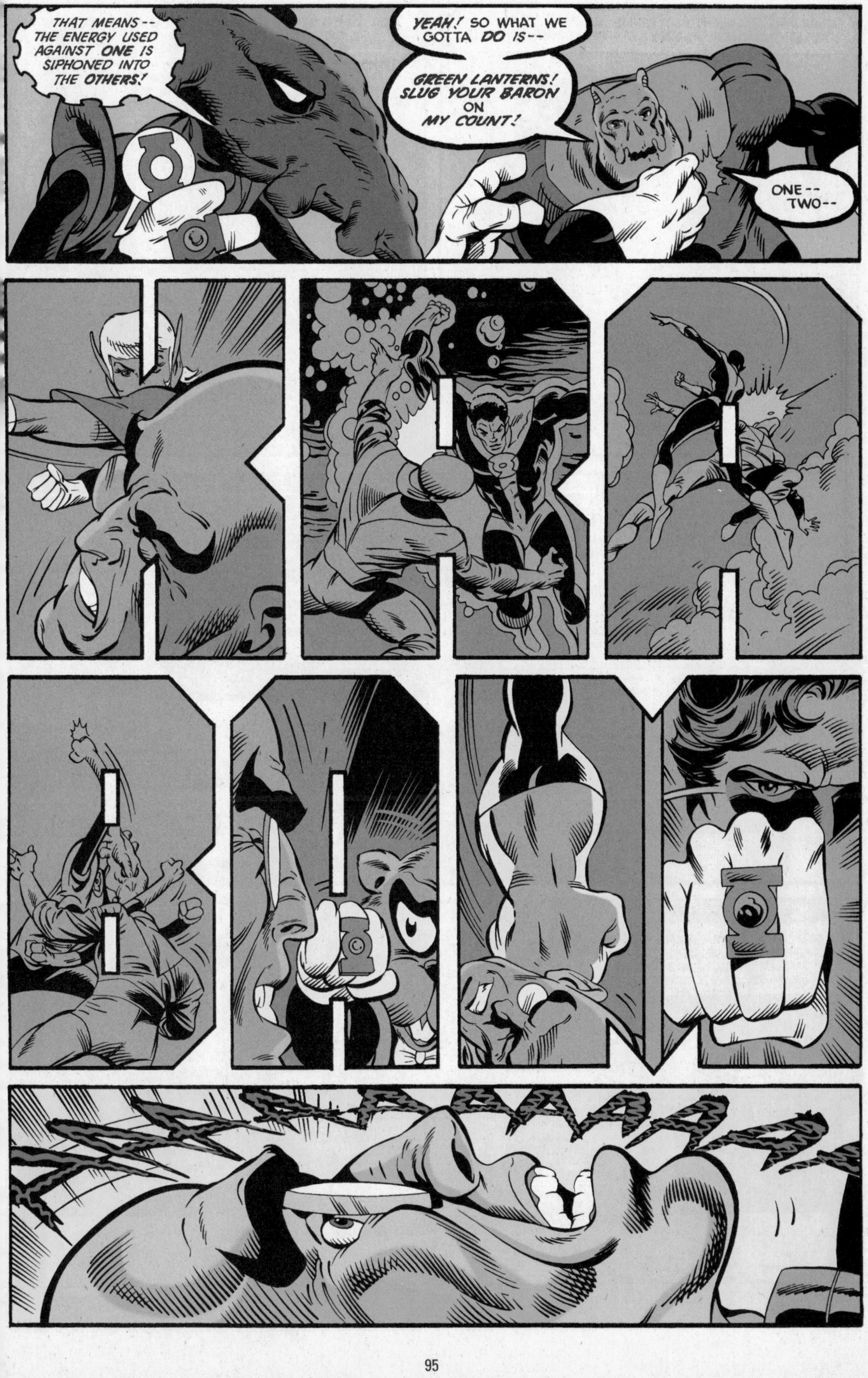
THAT MEANS-- THE ENERGY USED AGAINST ONE IS SIPHONED INTO THE OTHERS!
YEAH! SO WHAT WE GOTTA DO IS--
GREEN LANTERNS! SLUG YOUR BARON ON MY COUNT!
ONE-- TWO--

IT *WORKED!* WHEN ANY OF US HIT ANY OF THEM *ONE-ON-ONE*, THE ENERGY WAS SPLIT *SEVEN WAYS*--

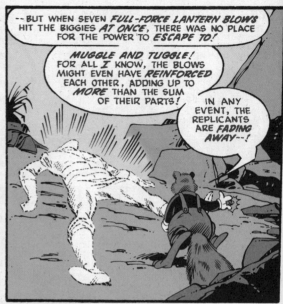

--BUT WHEN SEVEN *FULL-FORCE LANTERN BLOWS* HIT THE BIGGIES *AT ONCE*, THERE WAS NO PLACE FOR THE POWER TO *ESCAPE TO!*

MUGGLE AND TUGGLE! FOR ALL *I* KNOW, THE BLOWS MIGHT EVEN HAVE *REINFORCED* EACH OTHER, ADDING UP TO *MORE* THAN THE SUM OF THEIR PARTS!

IN ANY EVENT, THE REPLICANTS ARE *FADING AWAY*--!

"I WONDER WHAT HAPPENED TO THE *REAL BIGGIE!*"

EMERGENCY! EMERGENCY! THE BARON HAS SLIPPED INTO *UNCONSCIOUSNESS!* *EMERGENCY!*

BUT THE ATTENDANTS WHO *SURROUND* THE MAN IN THE IRON LUNG MAKE NO MOVE TO AID THEIR *MASTER!*

NO, THEY SIMPLY *FADE AWAY* LIKE THE *OTHER* REPLICANTS, WITHOUT THE BARON'S MENTAL ENERGY TO *DRIVE* THEM--

EMERGENCY! EMERGENCY!

--AND THE MAN WHO DESTROYED THE *REAL* MEN AND WOMEN IN HIS LIFE, IN FAVOR OF HIS *TELEVISION FRIENDS*--

--FINDS THAT *EVERYTHING* GETS CANCELED *EVENTUALLY*...!

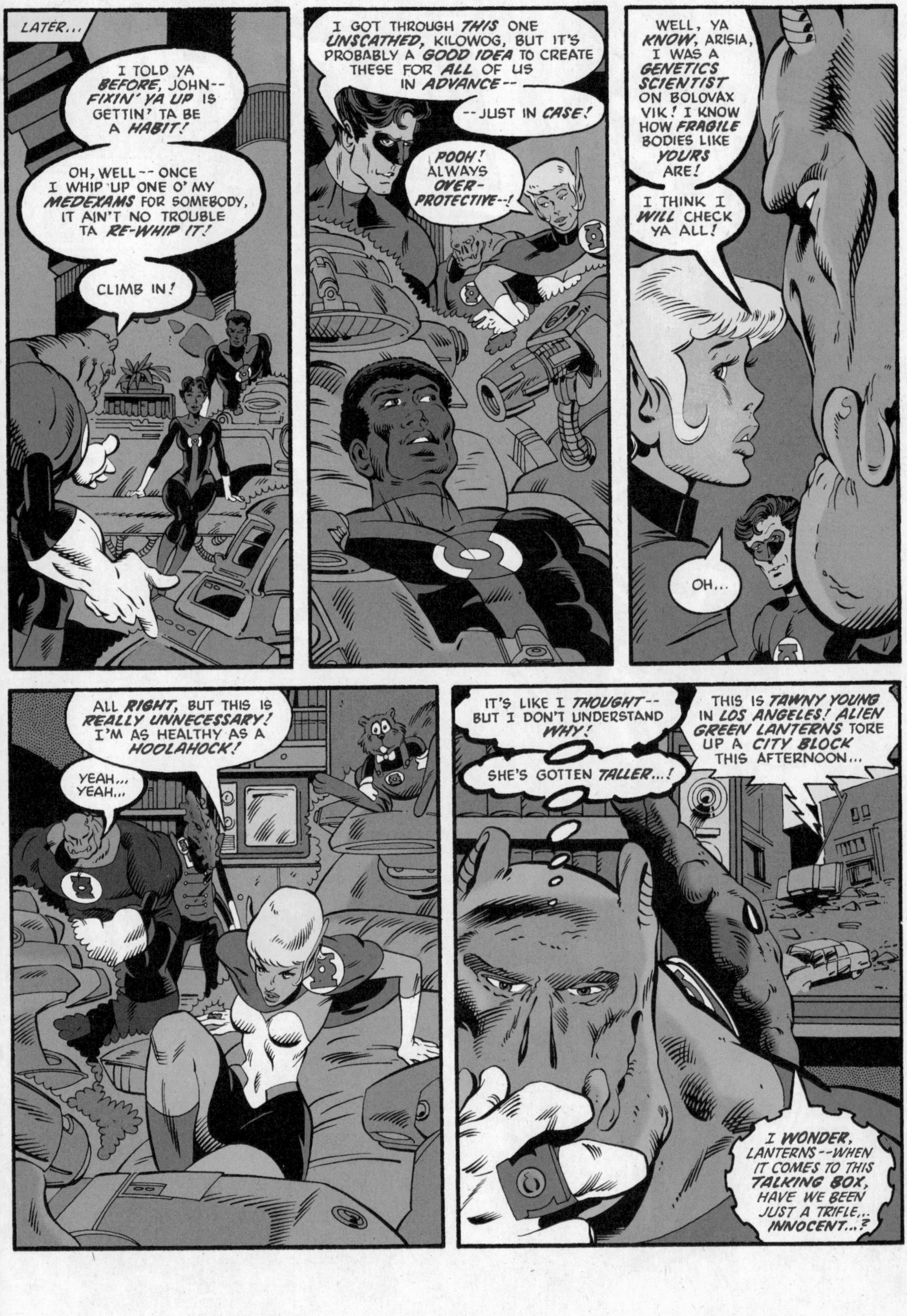
LATER...
I TOLD YA BEFORE, JOHN-- FIXIN' YA UP IS GETTIN' TA BE A HABIT!
OH, WELL-- ONCE I WHIP UP ONE O' MY MEDEXAMS FOR SOMEBODY, IT AIN'T NO TROUBLE TA RE-WHIP IT!
CLIMB IN!
I GOT THROUGH THIS ONE UNSCATHED, KILOWOG, BUT IT'S PROBABLY A GOOD IDEA TO CREATE THESE FOR ALL OF US IN ADVANCE--
--JUST IN CASE!
POOH! ALWAYS OVER-PROTECTIVE--!
WELL, YA KNOW, ARISIA, I WAS A GENETICS SCIENTIST ON BOLOVAX VIK! I KNOW HOW FRAGILE BODIES LIKE YOURS ARE!
I THINK I WILL CHECK YA ALL!
OH...
ALL RIGHT, BUT THIS IS REALLY UNNECESSARY! I'M AS HEALTHY AS A HOOLAHOCK!
YEAH... YEAH...
IT'S LIKE I THOUGHT-- BUT I DON'T UNDERSTAND WHY!
SHE'S GOTTEN TALLER...!
THIS IS TAWNY YOUNG IN LOS ANGELES! ALIEN GREEN LANTERNS TORE UP A CITY BLOCK THIS AFTERNOON...
I WONDER, LANTERNS--WHEN IT COMES TO THIS TALKING BOX, HAVE WE BEEN JUST A TRIFLE... INNOCENT...?

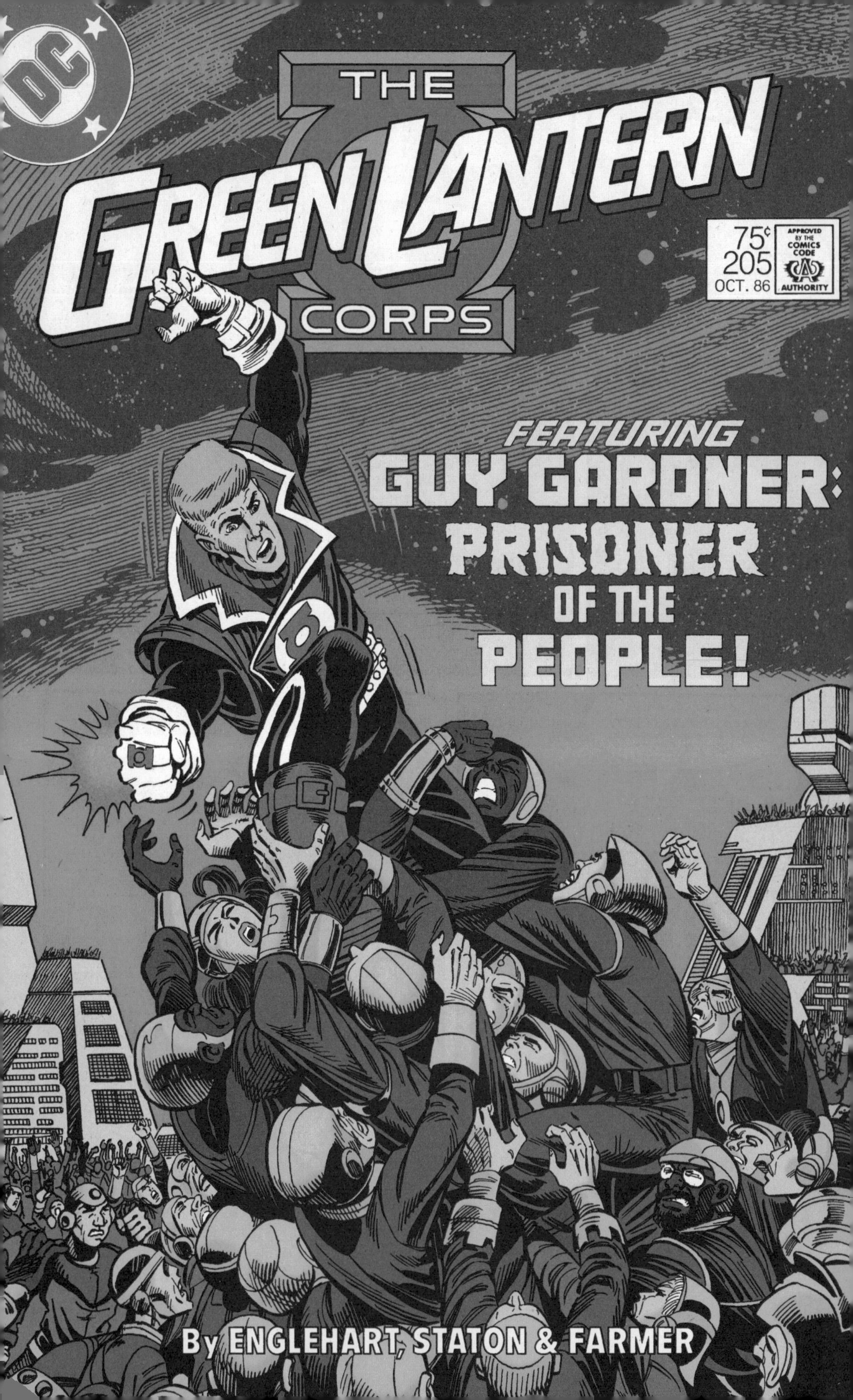
DC
THE
GREEN LANTERN
CORPS
75¢
205
OCT. 86
APPROVED BY THE COMICS CODE AUTHORITY
FEATURING
GUY GARDNER:
PRISONER
OF THE
PEOPLE!
By ENGLEHART, STATON & FARMER

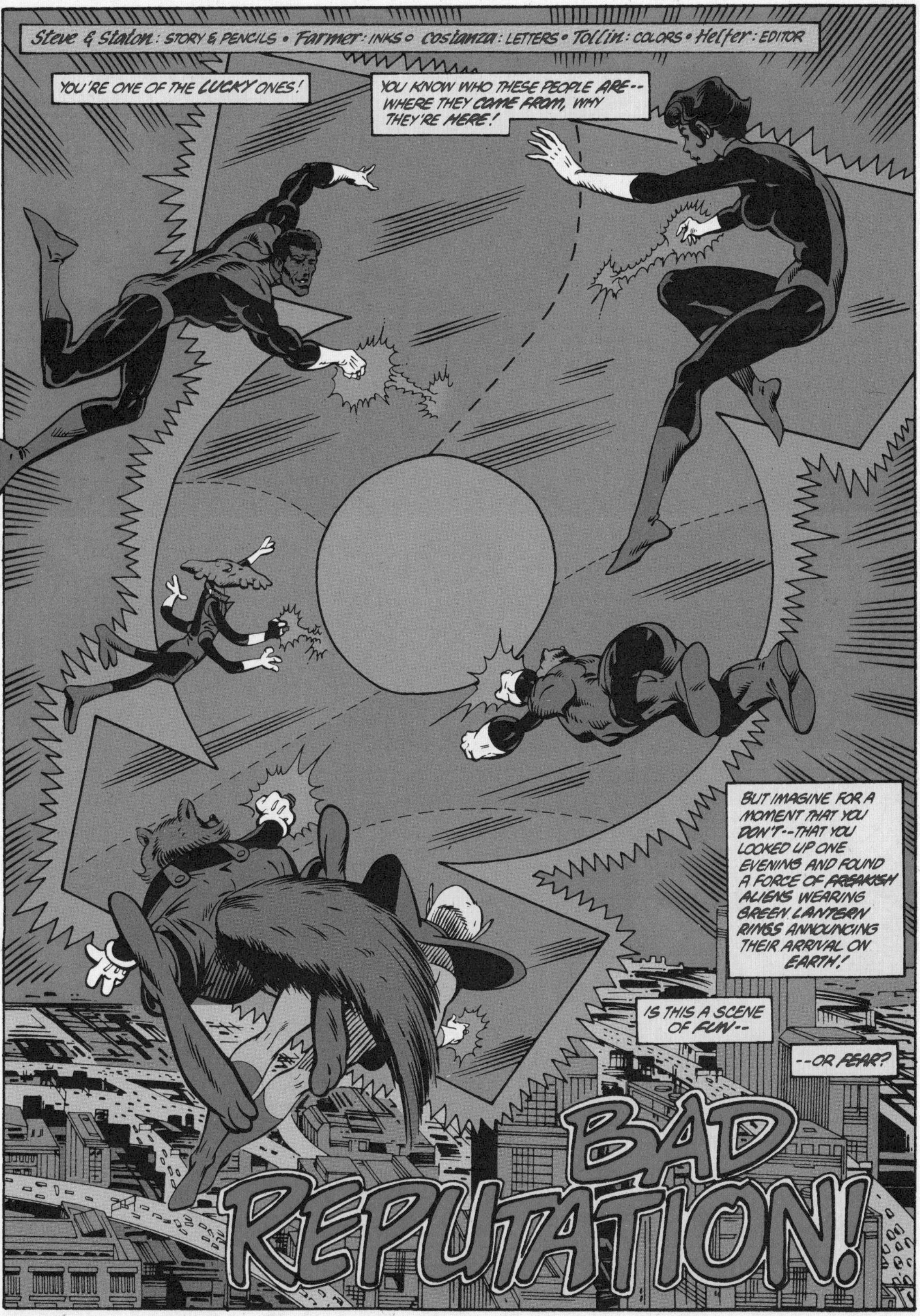
Steve & Staton: STORY & PENCILS • Farmer: INKS • Costanza: LETTERS • Tollin: COLORS • Helfer: EDITOR
YOU'RE ONE OF THE LUCKY ONES!
YOU KNOW WHO THESE PEOPLE ARE-- WHERE THEY COME FROM, WHY THEY'RE HERE!
BUT IMAGINE FOR A MOMENT THAT YOU DON'T--THAT YOU LOOKED UP ONE EVENING AND FOUND A FORCE OF FREAKISH ALIENS WEARING GREEN LANTERN RINGS ANNOUNCING THEIR ARRIVAL ON EARTH!
IS THIS A SCENE OF FUN--
--OR FEAR?
BAD REPUTATION!

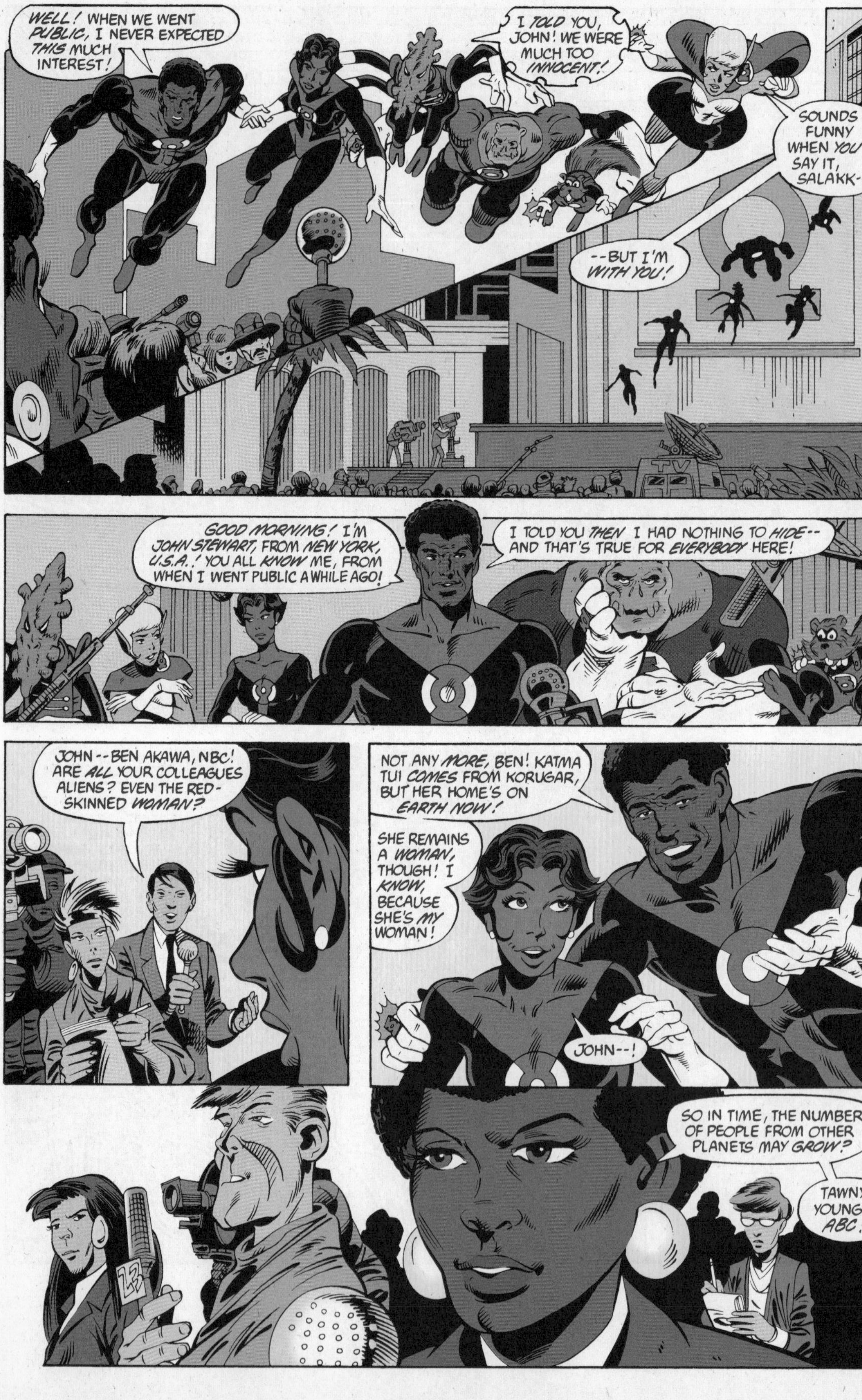

WELL! WHEN WE WENT PUBLIC, I NEVER EXPECTED THIS MUCH INTEREST!
I TOLD YOU, JOHN! WE WERE MUCH TOO INNOCENT!
SOUNDS FUNNY WHEN YOU SAY IT, SALAKK--
--BUT I'M WITH YOU!
TV
GOOD MORNING! I'M JOHN STEWART, FROM NEW YORK, U.S.A.! YOU ALL KNOW ME, FROM WHEN I WENT PUBLIC A WHILE AGO!
I TOLD YOU THEN I HAD NOTHING TO HIDE-- AND THAT'S TRUE FOR EVERYBODY HERE!
JOHN--BEN AKAWA, NBC! ARE ALL YOUR COLLEAGUES ALIENS? EVEN THE RED-SKINNED WOMAN?
NOT ANY MORE, BEN! KATMA TUI COMES FROM KORUGAR, BUT HER HOME'S ON EARTH NOW!
SHE REMAINS A WOMAN, THOUGH! I KNOW, BECAUSE SHE'S MY WOMAN!
JOHN--!
SO IN TIME, THE NUMBER OF PEOPLE FROM OTHER PLANETS MAY GROW?
TAWNY YOUNG, ABC!

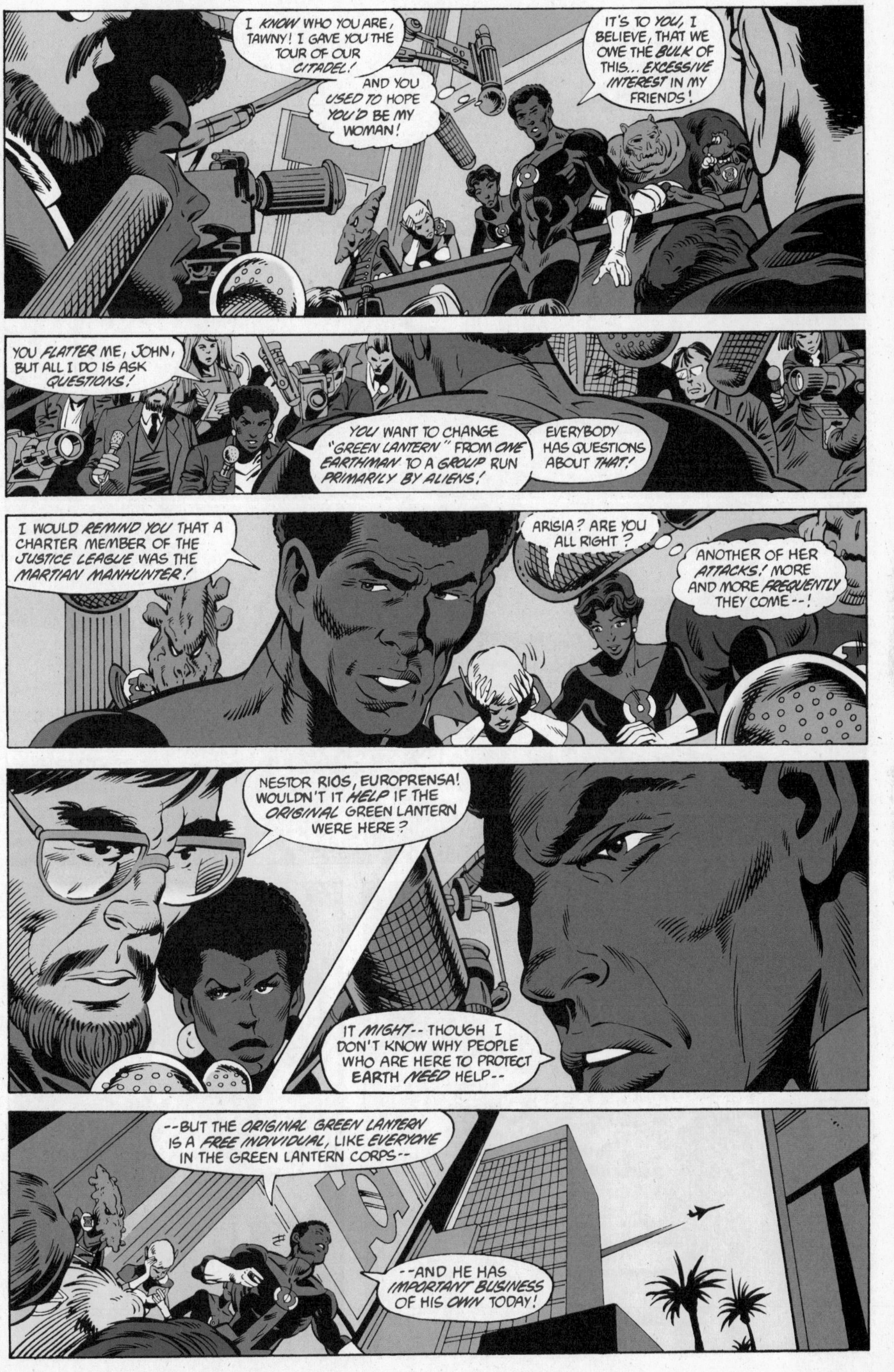
I KNOW WHO YOU ARE, TAWNY! I GAVE YOU THE TOUR OF OUR CITADEL!
AND YOU USED TO HOPE YOU'D BE MY WOMAN!
IT'S TO YOU, I BELIEVE, THAT WE OWE THE BULK OF THIS... EXCESSIVE INTEREST IN MY FRIENDS!
YOU FLATTER ME, JOHN, BUT ALL I DO IS ASK QUESTIONS!
YOU WANT TO CHANGE "GREEN LANTERN" FROM ONE EARTHMAN TO A GROUP RUN PRIMARILY BY ALIENS!
EVERYBODY HAS QUESTIONS ABOUT THAT!
I WOULD REMIND YOU THAT A CHARTER MEMBER OF THE JUSTICE LEAGUE WAS THE MARTIAN MANHUNTER!
ARISIA? ARE YOU ALL RIGHT?
ANOTHER OF HER ATTACKS! MORE AND MORE FREQUENTLY THEY COME--!
NESTOR RIOS, EUROPRENSA! WOULDN'T IT HELP IF THE ORIGINAL GREEN LANTERN WERE HERE?
IT MIGHT-- THOUGH I DON'T KNOW WHY PEOPLE WHO ARE HERE TO PROTECT EARTH NEED HELP--
--BUT THE ORIGINAL GREEN LANTERN IS A FREE INDIVIDUAL, LIKE EVERYONE IN THE GREEN LANTERN CORPS--
--AND HE HAS IMPORTANT BUSINESS OF HIS OWN TODAY!

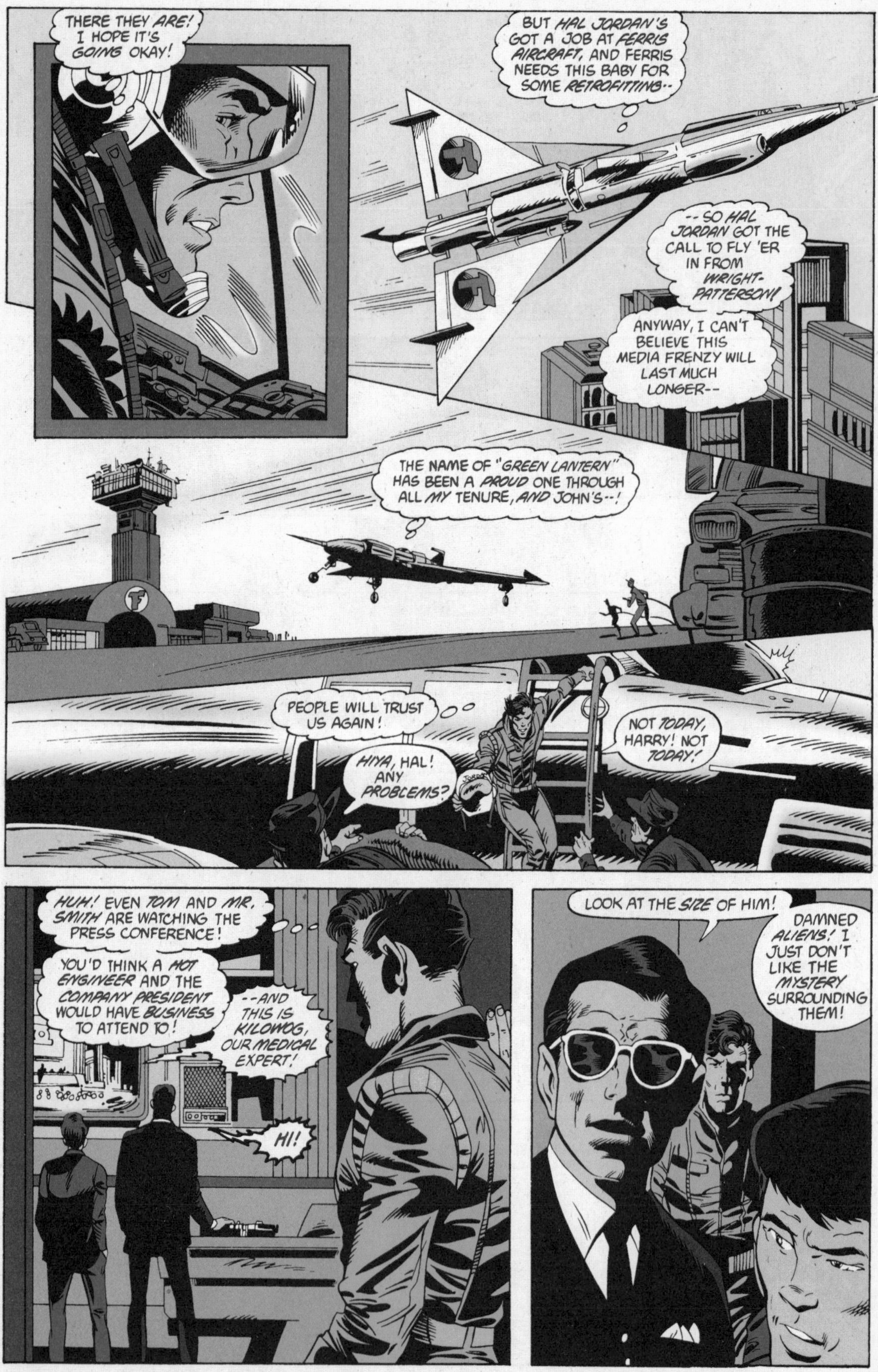
THERE THEY ARE! I HOPE IT'S GOING OKAY!
BUT HAL JORDAN'S GOT A JOB AT FERRIS AIRCRAFT, AND FERRIS NEEDS THIS BABY FOR SOME RETROFITTING--
--SO HAL JORDAN GOT THE CALL TO FLY 'ER IN FROM WRIGHT-PATTERSON!
ANYWAY, I CAN'T BELIEVE THIS MEDIA FRENZY WILL LAST MUCH LONGER--
THE NAME OF "GREEN LANTERN" HAS BEEN A PROUD ONE THROUGH ALL MY TENURE, AND JOHN'S--!
PEOPLE WILL TRUST US AGAIN!
HIYA, HAL! ANY PROBLEMS?
NOT TODAY, HARRY! NOT TODAY!
HUH! EVEN TOM AND MR. SMITH ARE WATCHING THE PRESS CONFERENCE!
YOU'D THINK A HOT ENGINEER AND THE COMPANY PRESIDENT WOULD HAVE BUSINESS TO ATTEND TO!
--AND THIS IS KILOWOG, OUR MEDICAL EXPERT!
HI!
LOOK AT THE SIZE OF HIM!
DAMNED ALIENS! I JUST DON'T LIKE THE MYSTERY SURROUNDING THEM!

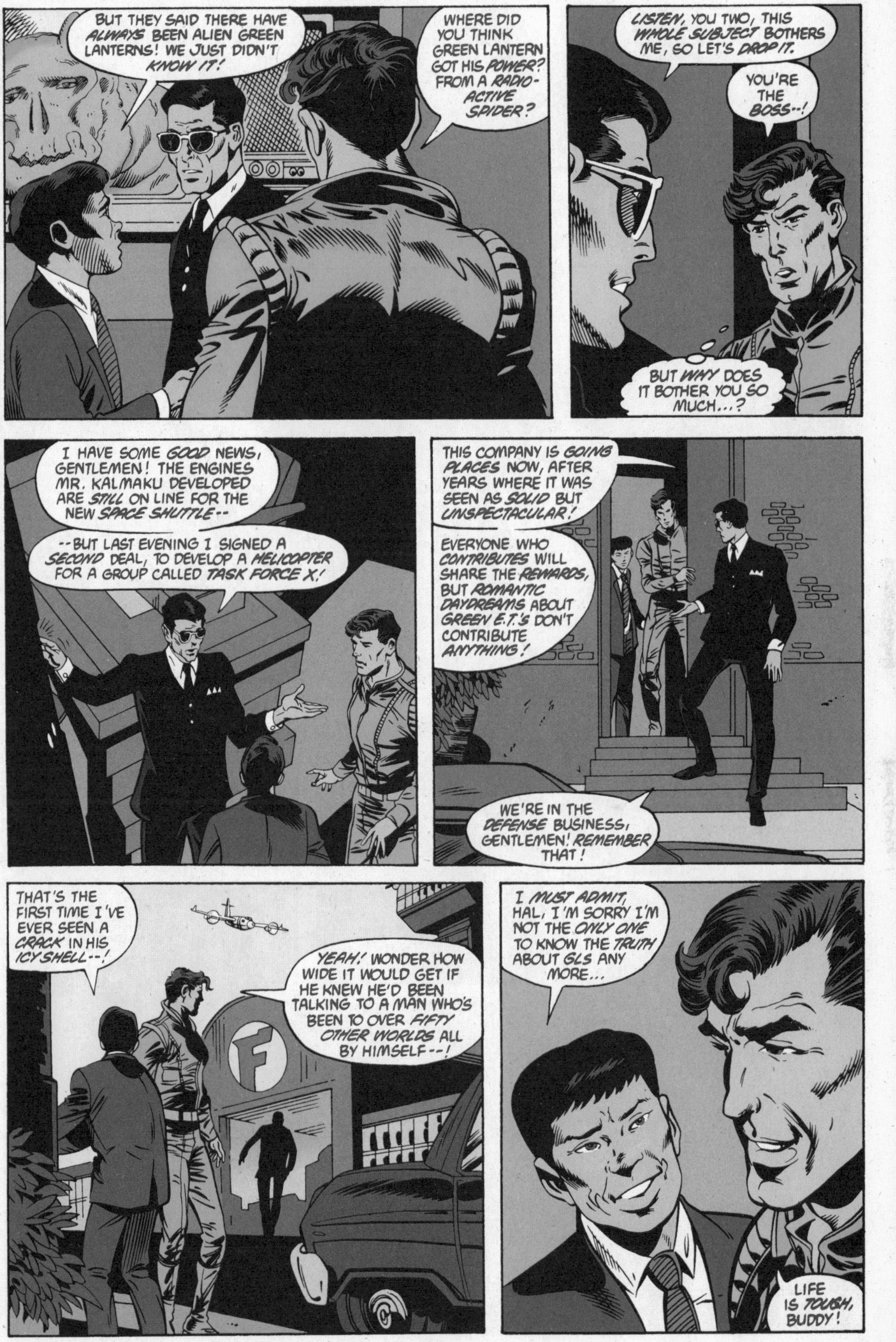
BUT THEY SAID THERE HAVE ALWAYS BEEN ALIEN GREEN LANTERNS! WE JUST DIDN'T KNOW IT!
WHERE DID YOU THINK GREEN LANTERN GOT HIS POWER? FROM A RADIO-ACTIVE SPIDER?
LISTEN, YOU TWO, THIS WHOLE SUBJECT BOTHERS ME, SO LET'S DROP IT.
YOU'RE THE BOSS--!
BUT WHY DOES IT BOTHER YOU SO MUCH...?
I HAVE SOME GOOD NEWS, GENTLEMEN! THE ENGINES MR. KALMAKU DEVELOPED ARE STILL ON LINE FOR THE NEW SPACE SHUTTLE--
--BUT LAST EVENING I SIGNED A SECOND DEAL, TO DEVELOP A HELICOPTER FOR A GROUP CALLED TASK FORCE X!
THIS COMPANY IS GOING PLACES NOW, AFTER YEARS WHERE IT WAS SEEN AS SOLID BUT UNSPECTACULAR!
EVERYONE WHO CONTRIBUTES WILL SHARE THE REWARDS, BUT ROMANTIC DAYDREAMS ABOUT GREEN E.T.'S DON'T CONTRIBUTE ANYTHING!
WE'RE IN THE DEFENSE BUSINESS, GENTLEMEN! REMEMBER THAT!
THAT'S THE FIRST TIME I'VE EVER SEEN A CRACK IN HIS ICY SHELL--!
YEAH! WONDER HOW WIDE IT WOULD GET IF HE KNEW HE'D BEEN TALKING TO A MAN WHO'S BEEN TO OVER FIFTY OTHER WORLDS ALL BY HIMSELF--!
I MUST ADMIT, HAL, I'M SORRY I'M NOT THE ONLY ONE TO KNOW THE TRUTH ABOUT GLS ANY MORE...
LIFE IS TOUGH, BUDDY!

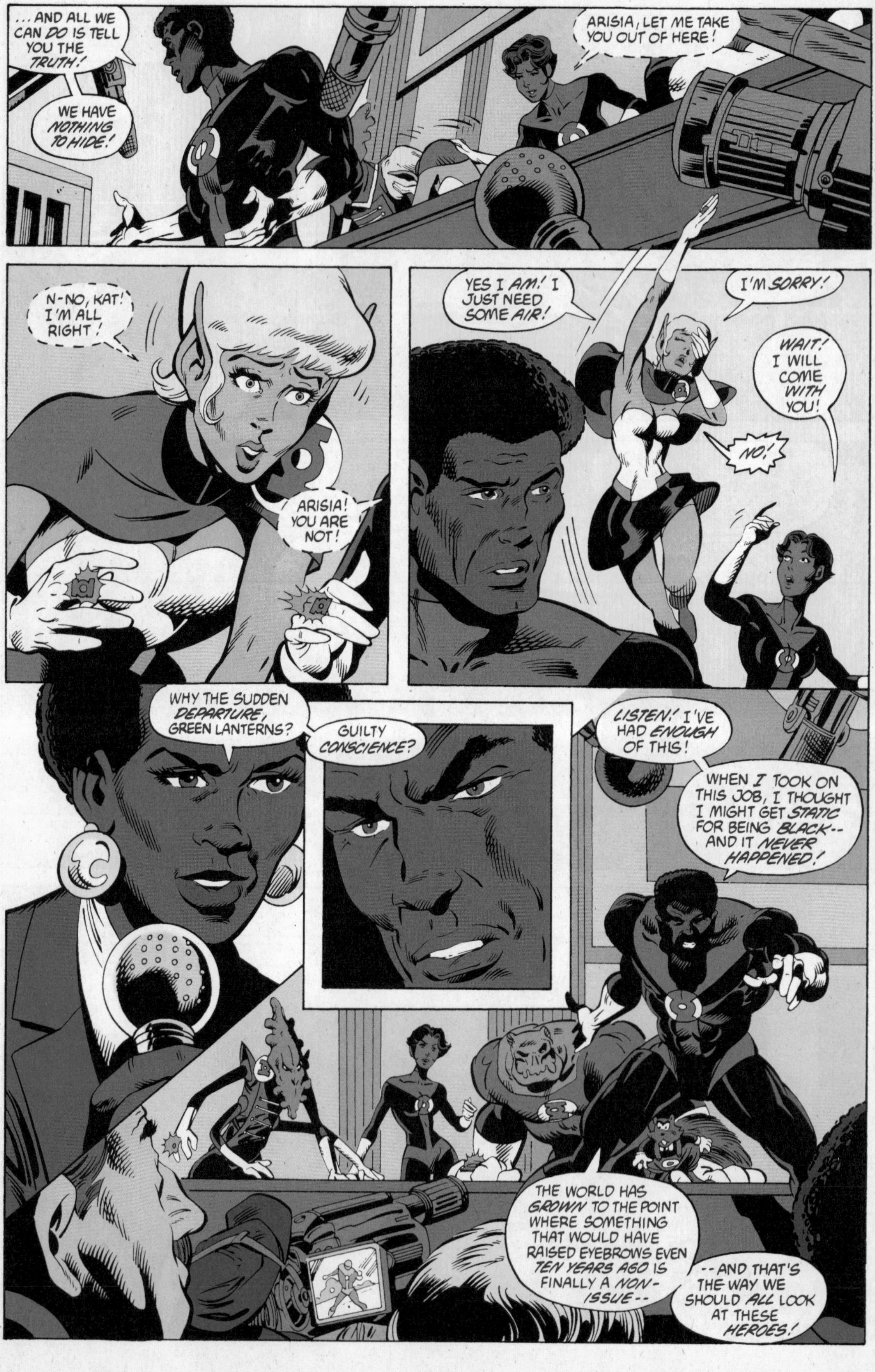
...AND ALL WE CAN DO IS TELL YOU THE TRUTH!
WE HAVE NOTHING TO HIDE!
ARISIA, LET ME TAKE YOU OUT OF HERE!
N-NO, KAT! I'M ALL RIGHT!
ARISIA! YOU ARE NOT!
YES I AM! I JUST NEED SOME AIR!
I'M SORRY!
WAIT! I WILL COME WITH YOU!
NO!
WHY THE SUDDEN DEPARTURE, GREEN LANTERNS?
GUILTY CONSCIENCE?
LISTEN! I'VE HAD ENOUGH OF THIS!
WHEN I TOOK ON THIS JOB, I THOUGHT I MIGHT GET STATIC FOR BEING BLACK-- AND IT NEVER HAPPENED!
THE WORLD HAS GROWN TO THE POINT WHERE SOMETHING THAT WOULD HAVE RAISED EYEBROWS EVEN TEN YEARS AGO IS FINALLY A NON-ISSUE--
--AND THAT'S THE WAY WE SHOULD ALL LOOK AT THESE HEROES!

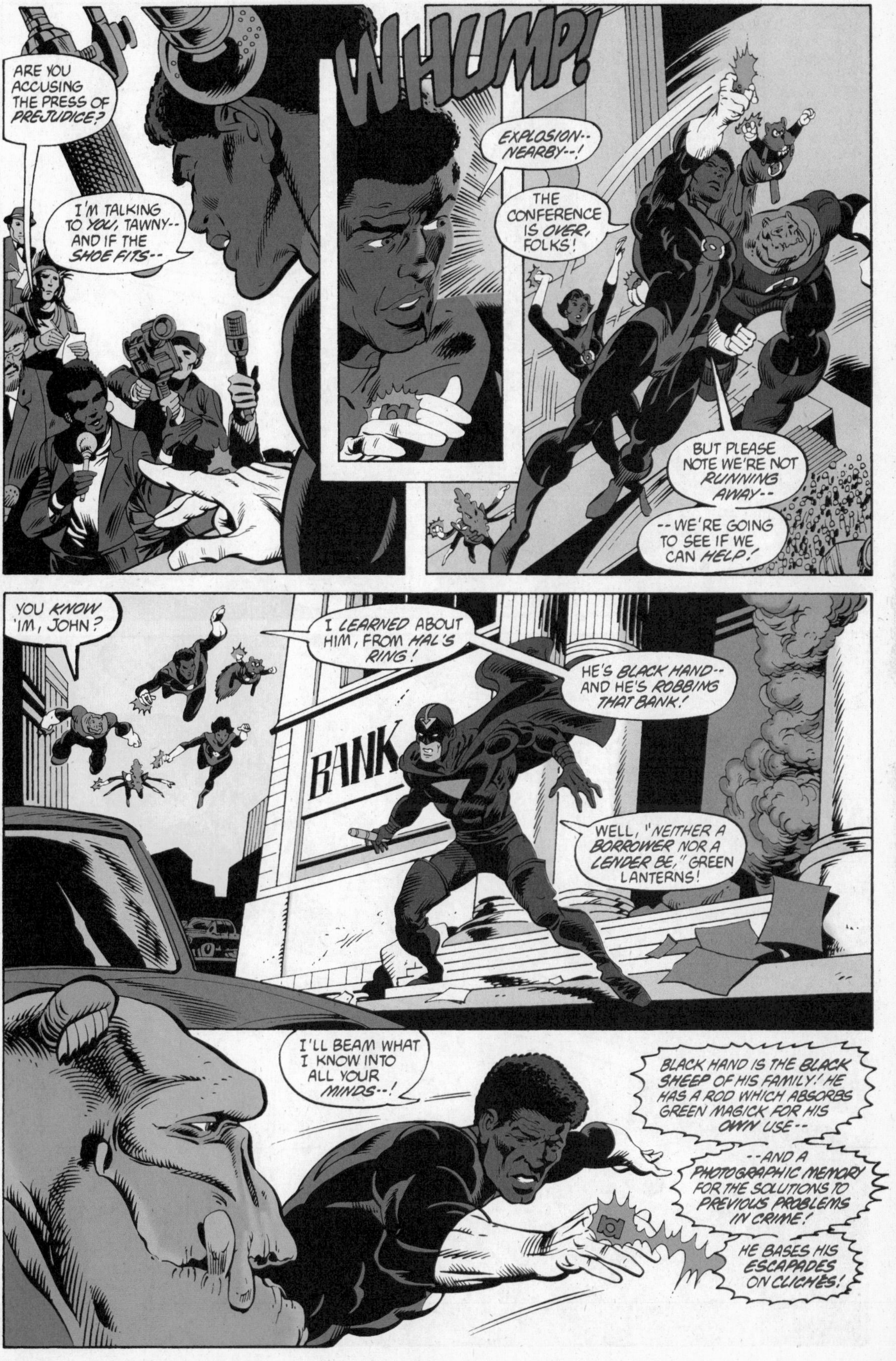

ARE YOU ACCUSING THE PRESS OF PREJUDICE?
I'M TALKING TO YOU, TAWNY-- AND IF THE SHOE FITS--
WHUMP!
EXPLOSION-- NEARBY--!
THE CONFERENCE IS OVER, FOLKS!
BUT PLEASE NOTE WE'RE NOT RUNNING AWAY--
--WE'RE GOING TO SEE IF WE CAN HELP!
YOU KNOW 'IM, JOHN?
I LEARNED ABOUT HIM, FROM HAL'S RING!
HE'S BLACK HAND-- AND HE'S ROBBING THAT BANK!
BANK
WELL, "NEITHER A BORROWER NOR A LENDER BE," GREEN LANTERNS!
I'LL BEAM WHAT I KNOW INTO ALL YOUR MINDS--!
BLACK HAND IS THE BLACK SHEEP OF HIS FAMILY! HE HAS A ROD WHICH ABSORBS GREEN MAGICK FOR HIS OWN USE--
--AND A PHOTOGRAPHIC MEMORY FOR THE SOLUTIONS TO PREVIOUS PROBLEMS IN CRIME!
HE BASES HIS ESCAPADES ON CLICHÉS!

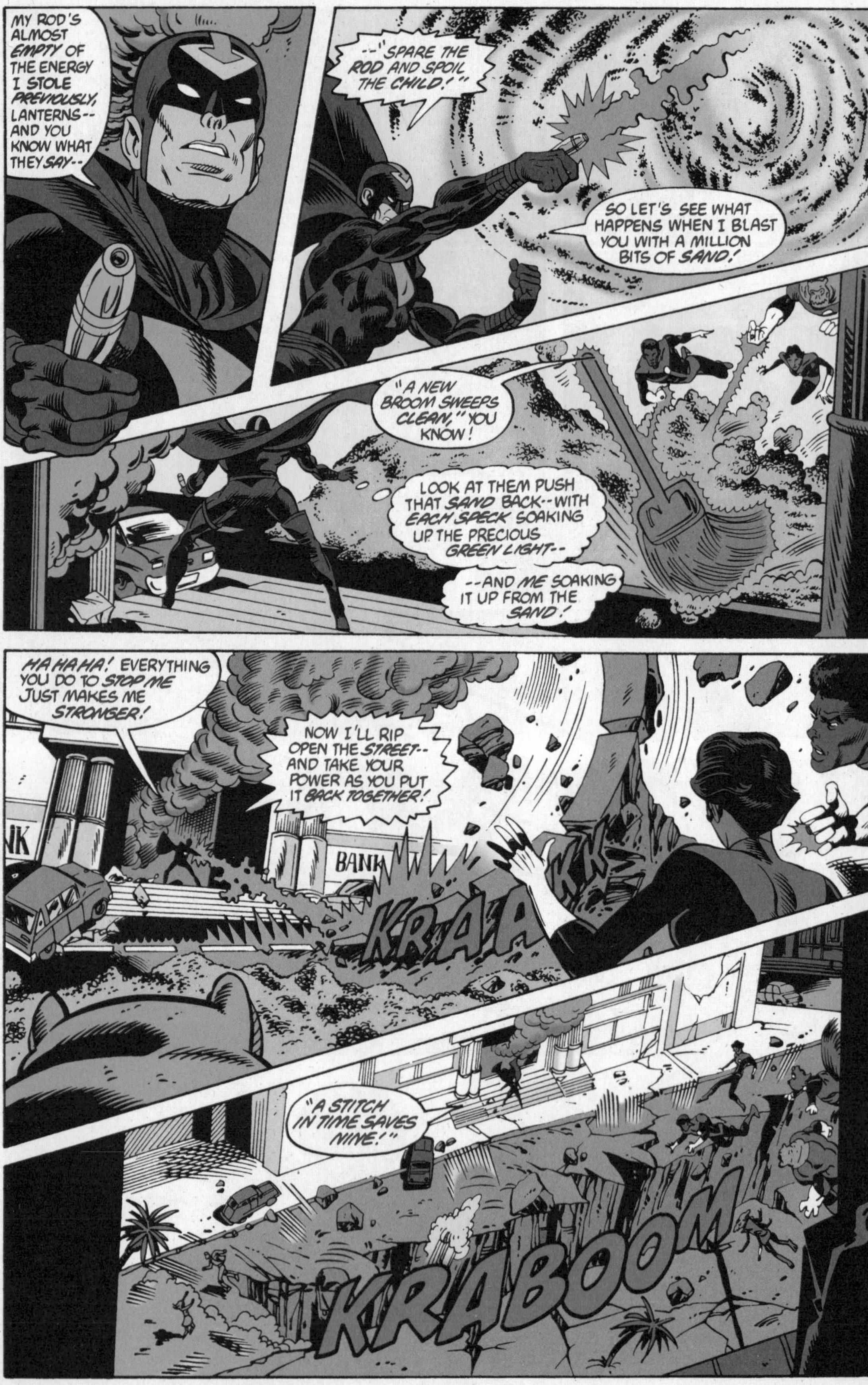
MY ROD'S ALMOST EMPTY OF THE ENERGY I STOLE PREVIOUSLY, LANTERNS-- AND YOU KNOW WHAT THEY SAY--
--"SPARE THE ROD AND SPOIL THE CHILD!"
SO LET'S SEE WHAT HAPPENS WHEN I BLAST YOU WITH A MILLION BITS OF SAND!
"A NEW BROOM SWEEPS CLEAN," YOU KNOW!
LOOK AT THEM PUSH THAT SAND BACK--WITH EACH SPECK SOAKING UP THE PRECIOUS GREEN LIGHT--
--AND ME SOAKING IT UP FROM THE SAND!
HA HA HA! EVERYTHING YOU DO TO STOP ME JUST MAKES ME STRONGER!
NOW I'LL RIP OPEN THE STREET-- AND TAKE YOUR POWER AS YOU PUT IT BACK TOGETHER!
BANK
BANK
KRAAAKK
"A STITCH IN TIME SAVES NINE!"
KRABOOM

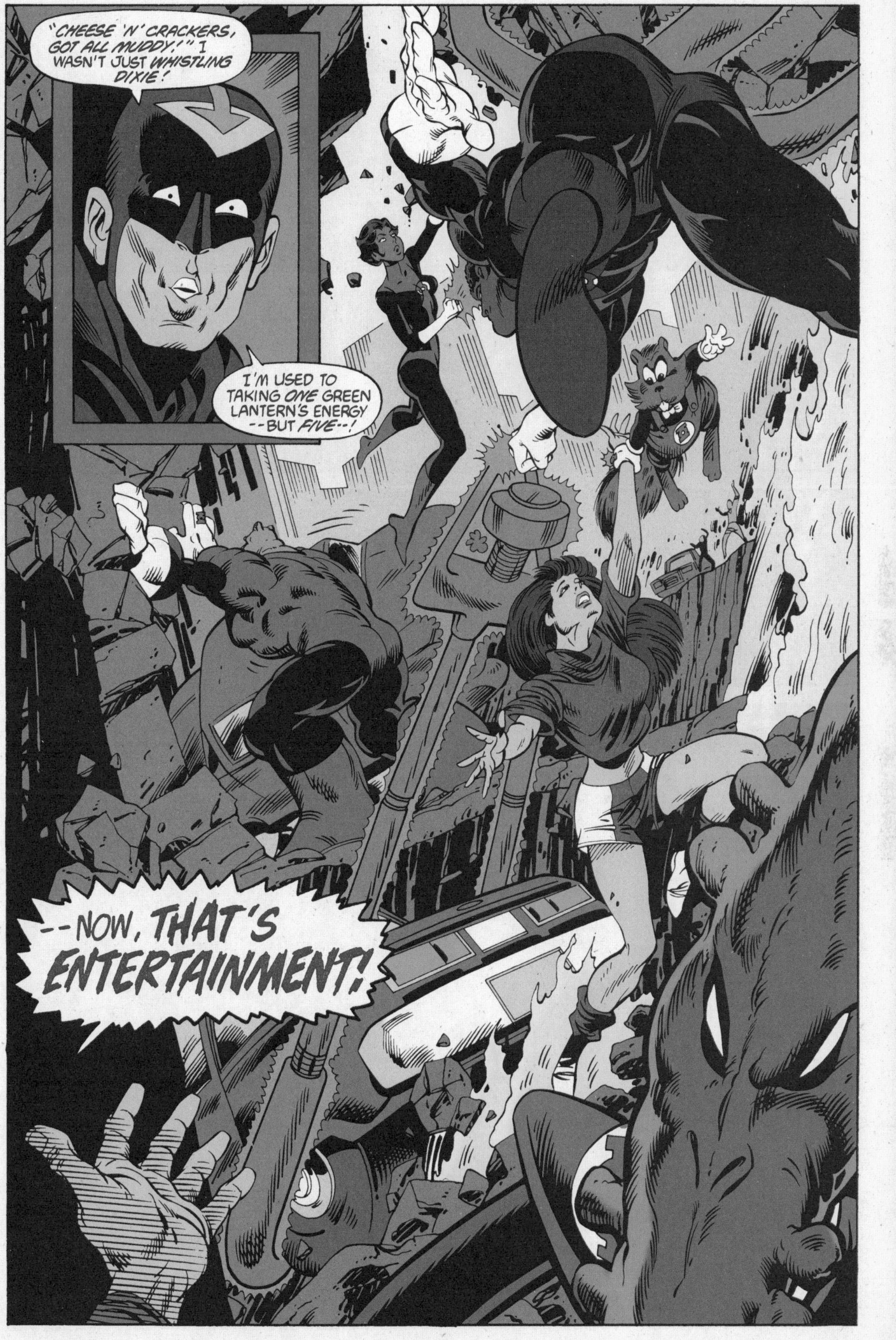
"CHEESE 'N' CRACKERS, GOT ALL MUDDY!" I WASN'T JUST WHISTLING DIXIE!
I'M USED TO TAKING ONE GREEN LANTERN'S ENERGY --BUT FIVE--!
--NOW, THAT'S ENTERTAINMENT!

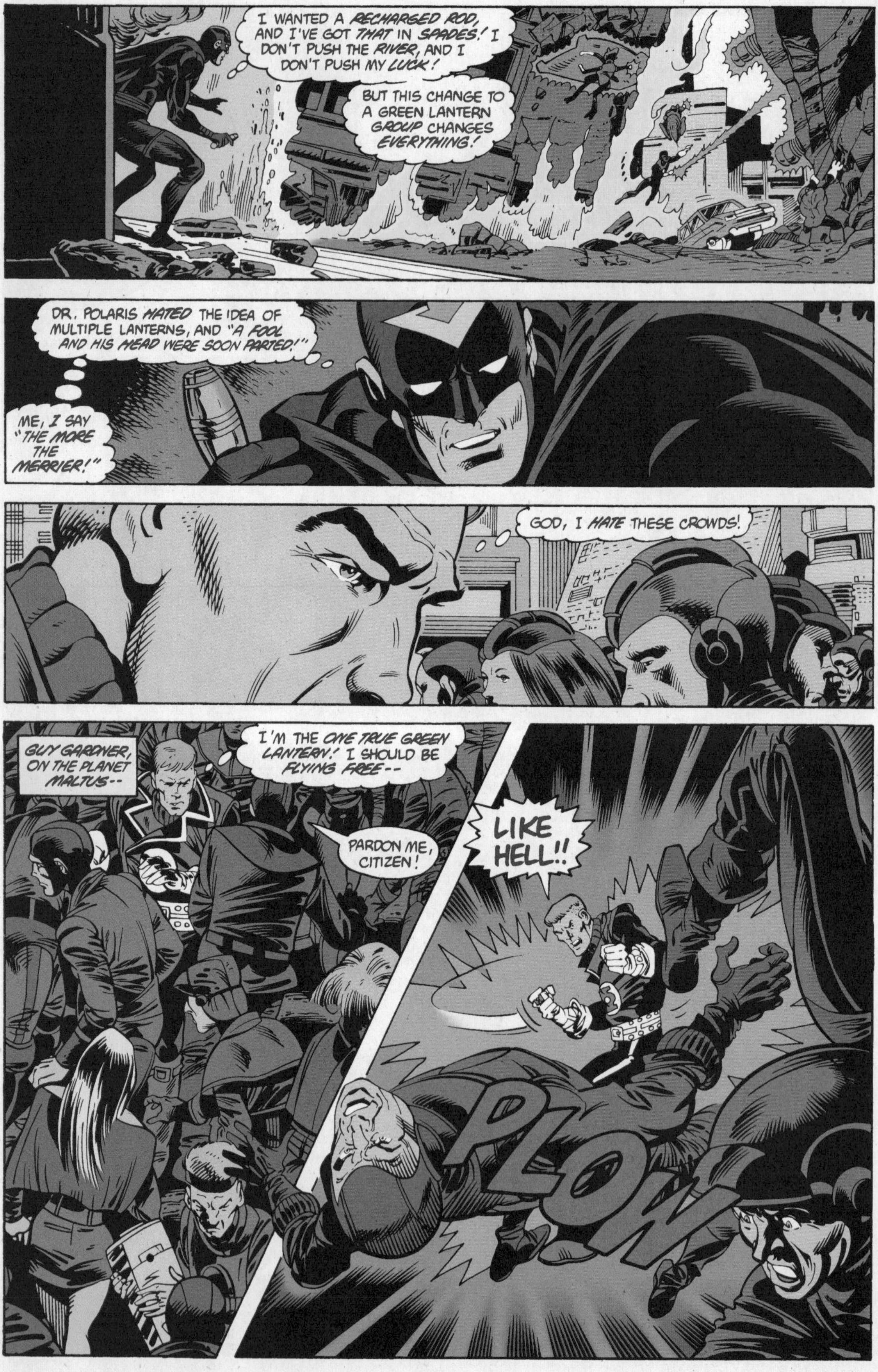
I WANTED A RECHARGED ROD, AND I'VE GOT THAT IN SPADES! I DON'T PUSH THE RIVER, AND I DON'T PUSH MY LUCK!
BUT THIS CHANGE TO A GREEN LANTERN GROUP CHANGES EVERYTHING!
DR. POLARIS HATED THE IDEA OF MULTIPLE LANTERNS, AND "A FOOL AND HIS HEAD WERE SOON PARTED!"
ME, I SAY "THE MORE THE MERRIER!"
GOD, I HATE THESE CROWDS!
GUY GARDNER, ON THE PLANET MALTUS--
I'M THE ONE TRUE GREEN LANTERN! I SHOULD BE FLYING FREE--
PARDON ME, CITIZEN!
LIKE HELL!!
PLOW

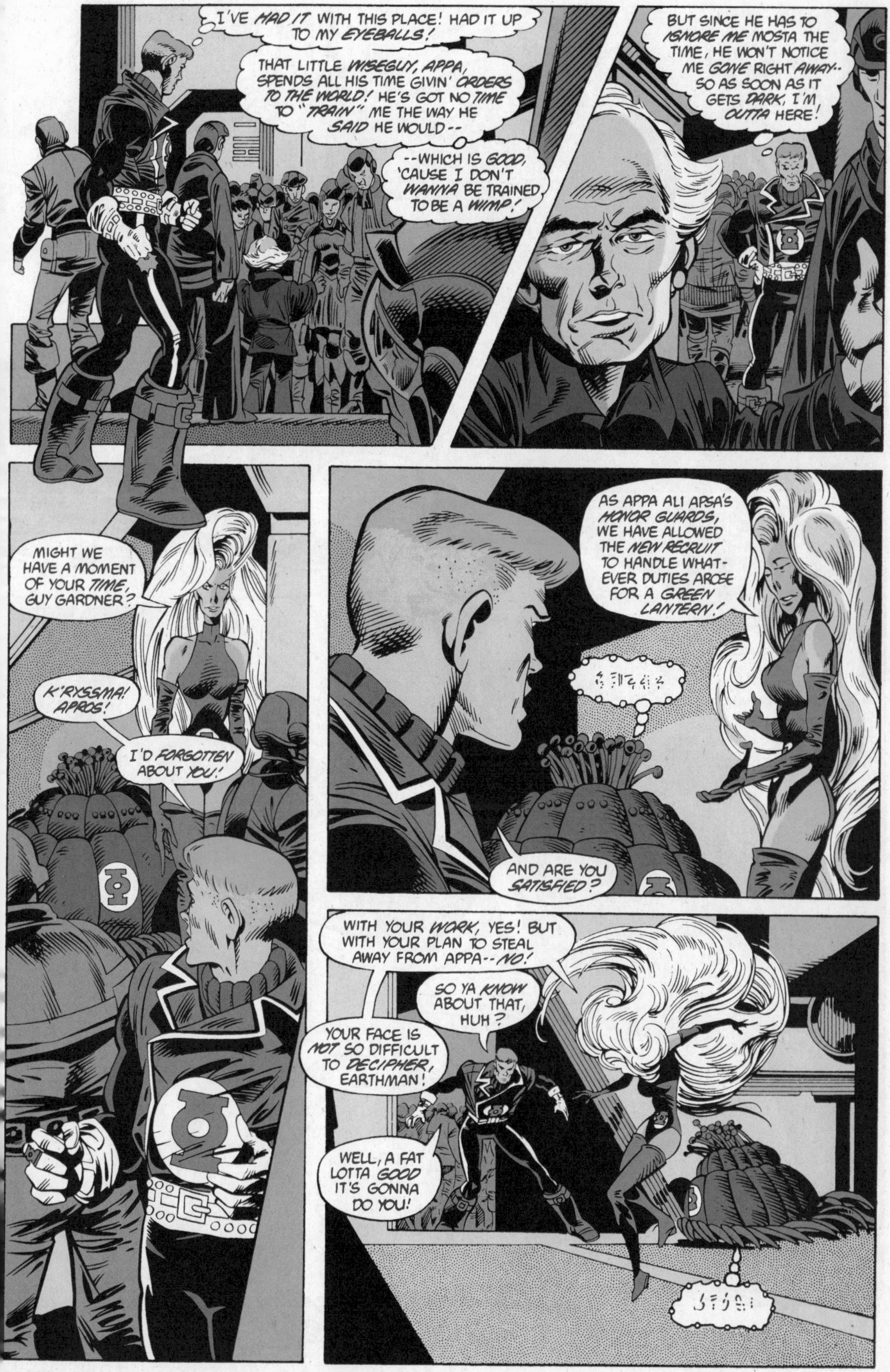
I'VE HAD IT WITH THIS PLACE! HAD IT UP TO MY EYEBALLS!
THAT LITTLE WISEGUY, APPA, SPENDS ALL HIS TIME GIVIN' ORDERS TO THE WORLD! HE'S GOT NO TIME TO "TRAIN" ME THE WAY HE SAID HE WOULD--
--WHICH IS GOOD, 'CAUSE I DON'T WANNA BE TRAINED TO BE A WIMP!
BUT SINCE HE HAS TO IGNORE ME MOSTA THE TIME, HE WON'T NOTICE ME GONE RIGHT AWAY-- SO AS SOON AS IT GETS DARK, I'M OUTTA HERE!
MIGHT WE HAVE A MOMENT OF YOUR TIME, GUY GARDNER?
K'RYSSMA! APROS!
I'D FORGOTTEN ABOUT YOU!
AS APPA ALI APSA'S HONOR GUARDS, WE HAVE ALLOWED THE NEW RECRUIT TO HANDLE WHATEVER DUTIES AROSE FOR A GREEN LANTERN!
AND ARE YOU SATISFIED?
WITH YOUR WORK, YES! BUT WITH YOUR PLAN TO STEAL AWAY FROM APPA--NO!
SO YA KNOW ABOUT THAT, HUH?
YOUR FACE IS NOT SO DIFFICULT TO DECIPHER, EARTHMAN!
WELL, A FAT LOTTA GOOD IT'S GONNA DO YOU!

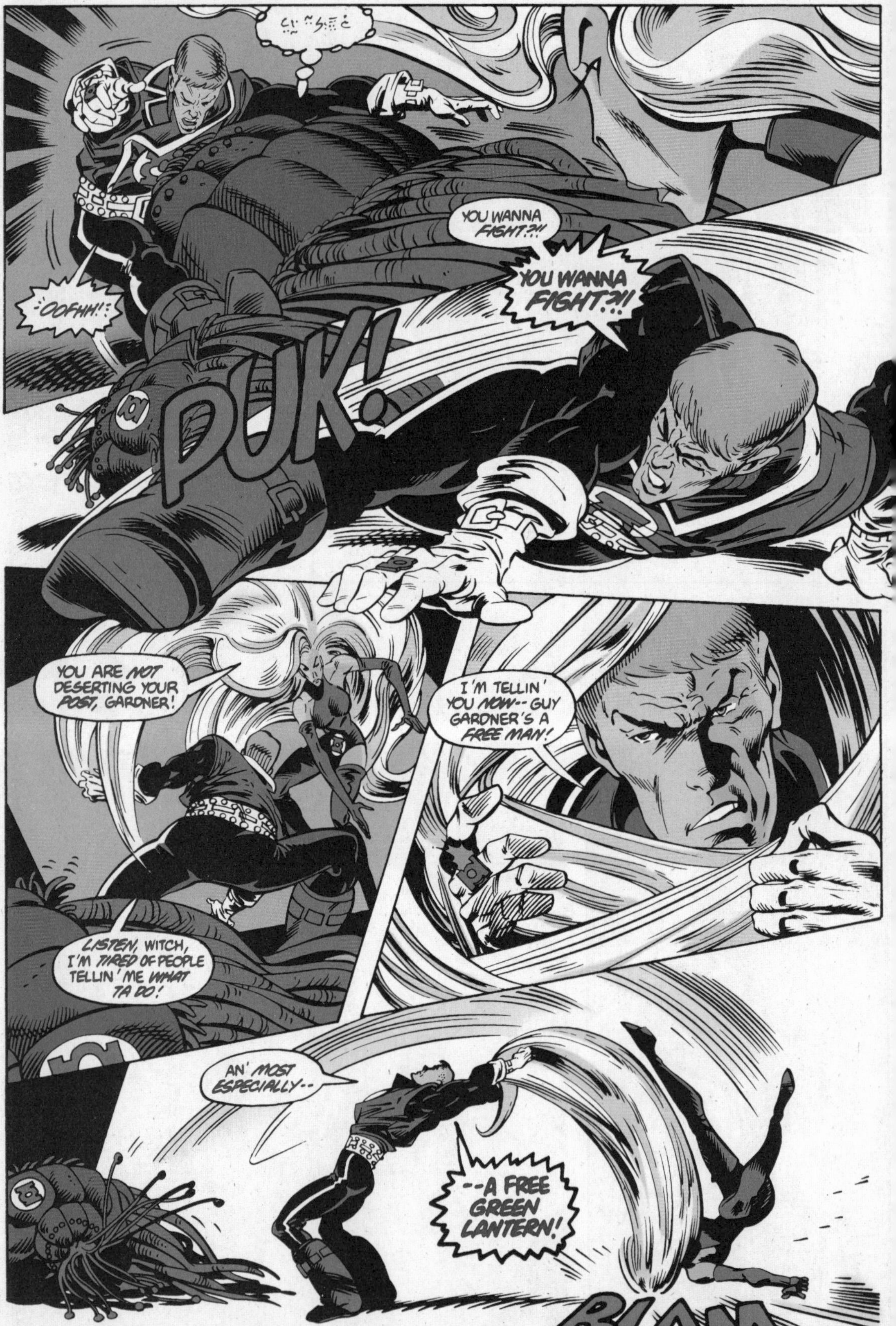

YOU WANNA FIGHT?!!
YOU WANNA FIGHT?!!
OOFHH!
PUK!
YOU ARE NOT DESERTING YOUR POST, GARDNER!
I'M TELLIN' YOU NOW-- GUY GARDNER'S A FREE MAN!
LISTEN, WITCH, I'M TIRED OF PEOPLE TELLIN' ME WHAT TA DO!
AN' MOST ESPECIALLY--
--A FREE GREEN LANTERN!
BLAM

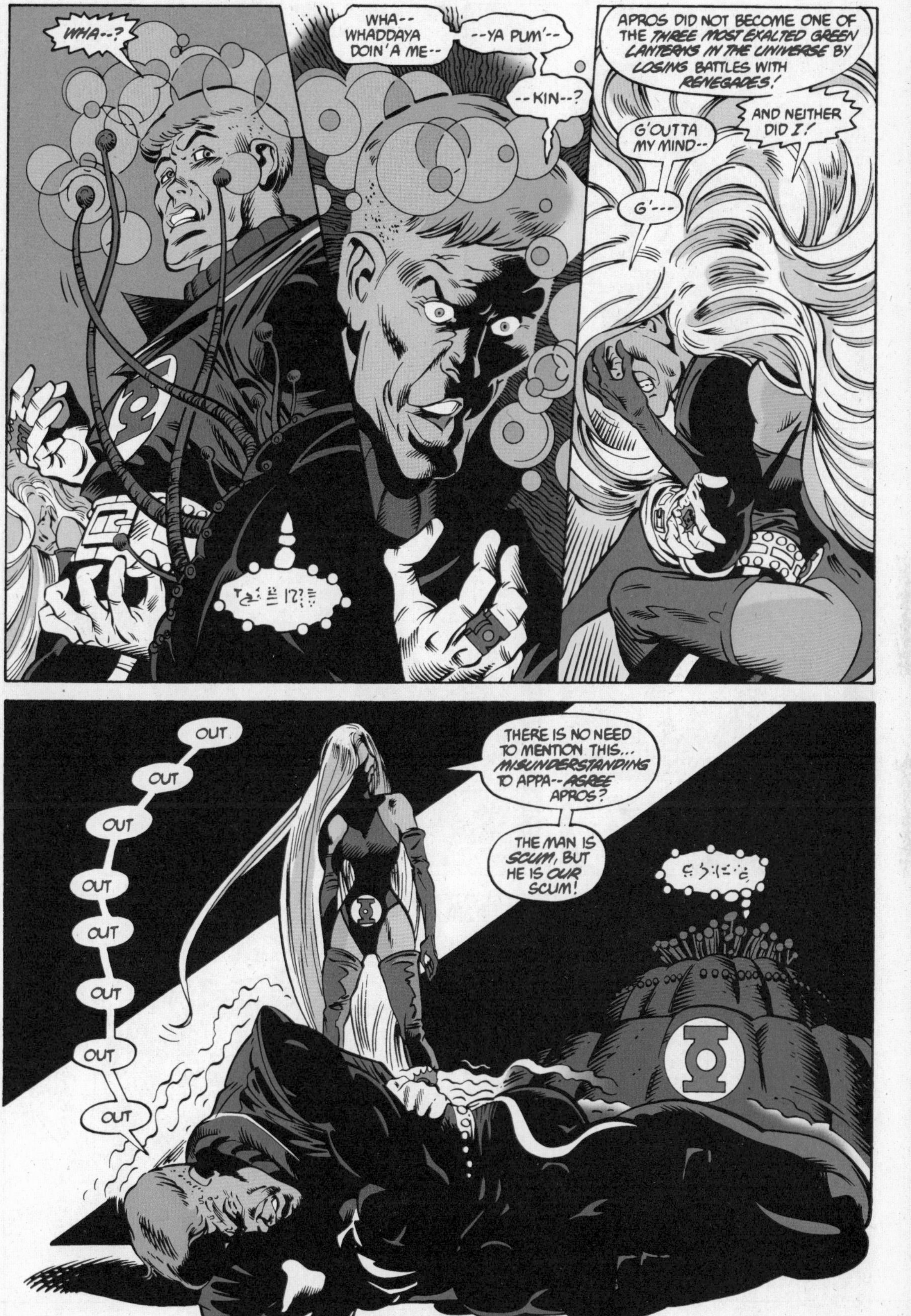
WHA--?
WHA-- WHADDAYA DOIN' A ME--
--YA PUM'--
--KIN--?
APROS DID NOT BECOME ONE OF THE THREE MOST EXALTED GREEN LANTERNS IN THE UNIVERSE BY LOSING BATTLES WITH RENEGADES!
G'OUTTA MY MIND--
AND NEITHER DID I!
G'---
OUT
OUT
OUT
OUT
OUT
OUT
OUT
OUT
THERE IS NO NEED TO MENTION THIS... MISUNDERSTANDING TO APPA--AGREE APROS?
THE MAN IS SCUM, BUT HE IS OUR SCUM!

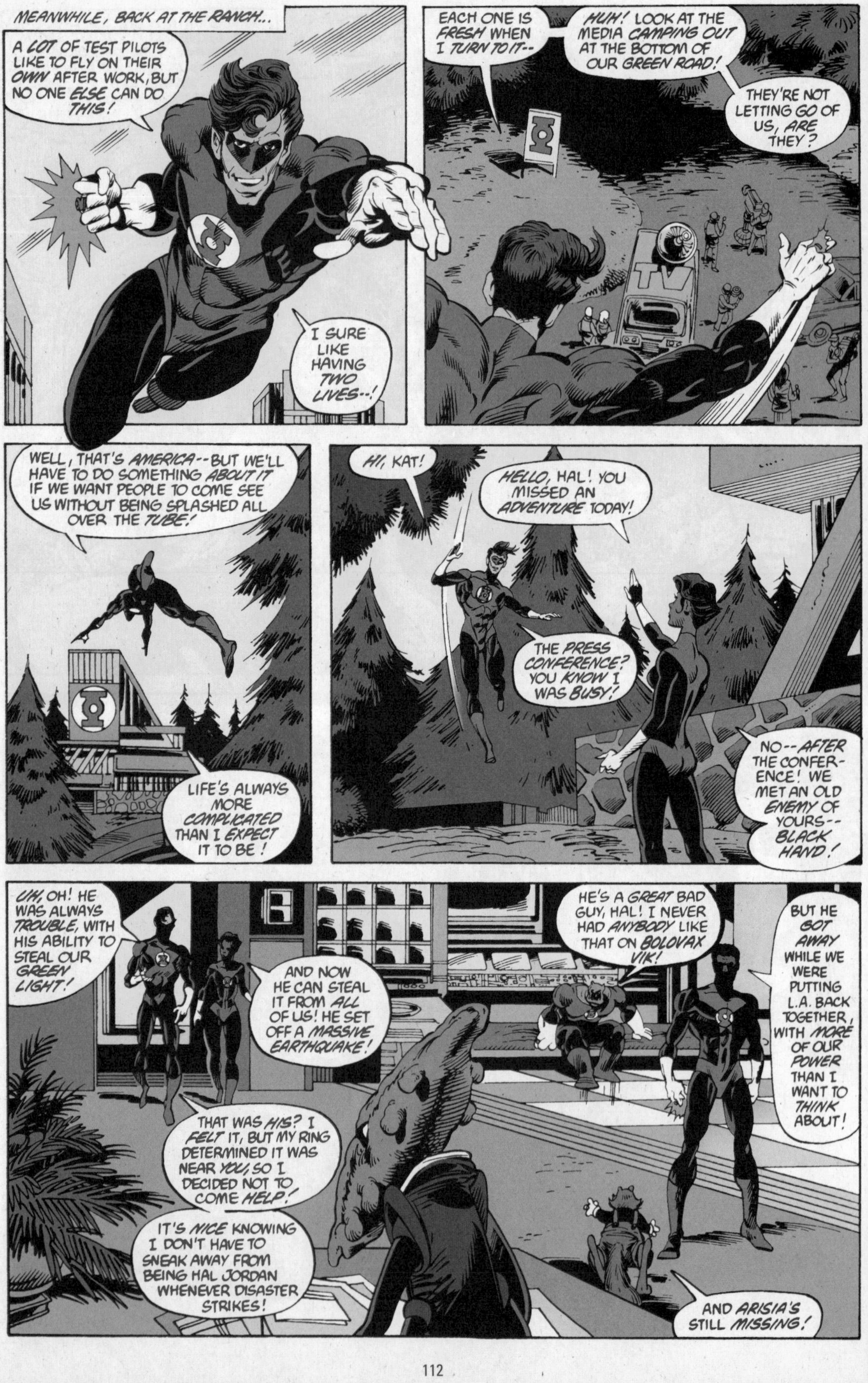
MEANWHILE, BACK AT THE RANCH...
A LOT OF TEST PILOTS LIKE TO FLY ON THEIR OWN AFTER WORK, BUT NO ONE ELSE CAN DO THIS!
I SURE LIKE HAVING TWO LIVES--!
EACH ONE IS FRESH WHEN I TURN TO IT--
HUH! LOOK AT THE MEDIA CAMPING OUT AT THE BOTTOM OF OUR GREEN ROAD!
THEY'RE NOT LETTING GO OF US, ARE THEY?
TV
WELL, THAT'S AMERICA--BUT WE'LL HAVE TO DO SOMETHING ABOUT IT IF WE WANT PEOPLE TO COME SEE US WITHOUT BEING SPLASHED ALL OVER THE TUBE!
LIFE'S ALWAYS MORE COMPLICATED THAN I EXPECT IT TO BE!
HI, KAT!
HELLO, HAL! YOU MISSED AN ADVENTURE TODAY!
THE PRESS CONFERENCE? YOU KNOW I WAS BUSY!
NO--AFTER THE CONFERENCE! WE MET AN OLD ENEMY OF YOURS--BLACK HAND!
UH, OH! HE WAS ALWAYS TROUBLE, WITH HIS ABILITY TO STEAL OUR GREEN LIGHT!
AND NOW HE CAN STEAL IT FROM ALL OF US! HE SET OFF A MASSIVE EARTHQUAKE!
HE'S A GREAT BAD GUY, HAL! I NEVER HAD ANYBODY LIKE THAT ON BOLOVAX VIK!
BUT HE GOT AWAY WHILE WE WERE PUTTING L.A. BACK TOGETHER, WITH MORE OF OUR POWER THAN I WANT TO THINK ABOUT!
THAT WAS HIS? I FELT IT, BUT MY RING DETERMINED IT WAS NEAR YOU, SO I DECIDED NOT TO COME HELP!
IT'S NICE KNOWING I DON'T HAVE TO SNEAK AWAY FROM BEING HAL JORDAN WHENEVER DISASTER STRIKES!
AND ARISIA'S STILL MISSING!

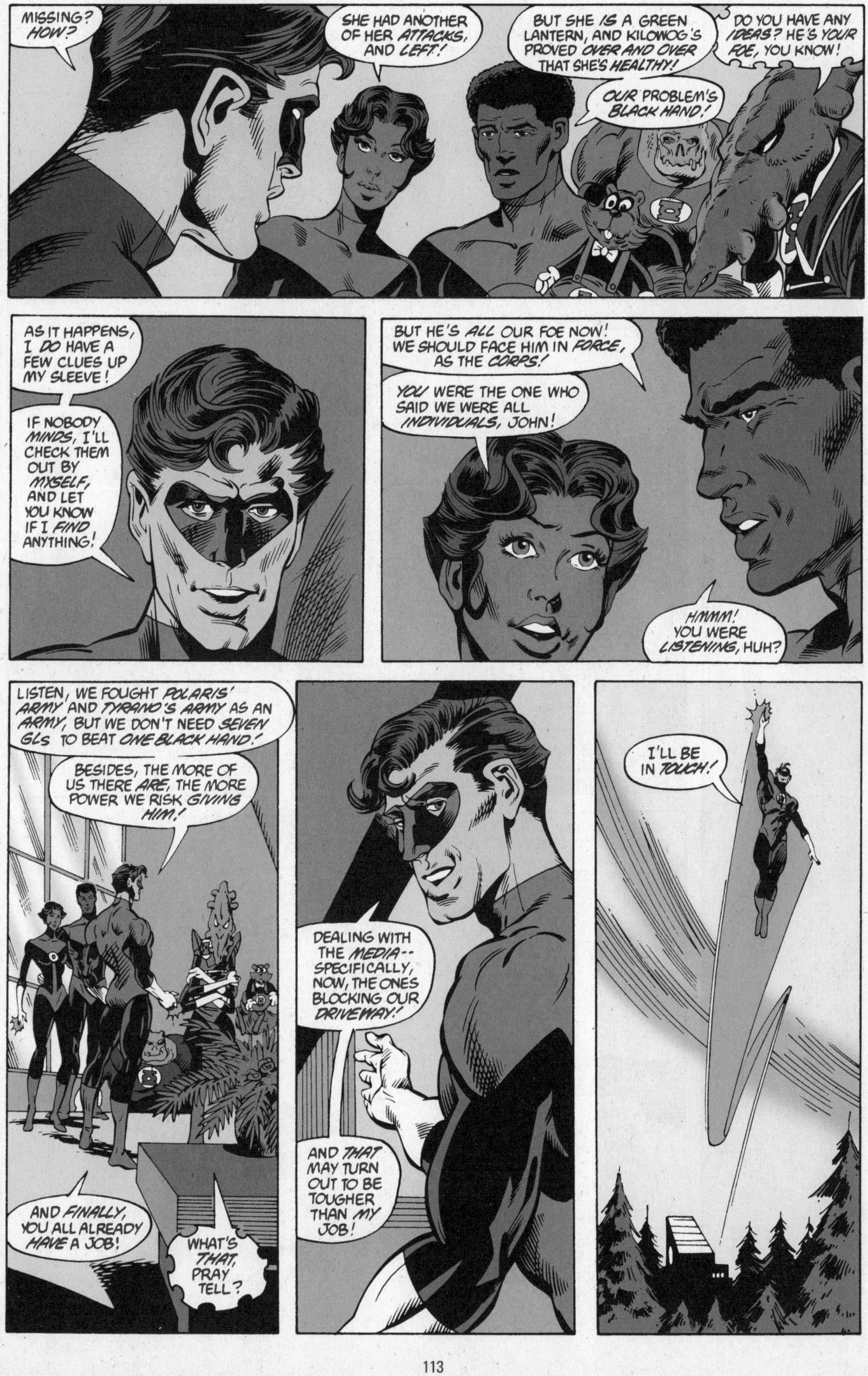

MISSING? HOW?
SHE HAD ANOTHER OF HER ATTACKS, AND LEFT!
BUT SHE IS A GREEN LANTERN, AND KILOWOG'S PROVED OVER AND OVER THAT SHE'S HEALTHY!
DO YOU HAVE ANY IDEAS? HE'S YOUR FOE, YOU KNOW!
OUR PROBLEM'S BLACK HAND!
AS IT HAPPENS, I DO HAVE A FEW CLUES UP MY SLEEVE!
IF NOBODY MINDS, I'LL CHECK THEM OUT BY MYSELF, AND LET YOU KNOW IF I FIND ANYTHING!
BUT HE'S ALL OUR FOE NOW! WE SHOULD FACE HIM IN FORCE, AS THE CORPS!
YOU WERE THE ONE WHO SAID WE WERE ALL INDIVIDUALS, JOHN!
HMMM! YOU WERE LISTENING, HUH?
LISTEN, WE FOUGHT POLARIS' ARMY AND TYRANO'S ARMY AS AN ARMY, BUT WE DON'T NEED SEVEN GLs TO BEAT ONE BLACK HAND!
BESIDES, THE MORE OF US THERE ARE, THE MORE POWER WE RISK GIVING HIM!
AND FINALLY, YOU ALL ALREADY HAVE A JOB!
WHAT'S THAT, PRAY TELL?
DEALING WITH THE MEDIA-- SPECIFICALLY, NOW, THE ONES BLOCKING OUR DRIVEWAY!
AND THAT MAY TURN OUT TO BE TOUGHER THAN MY JOB!
I'LL BE IN TOUCH!

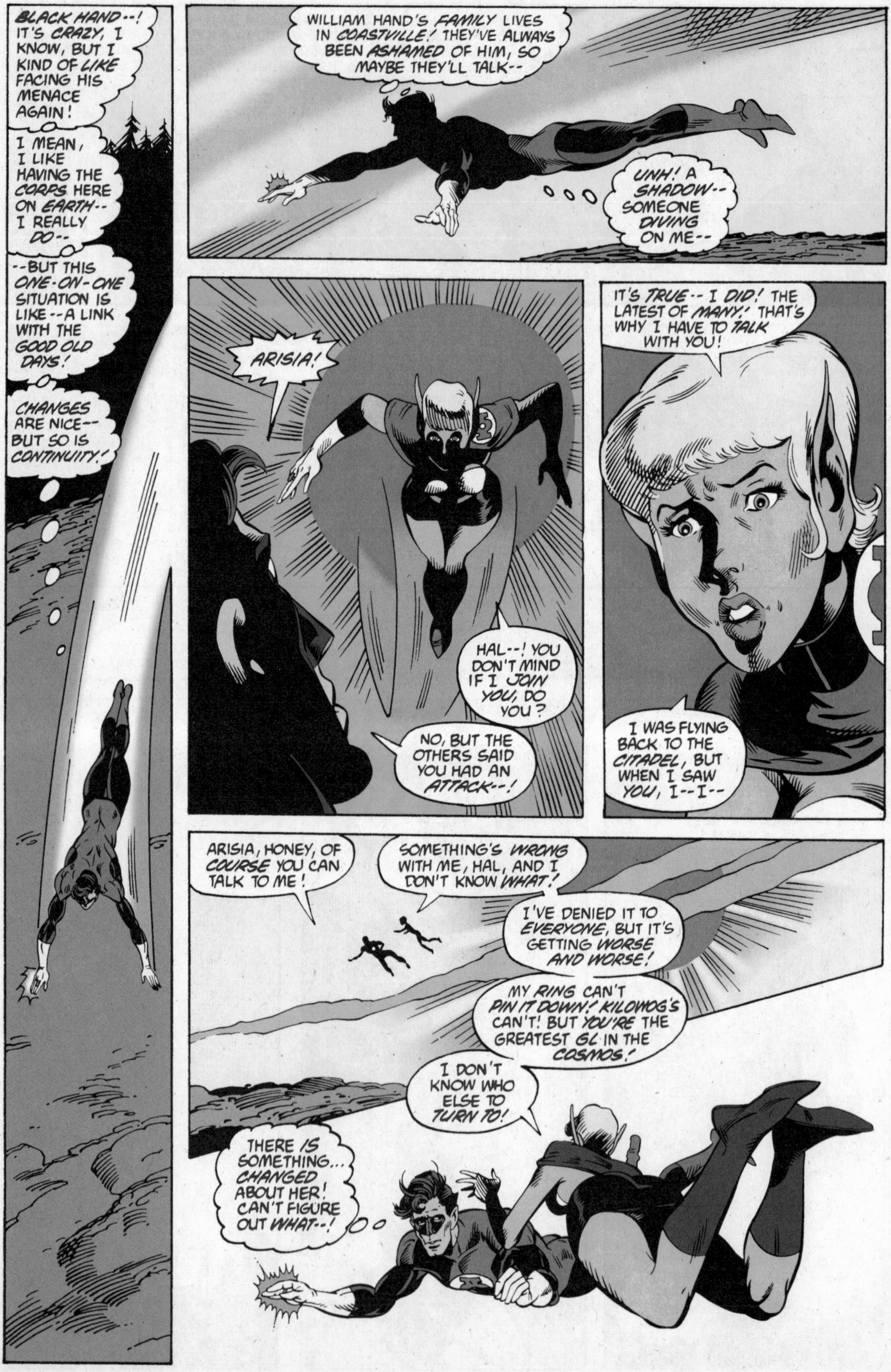
BLACK HAND--! IT'S CRAZY, I KNOW, BUT I KIND OF LIKE FACING HIS MENACE AGAIN!
I MEAN, I LIKE HAVING THE CORPS HERE ON EARTH-- I REALLY DO--
--BUT THIS ONE-ON-ONE SITUATION IS LIKE--A LINK WITH THE GOOD OLD DAYS!
CHANGES ARE NICE-- BUT SO IS CONTINUITY!
WILLIAM HAND'S FAMILY LIVES IN COASTVILLE! THEY'VE ALWAYS BEEN ASHAMED OF HIM, SO MAYBE THEY'LL TALK--
UNH! A SHADOW-- SOMEONE DIVING ON ME--
ARISIA!
HAL--! YOU DON'T MIND IF I JOIN YOU, DO YOU?
NO, BUT THE OTHERS SAID YOU HAD AN ATTACK--!
IT'S TRUE-- I DID! THE LATEST OF MANY! THAT'S WHY I HAVE TO TALK WITH YOU!
I WAS FLYING BACK TO THE CITADEL, BUT WHEN I SAW YOU, I--I--
ARISIA, HONEY, OF COURSE YOU CAN TALK TO ME!
SOMETHING'S WRONG WITH ME, HAL, AND I DON'T KNOW WHAT!
I'VE DENIED IT TO EVERYONE, BUT IT'S GETTING WORSE AND WORSE!
MY RING CAN'T PIN IT DOWN! KILOWOG'S CAN'T! BUT YOU'RE THE GREATEST GL IN THE COSMOS!
I DON'T KNOW WHO ELSE TO TURN TO!
THERE IS SOMETHING... CHANGED ABOUT HER! CAN'T FIGURE OUT WHAT--!

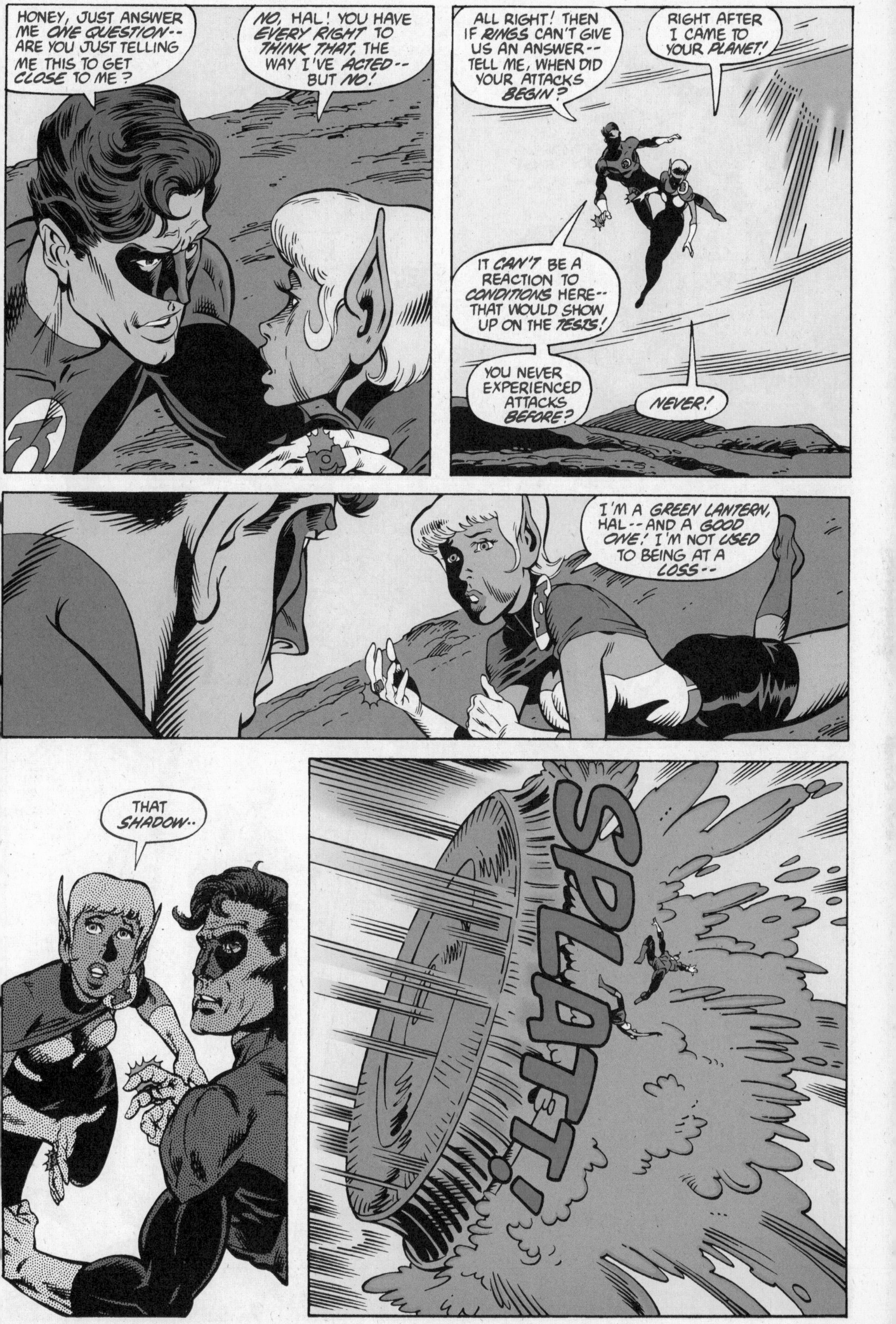

HONEY, JUST ANSWER ME ONE QUESTION-- ARE YOU JUST TELLING ME THIS TO GET CLOSE TO ME?
NO, HAL! YOU HAVE EVERY RIGHT TO THINK THAT, THE WAY I'VE ACTED-- BUT NO!
ALL RIGHT! THEN IF RINGS CAN'T GIVE US AN ANSWER-- TELL ME, WHEN DID YOUR ATTACKS BEGIN?
RIGHT AFTER I CAME TO YOUR PLANET!
IT CAN'T BE A REACTION TO CONDITIONS HERE-- THAT WOULD SHOW UP ON THE TESTS!
YOU NEVER EXPERIENCED ATTACKS BEFORE?
NEVER!
I'M A GREEN LANTERN, HAL--AND A GOOD ONE! I'M NOT USED TO BEING AT A LOSS--
THAT SHADOW..
SPLATT!

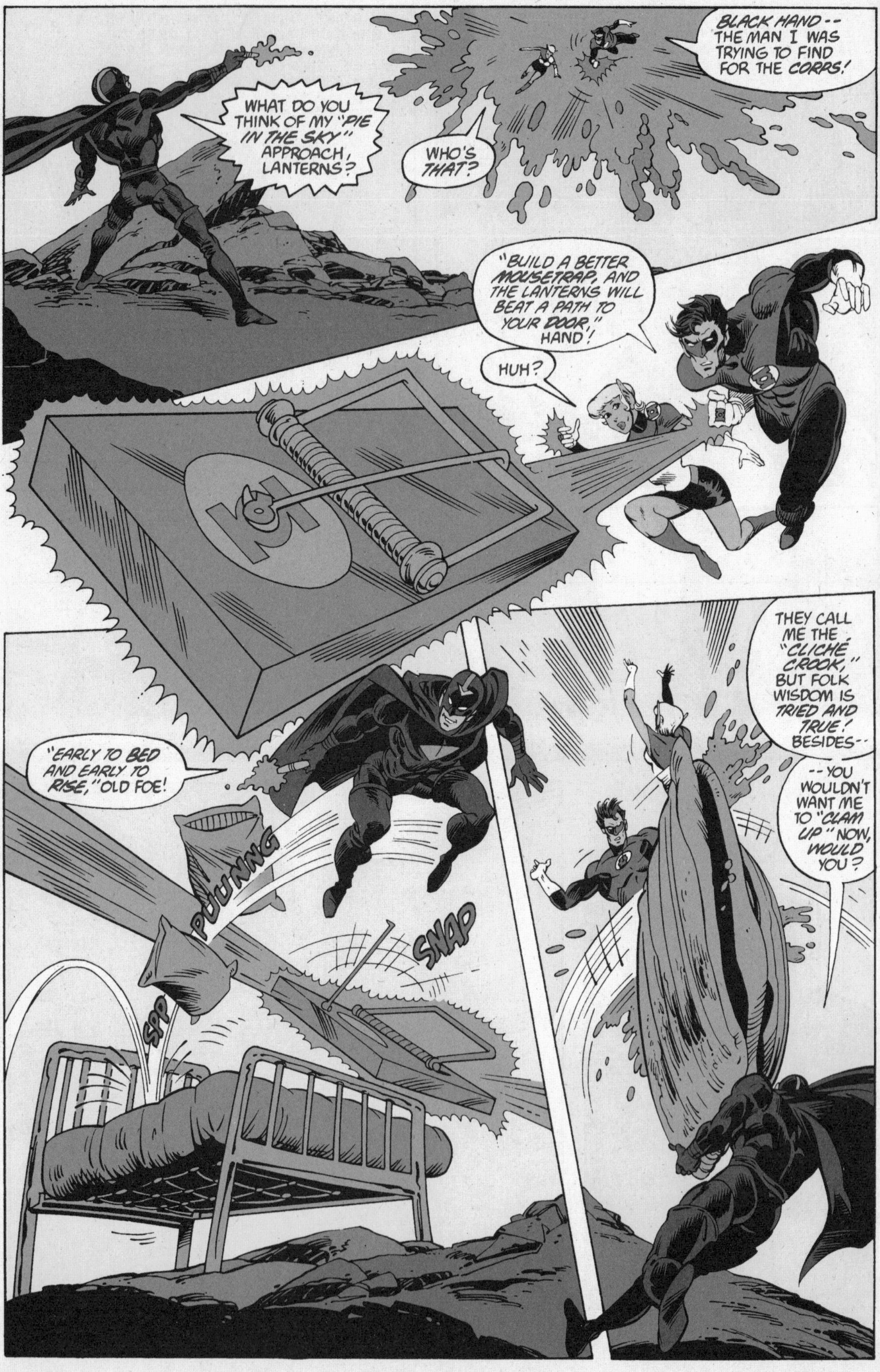
WHAT DO YOU THINK OF MY "PIE IN THE SKY" APPROACH, LANTERNS?
WHO'S THAT?
BLACK HAND -- THE MAN I WAS TRYING TO FIND FOR THE CORPS!
"BUILD A BETTER MOUSETRAP, AND THE LANTERNS WILL BEAT A PATH TO YOUR DOOR," HAND!
HUH?
"EARLY TO BED AND EARLY TO RISE," OLD FOE!
PUUNNG
SNAP
SPP
THEY CALL ME THE "CLICHE CROOK," BUT FOLK WISDOM IS TRIED AND TRUE! BESIDES--
--YOU WOULDN'T WANT ME TO "CLAM UP" NOW, WOULD YOU?

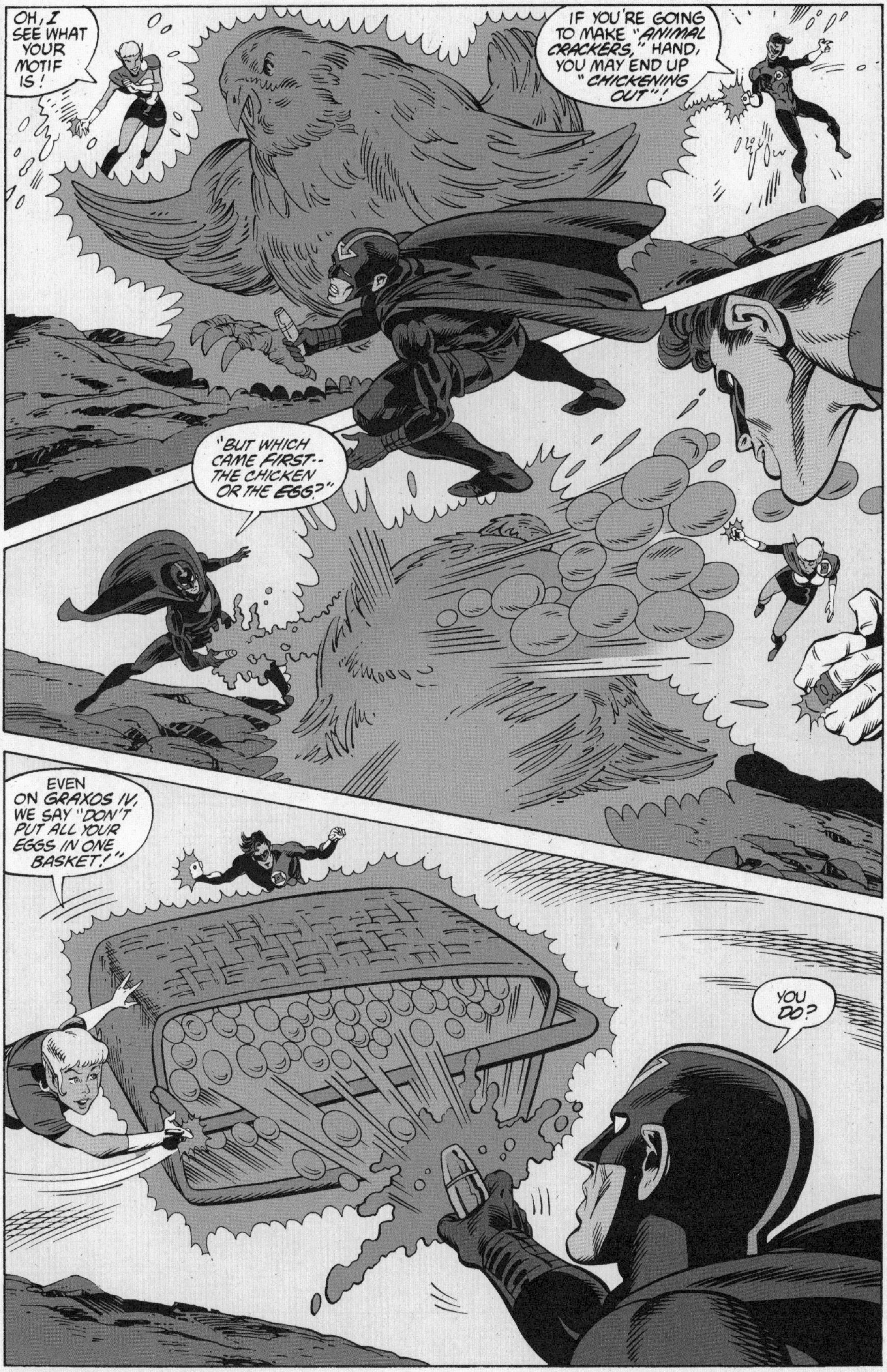
OH, I SEE WHAT YOUR MOTIF IS!
IF YOU'RE GOING TO MAKE "ANIMAL CRACKERS," HAND, YOU MAY END UP "CHICKENING OUT"!
"BUT WHICH CAME FIRST-- THE CHICKEN OR THE EGG?"
EVEN ON GRAXOS IV, WE SAY "DON'T PUT ALL YOUR EGGS IN ONE BASKET!"
YOU DO?

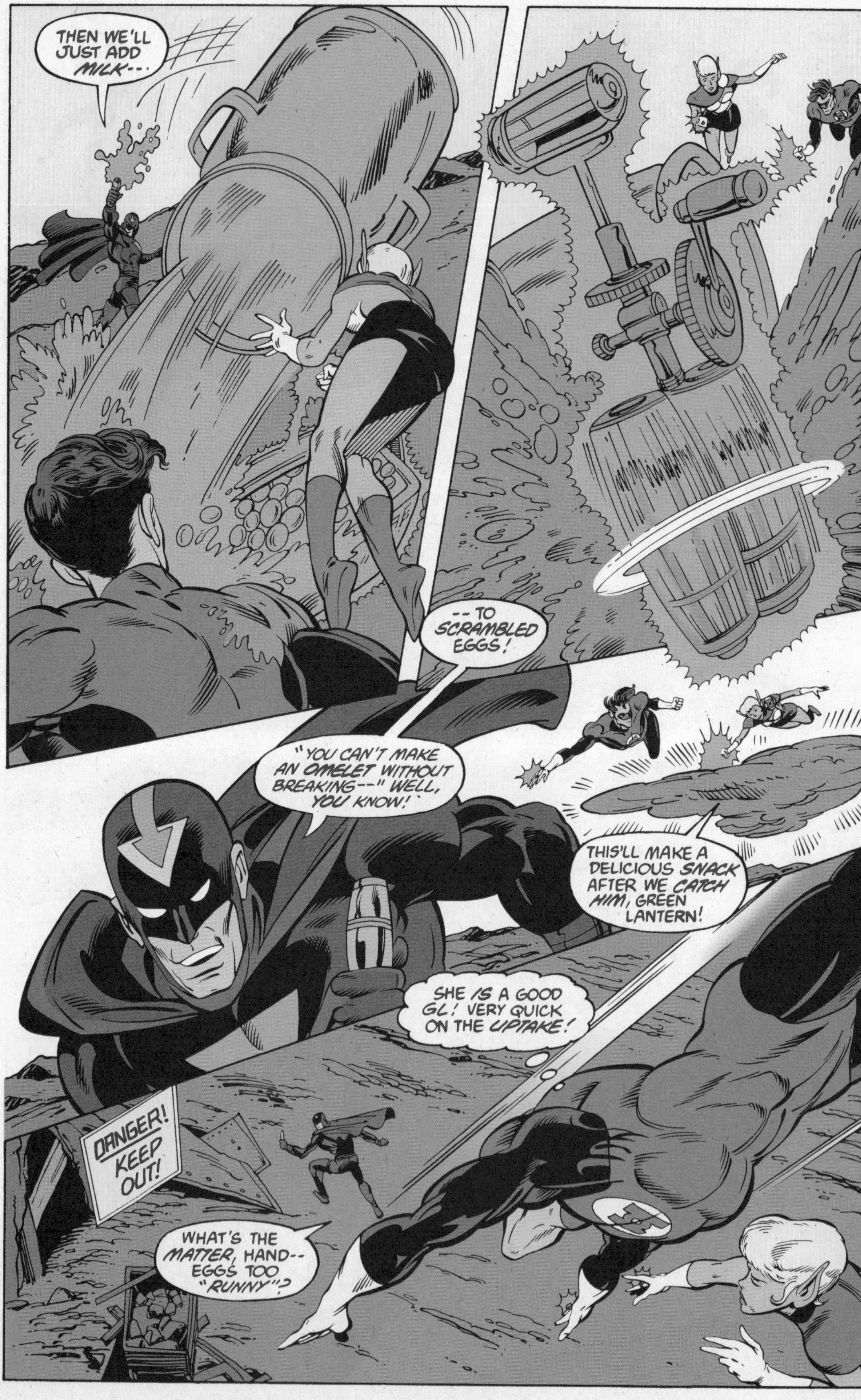
THEN WE'LL JUST ADD MILK--
--TO SCRAMBLED EGGS!
"YOU CAN'T MAKE AN OMELET WITHOUT BREAKING--" WELL, YOU KNOW!
THIS'LL MAKE A DELICIOUS SNACK AFTER WE CATCH HIM, GREEN LANTERN!
SHE IS A GOOD GL! VERY QUICK ON THE UPTAKE!
DANGER! KEEP OUT!
WHAT'S THE MATTER, HAND-- EGGS TOO "RUNNY"?

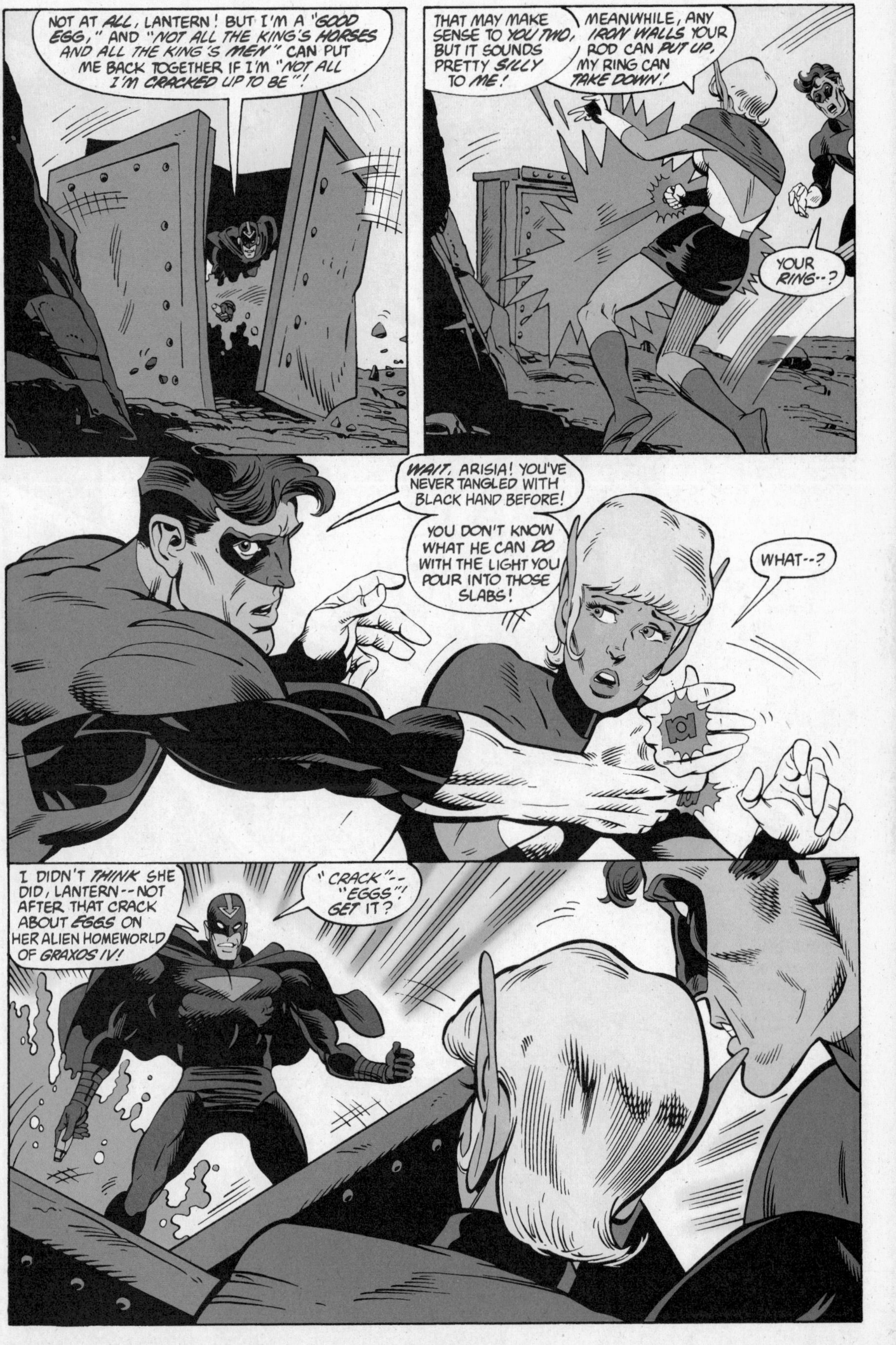
NOT AT ALL, LANTERN! BUT I'M A "GOOD EGG," AND "NOT ALL THE KING'S HORSES AND ALL THE KING'S MEN" CAN PUT ME BACK TOGETHER IF I'M "NOT ALL I'M CRACKED UP TO BE"!
THAT MAY MAKE SENSE TO YOU TWO, BUT IT SOUNDS PRETTY SILLY TO ME!
MEANWHILE, ANY IRON WALLS YOUR ROD CAN PUT UP, MY RING CAN TAKE DOWN!
YOUR RING--?
WAIT, ARISIA! YOU'VE NEVER TANGLED WITH BLACK HAND BEFORE!
YOU DON'T KNOW WHAT HE CAN DO WITH THE LIGHT YOU POUR INTO THOSE SLABS!
WHAT--?
I DIDN'T THINK SHE DID, LANTERN--NOT AFTER THAT CRACK ABOUT EGGS ON HER ALIEN HOMEWORLD OF GRAXOS IV!
"CRACK"--"EGGS"! GET IT?

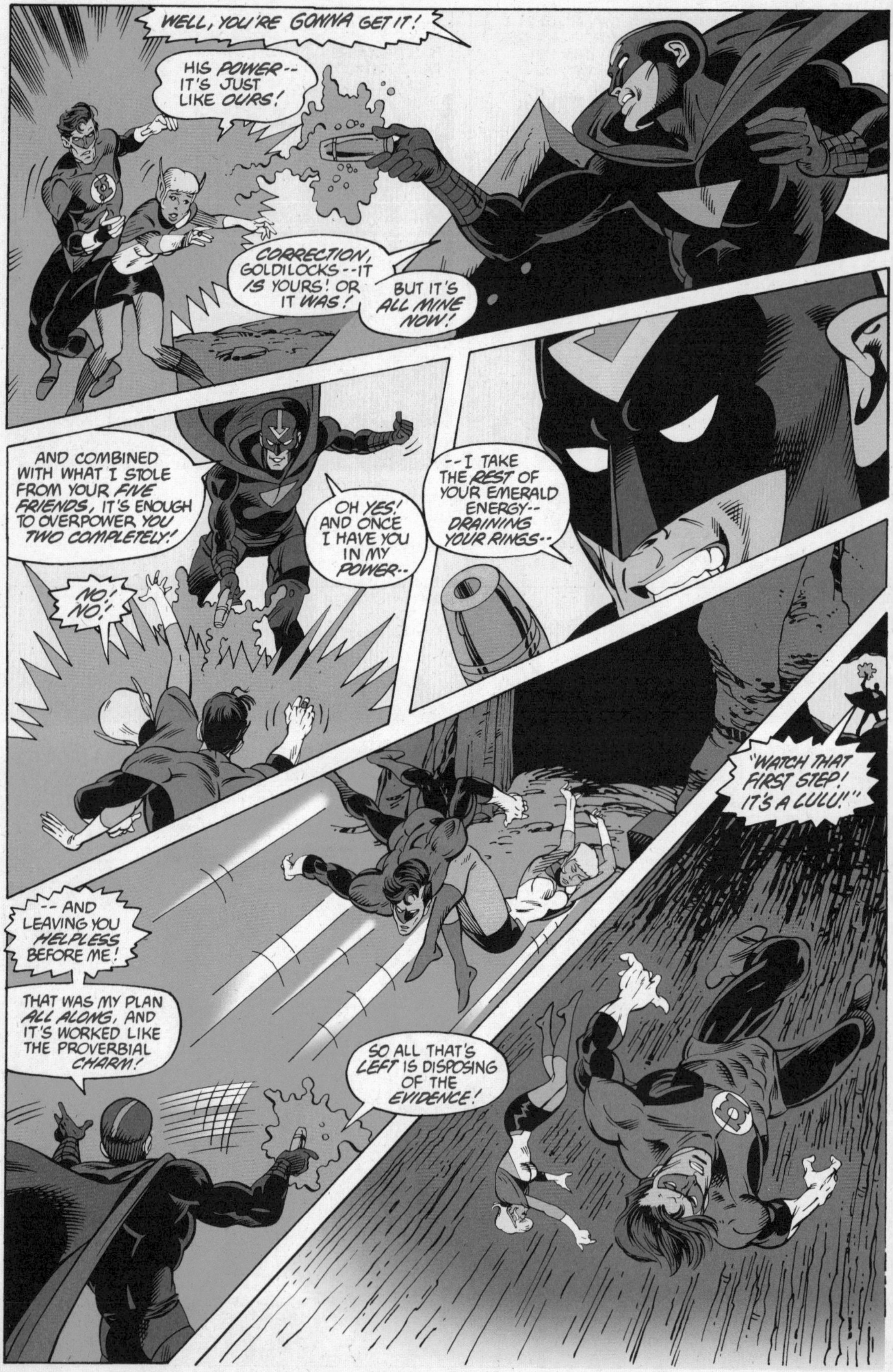
WELL, YOU'RE GONNA GET IT!
HIS POWER-- IT'S JUST LIKE OURS!
CORRECTION, GOLDILOCKS--IT IS YOURS! OR IT WAS!
BUT IT'S ALL MINE NOW!
AND COMBINED WITH WHAT I STOLE FROM YOUR FIVE FRIENDS, IT'S ENOUGH TO OVERPOWER YOU TWO COMPLETELY!
OH YES! AND ONCE I HAVE YOU IN MY POWER--
--I TAKE THE REST OF YOUR EMERALD ENERGY-- DRAINING YOUR RINGS--
NO! NO!
--AND LEAVING YOU HELPLESS BEFORE ME!
THAT WAS MY PLAN ALL ALONG, AND IT'S WORKED LIKE THE PROVERBIAL CHARM!
SO ALL THAT'S LEFT IS DISPOSING OF THE EVIDENCE!
"WATCH THAT FIRST STEP! IT'S A LULU!"

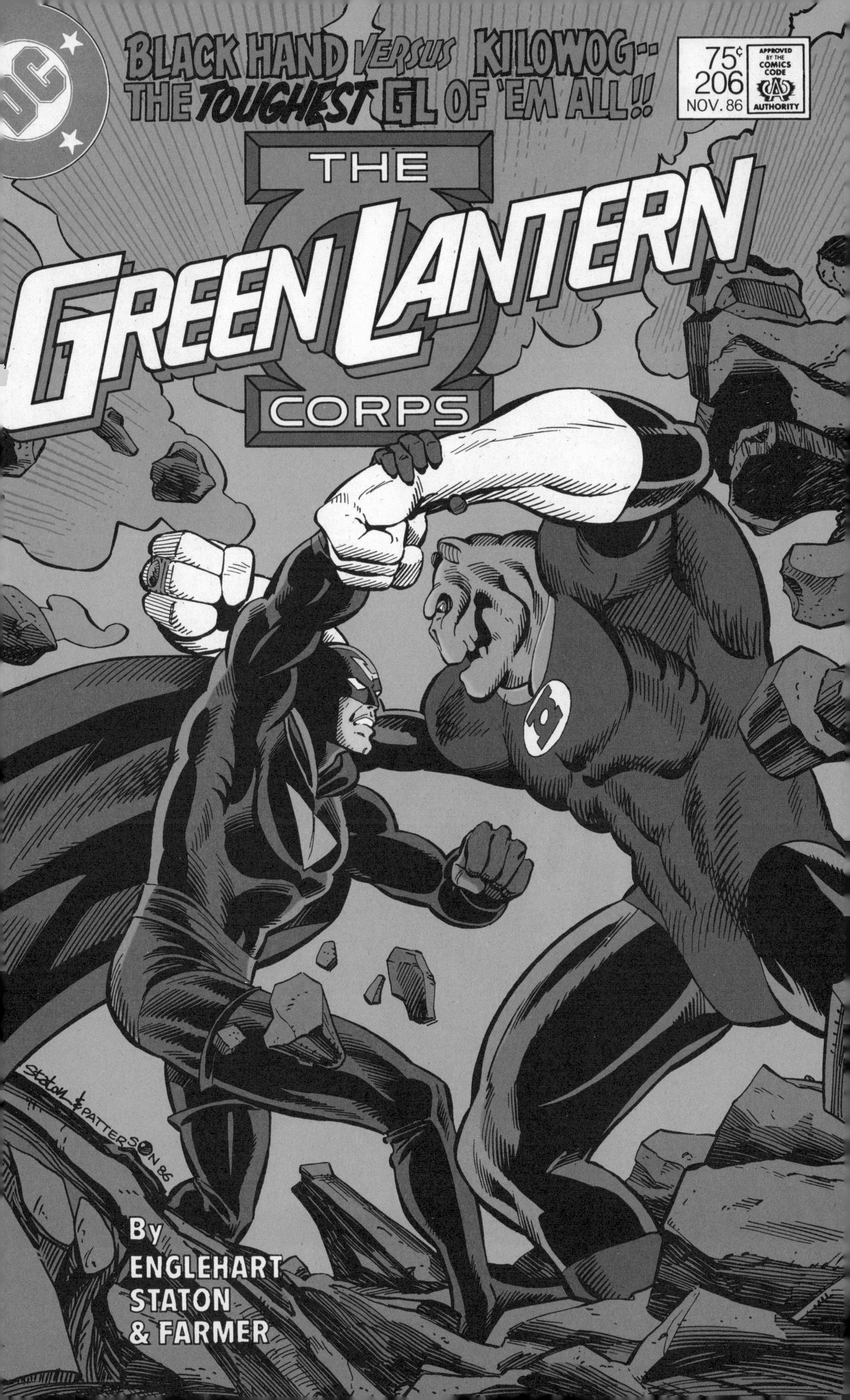

BLACK HAND VERSUS KILOWOG--
THE TOUGHEST GL OF 'EM ALL!!
75¢
206
NOV. 86
APPROVED BY THE COMICS CODE AUTHORITY
THE GREEN LANTERN CORPS
STATON & PATTERSON 86
By
ENGLEHART
STATON
& FARMER

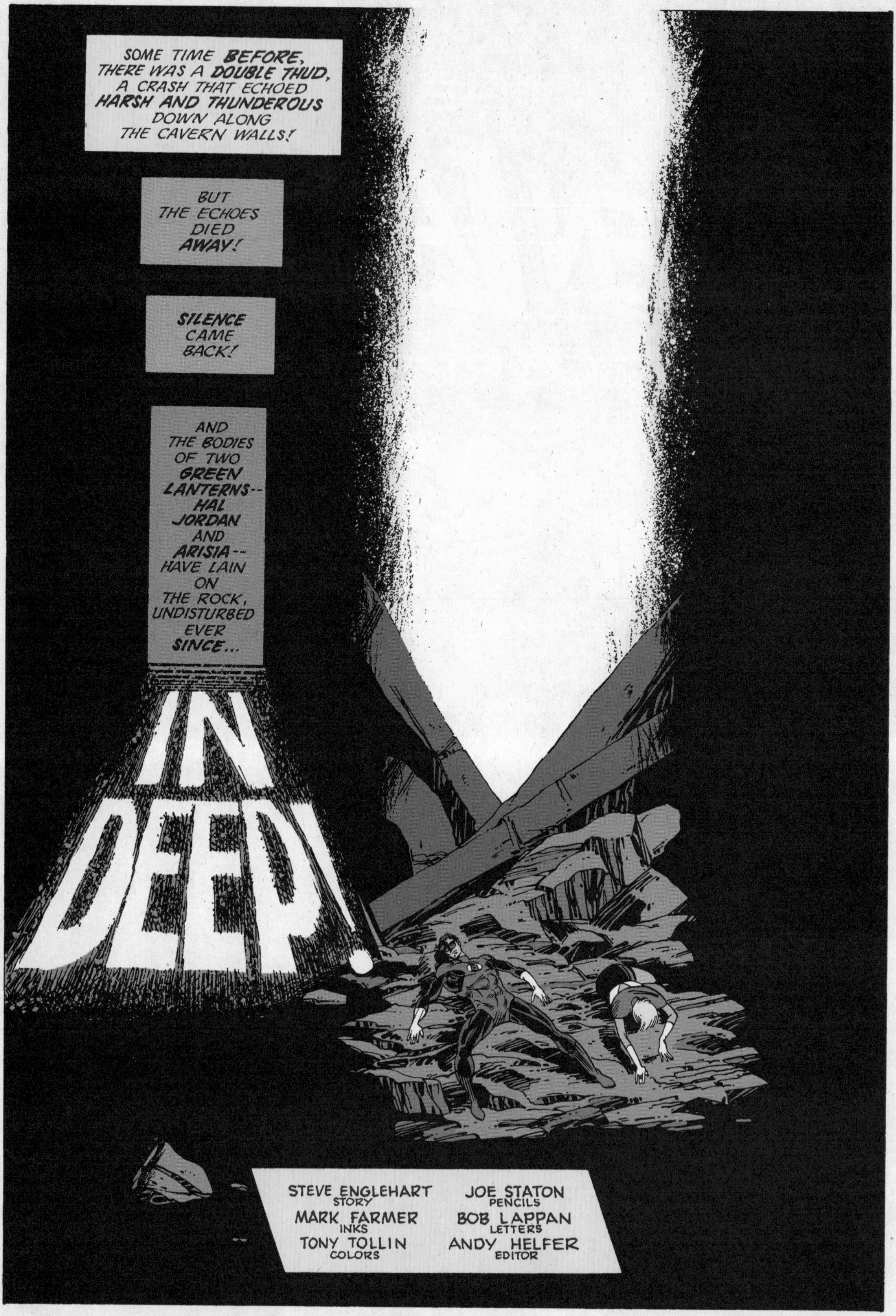

SOME TIME BEFORE, THERE WAS A DOUBLE THUD, A CRASH THAT ECHOED HARSH AND THUNDEROUS DOWN ALONG THE CAVERN WALLS!
BUT THE ECHOES DIED AWAY!
SILENCE CAME BACK!
AND THE BODIES OF TWO GREEN LANTERNS-- HAL JORDAN AND ARISIA-- HAVE LAIN ON THE ROCK, UNDISTURBED EVER SINCE...
IN DEEP!
STEVE ENGLEHART STORY
JOE STATON PENCILS
MARK FARMER INKS
BOB LAPPAN LETTERS
TONY TOLLIN COLORS
ANDY HELFER EDITOR

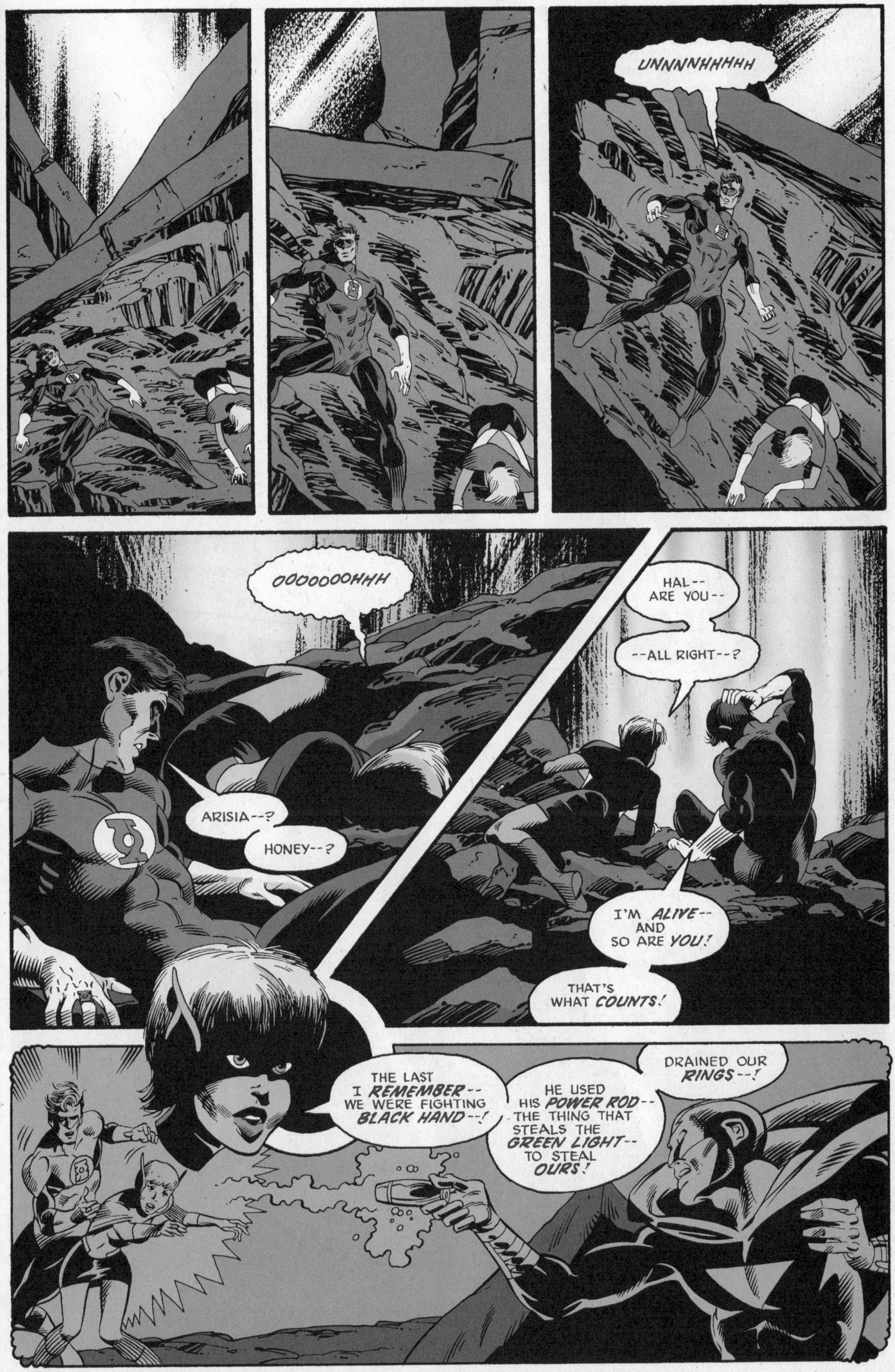
UNNNNHHHHH
OOOOOOOHHH
ARISIA--?
HONEY--?
HAL--
ARE YOU--
--ALL RIGHT--?
I'M ALIVE--
AND
SO ARE YOU!
THAT'S
WHAT COUNTS!
THE LAST
I REMEMBER--
WE WERE FIGHTING
BLACK HAND--!
HE USED
HIS POWER ROD--
THE THING THAT
STEALS THE
GREEN LIGHT--
TO STEAL
OURS!
DRAINED OUR
RINGS--!

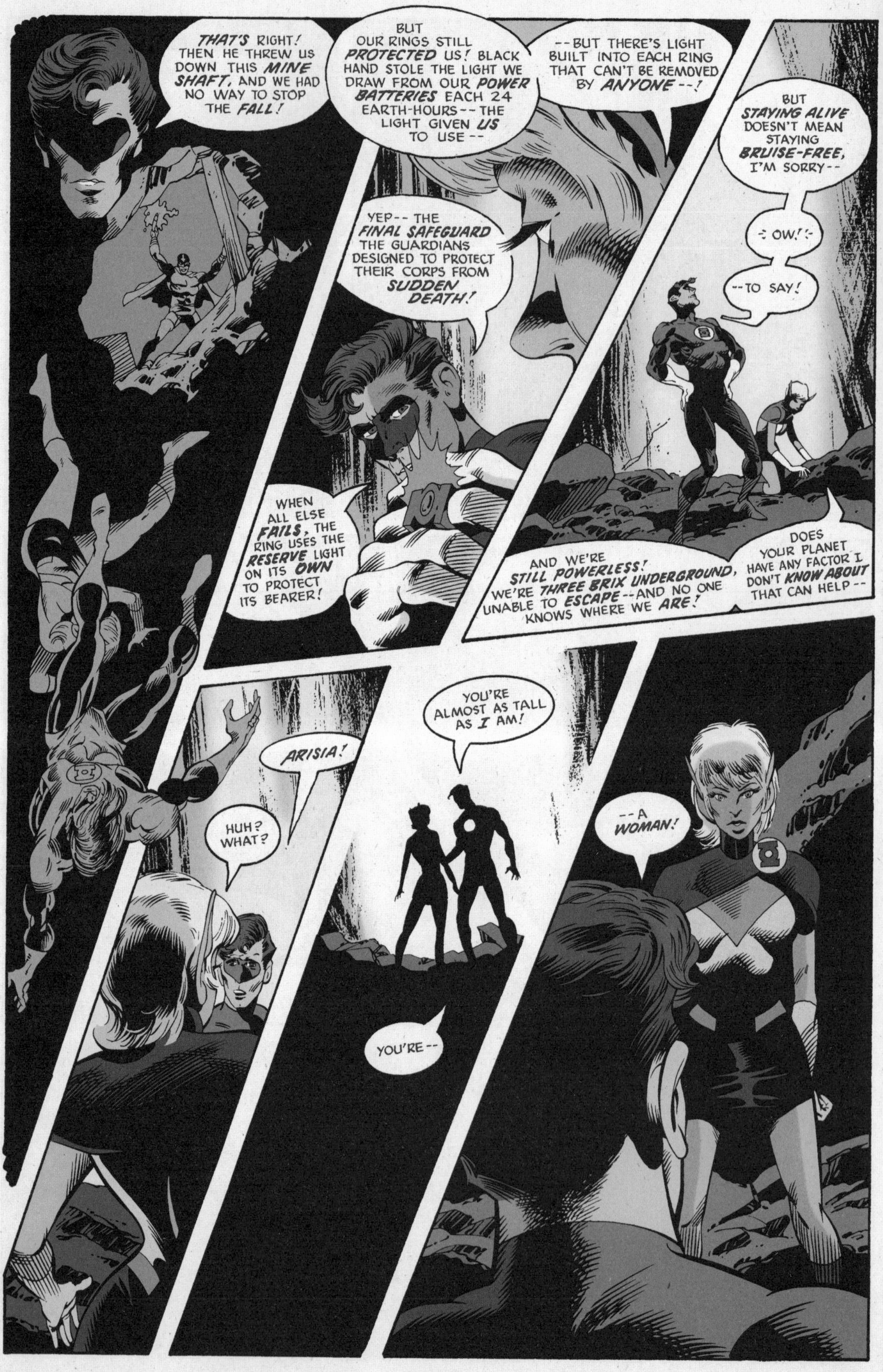
THAT'S RIGHT! THEN HE THREW US DOWN THIS MINE SHAFT, AND WE HAD NO WAY TO STOP THE FALL!
BUT OUR RINGS STILL PROTECTED US! BLACK HAND STOLE THE LIGHT WE DRAW FROM OUR POWER BATTERIES EACH 24 EARTH-HOURS -- THE LIGHT GIVEN US TO USE --
--BUT THERE'S LIGHT BUILT INTO EACH RING THAT CAN'T BE REMOVED BY ANYONE --!
YEP -- THE FINAL SAFEGUARD THE GUARDIANS DESIGNED TO PROTECT THEIR CORPS FROM SUDDEN DEATH!
WHEN ALL ELSE FAILS, THE RING USES THE RESERVE LIGHT ON ITS OWN TO PROTECT ITS BEARER!
BUT STAYING ALIVE DOESN'T MEAN STAYING BRUISE-FREE, I'M SORRY --
OW!
-- TO SAY!
AND WE'RE STILL POWERLESS! WE'RE THREE BRIX UNDERGROUND, UNABLE TO ESCAPE -- AND NO ONE KNOWS WHERE WE ARE!
DOES YOUR PLANET HAVE ANY FACTOR I DON'T KNOW ABOUT THAT CAN HELP --
ARISIA!
HUH? WHAT?
YOU'RE ALMOST AS TALL AS I AM!
YOU'RE --
-- A WOMAN!

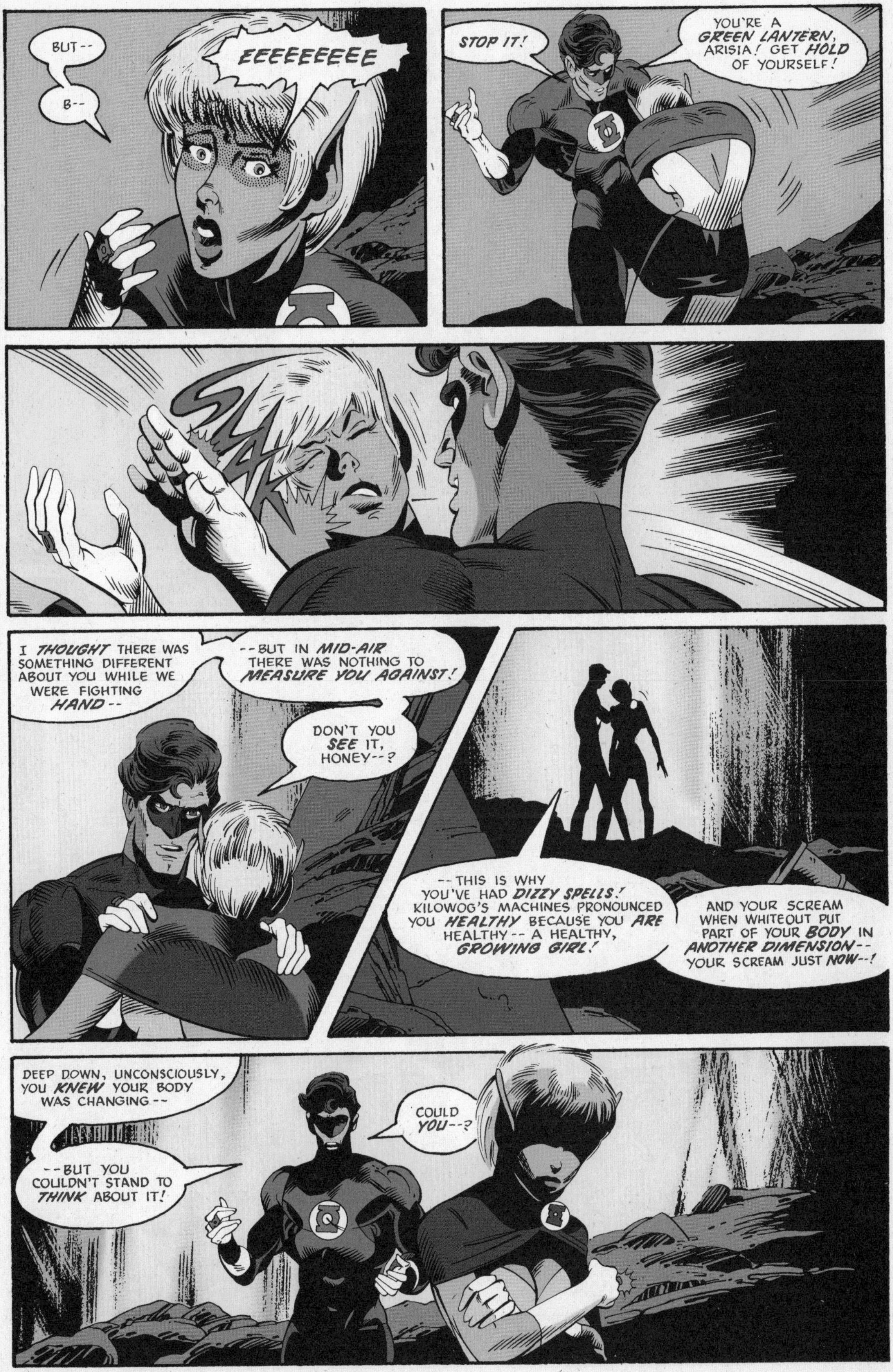
BUT--
B--
EEEEEEEEE
STOP IT!
YOU'RE A GREEN LANTERN, ARISIA! GET HOLD OF YOURSELF!
SMAK
I THOUGHT THERE WAS SOMETHING DIFFERENT ABOUT YOU WHILE WE WERE FIGHTING HAND--
--BUT IN MID-AIR THERE WAS NOTHING TO MEASURE YOU AGAINST!
DON'T YOU SEE IT, HONEY--?
--THIS IS WHY YOU'VE HAD DIZZY SPELLS! KILOWOG'S MACHINES PRONOUNCED YOU HEALTHY BECAUSE YOU ARE HEALTHY-- A HEALTHY, GROWING GIRL!
AND YOUR SCREAM WHEN WHITEOUT PUT PART OF YOUR BODY IN ANOTHER DIMENSION-- YOUR SCREAM JUST NOW--!
DEEP DOWN, UNCONSCIOUSLY, YOU KNEW YOUR BODY WAS CHANGING--
--BUT YOU COULDN'T STAND TO THINK ABOUT IT!
COULD YOU--?

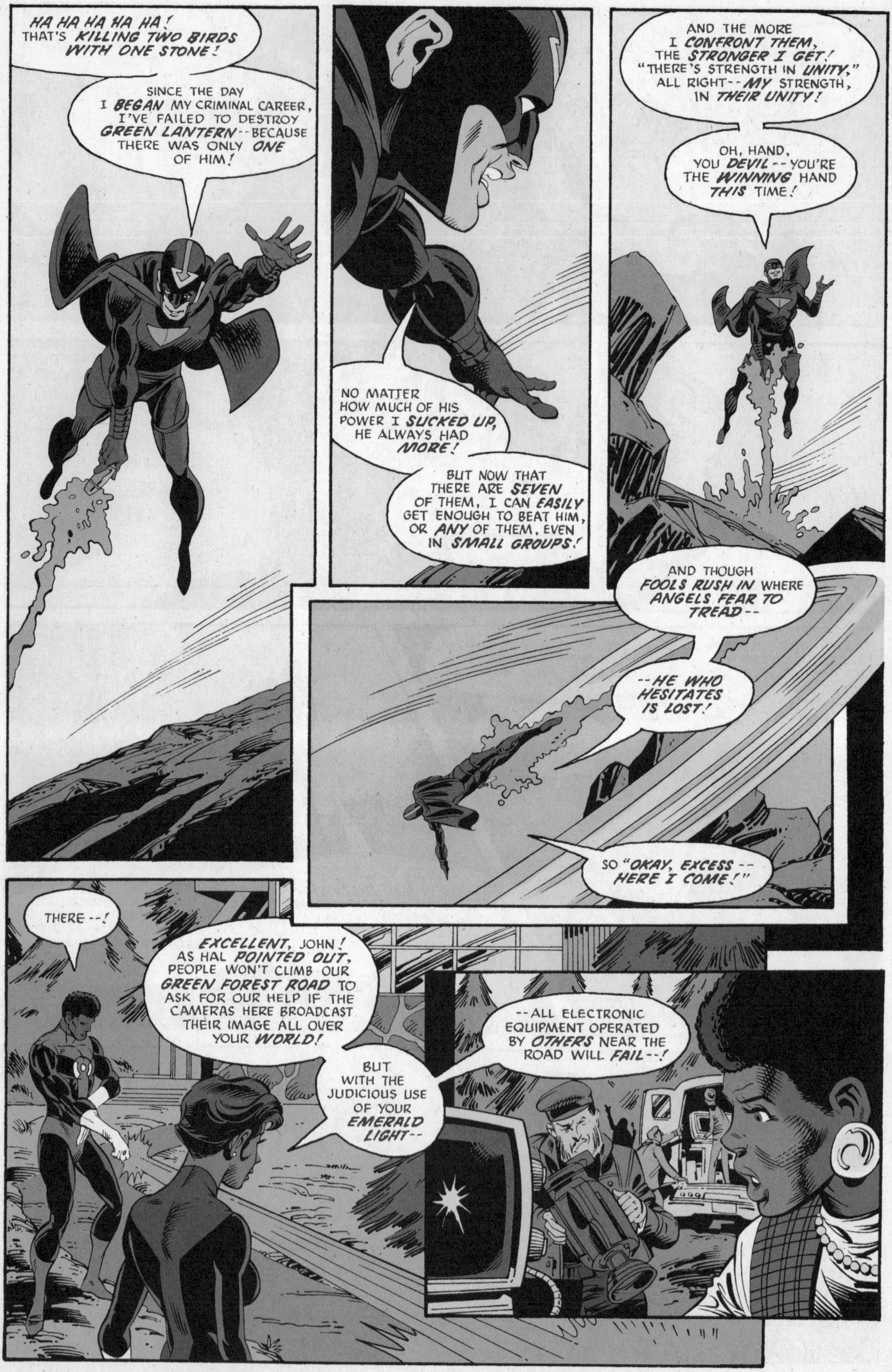
HA HA HA HA HA! THAT'S KILLING TWO BIRDS WITH ONE STONE!
SINCE THE DAY I BEGAN MY CRIMINAL CAREER, I'VE FAILED TO DESTROY GREEN LANTERN--BECAUSE THERE WAS ONLY ONE OF HIM!
NO MATTER HOW MUCH OF HIS POWER I SUCKED UP, HE ALWAYS HAD MORE!
BUT NOW THAT THERE ARE SEVEN OF THEM, I CAN EASILY GET ENOUGH TO BEAT HIM, OR ANY OF THEM, EVEN IN SMALL GROUPS!
AND THE MORE I CONFRONT THEM, THE STRONGER I GET! "THERE'S STRENGTH IN UNITY," ALL RIGHT--MY STRENGTH, IN THEIR UNITY!
OH, HAND, YOU DEVIL--YOU'RE THE WINNING HAND THIS TIME!
AND THOUGH FOOLS RUSH IN WHERE ANGELS FEAR TO TREAD--
--HE WHO HESITATES IS LOST!
SO "OKAY, EXCESS--HERE I COME!"
THERE--!
EXCELLENT, JOHN! AS HAL POINTED OUT, PEOPLE WON'T CLIMB OUR GREEN FOREST ROAD TO ASK FOR OUR HELP IF THE CAMERAS HERE BROADCAST THEIR IMAGE ALL OVER YOUR WORLD!
BUT WITH THE JUDICIOUS USE OF YOUR EMERALD LIGHT--
--ALL ELECTRONIC EQUIPMENT OPERATED BY OTHERS NEAR THE ROAD WILL FAIL--!

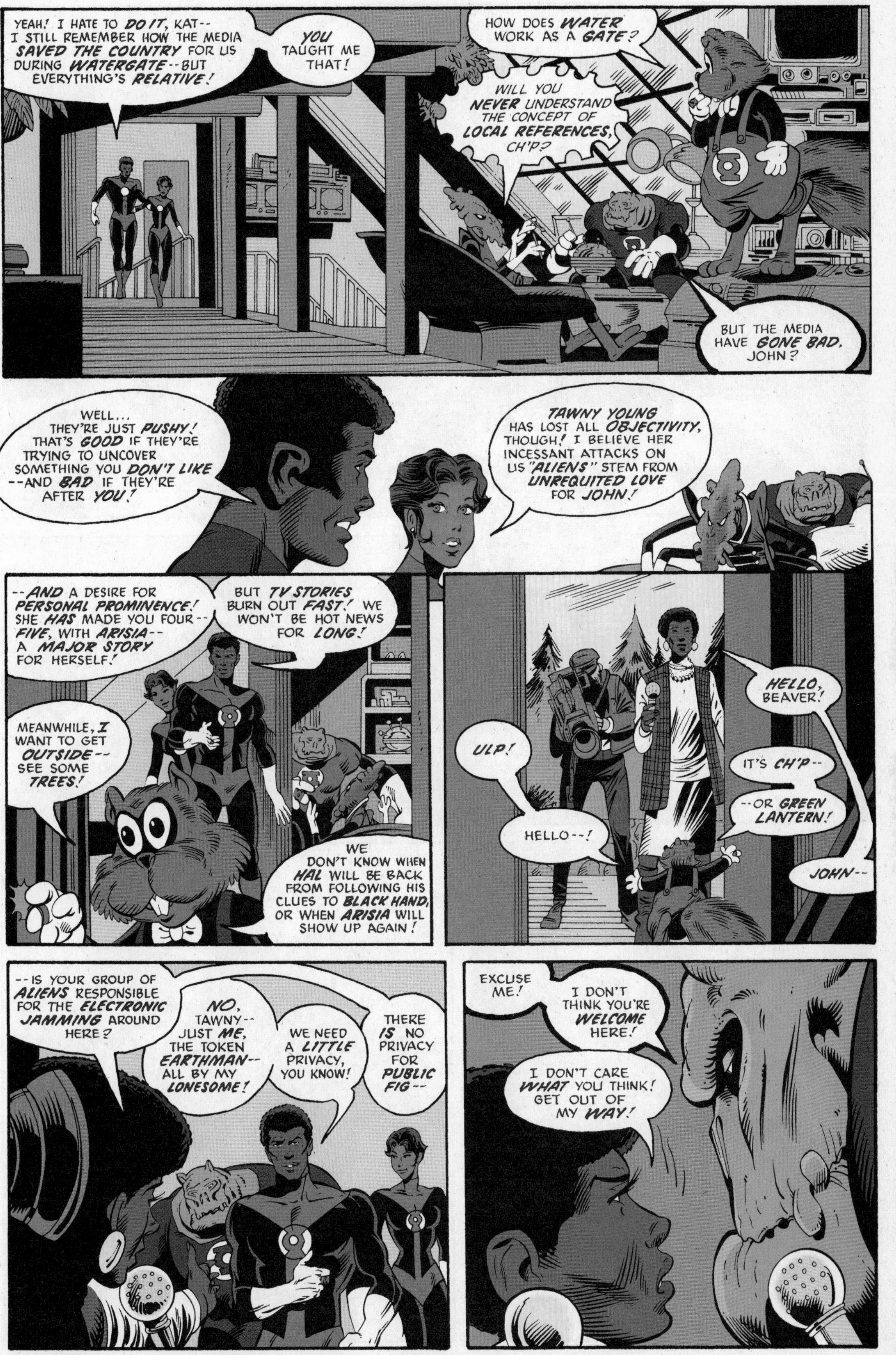
YEAH! I HATE TO DO IT, KAT-- I STILL REMEMBER HOW THE MEDIA SAVED THE COUNTRY FOR US DURING WATERGATE--BUT EVERYTHING'S RELATIVE!
YOU TAUGHT ME THAT!
HOW DOES WATER WORK AS A GATE?
WILL YOU NEVER UNDERSTAND THE CONCEPT OF LOCAL REFERENCES, CH'P?
BUT THE MEDIA HAVE GONE BAD, JOHN?
WELL... THEY'RE JUST PUSHY! THAT'S GOOD IF THEY'RE TRYING TO UNCOVER SOMETHING YOU DON'T LIKE --AND BAD IF THEY'RE AFTER YOU!
TAWNY YOUNG HAS LOST ALL OBJECTIVITY, THOUGH! I BELIEVE HER INCESSANT ATTACKS ON US "ALIENS" STEM FROM UNREQUITED LOVE FOR JOHN!
--AND A DESIRE FOR PERSONAL PROMINENCE! SHE HAS MADE YOU FOUR-- FIVE, WITH ARISIA-- A MAJOR STORY FOR HERSELF!
BUT TV STORIES BURN OUT FAST! WE WON'T BE HOT NEWS FOR LONG!
MEANWHILE, I WANT TO GET OUTSIDE-- SEE SOME TREES!
WE DON'T KNOW WHEN HAL WILL BE BACK FROM FOLLOWING HIS CLUES TO BLACK HAND, OR WHEN ARISIA WILL SHOW UP AGAIN!
HELLO, BEAVER!
ULP!
IT'S CH'P--
--OR GREEN LANTERN!
HELLO--!
JOHN--
--IS YOUR GROUP OF ALIENS RESPONSIBLE FOR THE ELECTRONIC JAMMING AROUND HERE?
NO, TAWNY-- JUST ME, THE TOKEN EARTHMAN-- ALL BY MY LONESOME!
WE NEED A LITTLE PRIVACY, YOU KNOW!
THERE IS NO PRIVACY FOR PUBLIC FIG--
EXCUSE ME!
I DON'T THINK YOU'RE WELCOME HERE!
I DON'T CARE WHAT YOU THINK! GET OUT OF MY WAY!

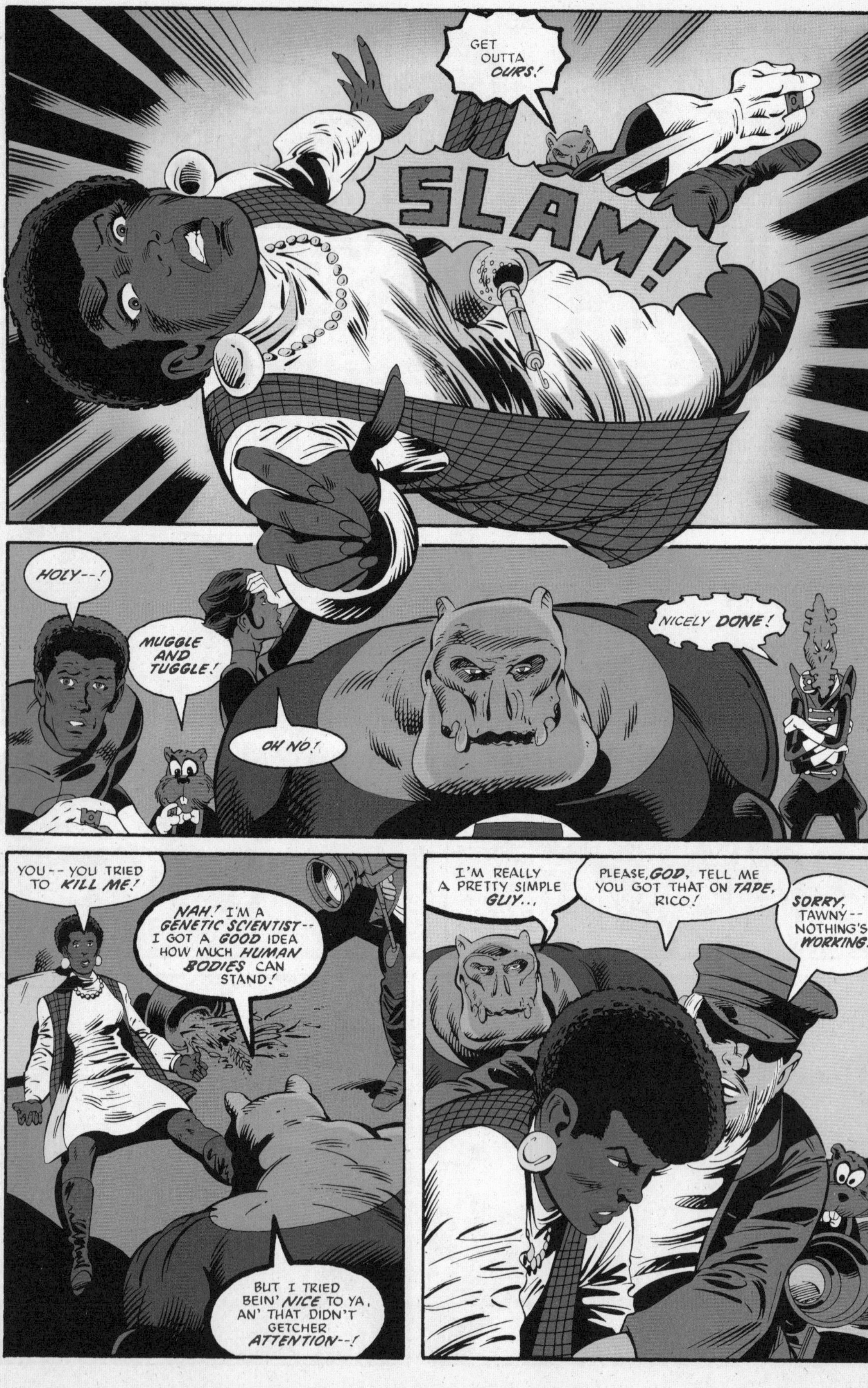
GET OUTTA OURS!
SLAM!
HOLY--!
MUGGLE AND TUGGLE!
OH NO!
NICELY DONE!
YOU--YOU TRIED TO KILL ME!
NAH! I'M A GENETIC SCIENTIST--I GOT A GOOD IDEA HOW MUCH HUMAN BODIES CAN STAND!
BUT I TRIED BEIN' NICE TO YA, AN' THAT DIDN'T GETCHER ATTENTION--!
I'M REALLY A PRETTY SIMPLE GUY...
PLEASE, GOD, TELL ME YOU GOT THAT ON TAPE, RICO!
SORRY, TAWNY--NOTHING'S WORKING!

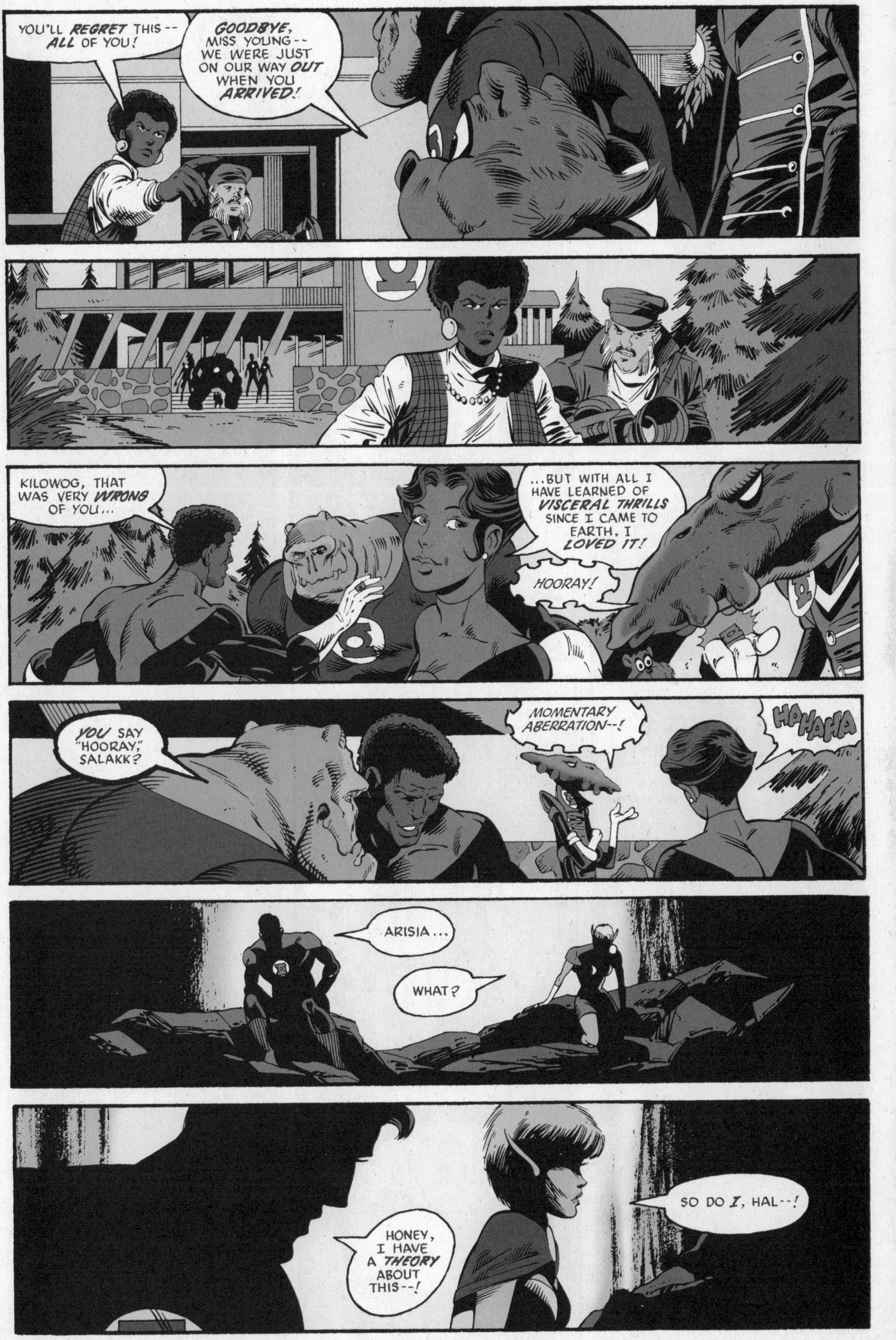
YOU'LL REGRET THIS -- ALL OF YOU!
GOODBYE, MISS YOUNG -- WE WERE JUST ON OUR WAY OUT WHEN YOU ARRIVED!
KILOWOG, THAT WAS VERY WRONG OF YOU...
...BUT WITH ALL I HAVE LEARNED OF VISCERAL THRILLS SINCE I CAME TO EARTH, I LOVED IT!
HOORAY!
YOU SAY "HOORAY," SALAKK?
MOMENTARY ABERRATION--!
HAHAHA
ARISIA...
WHAT?
HONEY, I HAVE A THEORY ABOUT THIS--!
SO DO I, HAL--!

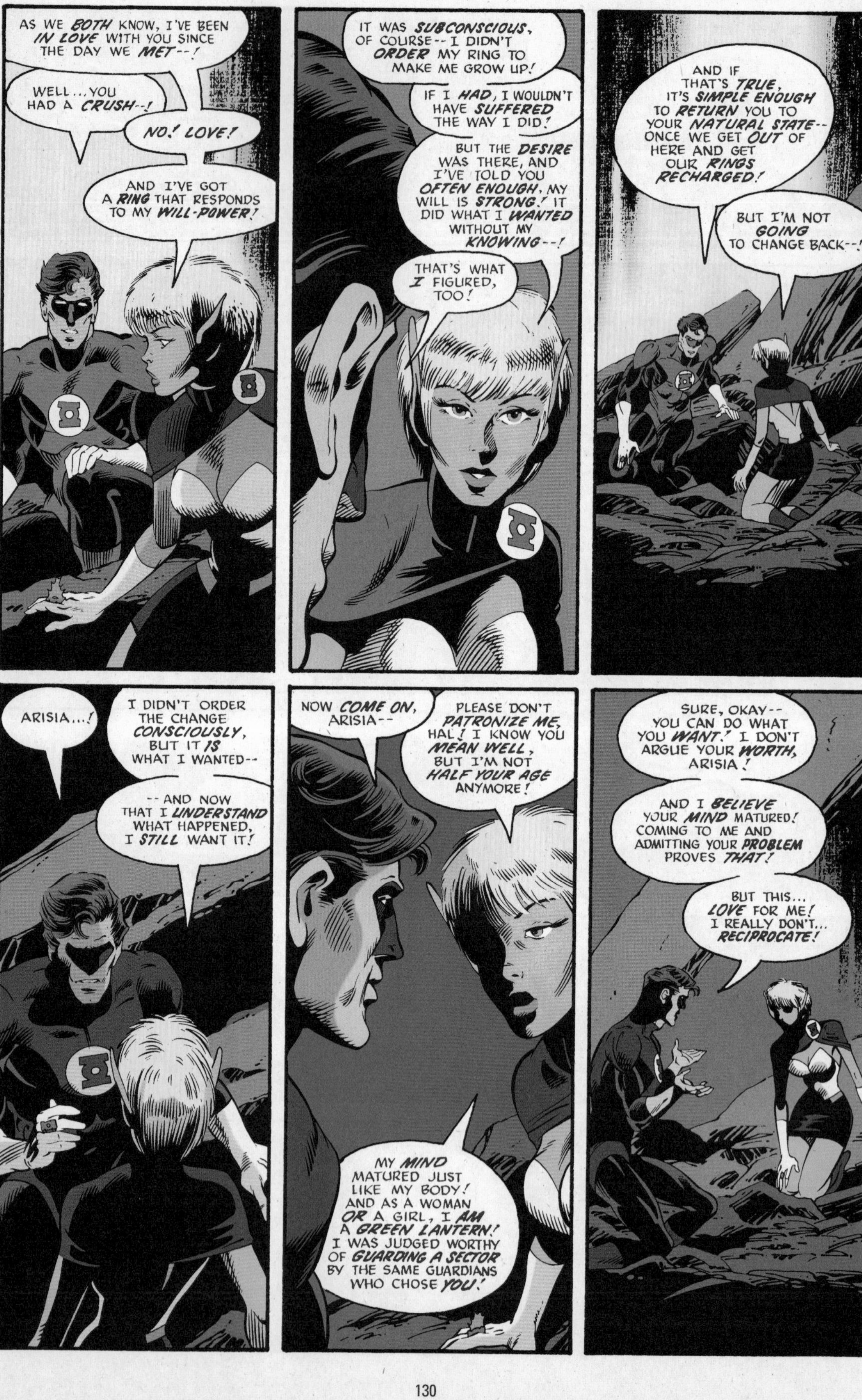
AS WE BOTH KNOW, I'VE BEEN IN LOVE WITH YOU SINCE THE DAY WE MET--!
WELL... YOU HAD A CRUSH--!
NO! LOVE!
AND I'VE GOT A RING THAT RESPONDS TO MY WILL-POWER!
IT WAS SUBCONSCIOUS, OF COURSE-- I DIDN'T ORDER MY RING TO MAKE ME GROW UP!
IF I HAD, I WOULDN'T HAVE SUFFERED THE WAY I DID!
BUT THE DESIRE WAS THERE, AND I'VE TOLD YOU OFTEN ENOUGH, MY WILL IS STRONG! IT DID WHAT I WANTED WITHOUT MY KNOWING--!
THAT'S WHAT I FIGURED, TOO!
AND IF THAT'S TRUE, IT'S SIMPLE ENOUGH TO RETURN YOU TO YOUR NATURAL STATE-- ONCE WE GET OUT OF HERE AND GET OUR RINGS RECHARGED!
BUT I'M NOT GOING TO CHANGE BACK--!
ARISIA...!
I DIDN'T ORDER THE CHANGE CONSCIOUSLY, BUT IT IS WHAT I WANTED--
--AND NOW THAT I UNDERSTAND WHAT HAPPENED, I STILL WANT IT!
NOW COME ON, ARISIA--
PLEASE DON'T PATRONIZE ME, HAL! I KNOW YOU MEAN WELL, BUT I'M NOT HALF YOUR AGE ANYMORE!
MY MIND MATURED JUST LIKE MY BODY! AND AS A WOMAN OR A GIRL, I AM A GREEN LANTERN! I WAS JUDGED WORTHY OF GUARDING A SECTOR BY THE SAME GUARDIANS WHO CHOSE YOU!
SURE, OKAY-- YOU CAN DO WHAT YOU WANT! I DON'T ARGUE YOUR WORTH, ARISIA!
AND I BELIEVE YOUR MIND MATURED! COMING TO ME AND ADMITTING YOUR PROBLEM PROVES THAT!
BUT THIS... LOVE FOR ME! I REALLY DON'T... RECIPROCATE!

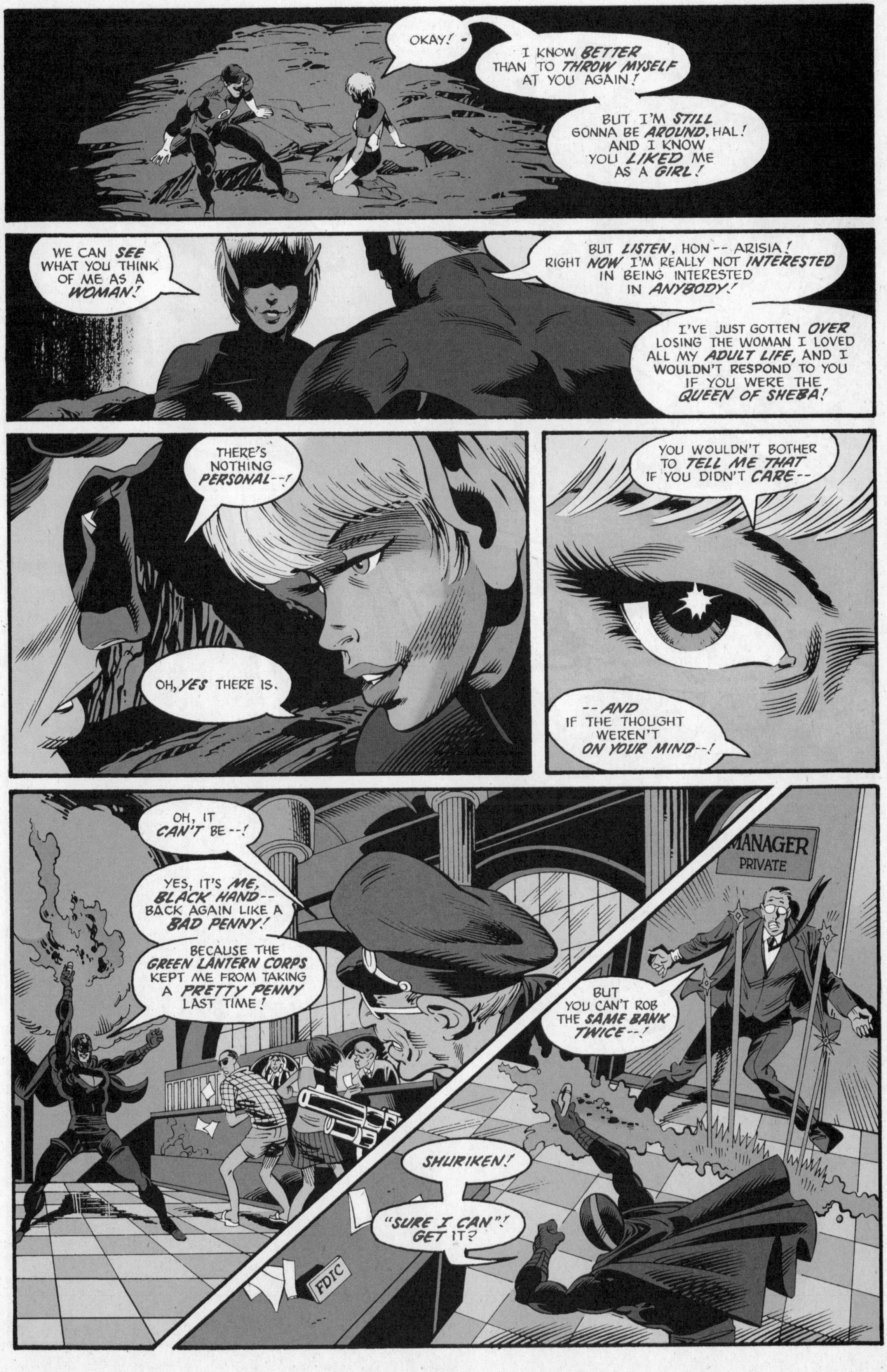
OKAY! -
I KNOW BETTER THAN TO THROW MYSELF AT YOU AGAIN!
BUT I'M STILL GONNA BE AROUND, HAL! AND I KNOW YOU LIKED ME AS A GIRL!
WE CAN SEE WHAT YOU THINK OF ME AS A WOMAN!
BUT LISTEN, HON -- ARISIA! RIGHT NOW I'M REALLY NOT INTERESTED IN BEING INTERESTED IN ANYBODY!
I'VE JUST GOTTEN OVER LOSING THE WOMAN I LOVED ALL MY ADULT LIFE, AND I WOULDN'T RESPOND TO YOU IF YOU WERE THE QUEEN OF SHEBA!
THERE'S NOTHING PERSONAL--!
OH, YES THERE IS.
YOU WOULDN'T BOTHER TO TELL ME THAT IF YOU DIDN'T CARE--
--AND IF THE THOUGHT WEREN'T ON YOUR MIND--!
OH, IT CAN'T BE--!
YES, IT'S ME, BLACK HAND-- BACK AGAIN LIKE A BAD PENNY!
BECAUSE THE GREEN LANTERN CORPS KEPT ME FROM TAKING A PRETTY PENNY LAST TIME!
MANAGER
PRIVATE
BUT YOU CAN'T ROB THE SAME BANK TWICE--!
SHURIKEN!
"SURE I CAN"! GET IT?
FDIC

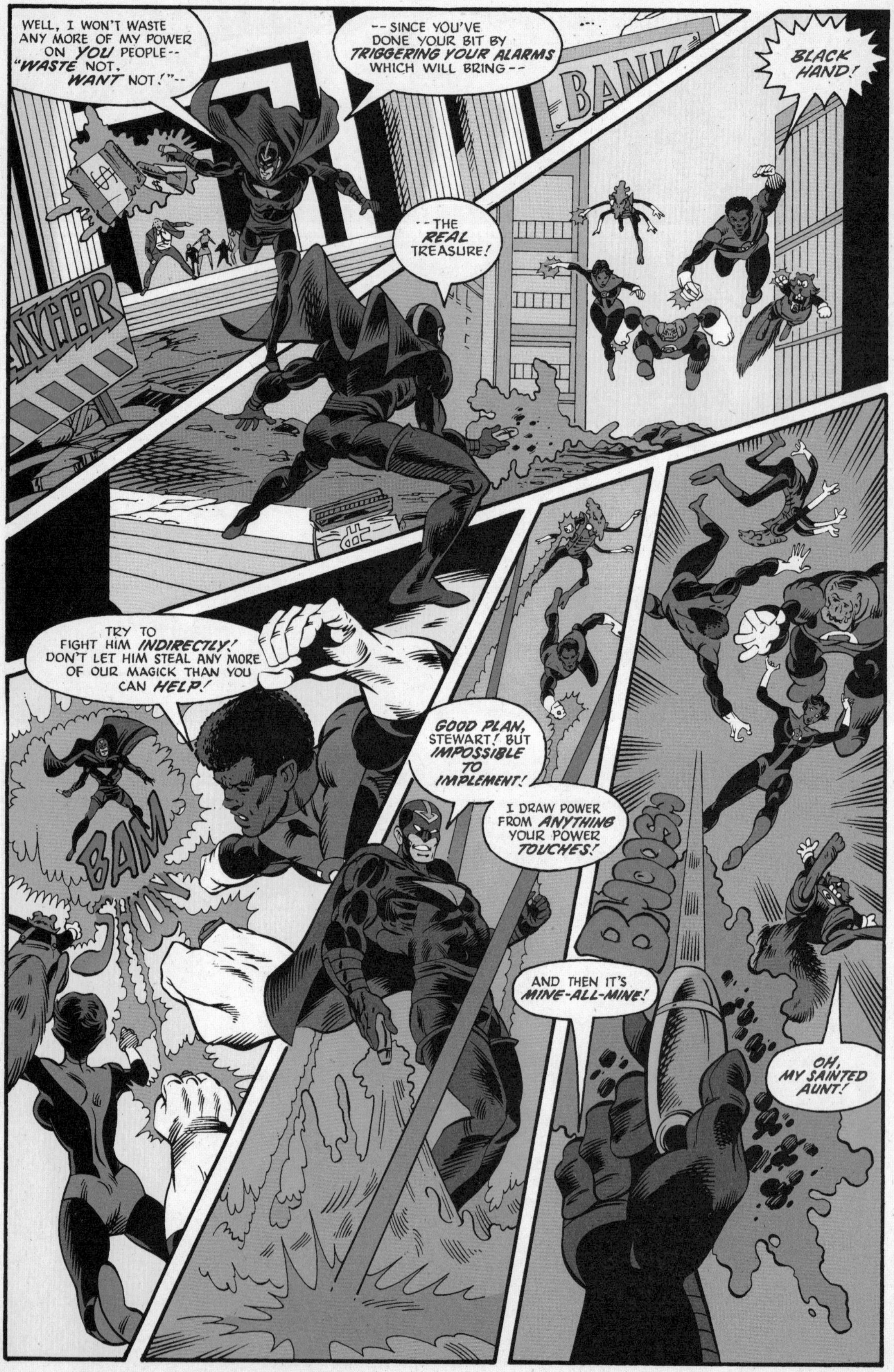
WELL, I WON'T WASTE ANY MORE OF MY POWER ON YOU PEOPLE-- "WASTE NOT. WANT NOT!"--
--SINCE YOU'VE DONE YOUR BIT BY TRIGGERING YOUR ALARMS WHICH WILL BRING--
BANK
BLACK HAND!
--THE REAL TREASURE!
TRY TO FIGHT HIM INDIRECTLY! DON'T LET HIM STEAL ANY MORE OF OUR MAGICK THAN YOU CAN HELP!
BAM
GOOD PLAN, STEWART! BUT IMPOSSIBLE TO IMPLEMENT!
I DRAW POWER FROM ANYTHING YOUR POWER TOUCHES!
AND THEN IT'S MINE-ALL-MINE!
OH, MY SAINTED AUNT!

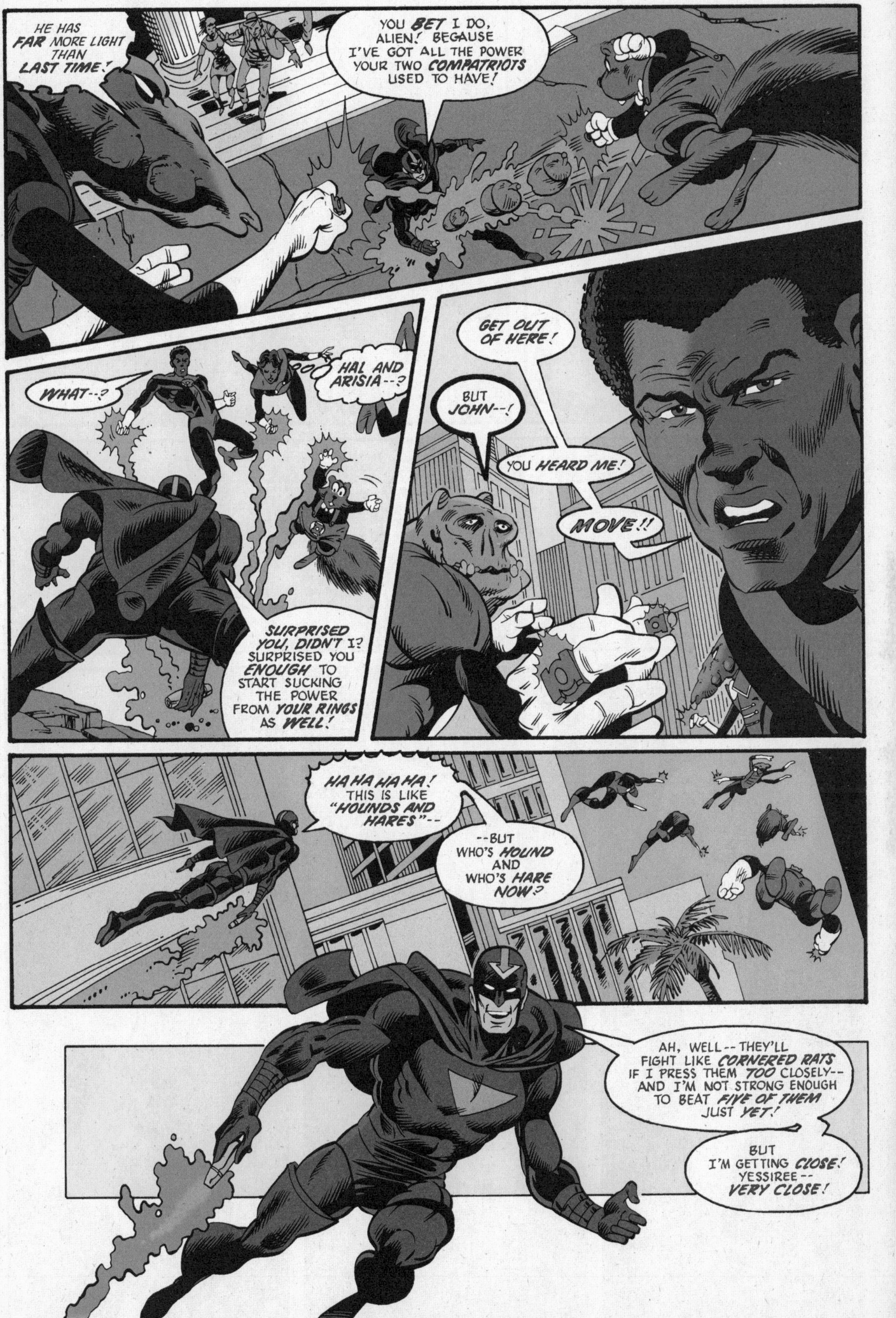
HE HAS FAR MORE LIGHT THAN LAST TIME!
YOU BET I DO, ALIEN! BECAUSE I'VE GOT ALL THE POWER YOUR TWO COMPATRIOTS USED TO HAVE!
WHAT--?
HAL AND ARISIA--?
SURPRISED YOU, DIDN'T I? SURPRISED YOU ENOUGH TO START SUCKING THE POWER FROM YOUR RINGS AS WELL!
GET OUT OF HERE!
BUT JOHN--!
YOU HEARD ME!
MOVE!!
HA HA HA HA! THIS IS LIKE "HOUNDS AND HARES"--
--BUT WHO'S HOUND AND WHO'S HARE NOW?
AH, WELL--THEY'LL FIGHT LIKE CORNERED RATS IF I PRESS THEM TOO CLOSELY--AND I'M NOT STRONG ENOUGH TO BEAT FIVE OF THEM JUST YET!
BUT I'M GETTING CLOSE! YESSIREE--VERY CLOSE!

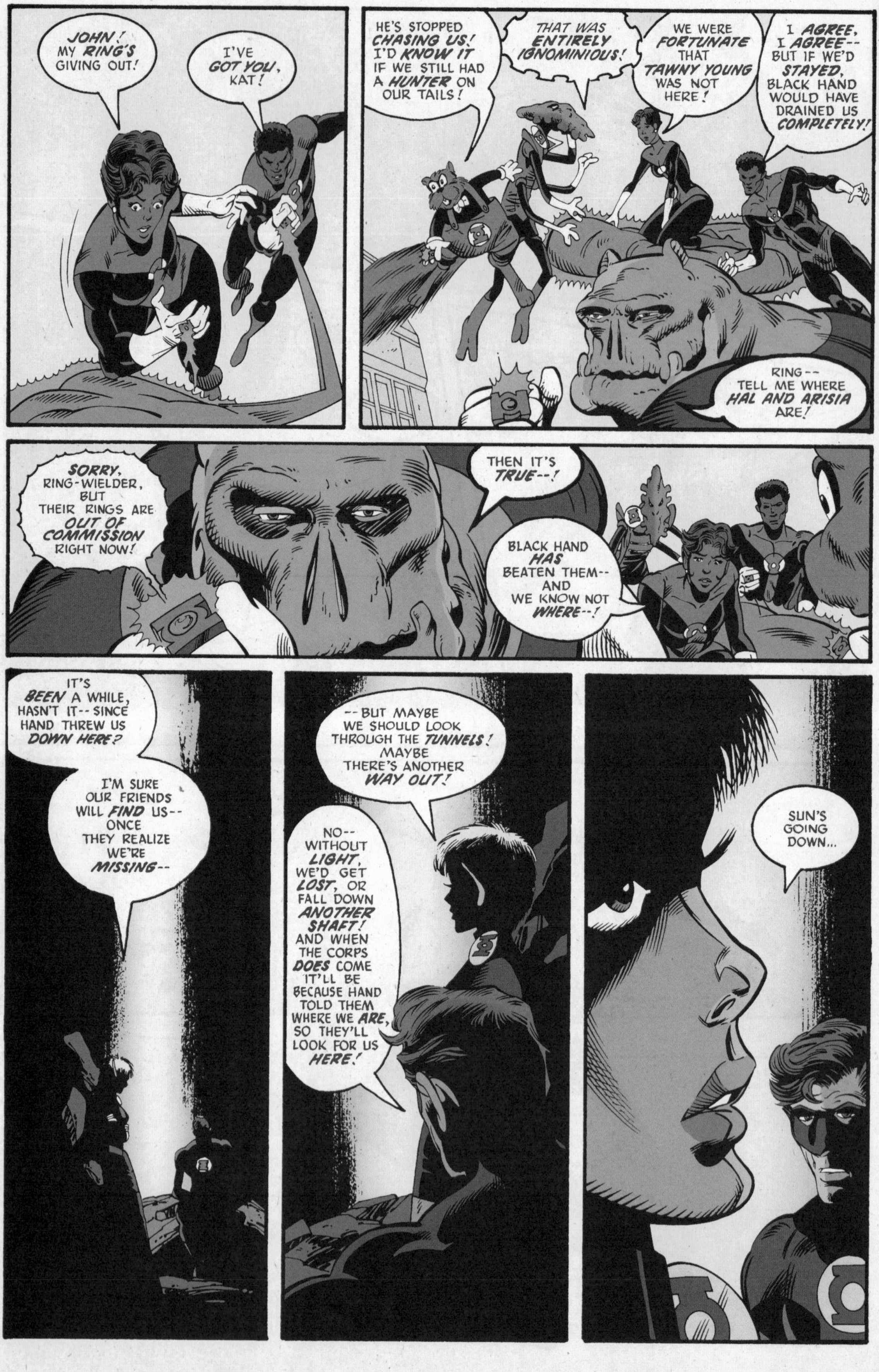
JOHN! MY RING'S GIVING OUT!
I'VE GOT YOU, KAT!
HE'S STOPPED CHASING US! I'D KNOW IT IF WE STILL HAD A HUNTER ON OUR TAILS!
THAT WAS ENTIRELY IGNOMINIOUS!
WE WERE FORTUNATE THAT TAWNY YOUNG WAS NOT HERE!
I AGREE, I AGREE-- BUT IF WE'D STAYED, BLACK HAND WOULD HAVE DRAINED US COMPLETELY!
RING-- TELL ME WHERE HAL AND ARISIA ARE!
SORRY, RING-WIELDER, BUT THEIR RINGS ARE OUT OF COMMISSION RIGHT NOW!
THEN IT'S TRUE--!
BLACK HAND HAS BEATEN THEM-- AND WE KNOW NOT WHERE--!
IT'S BEEN A WHILE, HASN'T IT-- SINCE HAND THREW US DOWN HERE?
I'M SURE OUR FRIENDS WILL FIND US-- ONCE THEY REALIZE WE'RE MISSING--
--BUT MAYBE WE SHOULD LOOK THROUGH THE TUNNELS! MAYBE THERE'S ANOTHER WAY OUT!
NO-- WITHOUT LIGHT, WE'D GET LOST, OR FALL DOWN ANOTHER SHAFT! AND WHEN THE CORPS DOES COME IT'LL BE BECAUSE HAND TOLD THEM WHERE WE ARE, SO THEY'LL LOOK FOR US HERE!
SUN'S GOING DOWN...

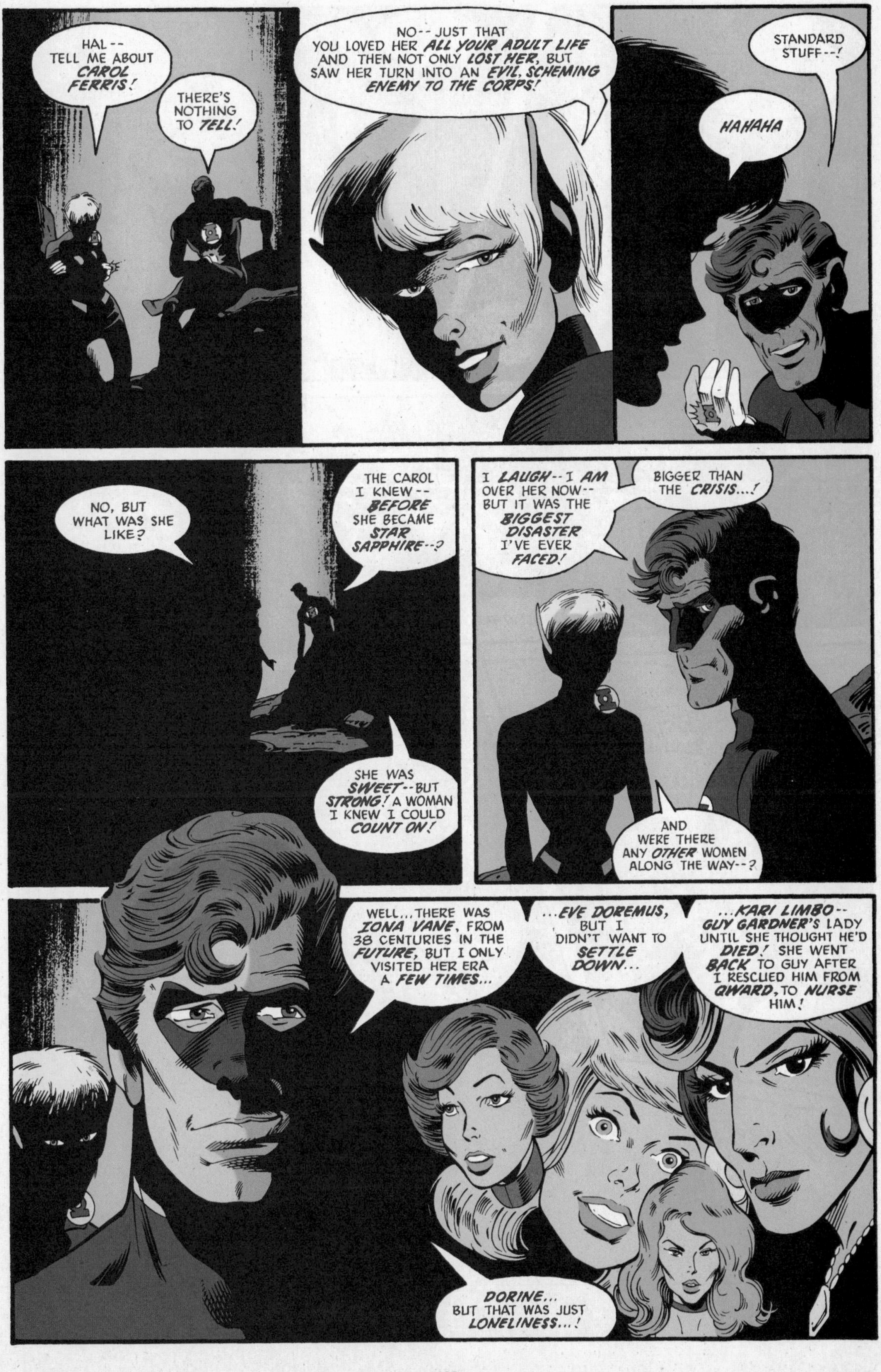
HAL -- TELL ME ABOUT CAROL FERRIS!
THERE'S NOTHING TO TELL!
NO -- JUST THAT YOU LOVED HER ALL YOUR ADULT LIFE AND THEN NOT ONLY LOST HER, BUT SAW HER TURN INTO AN EVIL, SCHEMING ENEMY TO THE CORPS!
STANDARD STUFF--!
HAHAHA
NO, BUT WHAT WAS SHE LIKE?
THE CAROL I KNEW -- BEFORE SHE BECAME STAR SAPPHIRE--?
SHE WAS SWEET--BUT STRONG! A WOMAN I KNEW I COULD COUNT ON!
I LAUGH -- I AM OVER HER NOW -- BUT IT WAS THE BIGGEST DISASTER I'VE EVER FACED!
BIGGER THAN THE CRISIS...!
AND WERE THERE ANY OTHER WOMEN ALONG THE WAY--?
WELL... THERE WAS IONA VANE, FROM 38 CENTURIES IN THE FUTURE, BUT I ONLY VISITED HER ERA A FEW TIMES...
...EVE DOREMUS, BUT I DIDN'T WANT TO SETTLE DOWN...
...KARI LIMBO -- GUY GARDNER'S LADY UNTIL SHE THOUGHT HE'D DIED! SHE WENT BACK TO GUY AFTER I RESCUED HIM FROM QWARD, TO NURSE HIM!
DORINE... BUT THAT WAS JUST LONELINESS...!

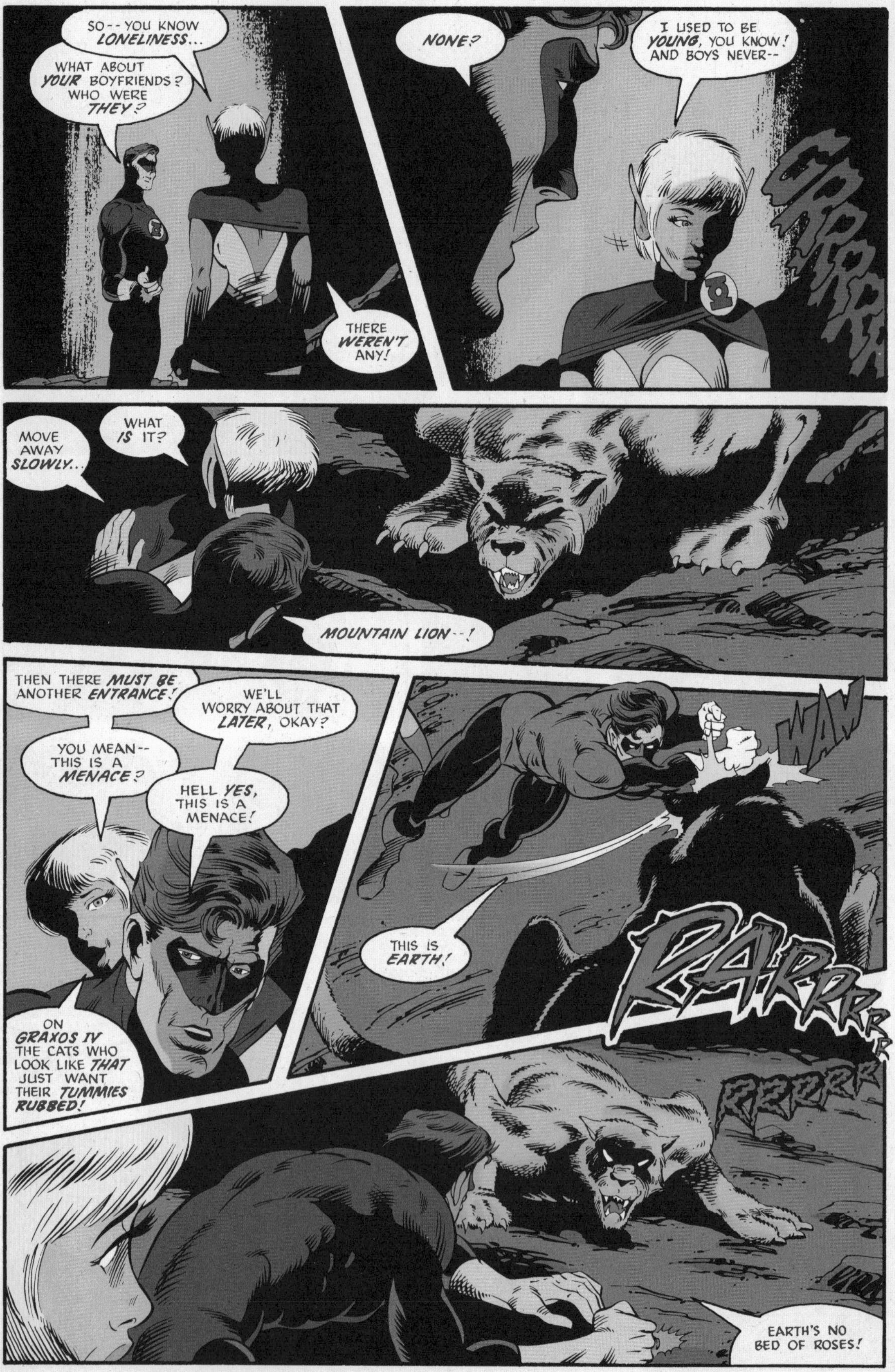

SO--YOU KNOW LONELINESS...
WHAT ABOUT YOUR BOYFRIENDS? WHO WERE THEY?
THERE WEREN'T ANY!
NONE?
I USED TO BE YOUNG, YOU KNOW! AND BOYS NEVER--
GRRRRR
WHAT IS IT?
MOVE AWAY SLOWLY...
MOUNTAIN LION--!
THEN THERE MUST BE ANOTHER ENTRANCE!
YOU MEAN-- THIS IS A MENACE?
WE'LL WORRY ABOUT THAT LATER, OKAY?
HELL YES, THIS IS A MENACE!
ON GRAXOS IV THE CATS WHO LOOK LIKE THAT JUST WANT THEIR TUMMIES RUBBED!
WAM
THIS IS EARTH!
RARRRRRR
RRRRR
EARTH'S NO BED OF ROSES!

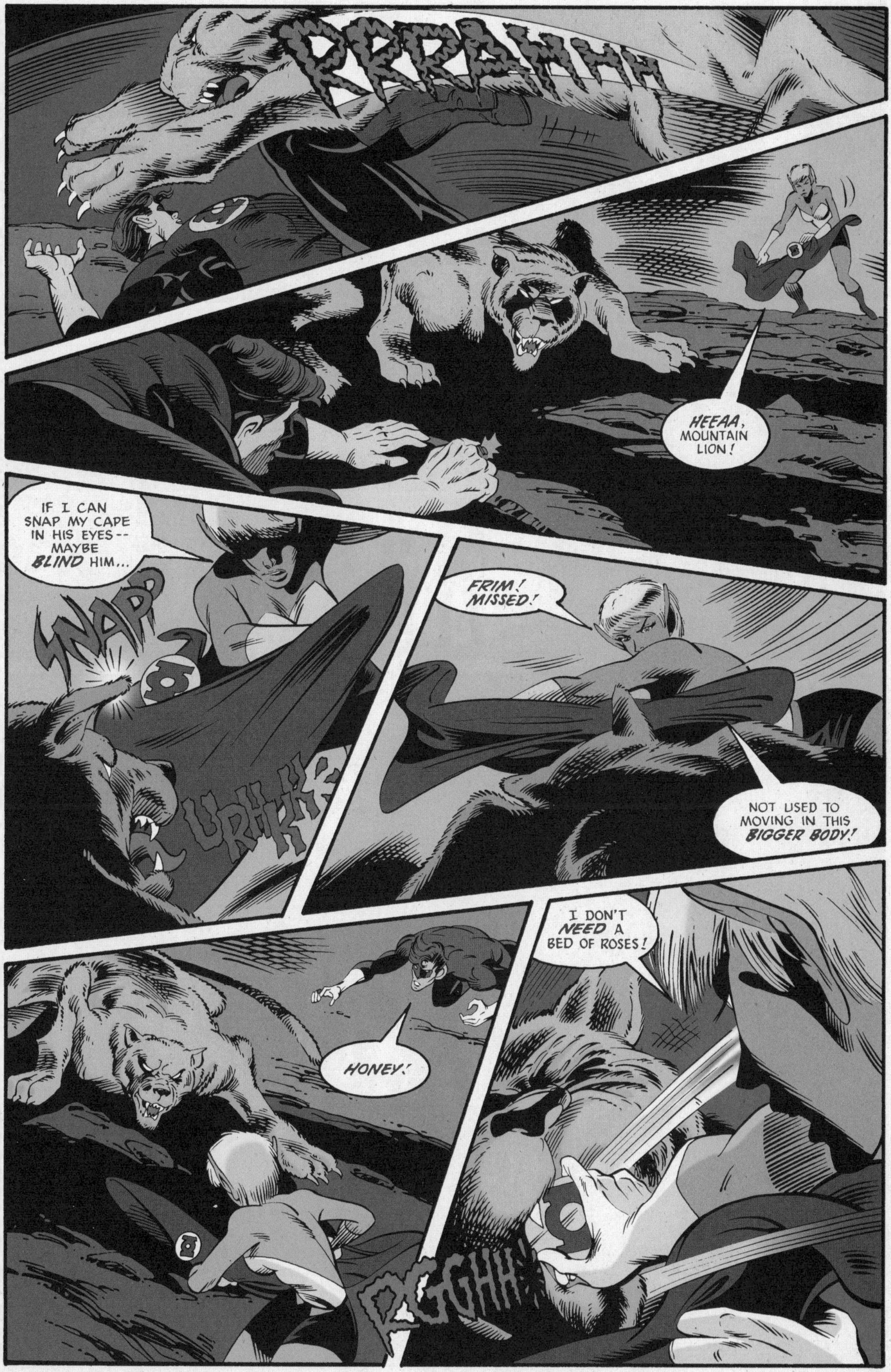

RRRAHHH
HEEAA, MOUNTAIN LION!
IF I CAN SNAP MY CAPE IN HIS EYES-- MAYBE BLIND HIM...
FRIM! MISSED!
NOT USED TO MOVING IN THIS BIGGER BODY!
HONEY!
I DON'T NEED A BED OF ROSES!

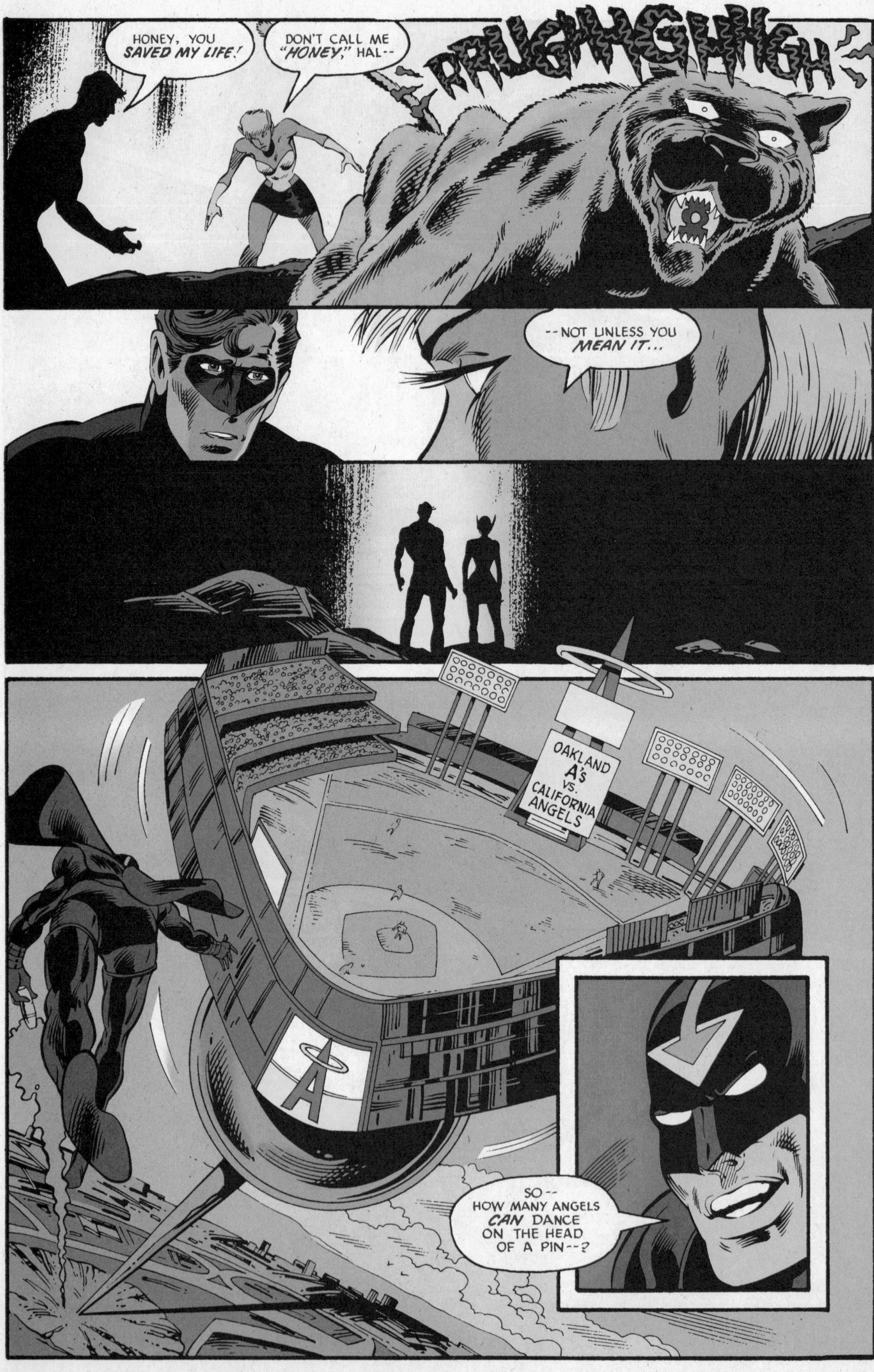
HONEY, YOU SAVED MY LIFE!
DON'T CALL ME "HONEY," HAL--
--NOT UNLESS YOU MEAN IT...
OAKLAND A's VS. CALIFORNIA ANGELS
SO-- HOW MANY ANGELS CAN DANCE ON THE HEAD OF A PIN--?

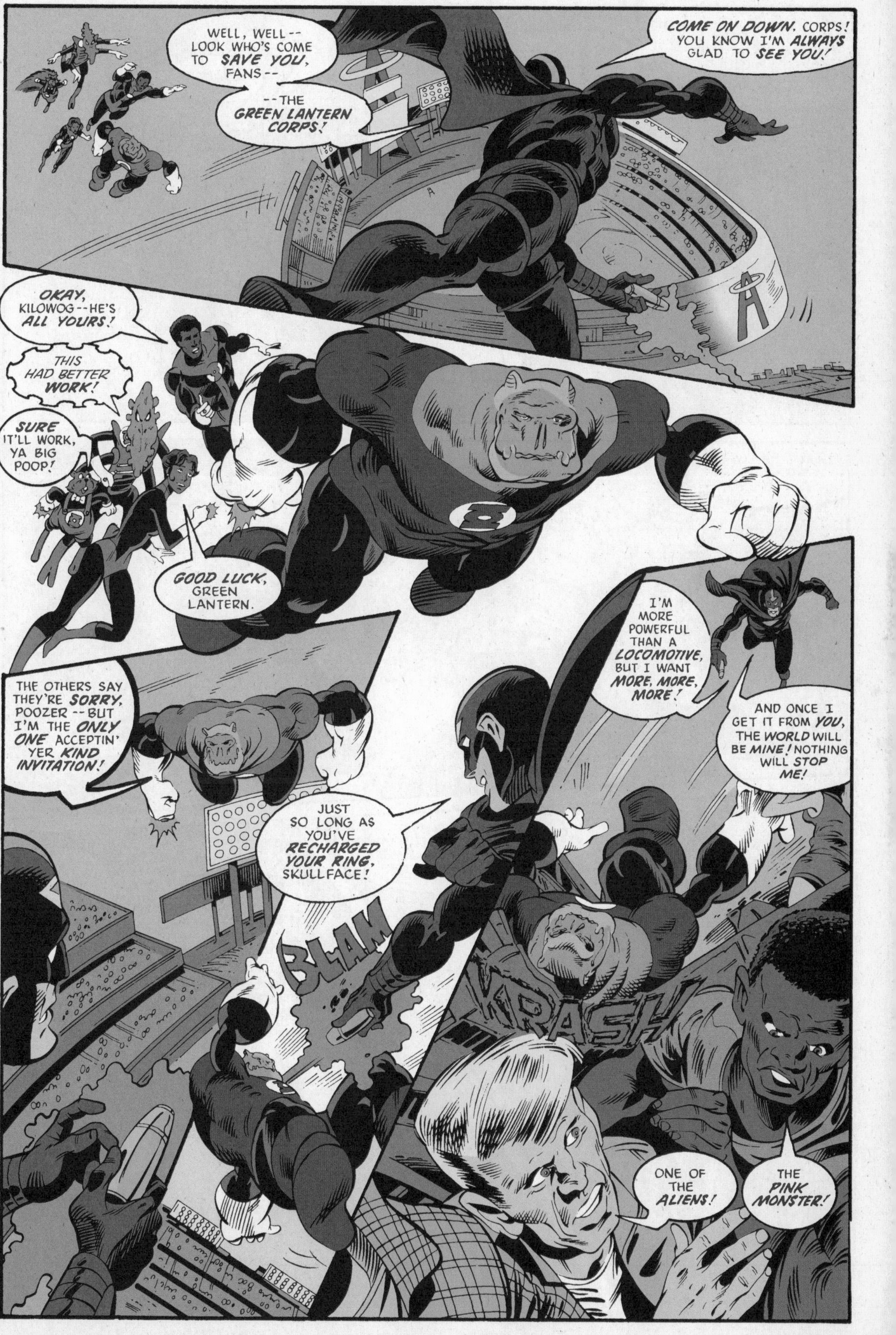

WELL, WELL-- LOOK WHO'S COME TO SAVE YOU, FANS--
--THE GREEN LANTERN CORPS!
COME ON DOWN, CORPS! YOU KNOW I'M ALWAYS GLAD TO SEE YOU!
OKAY, KILOWOG--HE'S ALL YOURS!
THIS HAD BETTER WORK!
SURE IT'LL WORK, YA BIG POOP!
GOOD LUCK, GREEN LANTERN.
I'M MORE POWERFUL THAN A LOCOMOTIVE, BUT I WANT MORE, MORE, MORE!
AND ONCE I GET IT FROM YOU, THE WORLD WILL BE MINE! NOTHING WILL STOP ME!
THE OTHERS SAY THEY'RE SORRY, POOZER--BUT I'M THE ONLY ONE ACCEPTIN' YER KIND INVITATION!
JUST SO LONG AS YOU'VE RECHARGED YOUR RING, SKULLFACE!
BLAM
KRASH
ONE OF THE ALIENS!
THE PINK MONSTER!

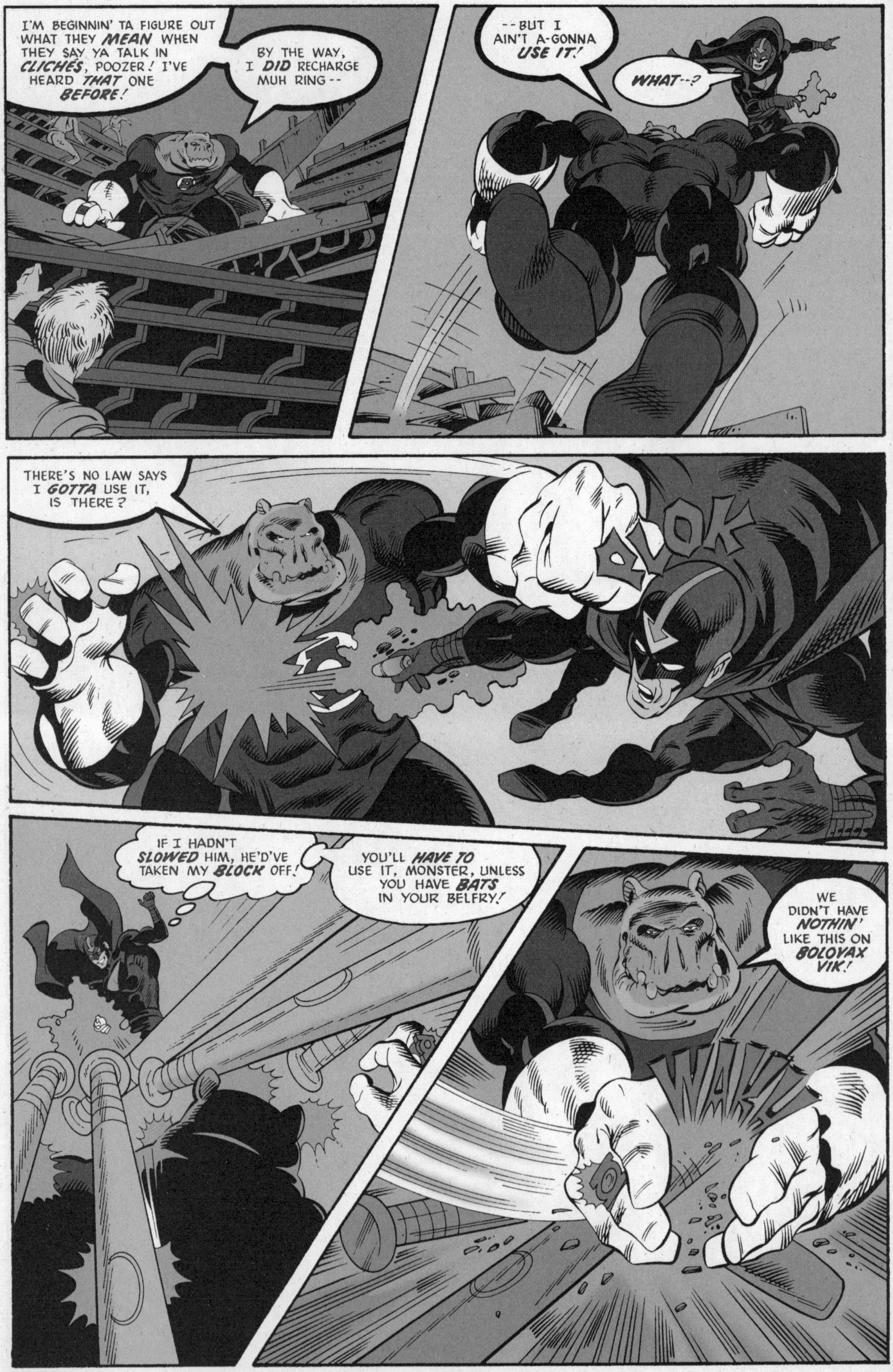
I'M BEGINNIN' TA FIGURE OUT WHAT THEY MEAN WHEN THEY SAY YA TALK IN CLICHÉS, POOZER! I'VE HEARD THAT ONE BEFORE!
BY THE WAY, I DID RECHARGE MUH RING--
--BUT I AIN'T A-GONNA USE IT!
WHAT--?
THERE'S NO LAW SAYS I GOTTA USE IT, IS THERE?
BLOK
IF I HADN'T SLOWED HIM, HE'D'VE TAKEN MY BLOCK OFF!
YOU'LL HAVE TO USE IT, MONSTER, UNLESS YOU HAVE BATS IN YOUR BELFRY!
WE DIDN'T HAVE NOTHIN' LIKE THIS ON BOLOVAX VIK!

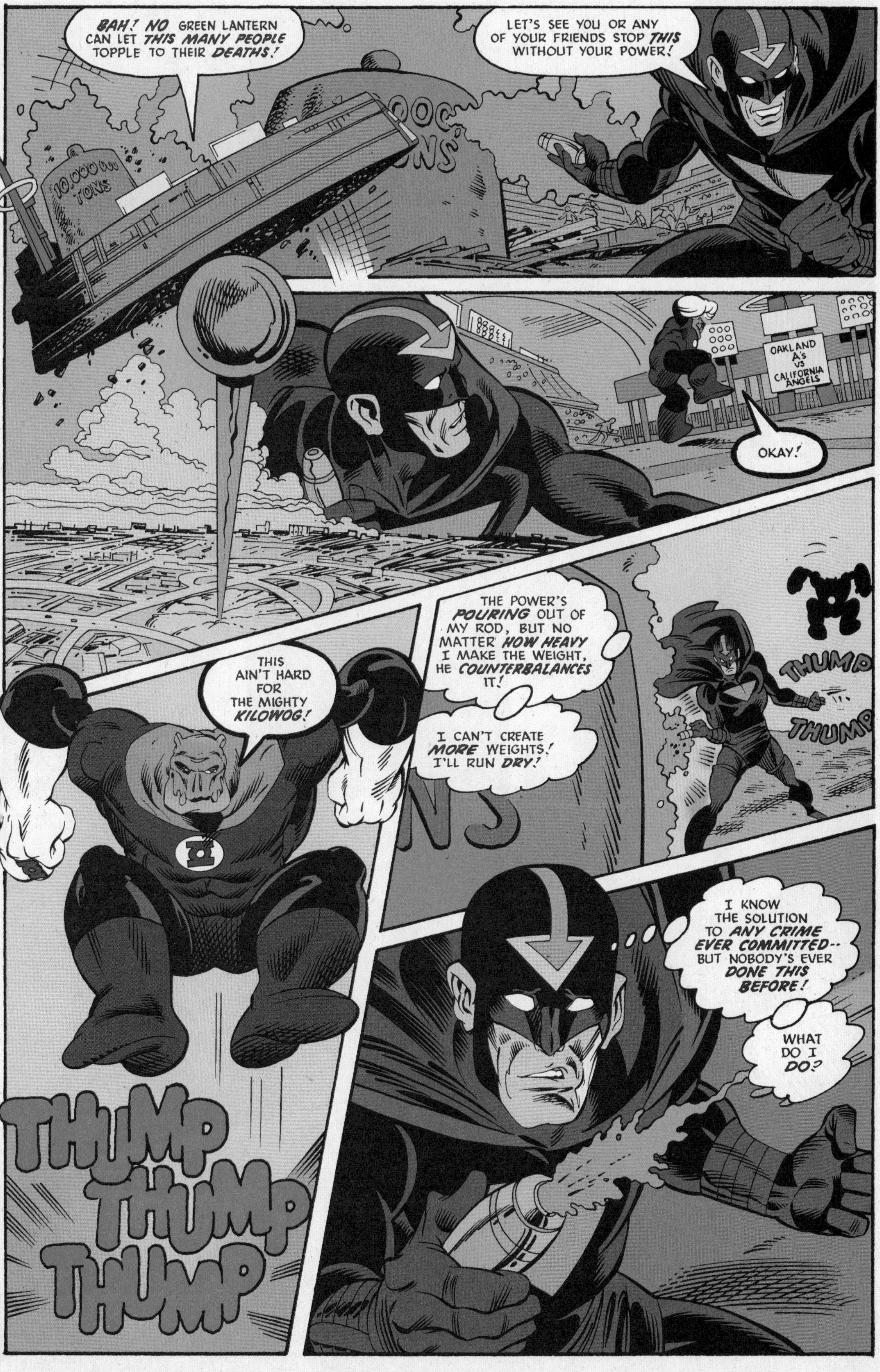

BAH! NO GREEN LANTERN CAN LET THIS MANY PEOPLE TOPPLE TO THEIR DEATHS!
LET'S SEE YOU OR ANY OF YOUR FRIENDS STOP THIS WITHOUT YOUR POWER!
10,000 TONS
OAKLAND A's VS CALIFORNIA ANGELS
OKAY!
THIS AIN'T HARD FOR THE MIGHTY KILOWOG!
THE POWER'S POURING OUT OF MY ROD, BUT NO MATTER HOW HEAVY I MAKE THE WEIGHT, HE COUNTERBALANCES IT!
I CAN'T CREATE MORE WEIGHTS! I'LL RUN DRY!
THUMP
THUMP
I KNOW THE SOLUTION TO ANY CRIME EVER COMMITTED-- BUT NOBODY'S EVER DONE THIS BEFORE!
WHAT DO I DO?
THUMP THUMP THUMP

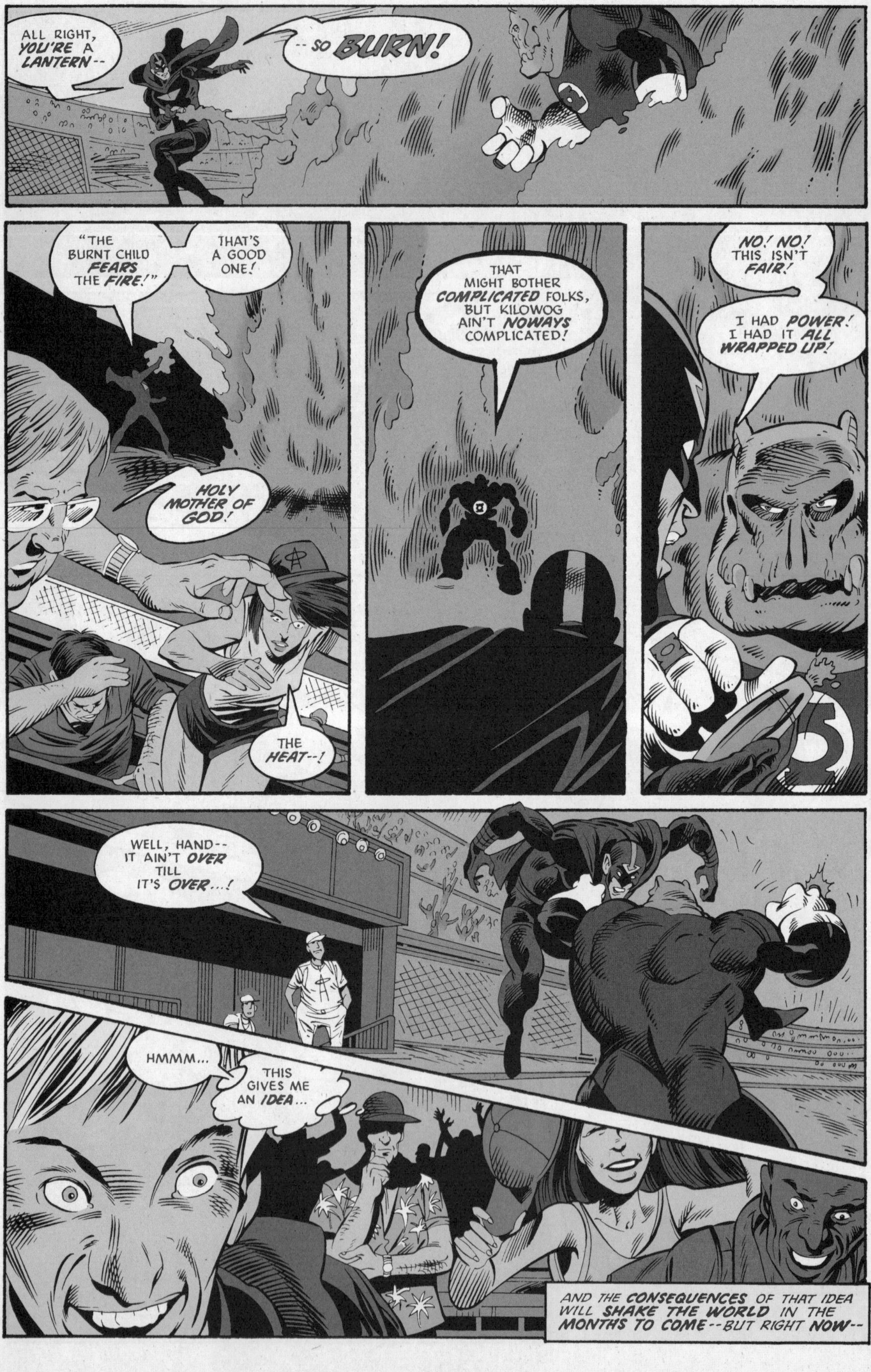
ALL RIGHT, YOU'RE A LANTERN--
--SO BURN!
"THE BURNT CHILD FEARS THE FIRE!"
THAT'S A GOOD ONE!
HOLY MOTHER OF GOD!
THE HEAT--!
THAT MIGHT BOTHER COMPLICATED FOLKS, BUT KILOWOG AIN'T NOWAYS COMPLICATED!
NO! NO! THIS ISN'T FAIR!
I HAD POWER! I HAD IT ALL WRAPPED UP!
WELL, HAND-- IT AIN'T OVER TILL IT'S OVER...!
HMMM...
THIS GIVES ME AN IDEA...
AND THE CONSEQUENCES OF THAT IDEA WILL SHAKE THE WORLD IN THE MONTHS TO COME--BUT RIGHT NOW--

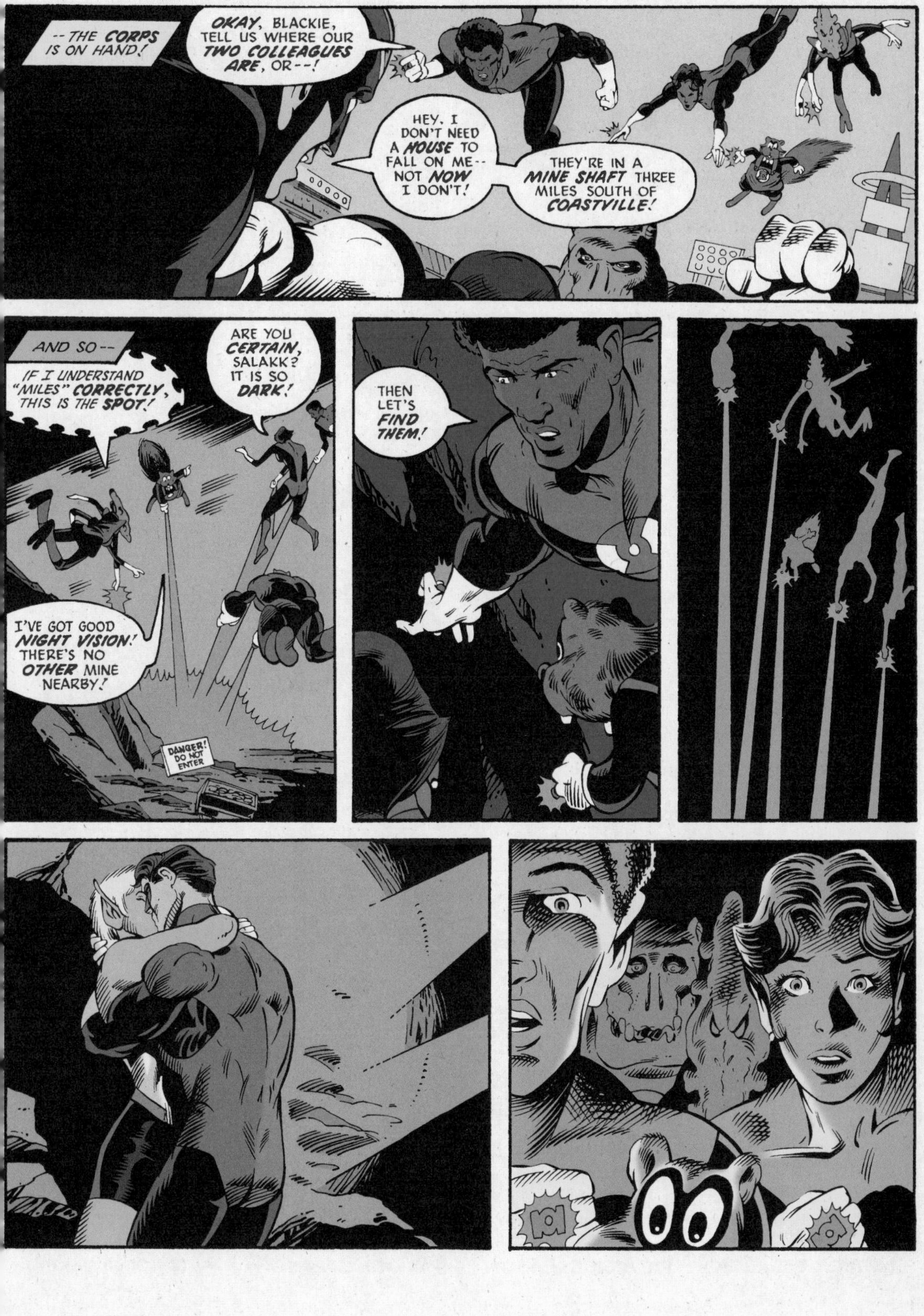
--THE CORPS IS ON HAND!
OKAY, BLACKIE, TELL US WHERE OUR TWO COLLEAGUES ARE, OR--!
HEY, I DON'T NEED A HOUSE TO FALL ON ME--NOT NOW I DON'T!
THEY'RE IN A MINE SHAFT THREE MILES SOUTH OF COASTVILLE!
AND SO--
IF I UNDERSTAND "MILES" CORRECTLY, THIS IS THE SPOT!
ARE YOU CERTAIN, SALAKK? IT IS SO DARK!
I'VE GOT GOOD NIGHT VISION! THERE'S NO OTHER MINE NEARBY!
DANGER! DO NOT ENTER
THEN LET'S FIND THEM!

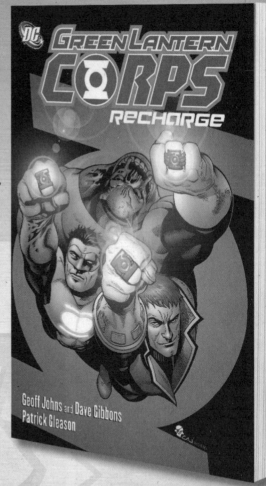

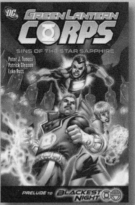